A History of Belize

A History of Belize

Narda Dobson

Longman Caribbean

Longman Caribbean Limited
Trinidad and Jamaica
Longman Group Limited
London

Associated companies, branches and representatives throughout the world

© Crown Copyright 1973

Published by Longman Group Limited by agreement with
the Controller of Her Majesty's Stationery Office

First published 1973
Reprinted 1979

ISBN 0 582 76601.X cased
ISBN 0 582 78512.X limp

Printed in Hong Kong by
Commonwealth Printing Press Ltd

To the people of Belize

Preface

My interest in the history of Belize owes its origins to a meeting in 1956 with Professor Rawle Farley, formerly extra-mural tutor there. His well-founded belief that the history of the country deserved further investigation persuaded me to embark on research into its social and constitutional history during the early nineteenth century. Two years afterwards I completed an Oxford thesis entitled 'Social and Administrative Developments in British Honduras 1798–1843'. When it was later suggested that I might write a comprehensive history of Belize, from its beginnings up to 1970, I was delighted at the opportunity to explore the country's history more widely. Yet I was also daunted by the difficulties posed by such a task. There were the difficulties which must confront the historian of any newly developing nation, increased in the case of Belize by the absence of any previous history based on original source material other than studies concerned specifically with the Guatemalan diplomatic struggle. Then too there were the demands of a very wide and varied audience which such a history must try to meet: this was to be a book which would both provide secondary school children in Belize with a clear and accurate survey of their country's past, and which would at the same time give students of Caribbean and British Imperial history a scholarly study of the territory.

But perhaps the difficulty of which I was most constantly aware was of writing a history of Belize at the present time. Changes in the political, social and economic situation of the country during the past few years have been considerable and are likely to continue in the immediate future. I finished writing this book in July 1970 with the knowledge that some of the information and interpretations in my final chapters will sooner or later need to be re-assessed in the light of subsequent events. One recent development cannot be allowed to pass without comment. Although the country is now generally known as Belize, it was originally known as the Honduras or Bay settlement and then, from the mid-nineteenth century, as British Honduras. I have consistently retained these older names to avoid historical anachronism and have restricted the term Belize to my reference to the present-day country. Similarly I have retained the use of Belize in referring to the city which is today known as Belize City.

During the long period in which I have been preparing and writing this book I have received so much kindness from so many individuals that I fear this may not be a complete list of my many acknowledgements. In the first place, however, I am grateful to the following institutions for permission to use their archives and papers as well as to the invaluable assistance provided by their Librarians and staff: Rhodes House Library, Oxford; the Bodleian Library, Oxford; the Public Record Office, the British Museum, the Royal Commonwealth Society Library; the Institute of Historical Research; the Foreign and Commonwealth Office Library; York University Library; the Jamaican Archives, Spanish Town; the Jubilee Library and the Registry, Belize. I am also grateful to the Earl of Clarendon for permission to use the Clarendon Papers in the Bodleian Library. Unpublished copyright material in the Public Record Office has been cited by permission of the Controller of H.M. Stationery Office.

At different times I have benefited greatly from conversation and correspondence with Sir Alan Burns, Mr Leo Bradley, Professor Wayne Clegern, Dr Kenneth Duncan, Dr Cedric Grant, Dr A. F. Madden and Professor David Waddell. I owe a particular debt to Professor R. A. Humphreys, Dr J. Eric S. Thompson and Dr James Walvin, each of whom read certain sections of the book and offered helpful advice. Without the assistance of the Overseas Development Administration, the West Indian Department of the Foreign Office and the Ministry of Education in Belize the book could never have been completed. I should also like to mention the great help I have received from the editorial staff of Longmans in the final stages of preparing the manuscript for press.

On a more personal note it is a real pleasure for me to be able to thank publicly everyone who made me so welcome in Belize. I am especially grateful to Louise and Willy Hoy for their generous hospitality, and to William Fonseca for his help in providing essential information—it is indeed difficult to express adequately how great has been his contribution to the writing of this history. At York I have been fortunate to have had the benefit of Colville Young's advice during his temporary exile from Belize, while Vicky Liversidge typed the book in her usual impeccable manner and with her customary cheerfulness.

Finally my husband and children bore my absences in Belize and my prolonged pre-occupation with its history with great patience and gave me constant encouragement. My husband, Barrie, has read every word of the book more times than he would care to remember and I am deeply grateful.

York 1972.

Publisher's note

Notes and references for each chapter appear in Appendix IV on pages 344 to 355.

Acknowledgements

We are grateful to the Library of the Royal Commonwealth Society for allowing us to photograph 'A View of Belize', reproduced on the cover, and the plan of Belize, pp. 6–7, both contained in *The Honduras Almanack*, 1829.

We are grateful to the following for permission to use photographs: Associated Press for p. 13; Belize Estate and Produce Company Limited for p. 10 (foot); Vivien Carrington for pp. 8 (foot), 9, 12 (foot) and 16 (top); the Government Information Service, Belize for pp. 5 (foot), 8 (top), 10 (top), 11 (foot), 12 (top), 14, 15 and 16 (foot); Norman Hammond for pp. 5 (top) and 11 (top); David Pendergast for pp. 1, 2, 3, and 4; Radio Times Hulton Picture Library for p. 7. The page numbers mentioned above refer to the pages of the illustration section.

Contents

There is an inset of photographs between pages 178 and 179

List of Maps

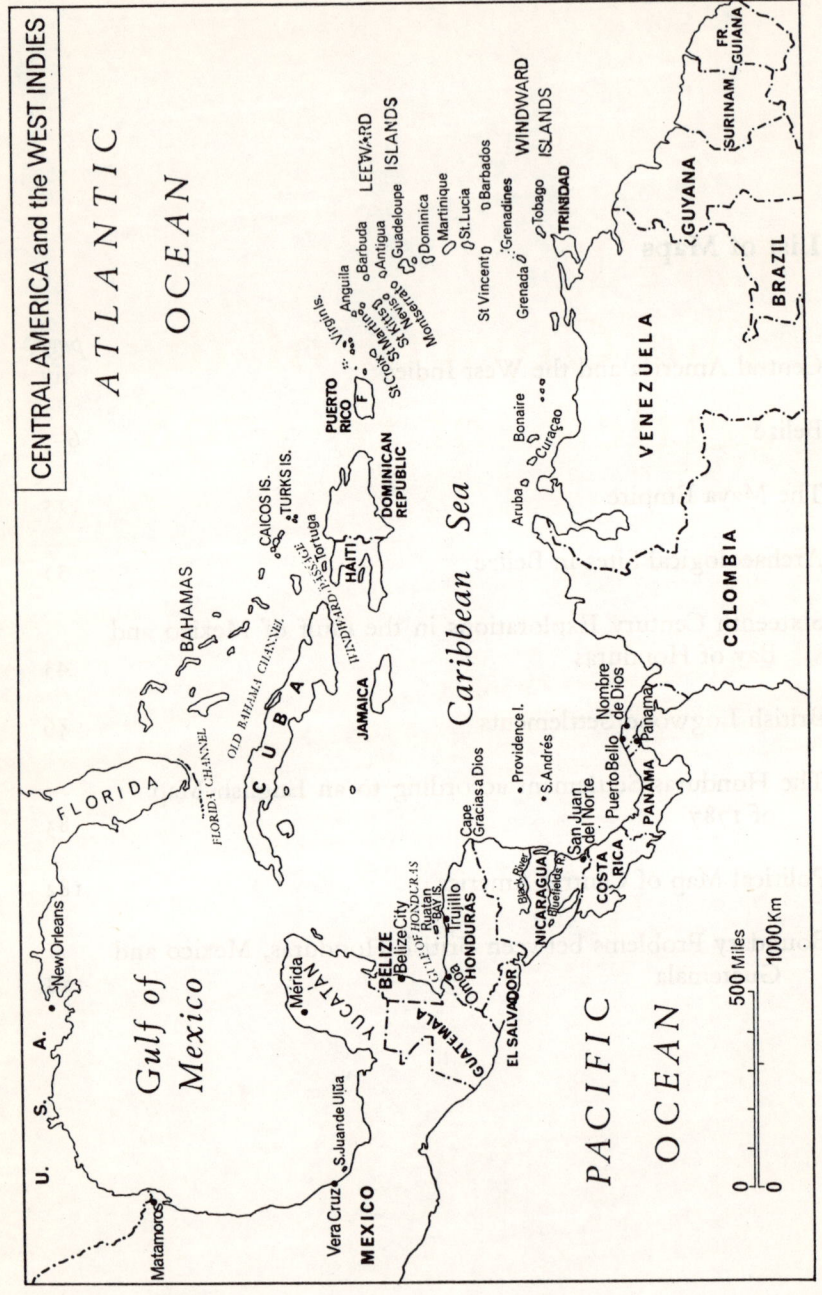

CENTRAL AMERICA and the WEST INDIES

ATLANTIC OCEAN

Gulf of Mexico

Caribbean Sea

PACIFIC OCEAN

U.S.A.

New Orleans

FLORIDA

BAHAMAS

CUBA

CAICOS IS.

TURKS IS.

OLD BAHAMA CHANNEL

FLORIDA CHANNEL

JAMAICA

HAITI

DOMINICAN REPUBLIC

Tortuga

WINDWARD PASSAGE

PUERTO RICO

Virgin Is.

Anguilla

St Martin

St Kitts

Nevis

Montserrat

Barbuda

Antigua

Guadeloupe

Dominica

Martinique

St Lucia

St Vincent

Barbados

LEEWARD ISLANDS

WINDWARD ISLANDS

Grenadines

Grenada

Tobago

TRINIDAD

Aruba

Bonaire

Curaçao

VENEZUELA

COLOMBIA

GUYANA

SURINAM

FR. GUIANA

BRAZIL

MEXICO

Vera Cruz

S.Juan de Ulua

Matamoros

Mérida

YUCATAN

BELIZE

Belize City

GUATEMALA

EL SALVADOR

HONDURAS

GULF OF HONDURAS

Ruatan

BAY IS.

Trujillo

Cape Gracias a Dios

Black River

NICARAGUA

Bluefields

Providence I.

S.Andrés

San Juan del Norte

COSTA RICA

Puerto Bello

Nombre de Dios

PANAMA

Panama

500 Miles

1000 Km

xiv

Part I
The Growth of the Settlement to 1798

I

Introduction

The Land and its Geographical Features

Belize lies on the east coast of Central America and is bounded on the north by Mexico and on the west and south by Guatemala. Although situated within the northern tropics, it can be said to have a sub-tropical climate. The coastal waters of the Caribbean are shallow for a distance of ten to twenty miles off shore and are dotted with small islets or cays which form a coral reef barrier. There are three other reef areas, the most easterly of which, Turneffe, lies forty-five miles east of Belize. If the cays are included the total area of Belize is 8,866 square miles. From the River Hondo in the north to the River Sarstoon in the south the country is 174 miles in length and at its widest point, between Belize City and Benque Viejo, is 68 miles in breadth. The country is about twice the size of Jamaica, and since it is slightly larger than the republic of El Salvador, it is the second smallest on the American continent.

Physical features

Physically the country can be divided into a northern low-lying plain which is swampy near the coast but rises to a slight plateau in the west, and a southern mountainous mass, the Maya Mountains, which falls away sharply towards the coast. Three-fifths of the total area is covered by hilly land while the remainder can be described as coastal plain. The Maya Mountains are com-

3

posed of very hard ancient rocks in which quartz and granite predominate. There are very few minerals in this mass of rocks and none such as phosphate, potash or sulphur which might make a valuable contribution to the soil and plant growth. Fortunately, the northern plain and parts of the west and south of the country are formed from a huge bed of limestone, which is a soil-forming rock and which usually creates very fertile soil. Among the most striking geographical features of the country are the rivers which, until quite recently, provided the most convenient system of communication. In the north of the country the River Hondo forms the boundary with Mexico; ten miles to the south and running parallel with it is the New River. Both these rivers flow in a north-easterly direction into Chetumal Bay. The Belize River, which in early days was often called the Old River, rises in the south-western hills, flows in a northerly direction and then turns eastwards towards the Caribbean. It has many tributaries and just to the south of it runs the Sibún River which is shorter and reaches the sea about ten miles to the south of Belize City. By contrast the rivers in the southern half of the country are short and steep, rising in the Maya Mountains then flowing in an easterly or south-easterly direction to the sea. Few of them are navigable for any distance and their rapids have always created a natural obstacle to man. It is partly for this reason and partly because of its more favourable climatic conditions that the northern part of the country was the first area to be settled and exploited commercially. Only modern methods of transport and forestry techniques have made possible the development of the southern half of the country.

Climate

The most important characteristic of the climate in Belize is its seasonal variation. Throughout the country there is a clearly marked dry and wet season, with considerable differences in the length of the seasons between the north and south. The onset of the dry season tends to vary from year to year. In the northern area it lasts for four months from February to May whereas in the extreme south, in the Toledo District, it may only last for the four weeks of March. Rainfall varies greatly from an average of 40 inches in Corozal to 160 inches in Punta Gorda. But there is also considerable change from year to year in one place; in Punta Gorda, for instance, the rainfall for September might be 12 inches one year but 36 inches the next. This obviously creates problems for the farmers. Corn is generally planted between April and May but in a very wet year the lowland areas might be flooded out or, in a dry year, the corn might wither on the hilly sites. In Belize City temperatures vary between 50° and 95° F. around an annual average mean of 79° or 80° F. In the Cayo District the cold days are often much colder than at Belize City, but in April or May temperatures as high as 100° F. may be reached in the shade. Atmospheric humidity is most oppressive on the coastal strip between Belize City and Punta Gorda but, in Belize City itself, sea breezes help to mitigate the effects of humidity.

It is apparent that climatic factors must have played, and still continue to play, an important part in the economic history of the country. The seasonal aspect of the rainfall led to a seasonal work cycle in the forestry industry which depended on a dry period for felling and a wet season for floating the logs to the sea. The difference in the length of the dry season gave the mahogany cutters much more opportunity to exploit the timber in the northern districts so that they strenuously resisted Spanish attempts to force them further south. The dependence of the timber industry on favourable climatic conditions made it a high risk venture and explains many of the short-term fluctuations in the volume of trade. Even today variation in rainfall affects agriculture and the communications within the country since certain roads are impassable in the wet season. Another unfortunate feature of the climate is the tendency to hurricanes, accompanied by winds of 100 m.p.h. Although less regular than in other parts of the Caribbean and the southern states of the United States, hurricanes have been responsible for very considerable damage to Belize in recent years. Although hurricanes are known to have occurred in 1785, 1805 and 1813, there was then no serious onslaught for over a hundred years with the result that it was widely believed that the country lay outside the hurricane belt. The devastating hurricane of 1931, which caused the loss of 150 lives and inflicted terrible damage on Belize City, marked the end of such a belief. Since then there have been a number of hurricanes including the serious Hurricane 'Hattie' of 1961 which led to the decision to build a new capital on a site 50 miles inland from Belize City. Hurricanes have struck other parts of the country; in 1945 Punta Gorda suffered devastation while ten years later Corozal was almost destroyed.

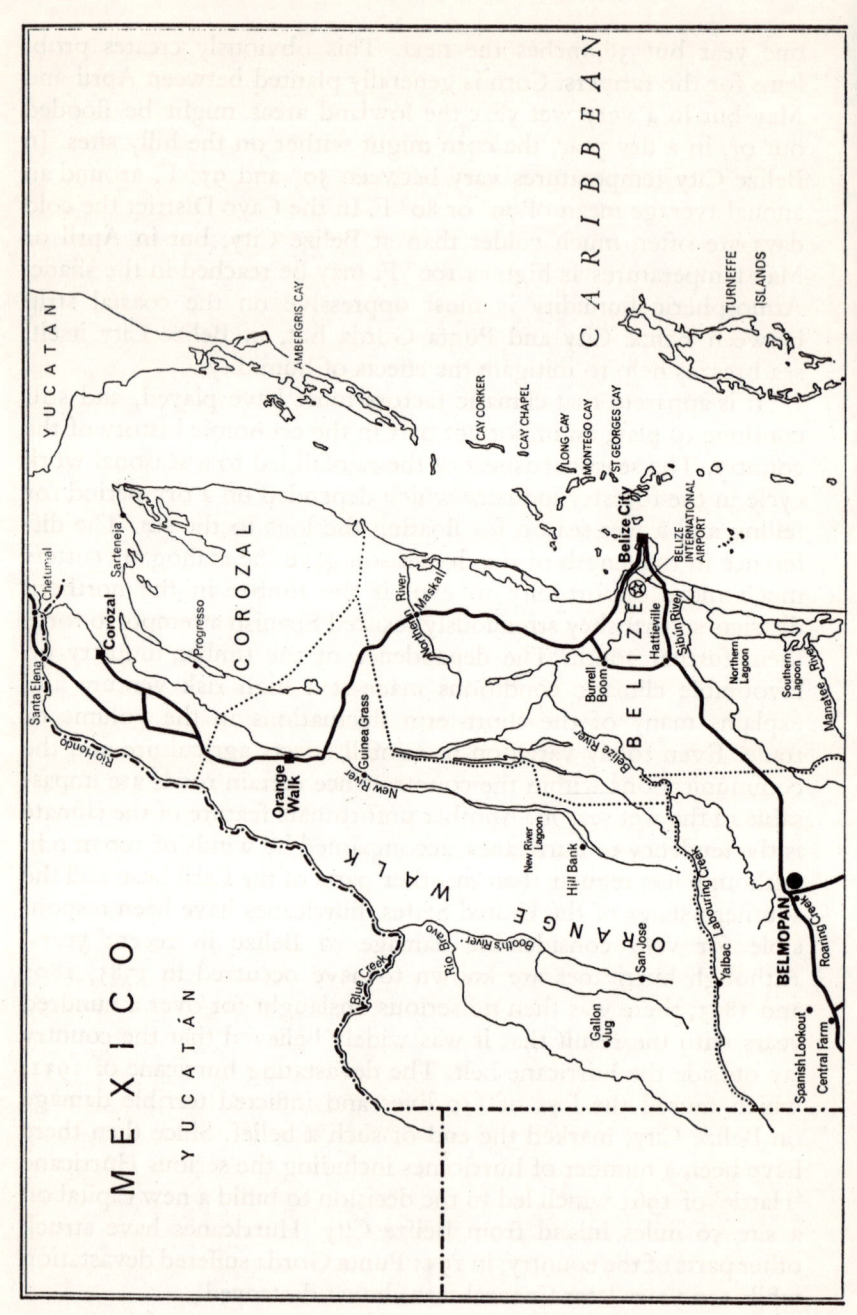

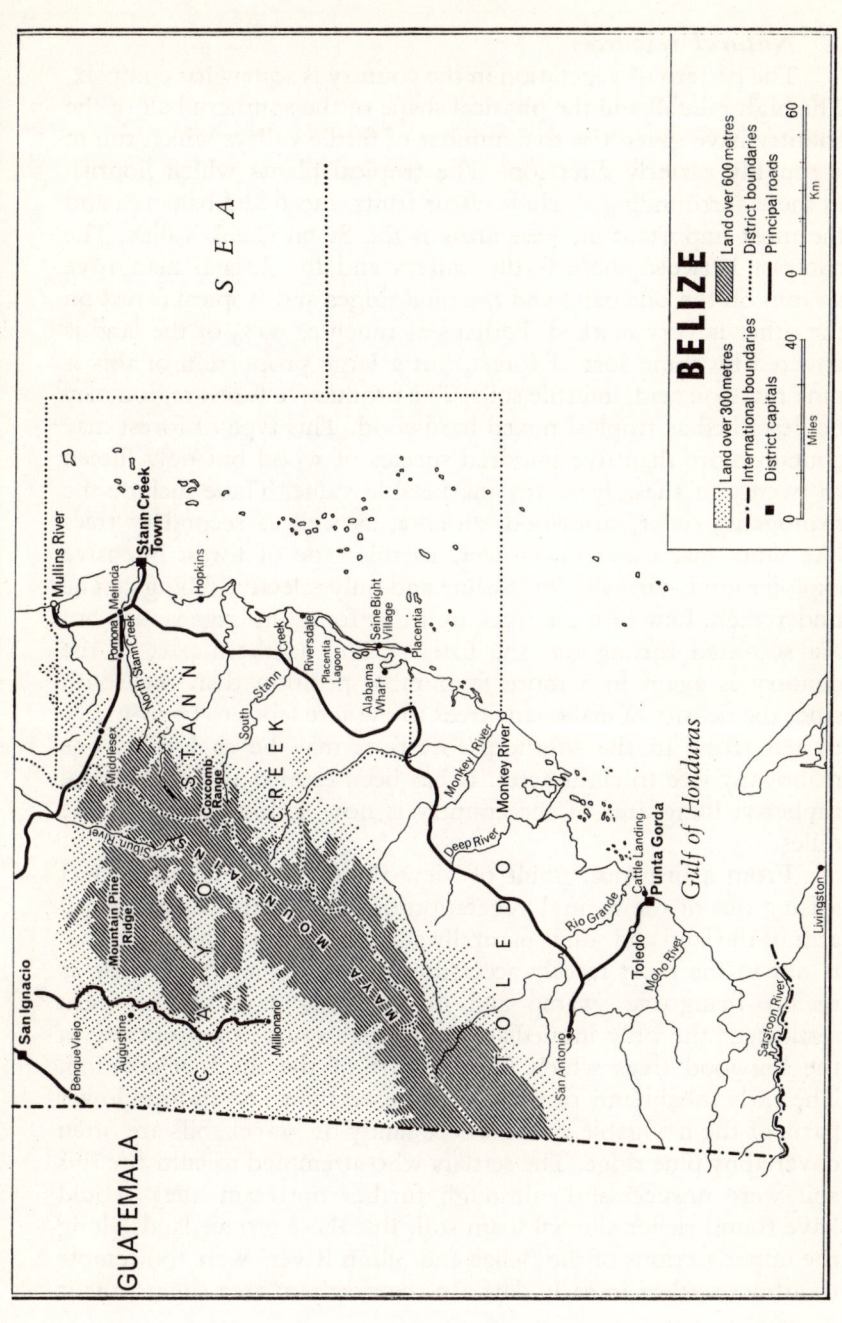

Natural resources

The pattern of vegetation in the country is somewhat complex. The high rainfall and the physical shape of the southern half of the country have given rise to a number of fertile valleys which run in a roughly easterly direction. The tropical plants which flourish in these surroundings include citrus fruits, cacao and bananas, and the most important of these areas is the Stann Creek Valley. The contrast between these fertile valleys and the coastal mangrove swamp on the one hand and the pine ridges and tropical forest on the other is very marked. Perhaps as much as 90% of the land is covered by some sort of forest, but a large proportion of this is pine ridge on acid, infertile soils. The productive forest region may be described as tropical mixed hardwood. This type of forest may contain more than five hundred species of wood but only fifteen to twenty of these have any marketable value. These include the mahogany, cedar, rosewood, ziricote, as well as secondary trees like santa maria and mayflower. In this type of forest intensive exploitation is virtually impossible and only selective felling can be undertaken. Few of these trees are to be found in large stands but are scattered throughout the forests. The northern part of the country is again in a more favourable position than the south since the density of mahogany trees to the acre tends to be from five to ten trees. In the southern forests it may be as low as one mahogany tree to eight acres. It has been estimated that the total timber-yielding area of the country is now as low as 120 square miles.

From a historical point of view there is one important fact arising out of the natural vegetation of the country. Only a small area of the land and soil is naturally suitable for agriculture and that is not in the most readily accessible regions. The coastal strip is mainly mangrove swamp and in the early days of European settlement the only immediately apparent source of profit lay in the logwood trees which formed part of the scrub vegetation. The early inhabitants of the country used the coast and the lower parts of the navigable rivers where sandy or gravel soils are often covered by pine ridge. The settlers who attempted to cultivate this soil were unsuccessful, although further upstream they would have found richer alluvial loam soil. But these terrace lands along the upper sections of the Belize and Sibún Rivers were too remote to attract settlers in early days. In the northern area sugar cane is now cultivated on suitable soil; but this is far enough removed from the main northern rivers for it not to have been apparent to prospective settlers until the influx of refugees from Yucatán in the mid-nineteenth century. Apart from the political fact of positive prohibition of agriculture by Spain there was a further obstacle to settlement and agriculture in the interior. Belize has been notorious from very early days for its insect life. The mosquito, sandfly, doctor fly and other insects thrive and, although modern systems of drainage and sanitation have done much to remove the health hazard of these insects in the cities, the fact remains that the unwary visitor is still liable to be severely bitten. Before the introduction of modern insecticides and mass spraying this proved a very real problem, especially in the interior of the country. The forest worker who knew that he was only spending a short period in the forests would tolerate the insect life, but to the prospective farmer likely to remain in one place the mosquitoes and sandflies proved very discouraging. A number of agricultural projects by foreign immigrants have been abandoned for this very reason.

Population and communication

Belize City has always been the centre of population and in recent years more than a third of the population has lived there. The other principal towns are also situated on the coast from Corozal in the north to Stann Creek and Punta Gorda in the south. The only inland towns of any size are San Ignacio and Benque Viejo in the western Cayo District, and Orange Walk which is situated between Belize City and Corozal in an area of potential agricultural importance. Communications between these towns were formerly by river. Despite innumerable surveys which were carried out in the late nineteenth century, and reports which recognized the need to build roads, little progress was made until the 1930s. The swampy land near the coast and the tropical forest in the interior do not favour road building and maintenance, but in the last few years great strides have been made in opening up the country by building all-weather roads between the most important centres. The use of light aircraft has greatly facilitated communications and the international airport near Belize City has now been extended to allow jet aeroplanes to land. Belize itself remains the principal port despite its lack of deep water facilities. Large ships have to anchor a mile or so off shore for all passengers and freight to be conveyed by launch or barge.

From the earliest days of the modern history of Belize geographical factors have played an all-important rôle in the economic life of the country. It was the abundance of logwood which drew the buccaneers to the swampy shores in the first place; it was the barrier reef formed by the cays which protected them from the Spaniards. Later, when the exploitation of the forests began with the felling of mahogany trees, the distribution of those trees together with the climate determined the way in which the timber industry functioned for well over a century. Geology, climate, vegetation and geographical position are all factors in the life and development of any country and must not be forgotten when we turn to consider the history of that country.

2

The Maya

The Maya civilization may seem very remote from the history of Belize, but in this land, over a thousand years ago, the ancient Maya lived and built their great ceremonial centres. The country which is now Belize formed only a small part of what was virtually a great cultural empire. Few traces of that empire remain for the historian, but the work of archaeologists has enabled us to know something of how the Maya people lived so long ago. Few Maya Indians of modern Belize are the direct descendants of those who once lived in the country, but nevertheless they tend their *milpas* in time-honoured fashion and have some of the same personal characteristics. Thus it is of some importance that a history should include an account of the people whose genius flowered in this land even before the birth of Christ and who lived there for many centuries longer than the period encompassed by the modern history of the country.

Early Man and his Environment in Central America

The earliest people to inhabit the American continent are now thought to have crossed from Asia to Alaska by the land bridge which connected the two continents before it was submerged by the sea about five thousand years ago. Human beings may have existed in Mexico as long ago as 20,000 B.C. and it is certain that they lived as far south as Chile 11,000 years ago. It is the task of archaeologists to discover the signs of early human occupation, to date their discoveries by scientific methods and to explain their importance. Other scientists have played a part in discovering and interpreting the facts about prehistoric man. For instance, botanists have recently been able to show from investigations in the Tehuacán region of Mexico that the area has been in almost continuous occupation since about 10,000 B.C. This conclusion emerged from an examination of the remains of corn cobs which revealed that corn had been cultivated by agriculturists there for over five thousand years.

It is unlikely that it will ever be possible to trace in detail the links between the civilized Maya and their primitive ancestors in Central America. Of all the civilizations which flowered in the New World before the Spanish Conquest the Maya reached the greatest heights; in some ways they even passed contemporaneous European cultures. The Maya people belonged to a larger group known as the Mesoamerican who inhabited the area between the dry Mexican plateau and a line running south from the republic of Honduras to El Salvador. Some of the features often ascribed to the Maya were in fact common to all Mesoamerican Indians. Among these were a form of hieroglyphic writing, a complicated calendar, a game played with a rubber ball in a special court, the use of cacao beans as money, books made of folded barkpaper and a religion which emphasized sacrifice to a large number of gods. The staple food of Mesoamerican Indians was maize, squash and beans, all of which were, and are, used in other parts of the Americas. Nevertheless it was only in this region that maize was prepared in such a way that it could be made into the characteristic tortilla. These similarities suggest that all the Mesoamerican Indians had some common origin far back in time and that over many centuries they had been in the habit of exchanging ideas and possessions. The Maya today number about two million people who still retain remarkable cohesion in spite of the intrusion of modern civilization. Moreover, unlike certain other tribes which are scattered throughout Mexico and Central America, the Maya-speaking peoples live in one area which includes Yucatán, Guatemala, Belize, parts of the Mexican states of Chiapas and Tabasco and the western parts of El Salvador and Honduras. Within this area fifteen Maya languages or dialects are spoken while two more became extinct in recent times. It is a remarkable fact that in this same area are to be found all the remains and ruins classified as part of the Maya civilization. This indicates that the Maya have never been inclined to wander far from their homes or to attempt the invasion of other lands. Estimates of the total Maya population at its height have varied so much and have so little factual basis that they are almost worthless. One archaeologist has suggested as many as thirteen million people in the Yucatán peninsula alone, but the more usual estimates range from between one and three million for the whole area.

Geographically, the area occupied by the Maya divides readily into the highlands, dominated by the volcanic range extending eastwards from Chiapas in a curve through El Salvador; and the lowland area of the Peten and the Yucatan peninsula. The Maya Mountains of Belize are isolated but must be considered as part of the highland region. In the highlands pine trees and grasses provide the natural vegetation. Although the same crops are grown as in the lowlands there are differences in farming methods. On the higher slopes the fields are cultivated for ten years and then allowed to lie fallow for as long as fifteen years. Lower down the slopes it is possible to till one field for up to fifteen years and then allow it only five years fallow. Where the population is dense, as in the highlands of Guatemala, different kinds of maize are planted through the year and secondary crops of squash, beans and chili peppers are planted between the maize. The lowland region is dominated by the limestone shelf of the Peten–Yucatan peninsula which juts up into the Gulf of Mexico to the north and west and forms a barrier reef along the east coast. The lowlands have only a few freely flowing rivers in the west and south-east: the Belize and Hondo Rivers being two of the more important. There are few lakes, and in Yucatán water supply has always been a problem: settlements often grew around the cenotes or large holes formed by the collapse of underground limestone caves. In the dry season the lowlands can be very hot and although, like the highlands, they enjoy a rainy season from May to October, the rainfall is sometimes sparse, especially in the north. In the southern part of the lowlands where the rainfall is higher, as in the Toledo district of Belize, the land is covered by monsoon forest. Apart from the mahogany, cedar and sapodilla trees, there are many fruit trees, such as the avocado, which have always provided an important part of the Maya diet. Intermingled with the forest are areas of broad savannah with coarse grasses and stunted trees. The savannahs are avoided by farmers but are burned by hunters to encourage the growth of new grasses which then attract game. Further north the forest becomes thorny jungle and finally scrub. The soil varies in its fertility from the rich soil of the Petén to the barren rock-like earth of Yucatán. The task of the Maya farmer in these regions has always been a hard one and has changed little over the centuries. The only possible method has been that of shifting cultivation where the forest has been cut down, burned and the resulting plot, or *milpa*, planted with maize seed by poking holes through the ashes with a stick. A *milpa* can only be cultivated for two years and must then remain fallow for at least four years in the more favourable areas of the Petén or as long as twenty years in Yucatán. It has only recently been appreciated that this primitive system of agriculture can be quite productive and that one farmer in the Petén may provide sufficient food for twelve people. This fact was of the utmost importance to the ancient Maya since it freed a sufficient number of men to build their great edifices and carry out the ceremonies connected with them. Another important difference between the Maya highlands and lowlands was the greater abundance of animals in the latter. There lived monkeys, deer and peccary, as well as the jaguars hunted for their skins and tapirs for their meat and tough hide. Of the many beautiful birds, including parrots and toucans, the quetzal, whose feathers were so highly prized by the ancient Maya, was only to be found in the highlands.

The Maya areas

The lands inhabited by the Maya in ancient times are usually classified into three main 'Areas'. The Southern Area included the highlands of Guatemala, Chiapas and the coastal plain along the Pacific with part of El Salvador. The Central Area was based on the Petén and stretched from Tabasco to Belize and the Río Motagua in Guatemala and included a small part of the Honduras Republic. The Northern Area of Yucatán formed a third centre of Maya civilization which, in spite of the poorer soils and dry climate, was never completely abandoned and where there are still many Maya Indians. It was in the Central Area that Maya civilization flowered most freely and where the characteristic buildings, stelae and hieroglyphic writing have been found by archaeologists. Since A.D. 1000 much of this area has been covered by tropical

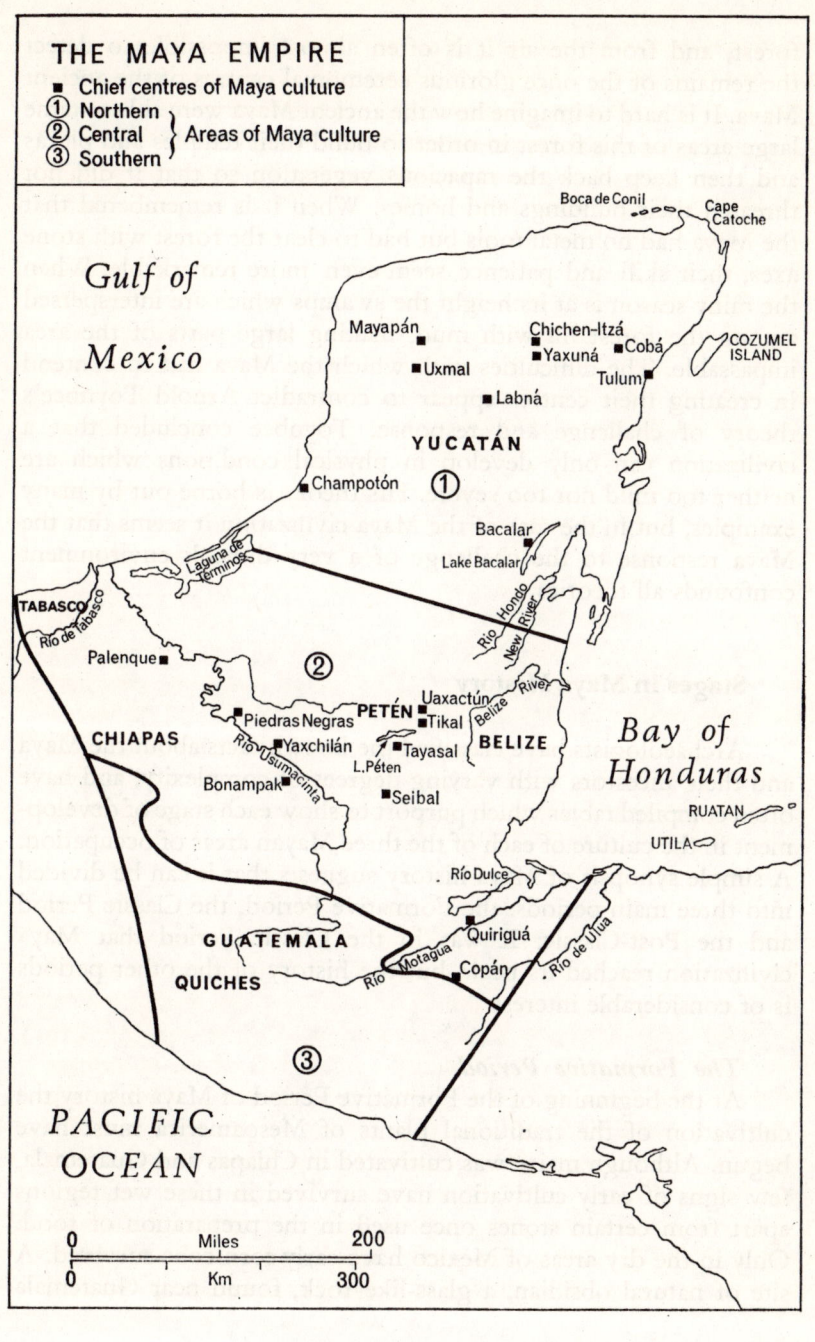

THE MAYA EMPIRE
■ Chief centres of Maya culture
① Northern
② Central   Areas of Maya culture
③ Southern

Gulf of
Mexico

Boca de Conil

Cape
Catoche

COZUMEL
ISLAND

Mayapán   Chichen-Itzá
                    ■Yaxuná   ■Cobá
    ■Uxmal
        ■Labná   Tulum■

YUCATÁN

①

■Champotón

Bacalar■

Lake Bacalar■

TABASCO

Laguna de
Términos

Río de Tabasco

Palenque■

Río Hondo

New River

②

PETÉN   Uaxactún■
Piedras Negras■   ■Tikal

CHIAPAS   ■Yaxchilán   ▲Tayasal
                    L.Péten
    Bonampak■   ■Seibal

Río Usumacinta

Belize River

BELIZE

Bay of
Honduras

RUATAN

UTILA

Río Dulce■

GUATEMALA   Quiriguá■
                    ■Copán
QUICHES

Río Motagua

Río de Ulúa

③

PACIFIC
OCEAN

0   Miles   200
0   Km   300

forest, and from the air it is often almost impossible to detect the remains of the once glorious ceremonial centres of the ancient Maya. It is hard to imagine how the ancient Maya were able to tame large areas of this forest in order to build their temples and plazas and then keep back the rapacious vegetation so that it did not threaten their buildings and homes. When it is remembered that the Maya had no metal tools but had to clear the forest with stone axes, their skill and patience seem even more remarkable. When the rainy season is at its height the swamps which are interspersed among the forest fill with mud, making large parts of the area impassable. The difficulties with which the Maya had to contend in creating their centres appear to contradict Arnold Toynbee's theory of challenge and response. Toynbee concluded that a civilization can only develop in physical conditions which are neither too mild nor too severe. His theory is borne out by many examples, but in the case of the Maya civilization it seems that the Maya response to the challenge of a very difficult environment confounds all theories.

Stages in Maya History

Archaeologists have classified the known facts about the Maya and their ancestors with varying degrees of complexity, and have often compiled tables which purport to show each stage of development in the culture of each of the three Mayan areas of occupation. A simple synopsis of Maya history suggests that it can be divided into three main periods: the Formative Period, the Classic Period and the Post-Classic. It was in the Classic Period that Maya civilization reached its peak, but the history of the other periods is of considerable interest.

The Formative Period

At the beginning of the Formative Period of Maya history the cultivation of the traditional plants of Mesoamerica must have begun. Although maize was cultivated in Chiapas and Guatemala, few signs of early cultivation have survived in these wet regions apart from certain stones once used in the preparation of food. Only in the dry areas of Mexico have early corn cobs survived. A site of natural obsidian, a glass-like rock, found near Guatemala

City has revealed thousands of crude tools and blades dating from this time and resembling similar artefacts found in Mexico. The Formative Period, which lasted from some time around 1500 B.C. to approximately A.D. 325, saw the growth of agriculture based on densely populated villages. This phase was common to all Middle America and there was a similar level of culture and religion throughout the region. Good pottery and figurines were produced and some pyramids were built. Towards the end of this phase an elementary calendar had evolved with the beginnings of hieroglyphic writing. The main centres of development appear to have been along the Pacific coast and in the Guatemala highlands. But there is also evidence that the lowland areas were occupied and were developing a simple culture. In fact it is now known that the distinctive achievements of the Classic Maya were beginning to emerge as early as 300 B.C. to A.D. 300.

The Classic Period

The Classic Period itself is often divided into two periods of Early and Late Classic with the division made about A.D. 600. By the time the Classic age of Maya splendour opened about A.D. 200 pyramids, platforms and elaborate tombs had already been constructed at the Petén sites of Tikal and Uaxactún. Moreover some of the early temples were decorated with vivid mural paintings. At this early date there were also important new ceramic features which may have originated or been elaborated in Belize. Among these was the use of polychrome in decorating pottery. Maya polychrome involved the application of a brilliant range of colours to a glossy orange underslip. Only at the beginning of the Classic Period were monuments erected with Long Count dates and hieroglyphic writing, although these two features were already in existence in the Southern Area of the highlands and the Pacific coast. During the Early Classic Period the distinctive features of Maya architecture were already making their appearance. The use of the corbelled vault, or arch, in building was widespread. Stelae were erected at many sites and the glyphs carved on these and other monuments show that the lowland Maya were using the Long Count calendar by A.D. 300. They can also be used to confirm the dates of buildings arrived at by other archaeological methods. At this time the highland centres were at their peak, but were shortly to come under the influence of Teotihuacán, a powerful city in central Mexico. From about A.D. 400 groups from that city profoundly influenced or perhaps even seized the main centres of Maya activity in the Southern Area and built there a miniature version of Teotihuacán. The individual Maya genius then gave way to Mexican influence and it was in the lowlands of the Central and Northern areas that Maya civilization continued to develop.

From about A.D. 600 these areas saw the enlargement of great ceremonial centres, embellished sometimes with elaborate carvings and sculpture as at Tikal, Quiriguá and Copán, or with vigorous paintings as at Bonampak and the much later ones at Santa Rita in Belize. Unfortunately the Santa Rita murals were destroyed by Indians out of superstitious fear as soon as they were discovered and before they could be completely copied. Beautifully made pottery figurines and articles in jade and other stones were designed at this time and were used as articles of trade between the various centres. In this period also the Maya elaboration of the calendar with an associated interest in arithmetic and astronomy was at its height. But already by A.D. 800 there were signs of collapse as the great ceremonial centres were gradually abandoned. Whereas in A.D. 790 no fewer than nineteen hieroglyphic monuments were dedicated at different centres, a hundred years later only three inscriptions seem to have been made to celebrate an important date in the Maya calendar.

The Post-Classic Period

Gradually the great ceremonial centres of the Petén were abandoned and by the beginning of the tenth century the ever-threatening forest was already encroaching upon the temples, the pyramids and plazas of the Classic Maya. The reasons for this collapse have not yet been satisfactorily explained. Among the many suggestions put forward have been disease, the decline of priestly authority, the failure of crops owing to soil exhaustion, and earthquakes. In the last few years it has become more fashionable to believe that the explanation is to be found in invasion and conquest from Mexico. Certainly by the middle of the ninth century there are signs of Mexican influence in the art of the western part of the Central area. Stelae erected during this period at Seibal show details of costumes with a definite Mexican flavour. Recent excavations at Altar de Sacrificios, Piedras Negras and Seibal revealed a type of fine paste pottery which is thought to have been made on the Gulf of Mexico. The conclusion has been drawn that during the ninth century people from the north invaded the Petén using the River Usumacinta system and leaving behind a trail of destruction. This invasion may have been part of a wider movement southwards from Mexico, or the conquerors of Seibal may have been Chontal Maya from the lower Usumacinta who had come under strong Mexican influence. In the tenth century there was probably a simple village culture similar to that of the Formative Period during which occasional visits were made to the abandoned centres for burials and other rites.

The Toltecs

By the end of the tenth century the independent Maya had yielded to a military race from the highlands of central Mexico. The Toltec people emerged to fill a vacuum caused by the collapse of older Mexican civilizations and settled in Tula soon after A.D. 900. Their king was one called Topíltzin, who also claimed to be Quetzalcóatl, a peaceful hero of Mexican myth. But there were also more military minded leaders and after a bitter conflict the king was forced to leave Tula. This city became the centre of an empire and has been identified as an archaeological site about fifty miles to the north-west of Mexico City. It was destroyed in the mid-twelfth century but its power and prestige was such that a good deal is known about the Toltecs. The king who left Tula, probably in A.D. 987, is said to have moved along the Gulf Coast and eventually established his capital at Chichen Itzá in northern Yucatán. Unfortunately the historical accounts of his arrival have been confused with that of the later Itzá people who did not reach Chichen until the thirteenth century and then gave their name to that city.

Although Topíltzin Quetzalcóatl was traditionally a peaceful ruler, all the evidence provided by murals from the Temple of Warriors at Chichen shows that the conquest of Yucatán by the Toltecs was a brutal business. The Maya were defeated in battle and the murals depict the heart sacrifices of their leaders. After this defeat the other great northern centres such as Uxmaal seem to have been deserted and Chichen Itzá became the splendid centre of a large kingdom. New styles of architecture and designs from Tula were absorbed into the old Maya art. Huge halls were built in which columns instead of solid walls were used to create a more spacious atmosphere; stone benches with carvings of Toltec warriors and feathered serpents were common and old Maya masks with long-nosed serpents were introduced. It was not only in art that Toltec and Maya practice was blended but also in religious and social life. The ball court built during this period is both the largest and best found anywhere; the game seems to have been played here in the Mexican fashion with two stone rings set high in the walls. When the rubber ball had been thrown through one of the rings the team which accomplished this feat not only won the game but was entitled to the clothing of the spectators. It is possible that even the lives of the players were at stake for nearby is a long platform carved with human skulls.

At every site occupied by the Toltecs in Yucatán, metal implements have been found. Most of these were probably imported and, as there was no local copper, it is hardly surprising that the surviving copper bells show signs of Mexican workmanship. The other significant find on Toltec sites is the glazed pottery known as plumbate, produced near the Pacific on the border between Chiapas and Guatemala. The centre at Chichen Itzá has yielded not only the bones of sacrificial victims, but gold disks dating from this period and many finely worked jades. However, in the days of the Toltecs the peak of the sacrificial cult was yet to come and most of the objects which have been recovered from the bottom of the well date from a later period in the history of Chichen Itzá.

The Itza people

At some time early in the thirteenth century, before 1224, Chichen seems to have been abandoned; nothing is known of what happened to the Toltecs except that they were succeeded by the Itzá people. To some extent the Maya of Yucatán had accepted the Toltecs and adapted their way of life to Toltec rule, but the Itzá were always regarded as foreigners and usually as rascals. During the Toltec ascendancy the Itzá probably lived at Champotón on the Campeche coast; later they seem to have been driven eastwards to Lake Petén Itzá and the coast of Belize, where they made their way northwards and eventually settled in the abandoned city of Chichen Itzá about 1230. The cult of the Sacred Well was intensified and that to the Goddess of Medicine introduced, with its shrine on the island of Cozumel. Some thirty or forty years later the city of Mayapán was founded by the Itzá and for a time became the capital of Yucatan. Mayapán was the first genuine city to appear in the Maya area. It covered about two and a half square miles and was surrounded by a defensive wall. It has been estimated that nearly 12,000 people lived within its walls, albeit in poor and cramped conditions. In the centre of Mayapán stood the temple, a poor copy of the Castillo at Chichen Itzá, while nearby were the stone houses of the more important citizens. The poorer people lived in thatched roof houses nearer the perimeter of the city.

The decline of the Maya

Meanwhile the Quiche had established a similar empire in the Guatemala highlands where, as in Mayapán, the rulers exercised tyranny over the people. Gradually the influence of Mexican culture declined and once again the ruling families spoke the Maya language and practised the Maya religion. Nevertheless the traditional Maya arts were in decay and by the mid-fifteenth century anarchy was so widespread that petty tribal revolts brought about the ruin of Mayapán. The Itza people once again wandered through the scrubland of Yucatan to the jungles of the Petén where they found refuge on an island in the middle of Lake Petén. There they built Tayasal, the modern Guatemalan city of Flores, where they remained unmolested by the Spaniards until as late as 1697. Cortés was received there on his great journey of 1524 and although several missionaries were sent during the sixteenth and seventeenth centuries in an attempt to convert the people, they were able to retain their traditional beliefs and rites in isolation. Once Mayapan had fallen Yucatán ceased to be one kingdom, but became the battle-ground of sixteen rival states with petty princelings engaged in endless disputes over land. There was little opportunity for any form of culture but town life continued in each area. The only site to survive from this period was Tulum, founded during the Mayapán era, on the Caribbean coast. The other sites were used by the Spaniards and therefore destroyed or rebuilt in accordance with Spanish taste. Like Mayapán Tulum was surrounded by a defensive wall, but the architecture was of poor quality and the workmanship of the decorations shoddy. Some of the frescoes found there are Maya in character but also show signs of the influence of the Mixtec people. Apart from the usual scenes illustrating the activities of the gods, the Tulum frescoes show the Rain God seated upon a four-legged animal. Obviously the artists of Tulum had learned about the Spanish horses before the subjugation of the town or else Tulum must have survived the Spanish Conquest.

The Book of Chilam Balam predicted that men with beards would come from the east and they would be received by the Maya. But the discovery of Yucatán in 1517 was not immediately followed up because the Spaniards were more interested in the tales of Mexican gold. The conquest of Yucatán proved to be a prolonged struggle: the Maya were no mean fighters and they knew how to live on the difficult terrain of the peninsula. However, by 1542, the Conquistadores had established their capital at Mérida and the Maya civilization was finally broken.

Maya Achievements

What were the achievements of the Mayan civilization? Why is it regarded as the greatest of the pre-Columbian civilizations in the New World? These questions are not as easy to answer as might be assumed. One of the difficulties is to state with any certainty the unique qualities and achievements of the Maya since so many were shared with the other Indians of Mesoamerica.

Inventions and discoveries

The difficulty is immediately apparent in trying to discover the source of certain inventions which were undoubtedly made in the region. Among these was the manufacture of rubber and its use for making balls, sandals and other articles. The brilliant turquoise blue known as Maya blue was much used in painting murals and was probably discovered by the Maya, as was the dye obtained from the logwood tree. An immense number of wild plants and fruits were first domesticated by the American Indian, but again it is difficult to attribute the discoveries to any one area or people. It seems possible that the Maya were the first to cultivate the important cacao, papaya and aguacate, or avocado pear, as all these trees grow wild in the Maya area. Maya farmers also kept stingless bees, and honey was a valuable export from Yucatán, together with the salt which was found in great quantity there. Hunting of animals such as deer and peccary was done by means of traps and spears; the birds which formed part of the Maya diet, such as wild pigeon and partridge, were shot by clay pellets from blowguns. It was not until a much later date, when Mayapan dominated northern Yucatán, that the bow and arrow was introduced from Mexico. The general use of metals dates from about the same time, although gold and copper objects were known earlier. Bronze and copper axes were in use in Yucatan by the time of the Spanish Conquest but were still by no means common.

Building methods and architecture

The Maya built roads although they had no wheeled vehicles to use them. The longest Maya road known, that between Coba and Yaxuna, is 62½ miles long. The way in which the roads were built, often through swampy areas, demonstrates no mean engineering skill, although the Maya were never as adept as the Inca people in this type of construction. It is possible that the roads were first built as processional ways, but Cobá is the centre of a network of roads which must have been used for more normal purposes of trade. These Yucatán roads were built during the Classic Period, and other shorter ones have been found in the Petén around Uaxactun.

The Maya centres connected by these roads were better constructed than those of their neighbours. The Classic Maya sites have often been mistakenly described as cities, but it has been conclusively shown that the majority of the people lived in scattered villages separated from others by natural features such as swamps or savannahs. The houses in the villages were often in compounds and were constructed of pole and thatch. Many Maya Indians still build their homes in the same way using palm leaves for thatch and liana in place of nails. It has been estimated that for every 50–100 of these dwellings in the Central Maya area there was a small ceremonial centre comprising at least one temple-pyramid and other large buildings. This complex formed a zone, but since Maya settlements were unplanned it is often difficult to separate one zone from another. The larger and more impressive sites, such as Palenque or Tikal in the Central Area and Uxmal in the Northern Area, were the centres for districts which were sub-divided into several zones. Tikal is the only Maya site in which the surrounding area has been completely mapped; within six square miles there are about 3,000 structures of very varying kinds. In the Late Classic

Period the total population must have numbered approximately 10,000.

In appearance a Classic site contained a series of stone buildings arranged around plazas or courtyards. These comprised the huge temple-pyramids built from limestone with a rubble core and often incorporating structures of an earlier period. These temples contained at least one and often several plaster-covered rooms with corbelled vaults, but these rooms were so narrow that they can only have been used for private ceremonies and rites performed by the priests on special occasions. Far more in evidence are the single storied buildings, sometimes described as palaces. These contained many plastered rooms, but it is not clear whether they were occupied by the rulers or not. The courtyards had stucco surfaces, and in the principal centres rows of stelae were erected in front of the important temples and sometimes the palaces. Carved in relief on the stelae were Maya figures in rich attire often carrying an emblem or trampling on a wretched prisoner; the other faces of the stelae were inscribed with glyphs and Long Count dates. Frequently the stela had a low flat-topped altar in front of it.

Whereas the early Maya buildings were constructed of large stones, or block masonry, the later ones were made of solid concrete with a veneer of thin well-cut stones. The use of concrete, made from lime and marl, produced much stronger buildings. The corbelled vault or arch was the most distinctive feature of Maya architecture and shows that the Maya understood the problems of stress and stability. The use of corbelled vaults created many difficulties and it is perhaps surprising that in their architectural experiments the Maya never discovered the principle of the true arch. Another feature common to most sites was the ball court, one of the best of these is at Copán in the western part of Honduras. There beautiful sculptured macaw heads were used as markers for the game. At Copán good volcanic stone was available to the sculptors and the results can be seen in the brilliantly executed stone figures of the gods which decorate the temples, the stelae and the altars. The stairway up the main temple is inscribed with a lengthy text of over two thousand glyphs. Another outstanding ruin in the Central Area thirty miles north of Copán is Quiriguá, a smaller site distinguished by its gigantic sandstone stelae, one of which is thirty-five feet high. Tikal itself contained no fewer than six great temples, and although the stone carvings of Tikal are not among the greatest Maya sculptures the wooden lintels over the doorways of the temples were exquisitely carved. At Tikal there are also ten reservoirs which the Maya built for drinking water. At Yaxchilan the carved stone lintels provide valuable clues to history and to the meaning of the Maya glyphs. At Palenque stuccowork of the highest quality was used to decorate the pillars of the huge palace. Excavations there have revealed a number of tombs containing precious objects, but in 1952 a Mexican archaeologist made the greatest discovery of all. In examining the floor of the Temple of the Inscriptions he found a removable stone slab which led into the pyramid by means of a staircase which had been deliberately blocked with rubble. After four seasons of excavation Alberto Ruz at last opened up a great funeral chamber thirty feet long and twenty-three feet high, around which were huge relief carvings of men. Inside the tomb lay a middle-aged man of evident distinction for he was surrounded by jade treasures and his face was covered with a mosaic mask of the same precious stone. The corpse was in all probability that of a late seventh-century ruler of Palenque who had his funeral chamber made and possibly surmounted by the temple-pyramid during his own lifetime in a manner similar to that of the ancient Egyptians.

In the Northern Area the low Puuc hills have many Maya sites which flourished during the Classic Period. The Puuc buildings are superior in style to those of the Petén and are characterized by the use of fine limestone veneer over a cement and rubble core, round columns in doors, and the use of stone mosaics with an emphasis on serpent-style faces. Of these sites Uxmal is undoubtedly the finest and the site displays the full genius of the Maya architects and artists. The Governor's Palace at Uxmal is possibly the culmination of Maya architectural achievement.

Maya arts

Unfortunately Maya artistic triumphs have not survived the ravages of time and climate so well as their buildings, but at Bonampak, in 1946, clear evidence was found of Maya artistic skill. A series of immensely vigorous and skilfully executed paintings covered the walls of three rooms in one of the buildings. The paintings, dating from shortly after A.D. 800, illustrate in narrative form a battle and the celebrations of victory afterwards. They have thrown a new light on the warlike interests of the Maya and the organization of Maya society. This chance discovery serves to remind us that we may never know the full extent of Maya genius at the height of its civilization. Pottery vessels were often painted with animated scenes and some of the modelled pottery objects were works of great skill. Many small figurines designed to be used as whistle's were delicately carved and are objects of great beauty.

Although no Maya textiles have survived, great weaving skill is evident from the designs of costumes depicted in mural paintings and carved stelae. The elaborate headdresses and prized feathers, leatherwork and basketry have succumbed to the atmosphere, and there is not one place in the entire Maya area sufficiently dry to have preserved such objects. But the greatest loss of all is undoubtedly the books in which the Maya recorded their rituals and their learning. These books were written on long strips of paper made from bark and then folded like screens. Only three books have been found in legible condition and all are concerned with Maya rituals and astronomy, none of them dating from the Classic Period. The finest of the three is the Dresden Codex which may have been written during the Toltec period at Chichen Itzá; it measures eight inches in height and is over eleven feet long. The Madrid and Paris Codices are of later date and in much poorer condition. It is the dream of all Maya archaeologists that further books may yet come to light. That this is now unlikely is suggested by the recent discovery during the excavations at Altun Ha of the fragments of several codices. Other literary evidence for Maya civilization is to be found in the thousands of inscriptions carved at Classic sites, but not yet fully deciphered. Valuable information came from the post-Conquest accounts of men such as Bishop Landa and from the curious Books of Chilam Balam which were written in the colonial period in Maya but using Spanish script. It is from these few sources that modern knowledge of Maya learning and ritual is derived.

The Maya calendar

As far as can be known ancient Maya skills in astronomy, their use of numbers and their elaborate calendar were all developed for religious rather than secular purposes. In considering these achievements it must be remembered that the height of Maya civilization was reached during the so-called Dark Ages in Europe. As we have seen, many of the Maya achievements were shared by other

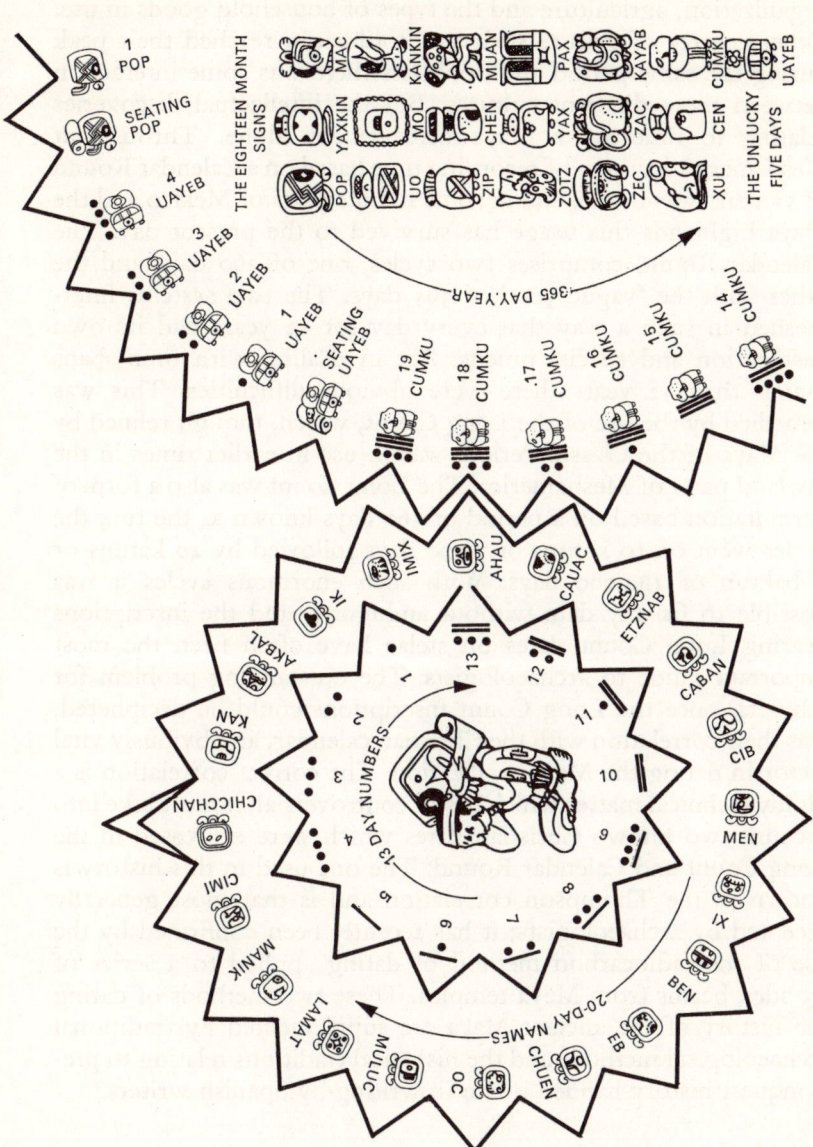

The very complicated calendar invented by the Mayas. The wheel on the left shows the sacred year of 260 days; the wheel on the right shows part of the calendar year of 365 days. The Maya calendar year contained eighteen months of twenty days each, and an unlucky period of five days.

Mesoamerican cultures; there were similarities in religion, social organization, agriculture and the types of household goods in use. Other centres of culture such as Teotihuacán reached their peak during the same period and doubtless there was some interaction between these different cultures. But the intellectual discoveries relating to time are a Maya achievement alone. Throughout Mesoamerica a system of recording time based on a Calendar Round of 52 years was in use, and in some remote parts of Mexico and the Maya highlands this usage has survived to the present day. The Calendar Round comprises two cycles, one of 260 days and the other with the 'vague year' of 365 days. The two systems intermeshed in such a way that every day for 52 years had its own designation and special omens. But in dealing with time spans longer than 52 years there were obvious difficulties. This was remedied by the use of the Long Count, which, though refined by the Maya of the Classic Period, was in use in earlier times in the lowland parts of Mesoamerica. The Long Count was also a form of permutation based on a period of 360 days known as the tun; the cycles went on to katuns of 7,200 days followed by 20 katuns or 1 baktun of 144,000 days. With such enormous cycles it was possible to fix any date without ambiguity, and the inscriptions bearing Long Count dates on stelae have often been the most important guide to archaeologists. The outstanding problem for scholars, once the Long Count inscriptions could be deciphered, was their correlation with the Christian calendar, an obviously vital factor in dating the Maya civilization. The correct correlation is a highly technical matter which is still controversial; it must take into account two known Christian dates which were expressed in the Long Count and Calendar Round. The one used in this history is known as the Thompson correlation and is that most generally accepted by archaeologists; it has recently been confirmed by the use of the radiocarbon method of dating applied to a series of wooden beams from Maya temples. These two methods of dating the history of the ancient Maya are supplemented by traditional archaeological methods and the historical traditions relating to pre-Conquest history handed down in writing by Spanish writers.

Mathematics

The Maya obsession with time caused them to inscribe Long Count dates on stelae and buildings throughout the Central and

Northern areas. The Long Count date went back to some far-distant point in time and in order to carry out the necessary calendrical calculations the Maya developed a positional system of

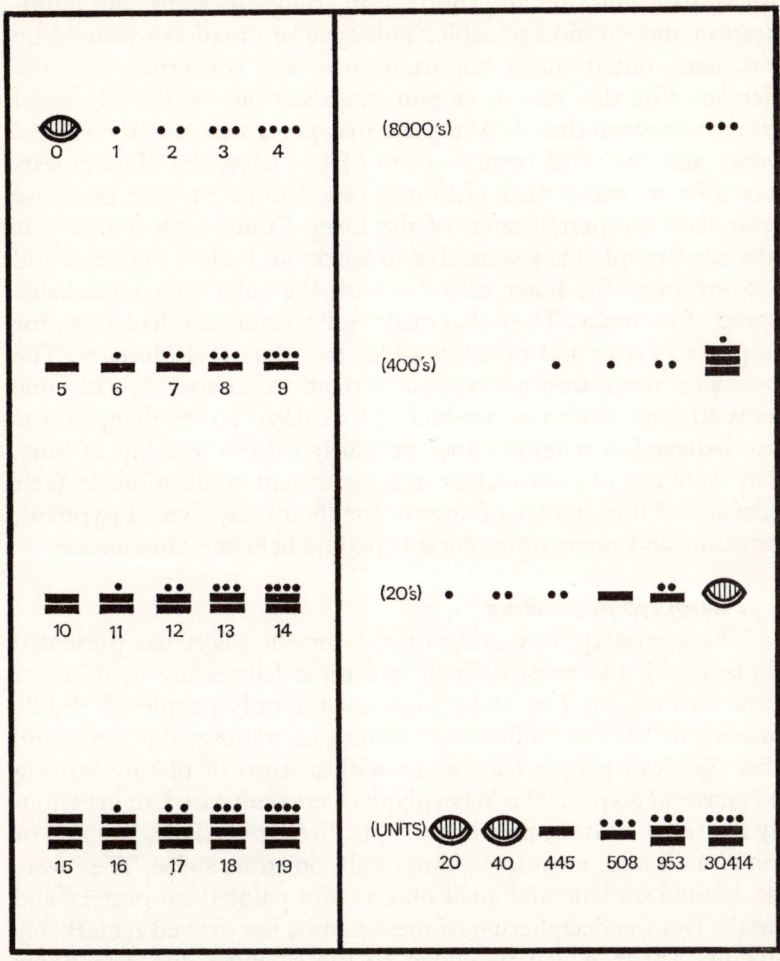

Maya numbers. Examples of larger numbers are shown on the right. These are counted from top to bottom.

numeration, that is to say the position of the symbols relative to one another was used to express numerical value. By using this method the Maya were able to make elaborate mathematical calculations with only three symbols—the dot for one, a bar for five and a shell for nought. The system adopted was a vigesimal[1] one, unlike our decimal one, and instead of increasing from right to left the Maya system increased from the bottom to the top of a column. The system made addition and subtraction straightforward, and multiplication and division possible. This type of notation was used by merchants, but its most important use was concerned with the calendar. For this reason certain modifications of the vigesimal system were introduced. When the first place was one, the second twenty and the third became a tun of 360 days, the Maya priests were able to make their elaborate calculations of time past and manipulate the permutation of the Long Count with the 52-year Calendar Round. They were able to work out tables of eclipses and to co-ordinate the lunar calendar with the solar to a remarkable degree of accuracy. They also made quite accurate calculations for the planet Venus and possibly tables for Mars and Mercury. The Maya were not astronomers as such: their preoccupation with time seems to have been the product of astrology rather than, as was once believed, a religion based primarily on the worship of time. They were not of course alone among ancient civilizations in their belief in the importance of augury for their daily lives: Egyptians, Etruscans and many other ancient people held the same beliefs.

Hieroglyphic writing

The hieroglyphic writing of the ancient Maya has presented scholars with the most difficult and most frustrating problem of Maya civilization. The Maya were not the only people of Middle America to have a rudimentary system of writing; the Aztec and other Mexican people had books with a form of picture writing and pictorial glyphs. The Maya glyphs were sculptured, or occasionally incised, on altars, panels, walls, ball-court markers, wooden or stone lintels and, most important of all, on stone stelae. They were also incised on jade and shell objects and painted on pottery and murals. But the deciphering of these glyphs has proved remarkably difficult. Those which pertained to the calendar and astronomy were the most straightforward: Bishop Landa's work enabled a nineteenth-century French Abbé to recognize day glyphs and numerals, and it was soon realized that Maya writing was arranged in double columns to be read from top to bottom. But after the early discoveries of glyphs for the months, Long Count, world

1. A counting system using twenties as basis.

directions and colours, progress was so slow that it has been suggested that the inscription and codices were meaningless except for the information they provide about the calendar. The most important and exciting discovery of recent years may eventually lead to the complete deciphering of the Maya hieroglyphic writing. In 1958 Heinrich Berlin demonstrated that there was a special 'Emblem Glyph' for specific Maya centres and he suggested that these represented the names of the centres or of the ruling dynasty and that their history might be recorded on the stelae and other monuments on each site. This suggestion was followed up by another scholar who analysed thirty-five monuments from Piedras Negras. It was then found that the stelae were in groups of seven and that the dates on the seven monuments in a group spanned only the lifetime of one person. It has now been proved that each group recorded the history of a single reign and included such facts as the date of the ruler's birth, his accession to power, his marriage and important events such as military victories. Some inscriptions are of special interest in that they reveal a connection between one Classic Maya centre and another. At Yaxchilán the stone lintels carved with glyphs have revealed the rule of a militant family in the eighth century. A similar deciphering of names and titles preceded the unravelling of the Egyptian script, and it is to be hoped that the Maya script will eventually yield to the work of scholars in the same way.

Religion

The Maya codices and the Books of Chilam Balam deal only with religious, annalistic and calendrical matters and their texts include many pictures of the Maya gods. What were the main features of the ancient Maya religion and what part did the Maya priests play in the daily lives of the people? The main source of information for the ancient Maya religion are the three codices which have survived together with the religious sculptures and inscriptions from the Classic sites. Other information is derived from the accounts of Spanish friars in the immediate post-Conquest period and similar sources which have been tainted by the introduction of Mexican and Spanish ideas and practices. It is dangerous to assume that Maya religion remained the same from the Classic Period until the Spanish Conquest. There were undoubtedly some variations over a period of time just as there were local differences. In the highland area of Guatemala, for instance, the mountains were personified and a cult of mountain gods developed which never spread to the lowlands of the Petén or Yucatán. The Maya view of the universe had features comparable with other Mesoamerican religions and among these was the notion of cyclical creation and destruction. The Maya seem to have regarded the earth as flat with four corners and a colour for each cardinal point, red for east and black for west. The sky had thirteen compartments or layers each inhabited by different gods, while the underworld had nine layers with nine 'Lords of the Night' in command. To this cold underworld most Maya were believed to descend after death.

The Maya gods themselves cannot be counted; their multiplicity is explained by the fact that they had many aspects. Each god was one and four individuals at the same time with his own world direction and colour; each god had good and bad aspects and each was at the same time both a heavenly god and a god of the underworld. The resulting confusion is readily understood. The sun and moon deities were among the most important and both had many legends surrounding them; but the Chacs or Rain Gods were also of immense importance. By the time of the Conquest there were many gods who were patrons of particular classes or professions such as Kukulcan, god of the ruling caste.

Of the most practical significance in the Maya practice of religion was the worship of maize, the foundation of their civilization. The Maya knew that without maize, leisure and prosperity would cease to exist and the very soil was regarded with reverence. Every farming task was accompanied by its own religious rituals so that before land was cleared or sown the Maya would fast and observe certain taboos, finally making offerings to the gods guarding the earth. The Maya attitude towards their gods was dominated by the belief that the gods did not simply grant favours but traded them for offerings of food, incense and blood. Although human sacrifice was practised by the Maya throughout their history, it seems to have become more common after the intrusion of Mexican influence in the post-Classic Period. Until then animals were the more regular sacrifice; among those used in these conciliatory ceremonies were dogs, turkeys and birds.

The performance of the Maya ceremonies and rituals was naturally in the hands of the priests. Unlike the Aztecs the Maya priests were allowed to marry and sons often followed their fathers into the priesthood. Not only Maya ritual but all Maya learning was in the hands of the priests, and it was they who were responsible for the computation of the calendar and the consequent omens and prophecies derived from it. They were also responsible for the cure of disease and the writing of books. No important task would be carried out or military enterprise undertaken unless the omens were favourable, every act was dictated by the calendar and especially by the 260 day count. If the omens were bad certain rites such as fire-walking could be performed by the priests in an attempt to placate the gods. Throughout the year the farmers, hunters, warriors and other groups performed their work only after their appropriate rituals had been carried out.

Society
The religious attitude of the Maya and their traditional cere-monies may have been responsible for the mistaken idea that Maya society was a theocracy. The priests were certainly very important members of ancient Maya society but they did not rule it; Maya society was organized by class and each class was clearly marked out. The social system was based on extended kinship groups which involved knowing one's ancestry in both the male and female line. Each adult Maya had two names, the first derived from the mother and passed on through the female line, the second from the father and passed through the male line. It has been estimated that there were about two hundred and fifty patrilineages in Yucatán at the time of the Conquest and they formed strict groups with definite rules of inheriting property and mutual obligation. The noble classes were those who could trace back their ancestry on both sides: they owned land and filled the most important administrative posts. They also formed a military élite and provided the merchants and the priests. The common people were the workers who prob-ably held an area of forest for their *milpas* from their patrilineage; it is possible that these were divided into two classes according to their wealth. There were also slaves who were the common people captured in war; the more exalted prisoners were usually killed. When the Spaniards reached Yucatán political power was held by rulers of Mexican origin. Each little state had a ruler, the 'real man' or *halach uinic*, who lived in a town and was supported by tribute and produce from his land worked by slaves. In former times the highland Maya at least had had kings, *ahau*, who had ruled much

larger areas. There was an equally well-defined system of rule in the smaller towns which were under the control of a *batab* appointed by the *halach uinic*. The *batabs* ruled through local councils and were the local war leaders as well as judges. War was a constant obsession of the Maya and was often begun by means of raids on enemy land, followed up by more formal warfare. A more detailed knowledge of Maya life and society may be hoped for if their hieroglyphic writing is ever completely deciphered.

Maya Sites in Belize

All studies of the Maya tend to survey their civilization in its entirety, or a particular aspect of it, or a specific site. But it would not be out of place in a history of Belize to give a brief survey of those Maya centres which are situated and survive there. Perhaps a dozen or more sites have been discovered and partially excavated in the country, but the expense involved is great and it has never been found possible to maintain all the sites after their excavation: the cost of protecting the ruins from the tropical forest would be prohibitive.

Many distinguished archaeologists have worked in Belize during the last fifty years, some of whom have been local men. Perhaps J. Eric S. Thompson worked at more archaeological sites over a longer period of time than any other man. Certainly he has written more freely of his experiences than any other archaeologist. His *Rise and Fall of Maya Civilization* is an admirable study of the Maya written for non-experts, while his book *Maya Archaeologist* paints a vivid picture of the work of an archaeologist and the customs and ceremonies which the Maya people still practised during the 1930s.

Lubaantun and Pusilha

Thompson was one of the men who worked on the first large-scale excavations in the country at Lubaantun during the late 1920s. The work was sponsored by the British Museum and, over a period of several seasons, excavations were undertaken at Lubaantun, Pusilha and other small sites. Lubaantun is situated on a low ridge within a short distance of San Pedro Colombia. The ancient Maya had levelled off the ridge and built it up in such a way that it formed

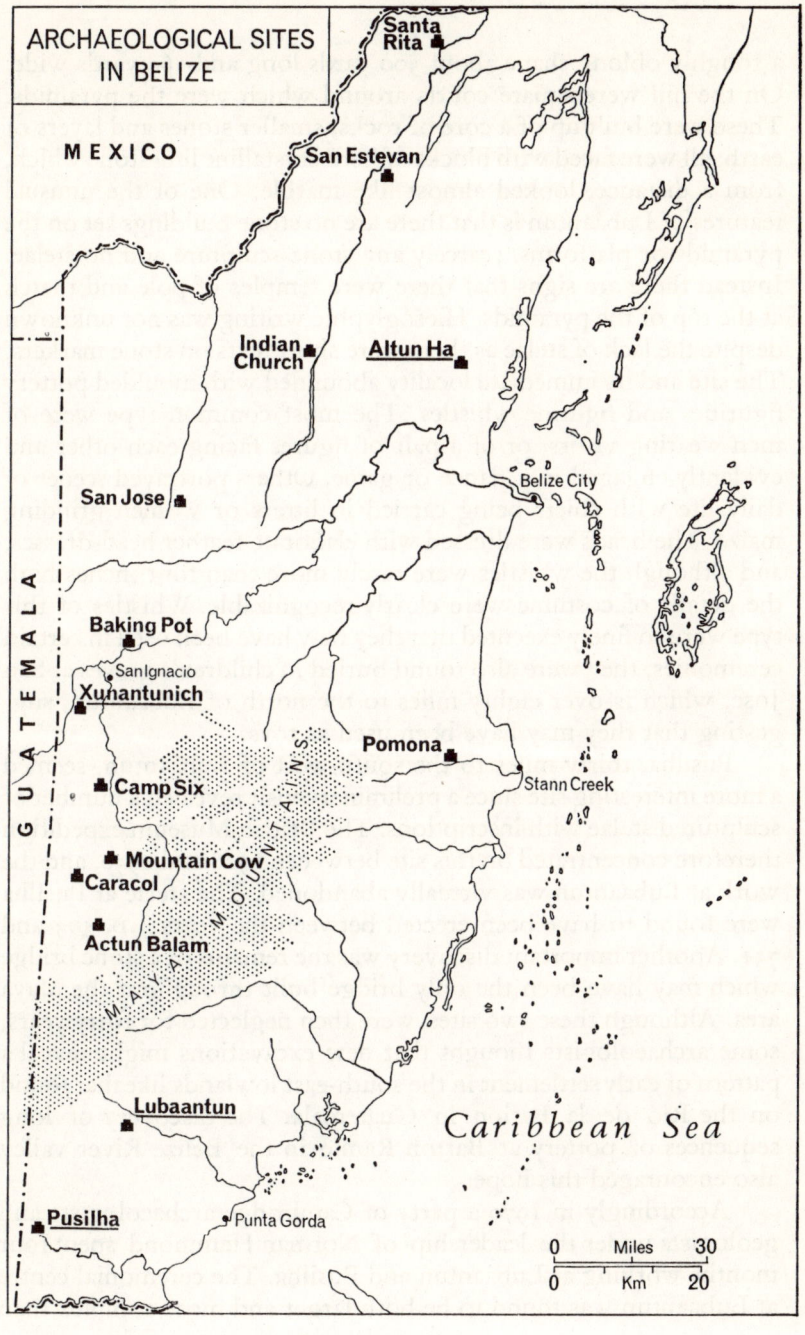

ARCHAEOLOGICAL SITES
IN BELIZE

MEXICO

Santa Rita

San Estevan

Indian Church

Altun Ha

San Jose

Belize City

GUATEMALA

Baking Pot

San Ignacio

Xunantunich

Pomona

Camp Six

Stann Creek

MAYA MOUNTAINS

Mountain Cow

Caracol

Actun Balam

Lubaantun

Caribbean Sea

Pusilha

Punta Gorda

Miles   30
0
0   Km   20

a roughly oblong shape about 300 yards long and 160 yards wide. On the hill were square courts around which were the pyramids. These were built up of a core of rocks, smaller stones and layers of earth; all were faced with blocks of hard crystalline limestone which, from a distance, looked almost like marble. One of the unusual features of Lubaantun is that there are no stone buildings set on the pyramids or platforms, scarcely any stone sculpture and no stelae. Instead there are signs that there were temples of pole and thatch at the top of the pyramids. Hieroglyphic writing was not unknown despite the lack of stelae as there were short texts on stone markers. The site and its immediate locality abounded with moulded pottery figurines and figurine whistles. The most common type were of men wearing visors, or of a pair of figures facing each other and evidently engaged in a dance or game. Others portrayed scenes of daily life with chiefs being carried in litters or women grinding maize. The heads were dressed with elaborate feather head-dresses, and although the whistles were rarely more than four inches high the details of costume were clearly recognizable. Whistles of this type were so finely executed that they may have been used in certain ceremonies; they were also found buried in children's graves at San Jose, which is over eighty miles to the north of Lubaantun, suggesting that they may have been used as toys.

Pusilha, thirty miles to the south-west of Lubaantun, seemed a more interesting site since a preliminary visit revealed a number of sculptured stelae with inscriptions. The British Museum expedition therefore concentrated on this site betweeen 1928 and 1930, and the work at Lubaantun was virtually abandoned. The stelae at Pusilha were found to have been erected between the years A.D. 573 and 731. Another important discovery was the remains of a stone bridge which may have been the only bridge built throughout the Maya area. Although these two sites were then neglected for forty years, some archaeologists thought that new excavations might reveal a pattern of early settlement in the south-east lowlands like that found on the Rió de la Pasión in Guatemala. The discovery of long sequences of pottery at Barton Ramie in the Belize River valley also encouraged this hope.

Accordingly in 1970 a party of Cambridge archaeologists and geologists under the leadership of Norman Hammond spent four months working at Lubaantun and Pusilha. The ceremonial centre at Lubaantun was found to be both larger and more complex than originally supposed, but the most significant discovery was the surprising one that the site dated only from the eighth century and that it was used for less than two hundred years. Most of the known Maya sites have revealed lengthy periods of settlement often pre-dating the establishment of a ceremonial centre on the site. However, it is clear that Lubaantun was only in use from about A.D. 700 to 889 or perhaps for as short a time as A.D. 730 to 750. It seems very probable that the ceremonial centre at Pusilha may have been moved to Lubaantun at some time near the beginning of the eighth century, and this theory is lent support by the similarity between the pottery found on the two sites.

Although the building stone used at Lubaantun was quarried locally, many small objects confirm the existence of trading routes to distant parts of the Maya area. Stones for many artefacts were imported, obsidian for blades from the Guatemalan highlands, while the material for stone axes came from the Maya mountains. An attempt to find a local source for jade failed and it seems probable that most of the jade found in Belize came from the Motagua valley. No stelae have been found at Lubaantun, which makes this centre unique; however, some stone carvings were found on ballcourt markers and on walls. The discovery of many moulds from which the figurines were made shows them to have been made at Lubaantun. The expedition was unable to throw any light on the vexed problem of the collapse of Maya civilization, but it did show that at Lubaantun at any rate the collapse came not as a sequel to a period of decline but at the very height of Maya architectural development.

Camp 6 and Mountain Cow

Among the other sites explored by Dr Thompson were two early sites in the Cayo region. Camp 6 was a small ceremonial centre with only three pyramid-type structures; but beneath one of these was found a votive cache containing the broken pieces of a large pottery urn. Scattered among the fragments of pottery and shell were three large pieces of carved jade, one of which was a round ear plug and another a beautifully carved human head. Offerings such as those found here were deposited in every Maya building either when it was dedicated or when it was enlarged: the offerings vary considerably in richness and some of the finest feather or woven articles have long since turned to dust. The other site, fourteen miles to the south, was Mountain Cow where an artificial underground chamber was found which had been used as a burial chamber. Pottery excavated was of the very late Formative stage or Proto-Classic period; several tombs at this site yielded a good deal of pottery but little jade. At San Jose, a small site reached from Hill Bank, pottery dating from the Late Formative to the Late Classic Periods was found by Thompson, but the most exciting find was the remains of some copper articles. At that date (1934) these copper remains were the first to be found at any Classic site and suggested that San Jose continued to be occupied or used after the larger ceremonial centres had been abandoned.

Throughout Belize there are reminders of the great Maya past; apart from the ceremonial centres mentioned above there were others at Caracol, Pomona and Benque Viejo, also called Xunantunich, all of which have been excavated to some extent. At Pomona was found a beautiful jade flare of an early date and at Santa Rita, near Corozal, the fifteenth-century frescoes which have been discussed; throughout the country Maya house mounds and caves are to be seen.

Altun Ha

The most recent excavation undertaken is possibly the most impressive and interesting since it is a rare example of a Maya coastal centre. Altun Ha is situated thirty miles to the north of Belize City and just a few miles from the coast. It was once thought that this area was a mere fringe of Maya activity in the later periods of its civilization, but one of the main results of the work carried out by the Royal Ontario Museum, under Dr David Pendergast, has been to show that this was far from the case. Altun Ha has proved to be a site of great significance since it shows that the Maya occupied this region from early times. The site lies on limestone which is only just above sea level, and it is separated from the Caribbean mainly by swamp. The soil is of little agricultural value and it seems most likely that the ancient Maya were attracted by the good water supply, for there are several large ponds including one fed from a spring. The site itself occupies nearly four and a half square miles and there may have been a considerable population judging from the remains of residential structures.[1] In order to support the inhabitants there must have been suitable arable land

1. It has been estimated that the population may have been as high as 8–10,000. D. Pendergast, *Altun Ha* 1969.

not too far from the centre, but as yet this area has not been discovered. However, the resources of the sea were available to the people of Altun Ha, and the fish and shellfish must have been a valuable addition to the more usual diet of maize, beans and game. In addition to using the sea and its shores for food supplies the people of Altun Ha collected many different types of shells which were made into beads and pendants. Many of the shells seem to have been traded, in their unmanufactured state, for articles from inland centres: material from the Caribbean has been recovered from Tikal for instance. The coastal situation of Altun Ha also lent itself to trade with large centres along the Yucatán Peninsula and along the coast to the south.

Altun Ha is similar to other Maya sites in its construction. Five pyramid-temples are arranged round two plazas, while another large structure lies 700 yards to the south near the largest pond. There are a great many smaller structures which include small temples, burial mounds and residences, but it is clearly impossible to excavate them all. The Temple of the Masonry Altars has produced information on eight phases of construction as well as seven priestly tombs. The Maya habit of rebuilding temples and other buildings was central to their way of life and their belief that every building had its own life span. Once the span of a particular building came to an end it could not be used for ceremonies and it was partially destroyed only to be rebuilt. This adds to the archaeologist's difficulties in dating the different phases of construction. However, it seems that there was some form of settlement at Altun Ha in the Formative Period, possibly as early as 200 B.C. By the end of the first century A.D. a society existed from which the developments of the Classic Period grew. Many of the buildings were constructed at the beginning of the Classic Period, and there is evidence of continual occupation until the tenth century. There are signs that at Altun Ha, at any rate, the end of the Classic Period of Maya civilization was accompanied by violence as some of the tombs have revealed the marks of deliberate destruction. One of the most interesting facts brought to light came from the excavation of a garbage dump which showed that some Maya were still living at Altun Ha as late as the fourteenth and fifteenth centuries. At what level of culture these Maya were living it is not yet possible to say, but it is now clear that the Central Maya area was not totally depopulated by the tenth century.

The burial tombs excavated at Altun Ha have yielded much material of interest. The tombs themselves seem to have been of much cruder construction than the vaulted and plastered crypts found at other centres. At Altun Ha they were simply made with walls of boulders and ceilings of flint slabs, but this crudeness is redeemed by the richness of the contents. Each tomb contained certain special objects. The group of tombs from the Temple of the Masonry Altars included large jade pendants; one of these weighed nearly one and a half pounds—carved with the figure of a priest on one side, the reverse contains a text of twenty glyphs. Jades with hieroglyphs are rare and this one seems to date from the second half of the sixth century. Another temple revealed one crypt now known as the Green Tomb which contained no less than 300 jade articles. But the most spectacular jade object of all was found in the seventh tomb at the top of the Temple of Masonry Altars. This was the carved head of the sun god, *Kinich Ahau*, and it weighed almost ten pounds. With it were a large number of other objects buried with the high priest towards the end of the seventh century and these suggest that this must have been a period of great prosperity in the life of Altun Ha. The altars themselves in this temple were unusual features; built of stone they are circular and vary in date from about A.D. 600–700. The plaster tops are charred by fire and excavations round their bases revealed burned incense and blackened jade beads and pendants. Destruction of such valuable objects is unusual in the Maya area and it is impossible to know for what purpose the offerings were made. The altars were certainly not used for human sacrifice.

The full story of Altun Ha will only be written when the excavations are completed; but enough work has been done to show that Maya civilization flourished in Belize throughout the first ten centuries of the Christian era and that, when Spain seized Yucatán in the sixteenth century, scattered remnants of the Maya people may have still been living in the forests of Belize. The ancient Maya were a highly civilized people in many ways, but they failed to solve certain fundamental problems such as the use of the true arch or the wheel, inventions which would have simplified their lives immeasurably. They have left few permanent legacies but many mysterious problems of which none is greater than the decline and final collapse of their civilization.

3

Discovery and Settlement

The Spanish Explorers

Just as the collapse of the Mayan civilization is shrouded in the mists of history so too is the early exploration and occupation of the country known today as Belize. From the journals and letters of the Spanish explorers and Conquistadores it is possible to piece together an account of the difficult and dangerous journeys which were made by land and sea. The main problem lies in identifying the rivers, falls and villages mentioned in these accounts, and scholars do not always agree as the old Mayan names were often used.

The first journeys

The voyages of Christopher Columbus are, however, well documented. It was on the fourth of his long journeys, in 1502, that Columbus saw and named the Bay of Honduras from the Spanish 'hondo' meaning 'deep'. Columbus was nearly fifty-one when he set sail from Seville in April 1502 on what was to be his last great voyage. He hoped to find a strait between Cuba, which he still believed was China, and the mainland of America which he had discovered in 1498. This, he thought, would lead him into the Indian Ocean as described by Marco Polo. Indeed he carried with him from his sovereigns, Ferdinand and Isabella of Spain, a letter of introduction to Vasco de Gama who was at that time sailing by the eastern route round the Cape of Good Hope to India. After riding out a terrible hurricane off Santo Domingo, Columbus and his small fleet of four vessels crossed the Caribbean, and on 30 July anchored at Bonacca or Guanaja as the island was then known. There they met with a very large canoe which had come to trade from the mainland, the skipper was seized and, having been renamed Juan Perez, was kept as an interpreter and guide. From Bonacca the fleet sailed the short distance to Cape Honduras where later the city of Trujillo grew up. At this point Columbus was undecided as to whether to sail west or east in his search for the strait. Had he turned west he might have sailed up the coast of Belize to Yucatan and discovered the Gulf of Mexico. In fact he sailed east and had an exhausting and tempestuous voyage to the Cape which he named Gracias a Dios. From there he explored the inhospitable Mosquito Shore, Veragua and Panama before he turned for home.

A few years after this Pinzon and De Solis reached the Gulf of Honduras and sailed west to the Rio Dulce and thence north along the coast of Belize. They were probably the first Europeans to see the Cockscomb or Maya Mountains, but it is not certain how far north they sailed. In 1511 some shipwrecked Spanish sailors landed on the coast of Yucatán where two of them survived to play a part in the expeditions of the great Conquistador Cortés. But it was not until 1517 that the earlier discovery of Yucatán was followed up by Francisco Hernandez de Cordoba.

The story of Córdoba's journey and subsequent ones to Yucatán is told by Bernal Díaz del Castillo in his *True history of the Conquest of New Spain*. He tells how in February 1517 Córdoba sailed from Havana and sighted land which was named Cape Catoche because the native Indians kept saying 'cones catoche' or 'come to our houses'. Despite this apparent welcome the Spaniards were attacked on several occasions; nevertheless Córdoba and his companions sailed westwards beyond Campeche to Champotón where Córdoba received a wound in a skirmish with Indians from which he later died. When the severely depleted force reached Cuba, the Governor, Velásquez, learned of signs that a civilized people with considerable wealth lived in Yucatán. Stone-built houses and painted temples, golden trinkets and cultivated fields had impressed the Spaniards who had come to seek their fortunes in the new world. It was not until many years later and after much hardship that they realized Yucatán was a poor province and greater riches were to be found in New Spain and

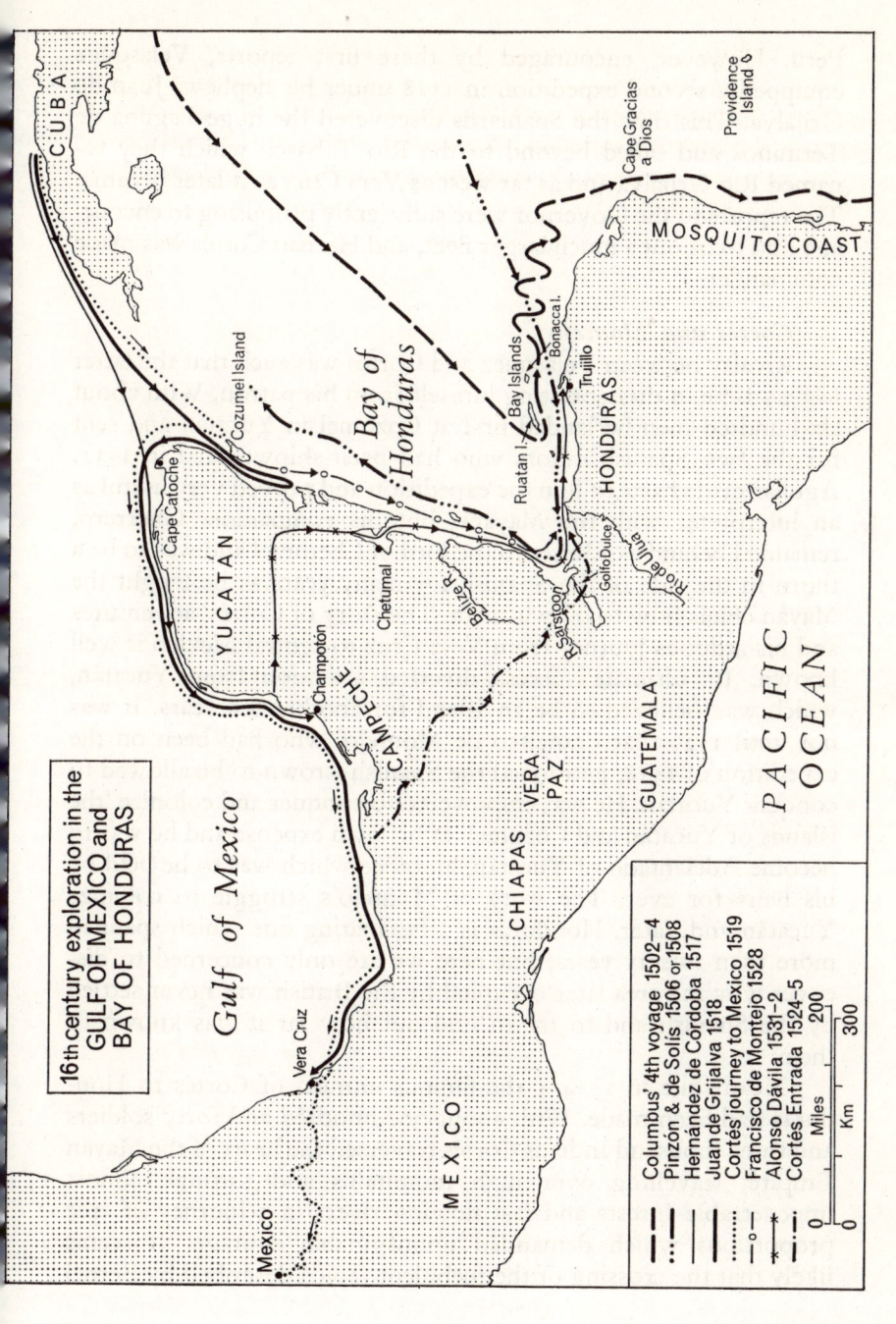

16th century exploration in the
GULF OF MEXICO and
BAY OF HONDURAS

Columbus' 4th voyage 1502–4
Pinzón & de Solís 1506 or 1508
Hernández de Córdoba 1517
Juan de Grijalva 1518
Cortés' journey to Mexico 1519
Francisco de Montejo 1528
Alonso Dávila 1531–2
Cortés Entrada 1524–5

Miles
Km

CUBA

Providence
Island

Cape Gracias
a Dios

MOSQUITO COAST

Bay of
Honduras

Cozumel Island

Cape Catoche

YUCATÁN

Chetumal

Belize R.

Ruatan I.   Bay Islands
Bonacca I.

Trujillo

HONDURAS

CAMPECHE

Champotón

Sarstoon R.

Golfo Dulce

Río Ulúa

GUATEMALA

CHIAPAS   VERA PAZ

PACIFIC
OCEAN

Gulf of Mexico

Vera Cruz

MEXICO

Mexico

Peru. However, encouraged by these first reports, Velasquez equipped a second expedition in 1518 under his nephew, Juan de Grijalva. This time the Spaniards discovered the huge Laguna de Términos and sailed beyond to the Río Tabasco which they renamed Río Grijalva and as far west as Vera Cruz as it later became. The reports to the Governor were sufficiently promising to encourage him to fit out a much larger fleet, and Hernan Cortés was made commander.

Cortés and Montejo

Rivalry between Velásquez and Cortés was such that the latter lost no time in disassociating himself from his patron. With about six hundred men he landed first at Cozumel in Yucatán and sent for the two Spanish sailors who had been shipwrecked in 1511. Aguilar made haste to join the expedition and proved very useful as an interpreter with the Mayans, but his companion, Guerrero, remained behind as adviser to the lord of Chetumal and was to be a thorn in the side of the Spanish for many years as he taught the Mayan chiefs how to outwit them. The story of Cortés' adventures and his arduous journey from Vera Cruz to central Mexico is well known. Its ultimate success diverted attention from Yucatán, which was believed to be an island for another ten years. It was not until 1526 that Francisco de Montejo, who had been on the expedition of 1518, petitioned the Spanish Crown to be allowed to conquer Yucatán. He was empowered to conquer and colonize 'the islands of Yucatán and Cozumel' at his own expense and he was to become Adelantado of Yucatán, an office which was to be held by his heirs for ever. The story of Montejo's struggle to colonize Yucatán and, later, Honduras is a fascinating one which spanned more than twenty years, but here we are only concerned to discover why the area later occupied by the British was never settled by the Spanish and to try to find out how far it was known to them.

Meanwhile in 1524–5 the famous entrada of Cortés to Honduras had been made. With about one hundred and forty soldiers and three thousand Indians Cortés traversed the heart of the Mayan Empire, travelling over high mountains and through almost impenetrable forests and fast flowing rivers in a journey of epic proportions which demanded unimaginable courage. It seems likely that the crossing of the turbulent rapids described by Bernal

Díaz were those of Gracias a Dios on the Sarstoon River. Certainly, on his route to the Golfo Dulce, Cortés may have passed through part of Belize. His mission of pacification in Honduras accomplished, he returned by sea to Mexico, and thus it can be said that Cortes, the great Conquistador, had encircled what was later to become British Honduras on his journey. Nevertheless there is less significance in this than in the efforts of Montejo and his lieutenants to explore the coast of Yucatan southwards from Cape Catoche to the Gulf of Honduras.

Both Montejo and his principal lieutenant, Alonso Dávila, had accompanied Grijalva in the entrada of 1518 and so had some knowledge of the difficult country and the fierce Mayan tribes when they reached Cozumel in September 1527. For some time they had a friendly reception, but their attempts to found a town which could be used as a base were frustrated by hostile Indians who were able to cut off supplies of food. In an attempt to find a suitable site it was decided that a joint expedition by land and sea should travel southwards. In 1528 Montejo sailed along the whole coast of Yucatan as far as the Río de Ulúa and at last realized that Yucatán was not an island. Meanwhile the cunning of Guerrero, the second of the two shipwrecked Spaniards of 1511, had separated Montejo from Dávila, both of whom believed the other to be dead, so it was with great rejoicing that they met again at Salamanca. Montejo now tried to establish himself in the Tabasco region, and it was not until 1531 that he sent Davila to found a town at Chetumal and to explore the interior. He did indeed found a settlement, but hostile attacks eventually forced Davila and his comrades to withdraw and take to canoes in which, pursued by Indians for some distance, they made the slow and difficult journey along the coast of Belize. At times they had to make desperate forays up rivers to raid Indian villages for food. The party finally reached Trujillo where they received little help from the Spanish authorities in Honduras, but were able to obtain a boat for the voyage back to Campeche where, after an absence of nearly two years, they were once again delighted to find Montejo safe and well.

Montejo's ambitions were vast: he dreamed of one huge administrative area under his authority which would include the whole of Yucatán, Tabasco, Chiapas and Honduras. Between 1535 and 1544 he was the Adelantado of Yucatán and Governor of the province of Honduras-Higueras, but he was obliged to leave the

45

further conquest and settlement of Yucatán to his son and nephew, while he dealt with the administration in the turbulent provinces to the south. When, in 1544, the Audiencia de los Confines was established by the Crown, Montejo lost the governorship of Honduras-Higueras, and the area between the Río de Copilco and the Río de Ulúa was transferred from Yucatan to the new Audiencia thus shattering Montejo's dream. After his return to Yucatán, now pacified by the efforts of his son, Montejo the Younger, he sent expeditions in 1546-7 to found a settlement in the Golfo Dulce region which he still considered part of Yucatán and which he thought would be a good trading centre. These expeditions passed through Belize and a town was founded to the west of the Golfo Dulce, but in the face of objections from the Dominican priests who were attempting to colonize Vera Paz by peaceful means, Montejo was obliged to withdraw from this position and by 1549 he was left with authority only in Yucatán. By this period towns such as Merida had been permanently established and when the Great Maya Revolt of 1546-7 failed Yucatán was held securely by the Spanish. Had the Spanish continued to hold the two provinces of Yucatan and Honduras under one jurisdiction it is likely that trading routes and some settlements would have been opened up along the coast of Yucatán and the British logwood cutters of the seventeenth century would never have been allowed to obtain a foothold in the region. The southern boundary of Yucatán was never clear, with the result that in later years there was some confusion as to whether the Captain-General of Yucatan or of Guatemala was responsible for the area occupied by the British.

Missionary activities

There is little record of further Spanish exploration after the mid-sixteenth century and Spanish interest seems to have been confined to the activities of a few courageous missionaries. About 1618 two Franciscans who could speak the Mayan language volunteered to preach to the Itzás of the Petén region. A mission was set up at Tipu, which may have been the village of Baking Pot on the Belize River. This proved fairly successful for a time, but attempts to convert the Itzás, working from this base, were abandoned. A later and more famous entrada was made by the Dominican, Fray Joseph Delgado, when in 1677 he travelled from Vera Paz to Bacalar. This journey took him through the southern part of Belize, across the Sarstoon River and then up the coast where, at the Tezach River, he was seized by some English who stole his clothes. This river has now been identified as the Manatee and the incident confirms that Englishmen were established on this part of the coast by 1677.

The British Adventurers

A century before this when Queen Elizabeth I sat on the throne of England there was growing rivalry between England and Spain: the Caribbean sea and the coast of the Spanish Main were the scene of much hostility between these two powerful European nations. For a time this hostility was unofficial as war was not declared until 1585, but for twenty years before this date great sailors such as John Hawkins and Francis Drake harried the Spanish. They wanted to share in the valuable trade to the Spanish colonies and to capture some of the rich prizes carried by the great silver fleets which sailed in convoy from Havana twice a year. The coast of Belize did not lie in the direct path of these fleets, one of which sailed from Vera Cruz and the other from Panama to Havana, but the Cockscomb or Maya Mountains must have been a familiar landmark to many of them who may have landed on the coast to shelter or renew supplies of food and water. Much of this can be little more than speculation, but in 1576 a Captain Andrew Barker attacked Trujillo and was later killed at Guanaja. Exactly twenty years later Master William Parker failed in an attack on Trujillo but explored some distance up the Río Dulce hoping to find a passage to the South Sea. A plan to travel overland was thwarted by the high mountains and difficult country and instead he sailed north along the coast as far as Cape Catoche and then westwards where he took the town of Campeche. He spent some weeks in this area and later reported that at the small Indian town of Sebo 'we found Campeche wood good to dye withall'. This is the first mention by an Englishman of the valuable dyewood which was to be all important in the history of Belize.

The first colonists
In the early years of the seventeenth century the ambitions of many Europeans turned away from adventures in clandestine

trade with the Spanish colonies towards more permanent settlements in the New World. English, Dutch and French struggled to obtain a footing in the Caribbean islands and on the mainland of North and South America. Individuals such as Raleigh sought El Dorado in South America; others formed trading companies under royal patronage and colonies were founded in Virginia, St Kitts, Nevis, Barbados, Antigua and Montserrat by the English. The Dutch settled Curacao and St Eustatius while the French occupied Martinique and Guadeloupe. Life for the pioneers in these early colonies was hard and the motives behind their foundation were varied. Some hoped to 'get rich quick', some sought toleration from persecution because of their religion and some simply sought employment because of difficult times at home.

The history of these colonies is known; the dates of their foundation and the leading colonists are recorded, often in letters to the patrons in London. Unfortunately this is not so with the history of Belize; its early years are largely a matter of conjecture. This may be because letters were lost at sea or because the type of people who settled there, by chance rather than by forethought, were not given to writing letters; or, indeed, fearful of attacks from Spain, they deliberately kept their activities secret. Whatever the reason it seems that the early years of the settlement will never be known with any degree of accuracy, and it remains a fascinating and tantalizing puzzle for historians.

The Providence Company

It has been suggested by E. O. Winzerling, a writer of German descent who lived at Monkey River for many years, that the history of the settlement is connected with the Providence Company. This company was founded by the Earl of Warwick and a group of leading English Puritans in 1629 to colonize the islands of Santa Catalina, or Providence, and Henrietta and adjacent islands off the Mosquito coast. The aim of the company was certainly profit, but conformity to Puritan precepts was expected and a chaplain sailed with the first group of colonists in 1630. The life of the colony was brief, a mere eleven years, but the record of its activities, the minutes of meetings held in London by the joint stock holders are available, and can be read in London.

The Earl of Warwick and his friends already had experience of privateering voyages in the Caribbean, but the new colony at

Providence was intended as a plantation. Detailed instructions were given for the planting of tobacco; each family was to plant twice as many foodstuffs as it would need to feed it and rewards would be given for the introduction of new staple commodities. The government of the colony was to be entrusted to Governor Philip Bell, with a council of six. In view of the colony's position, so close to the Spanish mainland, an unusual clause was inserted which allowed the colonists the right to reprisal if attacked. They were enjoined not to take the offensive but to be prepared with a system of forts for any attack that might be made.

The first colonists arrived in May 1631, but the land was not as fertile as had been hoped and the colony did not prosper. Moreover there were quarrels between the leaders and also with a group of dissidents who arrived from Bermuda. The company at home had little patience with the malcontents and continued to send detailed instructions in the hope that there would be a good return for their investment. Thus in May 1632 a letter to the Governor and Council from London stated: 'We wish silk grass to be planted and sent home and sugar cane for private use; cotton to be made trial of; mulberry trees to be procured, also bees and fruit from the main'. From the same letter the interesting observation was made that no more 'fustick wood' was to be sent 'being of so little value', yet it was not long before this dyewood was to become the foundation of the British settlements in Yucatán and the Bay of Honduras.

Soon the activities of the Providence Company were extended: the island of Tortuga, for long the resort of buccaneers of all nations, was included in the grant and became known as Association. On 15 May 1632 Governor Bell was ordered to see that all cards, dice and gaming tables were to be destroyed as gambling was abhorrent to the Puritans. The colonists were allowed to purchase negroes from the Dutch, who were also trading in the area, and several exploratory voyages to the mainland were made with a view to setting up trading posts. It is possible that the coast of Belize was explored, but it was a good distance from Providence, and Winzerling's theories that trading posts were set up at Stann Creek and a settlement made at Placentia cannot be substantiated by the company records. Winzerling's theories are largely deduced from place names; thus, for instance, he suggests that Commes Bight is a derivation from Captain Sussex Camock, who, he suggests, planted silk grass in the Stann Creek area. But the company records show that Camock was instructed to develop a trading centre with the Indians at Cape Gracias a Dios. The Mosquito Indians, who inhabited this shore, hated the Spanish, and it was Philip Bell and Camock who cultivated a friendship with them which was to last for two hundred years. A base was established near the Wanks River, known to the English as Cape River, and here silk grass was so successfully grown that it was known as Camock's flax and a special patent for it was granted. In 1635 when Camock returned to England and left the service of the Providence Company, he recommended Monkey Bay, near the Bluefields River, as a good harbour and suitable place for trade and settlement. This suggestion does not seem to have been followed although the Treasurer of the Company wrote in 1636 to commend the scheme. He said in the same letter that 'dettee' might be obtained for planting at Providence, and later in the year the company told the Governor that 'the planting of detee (should be) cherished; we are sorry to hear cattle have been permitted to eat it up'. This is interesting for it clearly shows that 'dettee' was a crop, whereas Winzerling takes it to be a place suitable for the planting of silk grass and links it with the Sittee River in Belize. It is mistakes such as this and the lack of specific evidence which makes it unwise for us to give too much credence to Winzerling's opinion that Belize was first settled by Englishmen on the Cockscomb coast during the 1630s. In 1635 the character of the settlement on Providence Island underwent a change as the result of a Spanish attack. The attack was beaten off, but from this time the colony was more of an armed camp than a plantation, from which raids were made on the mainland. In May 1641 a fierce Spanish attack was made by a fleet of nine ships and two thousand men. About four hundred of the colonists were taken prisoner and the remainder sought refuge elsewhere, including Ruatan which was already occupied by men from Providence.

If, then, so little connection can be traced between the colony at Providence with its small offshoots around Gracias a Dios, Bluefields River and Ruatan, and the settlement at Belize, where else can we look for the beginnings of occupation on that stretch of the coast?

The Wallace legend

Unfortunately historians have little more than legends to look at in the search for the truth about the foundation of the settlement.

Some of these legends have been accepted by earlier historians as actual facts so that now it is scarcely possible to disentangle the true story. Most of these legends are entwined around the figure of a Scottish buccaneer, one Peter Wallace or Willis. It is fairly certain that it was he who acted as leader of a group of French and British buccaneers on the island of Tortuga, but later he turned on the French and was driven from the island in 1640. This group may then have gone to Providence Island, abandoning it just before the final defeat of the English colonists by the Spaniards in 1641. This theory is based on the work of Charlevoix, a French Jesuit historian writing about 1730, and it has been adopted by others although Charlevoix makes no mention of Wallace founding a settlement at Belize. In the nineteenth century a number of Almanacks were published which attempted to give a brief history of the settlement at Honduras. That of 1826 mentions 1650 as the date when the English first sought refuge from the Spaniards in the Belize area. Those of 1827 and 1839 speak of a Lieutenant Wallace who had been expelled from Tortuga, while the one for 1829 speaks of a party of shipwrecked sailors who settled around the mouth of the Belize River in 1638. It is always possible that these Almanacks were based on records which have since been destroyed by fire, hurricane or tropical pest, but since they were written nearly two hundred years after the event they must be regarded with considerable caution.

Other nineteenth-century writers adopted these theories and linked the name Wallace with Belize. The *Annals of Jamaica*, written in 1827, state that: 'Willis the notorious Buccaneer, was the first Englishman who settled on the banks of the river to which he gave his name. The Spaniards called it Walis, and the corrupting influence of time has softened it to Belize'. An American writer, Bancroft, in his *History of Central America* of 1883, says that 'Peter Wallace, a Scotsman, landed with some eighty companions at the mouth of the Belize River, and erected on its banks a few houses, which he enclosed with a rude palisade. His name was given both to the river and to the settlement'. The modern Guatemalan historian, Asturias, goes further and states that Wallace was Sir Walter Raleigh's second-in-command on his Orinoco expedition and had visited Belize before 1620.

Whatever the truth may be about these assertions a modern Spanish historian has shown how the name Wallace or Willis has been written at various times until it has finally become Belize. But alternative explanations derive the name Belize from one of three Maya words, i.e. either *belakin* (land towards the sea), *balitza* (land of the Itzá) or *beliz* (muddy waters). The latter seems the most likely derivation, for it can certainly be applied to the Belize River during the rainy season. However, in the last resort the question of how the settlement began is perhaps of less importance than how it grew and of less interest than how its early inhabitants lived.

Wallixo   Yaléx,   Baléz,

Wallis,   Valis,   Bellese(

Walix   Valez.   Bellise

Walis,   Balixo   Belize

Waliz,   Balis

An illustration of the possible derivation of the word Belize.

4

From Buccaneering to Mahogany Cutting

Although it may never be known whether Peter Wallace was the first of the buccaneers to settle on the coast near Belize or even the exact date of such a settlement, it is certain that during the second half of the seventeenth century a number of woodcutting establishments grew up on the coasts of Yucatán.

The Spaniards had been exploiting the logwood which grew in the Gulf of Campeche since about 1550 and as long as they held the monopoly they could sell it on the European market at anything from £90 to £110 per ton. Logwood is a dyewood which grows prolifically in a tropical climate and requires no cultivation. The only expense involved lay in its felling and transport to Europe, where until the middle of the eighteenth century it was indispensable for the dyeing of woollen goods in black, grey, purple and dark red, especially as Brazil wood from Rio de Janeiro was in short supply. For nearly two hundred years the swampy coastland of the Yucatán peninsula was the main source of logwood. It was not until the 1740s that the Mosquito Shore also became an important source of supply. Until then only two harbours could be used for the export of this valuable timber, one in the Gulf of Campeche itself and the other used by the British when they were driven from Campeche, at Belize.

Buccaneering activities

The buccaneers who roamed the Caribbean and the coast of the Spanish mainland from the late sixteenth century until the

1670s were French, Dutch and British privateers, sometimes acting on the authority of their sovereigns and sometimes without it. For most of this period Spain was the common enemy, yet there was little sense of community among these highwaymen of the seas as they raided the Spanish treasure fleets. One of their main problems was to ensure a constant supply of food, and the method by which they preserved their meat gave them the name 'buccaneer'. On the island of Tortuga there were many wild cattle and the buccaneers found it a useful centre. There the Caribs showed them how to cut the meat into long thin strips and smoke it over a slow-burning fire or boucan.

Many of the buccaneers were superstitiously religious and although they were loyal to their comrades and usually fair in the division of their spoils from their exploits they often treated their prisoners with barbaric cruelty. They were feared throughout the Caribbean, and even though the European governments were not averse to using their services in time of war, efforts were gradually increased to suppress the activities of the buccaneers. It was therefore natural for these seafaring men to seek other outlets for their energies, and some of them gradually turned to logwood cutting. William Dampier, who spent two or three years among the men, provides much interesting information in his *Voyages round the World*. He tells us that after the English capture of Jamaica in 1655 the privateers came across many ships laden with logwood but so little did they appreciate its value that, having taken ships laden with it, they used it for firewood until a Captain James sold off a surplus and accidentally discovered its value. On his return to Jamaica the English started to seek it out and were often able to seize piles ready cut from the Champotón area in the Campeche gulf until the Spaniards put a stop to this. He continues:

> But by this time the English knew the trees, as growing; and understanding their value, began to rummage other coasts of the Main in search of it, till, they found large groves of it, first at Cape Catoch; . . . But it growing scarce there, they found out the Lagune of Trist in the Bay of Campeche, where they followed the same trade, and have ever since continued it.

By the 1670s there were small British logwood settlements at the Laguna de Términos, Trist and Beef Island in the Bay of Campeche and at Cape Catoche on the northernmost tip of Yucatán.

Dampier's account of life among the former buccaneers describes
the situation at that time:

> The Logwood Cutters (as I said before) inhabit the Creeks of
> the East and West Lagunes, in small Companies, building their
> Huts close by the Creeks sides for the benefit of Sea-breezes, as
> near the Logwood Groves as they can, removing often to be
> near their Business: yet when they are settled in a good open
> place, they chuse rather to go half a mile in their Canoes to
> work, than lose that convenience. Tho' they build their huts but
> slightly, yet they take care to thatch them very well with Palm
> or Palmetto leaves, to prevent the Rains, which are there very
> violent, from soaking in. For their Bedding they raise a
> Barbecue, or wooden frame 3 Foot and a half above Ground
> on one side of the House; and stick up 4 Stakes, at each corner
> one, to fasten their Pavilions; out of which here is no sleeping
> for Moskitoes.
> Another Frame they raise covered with Earth for a Hearth to
> dress their Victuals: and a third to sit at when they eat it.
> During the wet season, the Land where the Logwood grows
> is so overflowed, that they step from their Beds into the Water
> perhaps two feet deep, and continue standing in the wet all
> day, till they go to bed again; but nevertheless account it the
> best Season in the Year for doing a good Day's Labour in.
> Some fell the Trees, others saw and cut them into convenient
> Logs and one chips off the Sap, and he is commonly the prin-
> cipal man: and when a Tree is so thick, that after it is logg'd, it
> remains still too great a burthen for one man, we blow it up with
> Gunpowder.
> The logwood cutters are generally sturdy strong Fellows, and
> will carry Burthens of three or four hundred weight; but every
> Man is left to his choice to carry what he pleaseth, and com-
> monly they agree very well about it: For they are contented to
> labour very hard.
> But when ships come from Jamaica with Rum and Sugar, they
> are too apt to mispend both their Time and Money. If the
> commanders of these Ships are Free, and treat all that come the
> first Day with Punch, they will be much respected, and every
> Man will pay honestly for what he drinks afterwards; but if he
> be niggardly, they will pay him with their worst wood, and

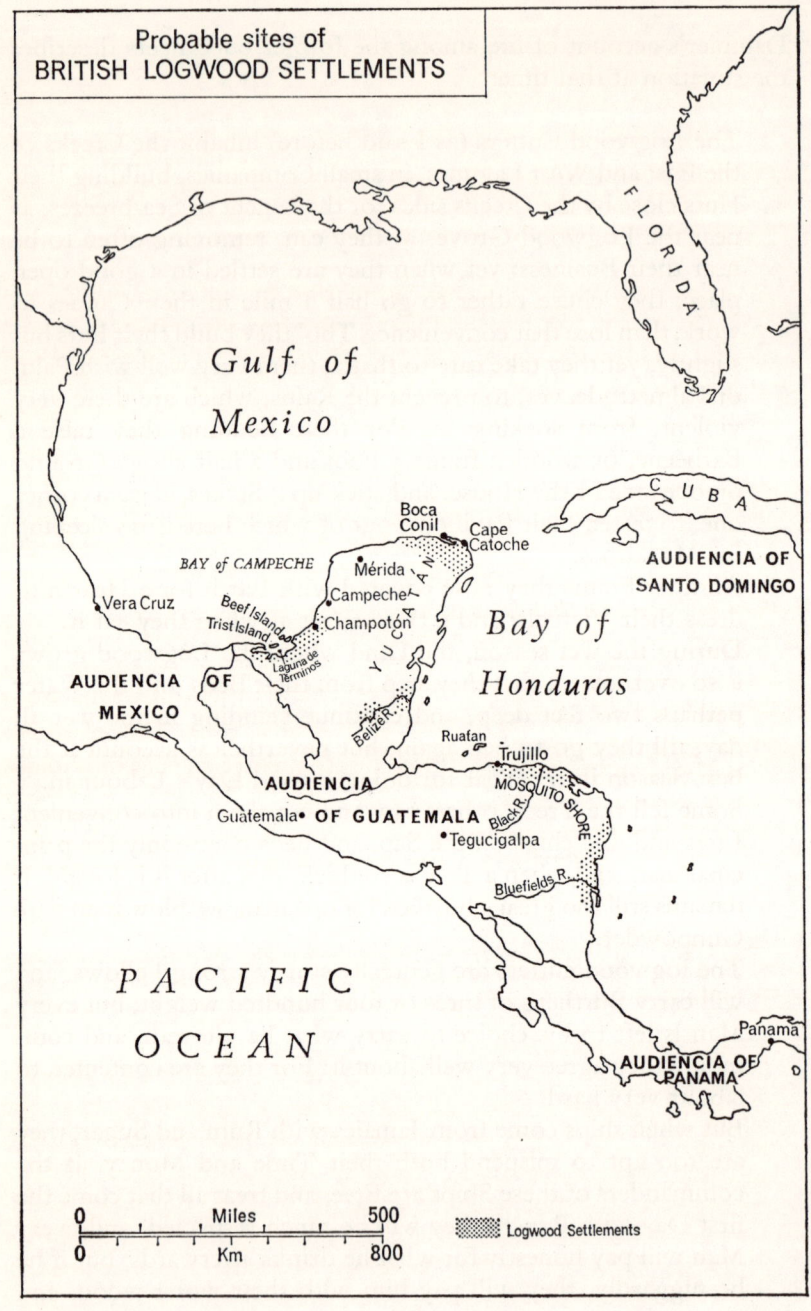

Probable sites of
BRITISH LOGWOOD SETTLEMENTS

FLORIDA

Gulf of
Mexico

CUBA

Boca
Conil
Cape
Catoche

AUDIENCIA OF
SANTO DOMINGO

BAY of CAMPECHE
Mérida
Campeche
Champotón

Vera Cruz
Beef Island
Trist Island
Laguna de
Términos

Y U C A T A N

Bay of

Honduras

AUDIENCIA OF
MEXICO

Belize R.

Ruatan
Trujillo
MOSQUITO SHORE
Black R.

AUDIENCIA
Guatemala • OF GUATEMALA
• Tegucigalpa

PACIFIC

Bluefields R.

OCEAN

Panama

AUDIENCIA OF
PANAMA

0   Miles   500
0   Km   800

Logwood Settlements

commonly they have a stock of such laid for that purpose; nay, they will cheat them with hollow Wood filled with dirt in the middle and both ends plugg'd with a piece of the same drove in hard, and then sawed off so neatly, that it's hard to find out the Deceit; but if any Man come to purchase with Bills payable at Jamaica, they will be sure to give him the best Wood.

It is evident from this description that the logwood cutters did not have an easy life, even if most of them had been used to the uncertainties of buccaneering ventures. In 1667 a treaty was passed to outlaw buccaneering with the result that more men turned to the logwood trade lest they should risk capture and be treated as pirates. The successive Governors of Jamaica found themselves almost powerless to assist the logwood cutters in the face of British indecision. The reasons for this lay in the contemporary situation in Europe where France under Louis XIV was all-powerful and threatening to engulf the whole of Europe. Confronted by this very real danger neither England nor Spain wished to offend the other in the Caribbean. In 1670 the Godolphin Treaty was signed between England and Spain, marking the first acknowledgement that England had a right to the countries and islands in the West Indies and America which she held at that time. Unfortunately these possessions were not defined in the treaty so that only those with a settled government such as Jamaica, Barbados and New England were free from dispute, while the more isolated settlements in Yucatán were in a rather questionable position. The logwood cutters regarded the Godolphin Treaty as the basis of their rights throughout the eighteenth century but the British Government gave little support to this view and the Spanish never acknowledged it at all.

Efforts to establish the trade
It is important to remember that at the time the Godolphin Treaty was passed the Spanish Government did not object to the activities of the British in Yucatán and the local Spanish officials tended to ignore the trade. The various Governors at Jamaica attempted to put the trade on a regular footing but were handicapped by the lack of response from London. In 1670 Governor Modyford reported to the Secretary of State, Lord Arlington: 'There are about a dozen vessels that only ply this trade (i.e. from

Jamaica) and make great profit selling the wood at £25–£30 a ton; they were privateers, but will not leave the trade again. They go to places either inhabited by Indians or void, and trespass not at all upon the Spaniard, and if encouraged, the whole logwood trade will be English and be very considerable to His Majesty paying £5 per ton custom.' He went on to ask for instructions with regard to the trade saying 'these new sucking colonies must have some help besides the native goodness of the soil'.

For the next few years appeals of this nature were addressed both to the Secretary of State and to the Committee of Trade in London. In 1671 the new Governor of Jamaica, Sir Thomas Lynch, reported to the Lords of the Council that as he had no instructions in the matter he had tried to regulate the trade since it employed one hundred ships a year and the Spaniards had not complained. A few months later he wrote with some desperation 'for God's sake to give your commands about the logwood', pointing out that it might lead to war with Spain. The following year Lynch reported that at least 2,000 tons of logwood had been cut in 1671 of which 600 tons had been carried to Boston. But by this time Spanish opposition to British interference with their monopoly was growing stronger and a Dutch privateer, by the name of Yallahs, was employed by Spain to raid the British settlement round the island of Trist. In October the same man was credited with having seized more than a dozen English ships laden with timber. Meanwhile Lynch, who clearly felt that the logwood trade should be promoted, had been taking evidence from some of the men taking part in it with a view to influencing the Council of Trade. Captains William and John Coxon swore that they had been engaged in the trade for two and a half years between Boca Conil and Cape Catoche and from there down to Cozumel where, they said, the English had always had huts and houses. They had met with no interruptions to the trade from Spaniards or Indians. Another man, Philip Osborne, swore that he had cut logwood at Beef Island for three years without any interruption. These depositions were used by the Council of Trade in 1717 when trying to claim that British rights in Campeche had been long established.

Meanwhile in June 1672 a new Spanish Royal Cedula was published which declared that anyone trading in a Spanish port without a licence would be proceeded against as a pirate. From this date attacks on the logwood ships increased, 75 ships being seized in the three years between 1671–4. The British Ambassador in Madrid, Godolphin, was unsuccessful in his attempts to obtain some recognition of British rights in the area. He suggested that if the logwood cutters acted with discretion he might manage to persuade the Spanish Government to connive at the trade but he held out no hopes of legalizing it. Spain was clearly not prepared to see her commercial monopoly on the mainland whittled away. British attempts to obtain reparation for the loss of her ships were unsuccessful, but despite the piratical attacks the trade continued. The Governor of Jamaica was advised by the Council of Trade to discourage the cutting of logwood and persuade the men involved to take to plantation work in Jamaica. In 1680 the island of Trist was attacked by Spain and all British subjects were marched off to Vera Cruz where they were imprisoned and treated very harshly.

When Sir Thomas Lynch returned to Jamaica in 1681 for a second term as Governor he took the warnings seriously and tried to prohibit the trade altogether. In one of the first letters which mentions logwood cutting in the Bay of Honduras he wrote, 'I have forbidden our cutting logwood in the Bay of Campeche and Honduras your Lordships having justly declared that the country being the Spaniards' we ought not to cut the wood'. Three months later he reported: 'I sent Captain John Coxon and two vessels to the Bay of Honduras to bring away our logwood cutters'. Up to this date most of the records and letters concerning logwood suggest that the main centres were either in the Bay of Campeche or on the northern tip of Yucatán around Cape Catoche. Belize itself is not mentioned until 1705 when it appears in a description of Yucatán by one John Fingas as 'the River of Bullys, where the English for the most part now load their logwood'. As the Spanish attacks on the cutters and their vessels in the Bay of Campeche increased they must have gradually shifted their activities to the area around Belize which was equally low lying and swampy and did provide a harbour. The last twenty years of the seventeenth century are filled with reports about the Spanish seizure of logwood vessels and, in 1696, it was reported that in a strong attack on the Bay of Campeche all the English who survived had been carried off to New Spain. Few of the prisoners taken escaped to tell their story. Three years later the Governor of New York reported that twenty-four ships had been captured in the Bay of Campeche, and all the evidence shows that a regular and profitable trade in logwood had been carried on between the British settlements and the New England colonies in North America. This evidence directs attention to another aspect of the logwood trade.

The Navigation Acts

Throughout the period under discussion, European trade was conducted according to the principles of mercantilism. In England these principles were embodied in a series of Navigation Acts which were designed to foster English trade and to promote the nation's shipping interests so that in time of war there would be a strong navy. The underlying assumption behind the theory was that only a limited amount of wealth, in the form of gold and silver bullion, existed and that therefore one country's trade could only prosper at the expense of another. The Navigation Acts, first passed under Cromwell in 1651, forced all trade between England and her colonies to be carried either in English ships or those of the colony which produced the goods. The enforcement of the Acts was the responsibility of the Admiralty court and the question of the trade to the Honduras settlement proved to be an extremely troublesome one. For if the settlers, or Baymen as they were becoming known, were to be given protection as British subjects, then the Navigation Acts should be applied to the settlement as a possession of the British Crown. For diplomatic reasons this was impossible and so a highly anomalous situation developed. This situation was not confined to trade, but extended to every aspect of life in the settlement and more especially to questions of law, order and government.

The logwood trade with New England caused problems because the logwood was being shipped directly to European markets which were thus obtaining their logwood as cheaply as was England. The English Crown derived no customs revenue and the English merchants were annoyed as they had to pay £5 per ton in customs duty. They complained that it was unfair for them both to have to pay duties and risk the loss of their cargoes at Spanish hands. Two specific cases illustrate the difficulties which arose in this connection. In 1686 the *Swallow* was seized at Jamaica for carrying logwood from Honduras without giving any bond that it would be taken to England or an English colony. When the owners of the vessel protested that Honduras was not an English colony and that therefore they did not come within the compass of the Navigation Act, Lieutenant-Governor Molesworth retorted that in that case they were robbers as they had no right to cut logwood there. The owners were obliged to submit. The Commissioners of the Customs, to whom the case was referred, said that the Acts of Trade should be enforced and that logwood must not be allowed to leave the Bay of Honduras without giving bond. For the time being matters were allowed to continue as before as the English Government feared that the trade might be discouraged altogether. In 1699 a second case was brought before the Council of Trade when the English sloop *Seaflower* was found to be carrying logwood from Honduras to Venice. After consultation with the Attorney General it was decided that this was perfectly legal unless the ship belonged to a colony since 'Honduras is no part of His Majesty's Plantation'. This seems to have been the first definite statement that the Navigation Acts could not be applied to the Honduras settlement and the decision was upheld for well over a hundred years resulting in some curious inconsistencies in the regulation of trade.

British interest in the logwood settlements, however little voiced by the government in the sixteenth and seventeenth centuries, was considerable. In the first place the commercial value of the native timber was always great, and during the eighteenth century it became an even more profitable commodity as mahogany imports into Europe rose dramatically. On the other hand, Spain naturally defended both her commercial monopoly and her territorial position with vigour: a serious conflict in the region became inevitable.

The Treaty of Utrecht, 1713

By the Treaty of Utrecht[1] in 1713 Spain refused to recognize any rights assumed by the logwood cutters and only confirmed the clause of the 1670 treaty regarding English occupation. Her grant of the Asiento[2] at the same time as Utrecht seems to have been a concession to English traders, but in practice it had little effect as far as the logwood trade was concerned. Yet the trade continued to flourish. Appeals to London to establish some form of regular government in the Campeche and Honduras settlements met with no success, but in 1717 the Council of Trade drew up an important

1. The Treaty of Utrecht ended the war of Spanish Succession in which England and Holland strove to prevent the union of the Spanish and French Crowns.
2. The Asiento gave the English the monopoly of supplying the Spanish colonies with negro slaves for thirty years and allowed her the privilege of sending an annual ship with goods to the great trade fair at Puerto Bello.

report in reply to Spanish complaints. The history of the English rôle in the logwood trade was outlined and for the first time the full right of British subjects to cut logwood was asserted. In the same report it was stated that the annual value of the trade was not less than £60,000 despite the reduction in price from £40 to £16 per ton.

The annual import of logwood to Britain continued to increase in the first half of the eighteenth century. In 1717 only 3,471 tons were imported while in 1756 the amount had risen to 18,000 tons, but in the second half of the century mahogany rapidly outstripped logwood in importance. New methods of dyeing cloth were being developed which rendered logwood redundant while at the same time, under the influence of the great cabinet makers Sheraton and Chippendale, the vogue for mahogany furniture was becoming widespread. The shipbuilding industry was also beginning to use mahogany and by 1763 the woodcutters were clamouring for their rights to cut not only logwood but mahogany.

5

The Conflict with Spain

The Atlantic Background

During the eighteenth century the story of the logwood settlement at the mouth of the Belize River was one of gradual consolidation in the face of repeated Spanish attempts to dislodge the British settlers. These attempts were usually conducted at a diplomatic level in Europe, but on several occasions the local Spanish officials used force in their efforts to drive the alien logwood cutters away. Too often the story of the Honduras settlement has been told without any understanding of the wider issues involved. But it cannot be considered in isolation and must be related to the foreign policies of the European powers, both within Europe and in the wider field of empire.

The principal antagonists were France and England who were both rivals for the prizes to be won from colonial expansion in North America, the Caribbean and India. For nearly thirty years after the Treaty of Utrecht, peace reigned between the two countries. During this period the Hanoverian dynasty was safely established on the English throne and the threat of war came from Spain, not France. Spain's resentment of the terms of Utrecht was fostered by her chief minister, Alberoni. He strengthened the Spanish forces and tried to restore her power but was opposed by the Quadruple Alliance of England, France, Holland and Austria. In 1718 Admiral Byng totally destroyed the Spanish fleet and demonstrated the English command of the Mediterranean.

The South Sea Company

In Caribbean waters events were less dramatic. The South Sea Company, formed to take advantage of the Asiento contract gained at Utrecht, found its privileges were somewhat illusory. It had the sole right to supply slaves to the Spanish colonies for thirty years and to send one ship a year to the trade fair at Puerto Bello. France bitterly resented these privileges but in practice the latter did little to break the Spanish trading monopoly and led to endless trouble. The South Sea Company complained that the Spanish bought few slaves, while the West Indian sugar planters grumbled that the Asiento had raised the price of their slaves and that the Company supplied all the strong and healthy ones to the Spanish. The profits obtained from the annual cargo to Puerto Bello were small, since the size of the ship was limited and the Spanish crown took a percentage of the profit. Moreover the Company was obliged to renounce all illicit trade, and infringements by other English smugglers led to retaliatory action against itself.

The legal trade was never very regular: twice interrupted by war in 1718 and 1727, only eight annual cargoes were actually sent and both sides would gladly have abandoned the arrangement if terms for compensation could have been agreed. Spanish insistence on her trading monopoly in the Caribbean was the cause of increasing bad feeling throughout this period. The guarda-costas which stopped and searched foreign ships were crewed by men more accustomed to pursuing the buccaneers than to policing the seas. On the discovery of any produce which could have come from a Spanish colony the ship was liable to be seized. Since such products as logwood, cocoa and indigo could also be found in the English islands angry disputes resulted.

Financial claims from the ship owners mounted and allegations were made by both sides. The Spanish attacked the Campeche logwood settlements, and in 1735 it was reported to the Council of Trade that all the woodcutters there had been carried off leaving only two hundred men in the Bay of Honduras. The Spanish themselves charged the South Sea Company with using its privileges to cloak an extensive illegal trade. The demand for war grew more vociferous each month, for the British trading community was well aware that illicit trade could flourish more easily once hostilities had begun. Sir Robert Walpole was conducting patient negotiations for peace throughout the 1730s, but Spain's offer to pay £95,000 as restitution for ships and cargoes seized came too late to avert the war. Captain Jenkins' appearance in London with his pickled ear— said to have been severed by the Spanish searching his ship—proved to be a sufficient *casus belli* and Walpole yielded to popular demand.

The War of Jenkins' Ear, 1739–1748

The War of Jenkins' Ear which broke out in 1739 was first and foremost concerned with trade. England was determined to challenge Spain's claim to sovereignty over the Indies and assert her own right to free navigation. Admiral Vernon's successful attack on Puerto Bello at the outset of the war was not repeated and a number of ambitious schemes for destroying Havana and other key Spanish possessions came to nothing. At the end of the war neither the question of navigation nor the thorny problem of the logwood settlements had been decided. Moreover this naval war against Spain led, as Walpole had foreseen, to a more serious conflict with France. All Europe became embroiled in the War of the Austrian Succession between 1743 and 1748; as a direct result of French intervention the Royal Navy had to contend with French naval squadrons in the Caribbean. The English system of permanently stationing small fleets at Port Royal and Antigua proved its worth and her command of the Caribbean was not seriously challenged. At the peace in 1748 the South Sea Company renounced all claims to the Asiento in return for the sum of £100,000. English merchants abandoned their attempts to persuade Spain to allow direct trade with her colonies and conflict in the area was diverted to the more central issue of dominance in the sugar markets of the world. Sugar production had increased during the war while prices had remained high—too high for some English importers who began to discuss (against all the principles of mercantilism) the possibility of obtaining sugar from the French West Indies. War benefited the British West Indian islands since it was the French trade which was more vulnerable to wartime conditions. Thus when fighting broke out again in 1756 the British sugar planters were not perturbed.

The Seven Years' War, 1756–1763

The Seven Years' War had its origins in European politics rather than in any colonial disputes, although the latter had been smouldering for some years in India, North America and the

West Indies. When Pitt the Elder took over the handling of the war after the disastrous loss of Minorca and failures in Prussia he quickly saw the importance of the colonial theatres of war. In India Clive's efforts to expel the French culminated in the great victory of Plassey in 1757 which secured Bengal. Three years later French ambitions in India were finally defeated at Wandewash. In North America the French attempt to build a chain of forts from Louisbourg at the mouth of the St Lawrence down the Ohio Valley to the Mississippi were frustrated by the capture of Quebec in 1759. In the West Indies large expeditions were mounted and a change of policy was evident in the orders to capture the enemy islands. This policy was forced upon the contestants by the desire to hold useful bargaining counters at the end of the war: the initial loss of Minorca by England and Louisbourg by France rankled on both sides and neither party wished for a simple exchange. By the time peace was made in 1763 England had achieved almost embarrassing success: the only West Indian island remaining in French hands was Saint-Domingue. Spanish entry into the war on the French side in 1762 did little to stop the run of English successes. At the peace table England was in a strong position but acted with moderation, keeping Canada but restoring Martinique and Guadeloupe to France. For the first time the English logwood settlements were recognized, but as no boundaries were agreed further disputes soon followed.

The American War of Independence, 1775–1783

For the next decade the English Government was increasingly concerned with her recalcitrant colonists in North America. The American War of Independence brought considerable loss of prestige. Moreover France, after recognizing American independence in 1778, seized the opportunity to recapture some of her former colonies. She took Dominica and Grenada while England seized St Lucia. The West Indian islands suffered severely from the interruption in their trade with the North American colonies from where they obtained most of their food supplies. In 1782 Rodney's great naval victory at the Saintes ended the threat to Jamaica, and by the end of the year peace negotiations were again in progress. At the Treaty of Versailles in 1783 American independence was recognized, several islands changed hands and an attempt was made to define the boundaries of the Honduras settlement.

The Settlement under Pressure, 1714-1779

Although the importance of the various treaties to the history of the settlement will be considered in greater detail in the next chapter, this history must now be placed in perspective against the background of wider conflict. We know little about the lives of the woodcutters. Occasional travellers' tales and reports from Spanish officials reveal only that life in the settlement must have been full of hardship. Despite continuous Spanish attacks, the tropical climate and the teeming insect life, the Baymen were determined to remain. John Atkins, a surgeon in the Royal Navy, writing after a visit in 1735 gave a vivid description of contemporary conditions. He stated that there were about five hundred merchants and slaves living about forty miles up the river. The river banks were infested with 'infinite numbers of sandflies and mosquitos. They live in Pavilions (tents); a Servant at the time of their lying down to rest, shaking them till cleared of the Vermin that are an insufferable plague and impediment to sleep . . . They have all good Arms, and knowing the Spanish clemency, defend themselves desperately if attacked, which has happened seldomer than at Campeche, and always by sea'. Fifty years later a Spanish observer wrote to Mérida: 'The populated rivers are the Walix and New and on all are a few camps in which there is no more wood, and only remain inhabited, particularly the Sibun, by poor people or negro slaves of little use for work, who keep themselves with plantains and fishing and hunting, having a most wretched life in wretched huts in a mortifying climate and surrounded by innumerable biting insects of different species'.

Rafael Llobet, a Spanish official, kept a diary during his annual tour of inspection in 1790. The diary tells us that by this date the principal establishment was at the mouth of the Walix or Belize River. This is useful information for it confirms the heading on letters and reports of meetings 'at the Belize River mouth' which appear from 1784 onwards. It seems that up to the abandonment of the settlement in 1779 the main dwelling places were on St George's Cay, for there the Baymen assembled to make their laws. Colonel Despard, the first official Superintendent, had his residence at the Haulover. This may have been the same place as 'the Belize River mouth' mentioned by contemporaries, probably the present site of Belize City, or it may have been the place still known as the Haulover. A sketch map drawn up in 1787 clearly marks the court house on the north side of the river and a substantial number of houses and other buildings. The south side was divided up into small lots but apparently unoccupied except for a burial ground. Llobet estimated that there were about one hundred houses built of good timber as well as huts constructed from poles and palm leaves. He also mentioned that there were four shops which supplied essential provisions such as salt meat, flour, biscuits, gunpowder and needles.

Population estimates

It is difficult to recapture the life led by the woodcutters during the eighteenth century; it is equally difficult to establish their numbers with any certainty. The population varied according to the state of relations with Spain and casual observers were easily deceived by the absence of the woodcutters and their slaves at the various timber camps. There were wide discrepancies in the estimates made. For instance, while John Atkins mentioned a total figure of five hundred in 1735, it was stated in 1742 that there were four hundred white men alone. Yet three years later a despatch from Ruatan to the Governor of Jamaica spoke of fifty whites and one hundred and twenty negroes. After a Spanish attack in 1754 as many as five hundred were said to have sought refuge on the Mosquito Shore. By the end of the century the population, swollen by the evacuees from the Shore, amounted to about three thousand. As the new arrivals were said to have outnumbered the original Baymen by five to one it is clear that for the greater part of the eighteenth century the population can have numbered only a few hundreds. In all the assaults made on the settlement during this period the Spaniards must therefore have had the advantage of superior numbers. It was only the strategic position of the place, coupled with the sheer determination of the settlers, that saved them from complete annihilation. Yet there were times when discretion was the wisest policy and on several occasions they sought temporary shelter at Ruatan or the Mosquito Shore.

Alarms and excursions

The accounts of the attacks made by Spain vary a good deal, even the years in which they took place being open to question.

The original records have frequently been lost and long delays in the reporting of incidents to the European courts led to much confusion. Later writers tended to glorify the story of the 'battles' with unfortunate results. The attempts to drive the woodcutters from the Campeche area in the late seventeenth century continued and there were innumerable complaints from both sides. In 1716 Spain launched a strong expedition to clear the English from the Laguna de Términos which seems to have been successful for a time. It is probable that this attack was authorized by the Governor-General of Yucatán rather than by Madrid. An official complaint by the Spanish Ambassador was made about the same time and was carefully considered by the Council of Trade. In the following year the Council issued a lengthy memorandum in reply to the complaints. For the first time it asserted the right of Englishmen to cut logwood, on the grounds that since they had been doing so before the 1670 Godolphin Treaty without any interruption they were at perfect liberty to continue. No mention was made of the settlement on the Belize River, but the logwood cutters there probably assumed this liberty applied to them too.

It must have been at about this time that the Belize River became the main centre of the logwood trade, although complaints relating to the Campeche area continued into the 1730s. The first attempt to dislodge the settlers from the Belize River is thought to have been made by a land expedition from Peten in 1718. A strong Spanish force made its way down river and built an outpost at the place still called Spanish Lookout. But this invasion is not mentioned in any official report nor does it appear in the list of attacks cited by the Spanish writer Calderón Quijano. Is it perhaps more probable that Spanish Lookout was a defensive site used by the settlers, the name indicating that it was a lookout place for signs of Spanish activity? Quijano also wrote of an unsuccessful Spanish attack in 1726, but English accounts suggest 1730 as the next year in which the settlers were disturbed. A brigantine captured seven vessels on the Belize River and another group was said to have travelled up the New River to the New River Lagoon and then overland to Belize taking about fifty prisoners on the way. This account is lent some support by Robert Hodgson who wrote from the Mosquito Shore in 1757 that the Baymen had been routed by the Spaniards in 1730 and taken refuge in the southern settlement. There is less support for the suggestion that Belize was sacked and burned in 1733 and again in 1737. If such disasters took place it is curious that no official complaint survives.

The news that war had broken out between England and Spain seems to have alarmed the settlers: the official records contain several requests for the appointment of a governor and for military protection. Their fears were not without foundation; June 1745 saw the destruction of the camps along the New River and the capture of several slaves. There was some response from the English Government to the pleas for help; an Order in Council was issued to Governor Trelawney in Jamaica 'to send some discreet person to Belize to take an account of the situation and condition of the place'. It is not clear whether any such person visited the settlement, but at least arms and troops were sent from Jamaica and Ruatan. In spite of this assistance Governor Trelawney had to report to London that in 1747 the Spaniards had 'swept down upon Belize' compelling the Baymen to remove themselves to Ruatan. The end of the war did little to ease the problems of the harassed Baymen and their vessels continued to be seized and the settlement attacked. In 1754 the Spaniards again attacked by way of the land route from Petén. The force of 1,500 men is said to have been halted at Labouring Creek by a small contingent of Baymen with their slaves. The traditional version of the story is that the enemy was routed by a small but heroic band of men; according to the Spanish account Belize was reached and taken, while a report from the Mosquito Shore states that the Baymen retreated to gather support but on their return found the Spaniards had already left. The last version does not explain why the 500 settlers found it necessary to seek safety at Black River.

Repercussions in Europe

On this occasion news of the affair did not go unnoticed in Europe. During the previous year the Spanish King had ordered the Governor of Havana to pay compensation for a dozen logwood ships; the latest news caused more trouble. The King learned that the Minister for the Indies, Ensenada, had given orders to exterminate the English woodcutters without any authority from him. He dismissed Ensenada and for a time the problem receded into the background. The Baymen were resettled without difficulty and a small company of soldiers in civilian dress was sent to support them. An engineer helped in the construction of a fort, probably at the Haulover, and Captain Hodgson, Superintendent on the Mosquito Shore, sent his son to assist the settlers. His orders were to inspect the fort on the Old River and choose a site for one on the New River. He was also to map the rivers, collect a sample of wood and report on the laws and regulations observed in the settlement. Furthermore he was to make it clear to the Baymen that they were to be responsible for providing the soldiers with food and rum and to warn them that unless they showed themselves deserving of protection they would be completely neglected.

The Baymen were hardly resettled before they were cutting timber as far north as the Rio Hondo. Spanish complaints against further encroachments on their territory grew ever more bitter. It was obvious that at the next peace treaty the logwood question would have to be settled. Indeed it was reported that the Spanish King considered that of the various points at issue between the two countries Honduras was the only essential one. The Paris Peace Treaty of 1763 failed to settle the question. It acknowledged the English right to cut logwood, but no boundaries were specified and it deprived the settlers of all protection by ordering the immediate destruction of all fortifications. This clause of the treaty had no sooner been carried out than the Governor of Yucatán, on a slight pretext, issued orders for the woodcutters to confine themselves to cutting on the Belize River until such time as the boundaries were settled. Troops were sent from Bacalar to enforce these orders so that the Baymen had little option but to obey. It took nearly two years and much correspondence before they were reinstated on the Hondo and New Rivers. In the meantime they found conditions very difficult since the logwood on the Belize River was exhausted; they complained that they could not cut enough to pay for even essential provisions. The English Government ordered Admiral Burnaby, Commander-in-Chief at Jamaica, to the Bay to see that orders from Madrid to reinstate the logwood cutters were carried out. By the time Burnaby arrived off Belize in March 1765 he was able to report that the Baymen were once more cutting wood at their former camps and were 'perfectly satisfied'. He had been treated with great courtesy by the new Governor of Yucatán who wished to see harmony preserved between his own people and the English cutters. As an extra precaution Burnaby arranged for a ship to visit the Bay at regular intervals.

Internal disorder in the settlement

The presence of a British warship had the desired effect. For the next few years the main problem in the settlement was internal anarchy and indiscipline. Burnaby warned the settlers not to commit excesses against the Spaniards and to strive for unanimity amongst themselves 'in order to merit His Majesty's protection'. Despite this warning the Captains of the ships which visited the Bay usually found the settlement far from peaceful. In 1768 Admiral Parry advised the Admiralty that a frigate should be kept permanently in the Bay of Honduras 'to prevent as much as possible Murders, Frauds and Confusion which are notoriously practised among the Baymen'. There were occasional rebellions amongst the negroes, and their regular enticement to Spanish territory was a major grievance. Nevertheless there was no open act of hostility until 1779 when Spain joined with France and the American colonies in the War of Independence.

The Settlement under Attack, 1779–1798

A fast boat was sent from the Mosquito Shore with the news of renewed war between Spain and England but it arrived too late to save the settlement from disaster. On the morning of 15 September 1779 the residents of St George's Cay were surprised by the arrival of a Spanish fleet numbering 19 vessels. The Commandant of Bacalar came in person to supervise the attack. There was no chance of resisting and about 140 prisoners were taken together with 250 slaves. A few men managed to hide and escape later to the Mosquito Shore where they were joined by the Baymen who had been absent from the Cay at the time. The unfortunate prisoners, including women and children, were marched overland to Mérida and then shipped to Havana. They were not released until 1782.

It seems probable that this disaster could have been avoided had Superintendent Lawrie at Black River sent a warning more promptly. The Bay settlement was abandoned for at least three years as a result of the attack, although St George's Cay itself was speedily retaken. In an unauthorized act of revenge against the Spanish, a Colonel Dalrymple led a party of sailors, Indians and Shoremen against Omoa. The Fort was taken in October and 207 of the Baymen were said to have taken part in this somewhat futile exercise. It was recaptured a month later. For the next few years correspondence between the settlers, or their agent, Robert White, and the Secretary of State was mainly concerned with the terms to be obtained from Spain at the next peace treaty. Demands for compensation for the losses incurred by the settlers were repeated in innumerable petitions and memorials for more than ten years. These claims amounted to more than £100,000 but never appear to have been met.

Treaties with Spain

Although representations were made on behalf of the settlers during the negotiations leading to the Versailles Peace Treaty of 1783 the relevant Article 6 was most unsatisfactory. It limited the cutting of logwood to the area between the Belize and Hondo Rivers, forbade the occupation of any of the islands or cays, and restricted fishing rights. As soon as the terms of the treaty were made known a number of petitions were drawn up by the Baymen and their agent, White. These were supported by the Governor of Jamaica and three years later a supplementary Convention was signed in London. By this Convention it was agreed that Britain would give up all claims to the Mosquito Shore. In return, certain concessions were granted to the Honduras settlement. Its limits were to be extended southwards to the Sibún River; mahogany and all other timber could be cut; the natural fruits of the earth could be used, but no sugar, cocoa or other plantations established; St George's Cay could be inhabited, the Southern Triangles used for refitting ships and the fishing rights extended. However, no fortifications of any kind were permitted and no system of government could be set up without Spanish approval. This clause was to bedevil the administration of the settlement for the next eighty years. Twice a year a Spanish officer, accompanied by an English one, was to make a tour of inspection to see that the treaty was enforced.

The first Superintendent of the settlement, Colonel Marcus Despard, took up his post in 1786 with instructions to see that the terms of the treaty were strictly observed. It was not long before the independent Baymen were quarrelling with the Spaniards and their new Superintendent. This was rather surprising, for not only had they been demanding the appointment of a Superintendent for some time, but they had actually asked for Despard to be given the position since he had impressed them favourably at Ruatan.

There were two reasons for their dissatisfaction. After the Mosquito Shore had been evacuated, over 2,000 people had made their way to the Honduras settlement, and the original inhabitants considered that Despard gave preferential treatment to the evacuees in his distribution of land. They also felt that his strict interpretation of the treaties and his support for the Spanish officers who destroyed their provision grounds could not be justified. So much ill-feeling was aroused that Despard was recalled to England in 1790.

When Colonel Hunter succeeded Despard it was made clear that his appointment was purely a temporary one, his main task being to restore order and harmony among the Bay settlers and to enforce the old established regulations and laws in place of Despard's 'Plan of Police'. In fact Hunter spent a year in the Bay because war was again threatened by the Nootka Sound crisis of May 1790 and he had to put the settlement in a state of defence.[1]

On his departure in March the following year he left the government of the settlement to its Magistrates with specific directions to guide them in their relations with the Spanish officials. Governor Effingham of Jamaica suggested that the expense of maintaining a permanent Superintendent was unnecessary and that occasional visits by a sloop from Jamaica would be sufficient. The Secretary of State seems to have agreed with this opinion for the settlement was without a Superintendent until the renewal of war in 1796. The proposed naval visits seem to have been infrequent, but in 1793 a Captain Lawford was sent to accompany the Spanish Commissary on his tour of inspection. He reported that the Baymen were making no attempt to observe the boundaries arranged with Spain and the fines imposed had no effect at all. Like most people who visited the Bay settlement in its early years his impression of the inhabitants was of their 'turbulent and unsettled disposition'. Colonel Hunter had expressed his opinion even more strongly to Secretary Grenville. Writing soon after his arrival in Honduras he said: 'The Banditti of the West Indian islands have always considered this country as the best asylum for them; and I am of opinion that at least one half of its present Inhabitants are of that description; however, there are certainly some people here of good

1. Spain seized some English fishing ships on the Pacific coast, claiming the West America coast, but was forced to allow English fishing rights.

character and possessed of property they can honestly call their own, but, I am sorry to say, their numbers are few'. It was, perhaps, the unruly behaviour of the people which was partly responsible for much of the neglect by the British Government and its representatives in Jamaica.

The defence of the settlement

But sometimes there were genuine difficulties which prevented the Jamaican Governor from affording the settlement the full protection its people requested. This was the case in 1796 when news of the outbreak of war between Spain and England reached the Bay. An immediate appeal for assistance was made by the Magistrates to Lord Balcarres in Jamaica. They pointed out that if they assembled in one place to defend the settlement their provisions could only last one month and they had no authority to command the Baymen in war. Balcarres was himself beset by problems. The Maroon war[1] had been causing trouble for the past two years; his troops were ravaged by disease and Admiral Hyde Parker was so uncooperative that Balcarres found it almost impossible to obtain transport for troops or provisions. Nevertheless a supply of gunpowder and small arms reached the settlement in October, and in December a Major Barrow was given the rank of Lieutenant-Colonel and ordered to the Bay as Superintendent. He was also given a special commission appointing him Commander-in-Chief in the event of hostilities. Barrow was warned that every effort must be made to defend the settlement as its evacuation would be a very difficult and expensive project.

Barrow set about his task with great energy and was soon holding regular parades and drilling both whites and slaves. At first all went smoothly but the settlers soon tired of the restrictions placed on them under the martial law which was in force almost continuously for eighteen months. In particular they resented the lack of food supplies and of troops from Jamaica. A crucial Public Meeting was held on 1 June 1797. The question before the Meeting was whether to defend the settlement or to evacuate it. By sixty-five votes to fifty-one the decision in favour of defence was made. After this important meeting it was arranged that the male population should divide their time between defence and their private

1. The Maroons were a separate community living in the mountainous area of Jamaica and provided a refuge for escaping slaves.

interests. Only a few days later Barrow reported to Balcarres that the situation amounted to anarchy and that, unless food arrived soon, there would be famine and the slaves would desert the settlement. Fortunately a transport ship arrived shortly afterwards carrying the news that troops were on the way. Barrow reported that the good news had 'stimulated the people to exertions hardly credible' and they had not only built a new fort but prepared barracks for the troops. This happy mood was soon dispelled and it was four months before the promised soldiers arrived. Even then Barrow complained that they were totally inadequate for the defence of the settlement. Three companies of the Irish Brigade had embarked at Jamaica but, out of the 210 men, 25 had died and 65 were sick. Barrow's request made through the Magistrates for 100 effective men to help the regular troops was refused. These difficulties were reported to Balcarres who arranged for more officers to be sent to the Bay on condition that 171 slaves were provided by the Baymen or alternatively purchased at £70 each. This expense proved unnecessary as sufficient slaves were released by the woodcutters. Early in 1798 Barrow suggested that an attack should be launched on Bacalar, but he was soon warned that nothing must be done to annoy the Spaniards and only defensive measures should be undertaken.

At this time Balcarres was much concerned with the problem of St Domingue. Brigadier-General Maitland proposed to evacuate the British defences in that island; but Balcarres considered its continued defence essential to the safety of all British possessions in the Caribbean. He was still receiving little or no support from Admiral Hyde Parker, but in June 1798 he managed to arrange for the sloop H.M.S. *Merlin* to be stationed in the Bay. The next few months was a time of considerable tension; an attack was constantly expected, and indeed Balcarres reported to London in July a rumour that a major attack had already taken place. This news was unfounded, but at two Public Meetings on July 20 and 21 it was thought necessary to call upon the entire male population to assist in the defensive preparations. Captain Moss of the *Merlin* clearly felt that more could be done. In a letter to the magistrates he complained of the 'tardiness, want of unanimity, and promptness in putting the Settlement, in that state of defence . . . the exigency of the present time requires'. He made certain proposals for strengthening the forts and equipping gun-flats, then declared that unless these measures were agreed upon by the next day H.M.S. *Merlin* would leave the settlement to its fate. This dire threat evidently had the desired effect. Martial law was renewed, the sale of liquor forbidden and all the men capable of fighting assembled in Belize. The usual self-interest seems to have been forgotten for a time as the settlers waived their rights to payment for certain contracts such as the hire of boats during the emergency. Moreover the owners of property on St George's Cay agreed to its destruction to prevent the Cay being used as a base for attack.

The Battle of St George's Cay, 1798

After almost two years of tension and alarms the news that the Spanish fleet had been sighted must have been welcomed by the troops and many of the settlers. The fleet was commanded by Arturo O'Neil, the Governor-General of Yucatán. It was reported to number thirty-two ships, including transports, manned by 500 sailors and carrying a force of 2,000 soldiers. The number of vessels and men assembled by the settlement was absurdly small in comparison with the large Spanish fleet. In addition to the *Merlin* and its crew there were three sloops, two schooners and seven gun-flats constructed from logwood rafts. These vessels had the improbable names of *Towser*, *Tickler*, *Mermaid*, *Swinger* and *Teaser*; they were commanded by local men and the Masters of merchant ships and carried about 240 men.

The famous battle of St George's Cay was more accurately a number of brief actions which took place between 3 and 10 September 1798. Full reports were made afterwards by both Colonel Barrow and Captain Moss as well as some of the settlers so that, far from there being room for dispute, this particular incident in the history of British Honduras is unusually well documented. The main part of the enemy fleet anchored between Cay Chapel and Long Cay; on 3 September five ships tried to force a passage between Montego Cay shoals but were repulsed. The next day a similar attempt was foiled by three armed vessels, and the stakes and beacons which the Spanish had put down to guide them through the treacherous reefs were removed. Captain Moss, realizing that the enemy would next try to take St George's Cay and attack Belize from there, sailed to the Cay to secure it. On seeing this the enemy fleet abandoned its attempt and withdrew to its anchorage. On the morning of the 10th, fourteen of the largest

Spanish ships weighed anchor and approached to within one mile
or so of the *Merlin* and the other craft. At first Moss believed that
the Spanish commander intended to attack the next day but then
'the enemy came down in a very handsome manner, and with a good
countenance, in a line abreast'. At 2.30 p.m. Moss gave the signal
to engage. The action lasted about two and a half hours, much to
the disappointment of Colonel Barrow and the regular troops who
arrived on the scene too late to play any part. The Spanish ships
had already cut their cables and departed in confusion towards
Cay Chapel. It was impossible for the *Merlin* to pursue the enemy
through the shallow waters. The fleet remained off Cay Chapel for
a few days and some prisoners were taken; it seemed that in the
confusion the enemy had suffered heavy losses but not one of the
defenders was killed. It is hard to find an explanation for the sudden panic on the part of the Spanish; the suggestion that they had
run short of water and supplies cannot explain their sudden flight
or the subsequent delay before sailing for Bacalar.

The battle of St George's Cay has acquired an unjustified pre-
dominance in the history of the country. It is true that the defence
of the settlement against such a strong force was a notable achievement, but, at the time, no-one imagined that this was the final
episode in the long conflict of the logwood trade. The settlement
continued in an uneasy state for some time; requests for further
naval assistance were made and more than two years later rumours
of Spanish naval preparations threw the place into renewed panic.
Moreover, the claim to hold the settlement by right of conquest
was not put forward until several years after 1798 and the claim
was never made officially. A suggestion made in a paper read at the
Public Meeting of October 1799 may have misled later writers
into thinking such a claim had government support. This statement maintained that 'Since the establishment of a Garrison at
Honduras the Tenure and possession of the Country is altered.
His Majesty holds it by force and it may in some degree be considered as a Conquered Country.' But the stationing of a garrison
for its protection in no way altered the status of the settlement.
The attitude adopted by some historians that the year 1798 'saw
British Honduras added to the Empire' has no foundation in fact.
The settlement did not become a British colony until 1862 and it
will be seen that the battle of St George's Cay did not alter the
legal position of the settlement at all.

6

The Status of the Settlement

The Problem of Sovereignty

The legal status of the settlement in the Bay of Honduras was
not in any way affected by the battle of St George's Cay. For many
years it remained what it had long been—'a settlement, for certain
purposes, in the possession and under the protection of His
Majesty, but not within the territory and dominion of his Majesty'.
This phrase, from a Parliamentary Act of 1817, represents the attitude of the British Government to the Bay settlement for more than
half a century. In legal terms, therefore, the Bay settlement was no
more than a place where British subjects had a right to cut timber.
The people who lived there were certainly regarded as British, but
all sovereign rights and powers lay with Spain. Nowhere else in the
British Empire was there such an anomalous situation. In New-
foundland, regarded for many years simply as a fishery, there were
comparable difficulties of administration but without the same
problem of a foreign sovereign power.

The question of sovereignty in the settlement was governed
by the treaties of 1763 and 1783 and, since it was so important to
the settlers, the problem must be considered in some detail. The
entire administrative and judicial structure of the settlement depended on the interpretation of these sovereign powers. Throughout the period from 1798 to 1862 neither the settlers nor the British
Government maintained a consistent attitude. The Government did
not in practice always observe the principle stated in 1817. In fact

the very business of legislating for the settlement at all in the British Parliament was quite exceptional and only carried out when the question at issue was of particular importance. Thus in 1819 a Supreme Court was established and during the 1820s and '30s many of the parliamentary acts relating to slavery and its abolition were made applicable to the settlement. As early as 1800 the Law Officers of the Crown pronounced that as the Bay of Honduras was now a British possession foreign ships should no longer be allowed to trade there. This opinion was not upheld for long and it was usually the Law Officers who objected to any change in legislation unless first approved by Spain. On several occasions plans were made to ask Spain to relinquish her sovereign powers, but it seems that only once, in 1835, was any serious attempt made to carry this out. The curious result was that long after Spain had abdicated all her other rights in Central and South America, Britain tacitly acknowledged her authority over the small settlement of British subjects in the Bay of Honduras.

The inhabitants of the settlement were themselves undecided in their attitude. They seem to have made use of this anomalous position in their struggle with authoritarian Superintendents. Occasionally it suited them to ignore the responsibilities of British citizenship. In 1809 the Magistrates argued that residence in the settlement could not confer naturalization on an alien since the Spanish King had the right to over-rule any act of the British Parliament. Superintendent Hamilton was so incensed at this lack of loyalty to the British throne that he issued a proclamation in which he published the offending letter and declared that 'I never will acknowledge or permit those of H.M.'s subjects under my Superintendence to acknowledge the right of any Power whatsoever, except the King and Parliament of Great Britain, to interfere in the execution of the internal Laws or Regulations of the said Settlement'. The following year the new Superintendent, Lieutenant-Colonel Smyth, reported that during a discussion on merchant law the Magistrates had said 'they did not know how far they were amenable to the Laws of Great Britain'. Smyth had then protested that 'it was a most extraordinary assertion for a Magistrate of a British Settlement to make'. In reality it was not so extraordinary for it was not until 1840 that the general body of English law was officially accepted as the law of the settlement. Even this was not achieved without considerable discussion in the Colonial

Office. The contradictory attitude of the settlers to their situation and to the status of their settlement is well illustrated by the step taken by their agent, Dyer, in 1810. Writing to the Colonial Department he explained that the increased trade to the Bay of Honduras made the settlement too important to be governed from Jamaica and he went on: 'I submit with great deference to Lord Liverpool that in future the civil proceedings of the Bay Settlement in the Province of Yucatán, ought to be brought under the immediate cognizance of H.M.'s Principal Secretary of State for the Colonial Department'. This was the first formal plea on behalf of the settlers for that colonial status which was not to be granted for another fifty years. There is little doubt that the general attitude of the settlers was as ambivalent as was that of the Colonial Office. In 1819 Superintendent Arthur explained to the Secretary of State that the settlers were very inconsistent: 'at one moment they are humbly submitting their neglected situation, at another they scarcely acknowledge that the Authority of the Crown extends over them'.

In view of the response by Colonial Office officials to the various problems presented by the settlement, it is hard to blame the settlers for their inconsistency. The question of Spanish sovereignty was kept open long after its reality had ceased. In 1846 James Stephen, then Permanent Under-Secretary, wrote: 'The Government of Spain assert their right to the place still; and tho' of course it will always remain the barren assertion of a right, yet to provoke a dispute with the Spaniards by an avowed exercise of Legislative authority in H.M.'s name, would be to incur an evil for which we should have no compensation whatever'. It was in fact many years since Spain had last attempted to interfere in any way with the settlement. In 1816 she had presented a Note complaining at the infringement of the 1783 treaty by the construction of three forts. At the same time she protested against the crowning of the Mosquito King at Belize. Her complaints appear to have been ignored. The inspection of the settlement by Spanish officials and the payment of a grain of corn as a token of Spanish authority seem to have ceased in 1796.

Anglo-Spanish Treaties, 1763–1814

The Treaties of 1763 and 1783

Spanish sovereignty derived from the general peace treaties made between England on the one hand and Spain and France on the other. The clauses relating to the Honduras settlement formed only a small part of those treaties, and in spite of the fact that in 1763, at least, England was in a powerful position at the conference table, they seem to have been drawn up with little consideration for the future of the British subjects in the Bay. Article XVII of the Paris Peace Treaty stated that in return for destroying all fortifications in the Bay of Honduras and other Spanish territories (i.e. the Mosquito Shore) within four months of its ratification, the Spanish authorities would no longer interfere with 'their occupation of cutting, loading and carrying away logwood'. As has already been seen, no attempt was made to define the limits in which the British could carry on their work and consequently trouble soon occurred. Thus although this treaty was important because it was the first acknowledgement of the British right to cut logwood in the Bay of Honduras, it failed to bring peace to the area and, moreover, left the settlers without any means of protection.

Twenty years later, when the Versailles treaty was negotiated, an effort was made to avoid the same mistake by defining the boundaries of the settlement. This proved no more satisfactory to the settlers. The area in which they were to cut logwood was restricted to the territory between the north bank of the Belize River and the south bank of the Hondo. The concession was still limited to logwood, although by this time Spanish logwood from the Campeche area had flooded the European market and the Baymen were becoming increasingly dependent on mahogany for their livelihood. While they were to be allowed to build houses and warehouses for their use, all forts were to be destroyed, there was to be no occupation of the off-shore Cays and fishing was to take place only along the coast between the two rivers. Lest there be any doubt on the matter it was stated that these privileges 'shall not be considered as derogating in any wise from his (i.e. the Spanish King) Rights of Sovereignty'. The treaty was signed in September 1783: at the end of the month a strongly worded memorial was sent to Lord North by a group calling themselves 'the late Settlers at Yucatán and the Bay of Honduras'. They protested that the map

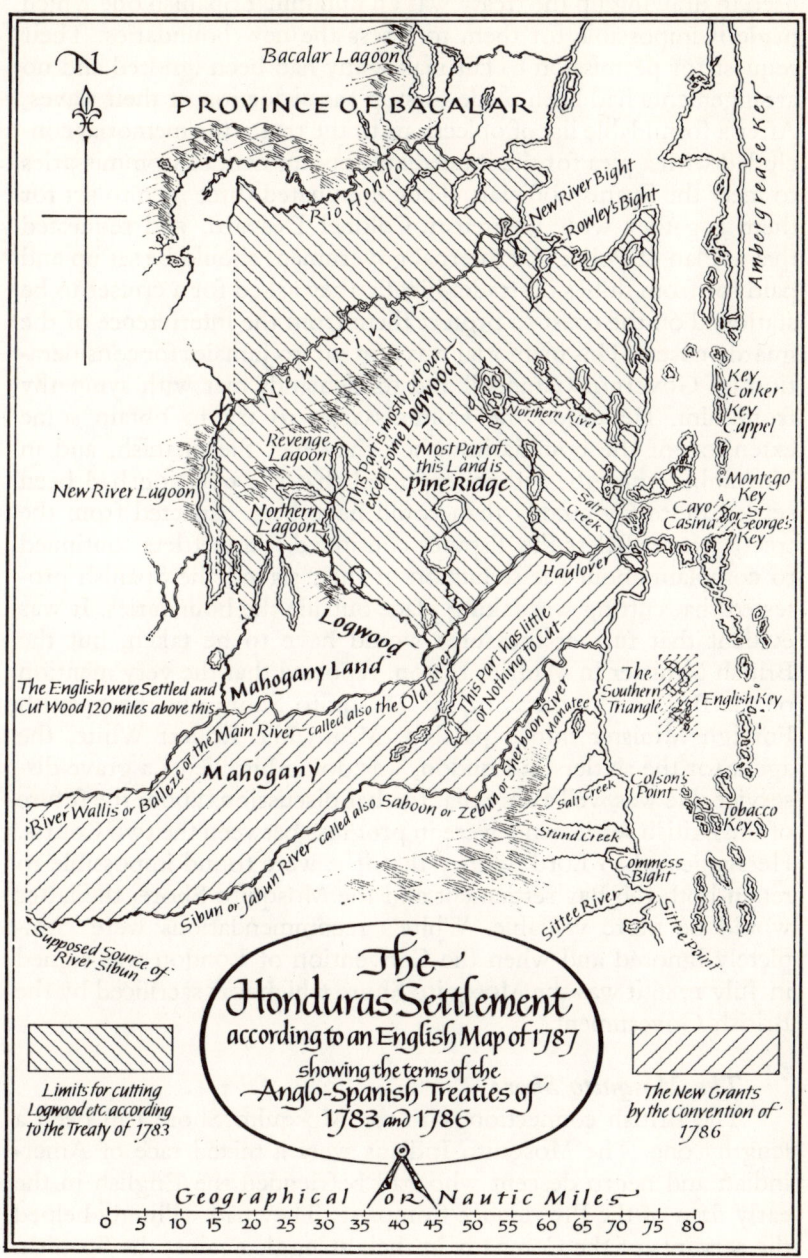

The
Honduras Settlement
according to an English Map of 1787
showing the terms of the
Anglo-Spanish Treaties of
1783 and 1786

Limits for cutting
Logwood etc. according
to the Treaty of 1783

The New Grants
by the Convention of
1786

Geographical or Nautic Miles

0 5 10 15 20 25 30 35 40 45 50 55 60 65 70 75 80

D

used in drawing up the treaty was an unfamiliar Spanish one which made it impossible for them to assess the new boundaries. Their request for permission to cut mahogany had been ignored and no arrangements had been made to stop the seduction of their slaves. After a formidable list of objections to the treaty the memorial concluded with a plea for the immediate appointment of Commissaries to meet the Spanish officials. They nominated three men to act for them together with Lieutenant-Colonel Despard, and requested that a 'Plan of Police' for internal government should be set up and paid for from duties on trade. Finally they asked for a cruiser to be stationed off the coast to protect them from the interference of the guarda-costas. This memorial was sent out to Jamaica for consideration by Governor Campbell and its demands met with sympathy from him. He urged the Commissaries to try to obtain some extension of the boundaries when they met the Spanish, and in November 1784 the settlers reported that the question had been settled more favourably than could have been expected from the treaty. Nevertheless the disputes continued. The settlers continued to complain about the seduction of their slaves; the Spanish protested that cutting was taking place outside the boundaries. It was evident that further measures would have to be taken, but the British Minister in Madrid, Liston, reported that the very mention of the Bay of Honduras or the Mosquito Shore put the Spanish Foreign Minister into a passion. Meanwhile Robert White, the agent for the settlers in London, was doing his clients a grave disservice. He was well aware that further discussions about the future of the British settlements were in progress between the two Courts. He suggested to Lord Sydney that if it were found impossible to retain both the Bay settlement and the Mosquito Shore, the latter would be more valuable. White's recommendations were completely ignored and when the Convention of London was signed in July 1786 it was the Mosquito Shore which was sacrificed by the British Government.

The Mosquito Shore

The British connection with the Mosquito Shore had been a lengthy one. The Mosquito Indians were a mixed race of Amerindian and negro descent who had befriended the English in the early days of the Providence Company. They had willingly helped the servants of the Company in their struggle against the Spanish.

During the eighteenth century British interests in the Mosquito Shore had expanded; the area concerned was a vast one stretching eastwards from Cape Honduras and then south along the present-day coast of Nicaragua to Greytown, or San Juan del Norte as it was then called. There were several British settlements of which the largest was at Black River where, in 1749, Captain Robert Hodgson took up his position as the first Superintendent. Nine years previously, during the War of Jenkins' Ear, he had obtained a formal cession of the country from the Mosquito King in return for British protection. A small force of troops was stationed there and the settlement came under the authority of the Governor of Jamaica. The fort then constructed at Black River was later destroyed in accordance with the terms of the Paris Peace Treaty and the troops withdrawn in 1764. This was bad enough, but the complete abandonment of the Mosquito Shore in return for concessions to the Belize settlers in 1786 was regarded as a terrible betrayal of British interest. By July 1787 more than 3,000 people had left the Shore, of whom more than 2,000 went to Belize. A few British subjects remained on the Mosquito coast and several of the mahogany cutters in Belize continued to have an interest in the Shore. The Spanish failed to establish themselves on the Shore at all permanently and the traditional friendship between the British and the Mosquito Indians was continued. Their chiefs still received presents, their princes were sent to Jamaica or even to England for their education and, after 1816, several of their kings were crowned in St John's Cathedral in Belize. The unofficial relationship between Great Britain and the Mosquito Shore, which was never formalized as a protectorate, lasted until the middle of the nineteenth century when growing American interest in the area brought it to an end.

The Convention of London, 1786

This digression on the history of the Mosquito Shore helps to explain the implications of the 1786 Convention. The Convention made a genuine attempt to deal with the problems raised by the settlers after the Treaty of Versailles. It extended the boundaries of the settlement southwards to the Sibún River, permitted the cutting of mahogany and all other timber, extended the fishing rights and gave permission to refit ships at the Southern Triangles. Moreover St George's Cay could henceforward be used as a settlement. But, at the same time, Spanish sovereignty was firmly asserted. No plantations or fortifications were to be permitted and Spanish officers were to make an inspection twice a year to see that these conditions were not infringed. Moreover the Convention explicitly prohibited 'the formation of any system of Government, either military or civil, further than such regulations as their Britannic and Catholic Majesties may hereafter judge proper to establish, for maintaining peace and good order amongst their respective Subjects'. This clause effectively prevented the formal establishment of any regular system of government or law for many years and was a great obstacle to the reforming plans of successive Superintendents. The settlers themselves were not slow to point out its deficiencies and were soon complaining that the extension of the boundaries was quite inadequate to deal with the expected immigration from the Mosquito Shore. They were also worried about the continued prohibition of plantations and much resented the prospect of regular visits from Spanish Commissioners. The strict enforcement of the clauses relating to plantations and the destruction of small provision grounds was the cause of much anger during the next few years. Colonel Despard justified the Spanish actions on the ground that the woodcutters had no intentions of remaining within the boundaries and were constantly going beyond them in their efforts to find new supplies of timber. But his successor, Colonel Hunter, reported that 'the present Honduras limits are expressly calculated to cause infractions'. He said that the Baymen had once cut as far south as Monkey River, though the timber there was of inferior quality, and he suggested that 'the ancient limits' should be restored. It is not clear exactly what he had in mind as there never had been any definite boundaries prior to 1786. His other suggestions that there should be some procedure for restoring runaway slaves to their owners and that there should be a time limit during which the inhabitants could evacuate themselves in the event of war, were more sensible but never put into effect. Indeed the 1786 Convention was the last treaty made between Spain and England which referred specifically to the Belize settlement. The Napoleonic wars brought about fresh peace treaties in 1802, 1809 and 1814, but in general these treaties merely reaffirmed existing ones between England and Spain. The Amiens Treaty of 1802 returned to Spain all her possessions conquered during the recent war, with the exception of Trinidad. Thus, even if the claim to have won Belize in battle in 1798 had any validity, it should have been handed over to

Spain in 1802. The fact that there was no mention of this possibility shows that neither Britain nor Spain held the view officially. The settlement continued to be held on the grounds of long possession with sovereign powers reserved to Spain.

The fact that the sovereignty of the settlement resided in the Spanish Crown and tacitly continued to do so long after Spain had asserted any claim to control affected almost every aspect of government for many years. The later developments in the constitution and the judicature will be considered fully in the next chapter; but how far had a regular form of government been established during the eighteenth century?

The Birth of Government, 1704–1798

As early as 1704 the Council for Trade in London discussed with the Governor of Jamaica the advisability of appointing an officer to superintend the logwood settlements in the Campeche region. The Governor even recommended a Mr John Lewis to act in this capacity, only to be told that there was no possibility of establishing any form of government at that time. The ever-present threat of attack to the settlement on the Belize River brought the question into the open once more during the 1740s. The outbreak of war induced the British Government to appoint two commissioners to visit and report on the settlement at Belize and the Bay islands of Bonacca and Ruatan. This was purely a temporary appointment and little came of it; three years later Governor Trelawney was ordered to send 'some discreet person' to Belize to make a report about the place and its inhabitants. A few months later it was recommended that a legislative body should be formed and empowered to draw up a constitution based on English law. No further action was taken; during the next twenty years a number of petitions for the establishment of a formal government under the protection of a small military force were ignored, despite the fact that a Superintendent was appointed for the Mosquito Shore.

Burnaby's Code
The first positive step taken by the British Government to control the situation in the Bay settlement was the mission of Admiral Burnaby, the Commander-in-Chief at Jamaica in the spring

of 1765. His task was the specific one of ensuring that the logwood cutters were freely allowed to cut timber in accordance with the recent peace treaty. On his arrival Burnaby found that relations between the settlers and the neighbouring Governor of Bacalar were more peaceful than they had been for some time but that the settlers themselves were 'in a state of Anarchy and Confusion'. He therefore took it upon himself to frame some simple laws and regulations for the government of the place and to obtain the signatures and acceptance of the laws by a large number of the leading citizens. The laws became known as Burnaby's Code and it was mistakenly assumed that the Admiral had himself devised the regulations. The significance of the Code lay in the fact that Burnaby, by giving it his name, also gave it an official blessing in the minds of the settlers. Although it was later regarded by them as the cornerstone of their rights and liberties, Burnaby himself attached little importance to it. He reported a few months later that the Baymen only complied with the regulations when it suited them. He also suggested that since the settlers were willing to pay half the salary, a Superintendent should be appointed.

Burnaby's regulations were extremely simple, merely intended to maintain some sort of order; the means by which they were to be enforced were equally simple and can scarcely be dignified with the name of a constitution. The spirit of the Code was very democratic and its aim was to administer rough and ready justice in difficult circumstances. The Code prohibited swearing and stealing and the enticement of sailors from their ships. It also insisted that the hiring of servants should be the subject of a written agreement signed by both parties. The seventh clause of the Code named seven of the leading settlers who were to act as Magistrates. It is clear from the wording of the clause that this was no innovation: a later document shows that the annual election of Magistrates had taken place at least as early as 1738. The Magistrates were to hold quarterly courts at St George's Cay or Kay Casine as it was sometimes called. They were to be supported in their task of maintaining the laws by a jury of thirteen householders, elected by a majority vote of the inhabitants. The Bench of Magistrates was given the power to seize property if its authority was resisted. Burnaby must have felt that the Magistrates might meet with difficulties in the enforcement of the Code for the next clause empowered the Commanding Officer of any Ship of War to enforce it and any future laws. Perhaps the most important clause was that which declared that all such future laws were to be approved by a majority of the inhabitants and then made by 'the Justices of the Bay in full Council'. In practice, any member of the Public Meeting could introduce a regulation and if it was approved by that body no further action on the part of the Magistrates was necessary. The Code made a distinction between the two Justices and the other five elected settlers, but in practice they all acted as Magistrates without any distinction. Burnaby had failed to state how often the Magistrates were to be elected, nor did he lay down any procedure for ascertaining the 'voice of the Inhabitants'. This apparent failure suggests that the practice of electing leading settlers as Magistrates was already well established, as was the habit of holding informal meetings to discuss matters of importance to the settlement as a whole. The Burnaby Code was important because it strengthened these informal practices and gave them a quasi-official status.

A year later the settlers themselves took the initiative in enlarging and refining the Code. The election of Magistrates was to take place annually on the first Monday in May, the quarterly courts were to be held alternately at St George's Cay and the Rio Hondo and there was to be no appeal to any other court for a sum less than £200. Regulations for the measurement of logwood works and for the payment of debts in logwood were added and provision was made for the appointment of a Clerk of the Court. Yet in spite of good intentions and the efforts of the Magistrates to enforce the laws it was soon all too clear that the majority of the woodcutters were as lawless as ever. Visiting naval officers all reported to their superiors that their authority was ignored. Admiral Parry suggested in 1768 that the settlement should be brought under military authority as the people 'are a most notorious lawless sett of Miscreants who are artful and cunning and who after having practised every ill fly from different parts thither to avoid justice where they pursue their licentious conduct with impunity'. The navy was not alone in its strong opinions; twenty years later one of the Magistrates wrote that the settlement was 'an open Receptacle for Out-Laws, Felons, Foreigners and all such men as fly from Justice, or are fond of a licentious life'. It seems that the buccaneering life of the seventeenth century had left its traces in the Bay of Honduras.

The first Superintendent

The return of the settlers to the Bay after the disastrous events of 1779 provided an opportunity for the confirmation of the Burnaby Code. At a Public Meeting on 12 June 1784 this confirmation was followed by the enactment of several new laws. Since so few people had returned to the Bay at that time some of these measures were designed to enable the public business to be carried on; one Magistrate and four other inhabitants could form a jury and a small committee was to be chosen by one or two Magistrates to transact public business. But the most important development of the year was the appointment of a Superintendent by the Secretary of State. On 1 December 1784 Captain Marcus Despard was instructed to proceed to Jamaica where he was to receive further directions from the Governor together with a salary of £500 per year. However, by the same mail, the Governor was told that Despard's departure for Honduras should be delayed so long as his services were still useful in the disturbed situation at the Mosquito Shore. The delay involved was perhaps longer than had been intended, for Despard did not take up his appointment and his new rank of Lieutenant-Colonel until June 1786. Meanwhile both he and the Governor of Jamaica had been unsuccessfully trying to persuade their superiors in London to adopt a system of government for the Bay which would give the new Superintendent some authority over the recalcitrant settlers.

Soon after his arrival in Belize Despard was informed of the London Convention and told that his main task was to see that its terms were kept and to maintain good relations with the local Spanish officials who would inspect the boundaries. The Superintendent took this part of his work so seriously that it was not long before he had antagonized the very men who had been pleading for his appointment. In December he wrote to the Governor of Jamaica to ask whether the existing government of Magistrates was contrary to the terms of the 1783 treaty. He also reported that within two days of publishing the Convention its terms had been violated, but he did not specify in what way. It was soon clear that there was no possibility of harmonious relations between the Superintendent and the settlers. Despard's distribution of the new lands to the evacuees from the Mosquito Shore and his strict enforcement of the treaties made the situation worse. At a Public Meeting in July 1787 it was resolved that the inhabitants themselves should be responsible for the division of lands and a committee was set up to revise the laws of the settlement. Among the new regulations were two concerning juries. In future juries were to consist of not less than eight freeholders, and a fine of £5 was to be imposed on a juror for absence.

During the next two years the correspondence between the Bay of Honduras and London was filled with increasingly bitter complaints about the despotic behaviour of the Superintendent. From London came the advice that Despard should try to conciliate the settlers, but it was all to no avail. When Don Gual complained that the system of government by Magistrates broke the terms of the Convention, Despard dissolved the Courts and forced the Magistrates to give up their office. He then set up an elected committee of fifteen ostensibly to act with the Superintendent but in reality giving the Superintendent complete authority over all laws and appointments. A large number of the settlers seem to have agreed to this scheme, possibly in desperation, but a number of others signed a petition protesting against 'the despotic government of an individual'. By this time a group of merchants in London and the agent Robert White had made so many protests to the Secretary of State that it was decided to recall the Superintendent. Colonel Hunter was to succeed him on a temporary basis and at the same time the Foreign Secretary asked the British Minister in Madrid to obtain the appointment of a Spaniard to join Colonel Hunter in devising an acceptable system of government for the settlement which would in no way 'derogate from the sovereignty of Spain'. Nothing came of this approach, probably the result of the strained relations with Spain over the Nootka Sound crisis of 1790. Hunter himself was instructed to declare Despard's so-called 'Plan of Police' null and void (but Despard himself took this step on his own initiative in November 1789), he was also to see that the Convention was observed and to prevent the growth of the settlement into anything more extensive which might resemble a 'Colonial Government'.

Colonel Hunter soon re-established the former system of government by Magistrates and then proceeded to draw up a simple scheme of administration. This was forwarded to the Law Officers of the Crown for their comments and in December 1790 was submitted to the Lord President of the Council; although the original intention was to obtain Spanish approval it is not clear whether the constitution was ever sent to Spain. When Hunter left the settlement he had restored harmony sufficiently to enable him to leave the government in the hands of the Magistrates. It was decided by the new Secretary of State, Dundas, not to re-appoint Despard to the Superintendency nor to fill the post for the time being. Despard's lengthy explanations of his conduct were evidently unsatisfactory and his later behaviour shows him to have been a man of ungovernable temper and pride. Embittered by his experiences, he became involved in a revolutionary plot against the government and was hanged for treason in 1803.

The beginning of government

It was not until 1796 that the office of Superintendent in the Bay of Honduras was permanently established. The threat of a renewed Spanish attack on the settlement led Earl Balcarres, then Governor of Jamaica, to appoint Colonel Barrow to the post and explain his action to London later. His initiative in the matter was approved and the Superintendent was also named as Commander-in-Chief in the event of war. Colonel Barrow's task was not an easy one: he had to put the settlement in a state of defence and maintain law and order at a time when the settlers resented being under martial law. He seems to have been quite successful and the only dispute about constitutional matters was a relatively minor one concerning the correct procedure for the election of the Magistrates. The Public Meeting responded to the Superintendent's query about the form of government by passing a resolution that 'the existing Laws and Regulations should be the form of Government in future', and there was no serious challenge to this resolution for some years.

By the end of the eighteenth century a rudimentary system of government existed in the Bay settlement. There was a paid Superintendent appointed by the Home Government; there was a Bench of seven Magistrates elected annually to act in both a judicial and executive capacity and there was also the Public Meeting. By this date the Public Meeting was the accepted legislative assembly although there seem to have been no precise rules to govern its procedure or its membership. It probably met for discussion of public topics after each quarterly court and in times of emergency. The definition and development of these institutions during the first part of the nineteenth century will be examined in the next chapter.

Part II
From Settlement
to Colony, 1798-1862

7

Government and the Law

At the beginning of the nineteenth century the forms of government in the Honduras settlement were still extremely simple; but during the course of the subsequent sixty years the social and economic pressures within the settlement gradually led to a more elaborate and less democratic form of government. Few of these developments were the result of deliberate policy on the part of either the settlers or the Colonial Office. Nevertheless by the time that the settlement officially achieved colonial status in 1862 its government was conducted in a fashion which varied little from the pattern familiar throughout the British West Indian colonies. It can be said that it was during the first half of the nineteenth century that British Honduras first became a definite political and administrative unit, a development which was by no means inevitable in 1800.

Although the Law Officers of the Crown continued to pay lip service to the maintenance of the Spanish treaties the men actually concerned with the day-to-day administration of government tended to ignore them. It has already been seen that when a matter of sufficient importance arose, such as the abolition of slavery, the Government did not hesitate to legislate in Parliament for the settlement. Although the treaties forbade the establishment of any regular constitution, as the population expanded so the machinery of government became more elaborate to meet the needs of the growing community. Every aspect of government reflected the need for growth, development and refinement during this crucial period in the establishment and development of British Honduras. A detailed study of the rôle and function of the offices of Superintendent and Magistrates reveal this process as clearly as in the case of the Public Meeting and the Judicature. Each will be examined in turn so that it can be seen how far the actual forms of government had altered by 1862.

The Superintendent

The Superintendent, as representative of the Crown, held the reins of government and, at first sight, his appears to be the best defined office in the constitution. In reality this was far from true and the rôle played by the Superintendent varied according to the character of the holder of the office. In 1838 James Stephen described the Superintendent's position with considerable perception: 'The Crown is represented by a Superintendent who is not much more than a Looker-on, and who supplies the want of authority by dexterity and address in acquiring and using influence over the general meeting and the Magistracy'. The lack of this 'dexterity' among many of the Superintendents was largely responsible for the incessant wrangling which went on between them and the Magistrates. In the first ten years of the century no fewer than seven men held the office of Superintendent: it was little wonder that the leading citizens felt 'that they can get His Majesty's Superintendent removed whenever they think proper'.

The normal method of appointing the Superintendent was for the Colonial Secretary to issue general Instructions from Downing Street, while the Governor of Jamaica was authorized to issue the Superintendent's Commission together with more specific Instructions. On some occasions temporary appointments were made on the sole authority of the Governor of Jamaica. For instance, in the emergency of 1796, Earl Balcarres appointed Major Barrow without reference to London and issued him with his ordinary Commission and a special Commission as Commander-in-Chief. This seems to have established a precedent; even in peacetime a special Commission was issued, and since the Superintendents were always army officers the dual nature of their authority was the cause of many difficulties.

Commission and Instructions

During the eighteenth century the procedure for the appointment of Governors in the American colonies had become well established and was later followed in the Crown Colonies. There were two instruments of authority: a Commission, in the form of Letters Patent under the Great Seal, and Royal Instructions in the form of Letters Close under the Royal Sign Manual. The Commission was the source of the Governor's powers, which it defined; while the Instructions were a more general guide intended to clarify the statements made in the Commission. The latter had legislative force and invested the Governor with certain of the Sovereign's prerogatives such as power over life and death, the right to summon the representative Assembly and to veto legislation passed by that Assembly. In the new Crown Colonies acquired by conquest during the Napoleonic wars these powers were even greater and usually extended to the control of public finance.

The Commission issued to the Superintendent of Honduras gave him none of these powers. The Crown had no sovereign territorial rights in the Bay of Honduras and therefore it could not delegate prerogative powers to the Superintendent. As a result his Commission was always phrased in very general terms and gave him no specific rights, powers or privileges. The one issued by the Duke of Manchester to Major George Arthur in 1814 is typical of these Commissions. After stating his appointment to the 'British Settlement on the coast of Honduras' he was instructed to take under his care British subjects there and to do everything possible to avoid misunderstanding with their Spanish neighbours. The Instructions were equally vague and were not even issued under the Royal Sign Manual: the only positive order being to uphold the existing customs and institutions. The Instructions issued by Lord Liverpool in 1810 for the guidance of Colonel Smyth were more precise than usual. After urging the new Superintendent to send regular information to London they went on to declare that 'His Majesty's Subjects shall be left in the full enjoyment of their ancient Customs in the convening of public Meetings, the election of Magistrates and other Public Offices; and in the raising and application of the Money required for the public Service'. Smyth was to uphold the courts and the civil authorities and to see that peace was maintained with the Spaniards. It is evident that these

Instructions asserted little authority on behalf of the representative of the Crown. The Superintendent's rôle was indeed anomalous and when confronted by a determined Magistracy or Public Meeting he was in a very weak position. Everything depended on the skill of the Superintendent in handling the leading merchants and woodcutters. But the basic weakness of his position was implicit in the lack of authority delegated to him and was emphasized by the innumerable quarrels which so often ended with his recall and the appointment of a new Superintendent.

The Superintendent as Commander-in-Chief

In the early years of the nineteenth century one of the most regular causes of dispute between the Superintendent and the Magistrates was the former's use of his military authority. The settlers saw no reason to be treated as troops under the command of an officer except in times of emergency. They resented the use of the military especially in the judicial sphere. In 1807, when Superintendent Hamilton used soldiers to arrest two slaves, the Magistrates immediately protested that troops had no right to enter civilian property. They were equally hostile when they felt that their own authority was being challenged by the Superintendent's protection of soldiers who were guilty of criminal offences. Since many of the murders and other felonies committed in the settlement were the work of soldiers there were frequent opportunities for friction. The attitude expressed by Superintendent Hamilton in a letter to the Governor of Jamaica was doubtless shared by many of his fellow Superintendents. He explained that he had directed military patrols to remove soldiers from negro quarters at night and to stop the beating of drums. His argument was that 'I consider this completely to be a Garrison Town'. Naturally enough the settlers had different ideas and the Magistrates would not tolerate such an attitude. In 1810 they arrested an officer on the grounds that his conduct during a fire had almost precipitated a riot, and when the Superintendent stopped the proceedings of the court and reported the incident to London the matter was taken up in the Public Meeting. A resolution was passed deploring 'the tendency to introduce military government amongst us' and a protest was promptly sent to Jamaica and to London urging that in future all military offenders should be tried in the civilian courts. In this case the use of a Court Martial to try military personnel was upheld by the Secretary of State, who pointed out that the settlers could not regard their courts as legally established tribunals such as those in the West Indian colonies. Here again the question of the status of the settlement was involved. One of the reasons for the Superintendents' insistence on their authority as Commanders-in-Chief was that thereby they could authorize the death sentence or transportation. In their civilian capacity they had no such sanction and several of them expressed the view that without it lawlessness would rule and murders be committed with impunity.

Salary arrangements

One factor which contributed to the weak position of the Superintendent was his dependence on the settlement for his salary. When Colonel Despard was appointed in 1786 he was paid a salary of £500 by the Governor of Jamaica, but ten years later the Governor could find no record of the amount paid and so Colonel Barrow was paid at the rate of one and a half guineas a day. On his appointment to a second term of office in 1803 the Public Meeting voted him a salary of £500. Although this may have been intended as a special mark of gratitude to Barrow for his services during the crisis of 1796–8 the practice of supplementing the amount paid by the British Treasury seems to have continued. The Public Meeting voted such a sum annually, a practice which later met with strong disapproval from the Colonial Office. In 1808 the money was withheld from Superintendent Hamilton as a result of his unpopularity. He was extremely angry and accused the Magistrates of using this sum as a bribe 'to permit the Magistrates to act as they might think proper without control'. This particular form of intimidation does not seem to have been used by the Magistrates or Public Meeting again. Indeed they showed their gratitude to Colonel Arthur for his services to the settlement by increasing his salary by £300 per annum. On certain occasions the Public Meeting also voted considerable sums of money towards the purchase of a piece of silver for a Superintendent who had achieved some desired objective. In 1819, for example, Arthur was rewarded by the gift of £1,000 'in recognition of his public services', probably in connection with the establishment of the Supreme Court in that year. By 1828 the financial position of the settlement was sufficiently prosperous for the Secretary of State to direct the Superintendent to pay himself his full salary of £1,000 from the funds of the settlement. This order was not at all pleasing to Superintendent Codd who pointed out that, as all expenditure was in the hands of the Magistrates, he could not pay himself a salary. He added that at present the settlement paid the Superintendent £1,000 annually in addition to the amount paid by the Crown, and that his expenses were so heavy that he could not manage without both salaries. A few months later his successor told the Public Meeting of the Government's decision that all the Superintendent's expenses should be voted as part of the general expenditure. Despite protests that the public could not bear the additional burden this practice seems to have been adopted in conformity with the system in other colonies. When the Public Meeting felt well disposed towards the Superintendent money was voted for the repair of Government House or for additions to its furnishings, but in times of distress Government House was often allowed to lapse into a state of disrepair.

The Superintendent's powers

In the early years of the nineteenth century it is clear that the Superintendent of Honduras had few, if any, real powers. It was only gradually that successive holders of the post assumed certain powers which in time came to be accepted by the Colonial Office as inherent in the position of Superintendent. The transfer of these powers from the Magistrates or Public Meeting to the Superintendent was not achieved without conflict; the changes were normally initiated by the Superintendent and only tardily supported by the Home Government. Colonel Arthur reported to Lord Bathurst after five years as Superintendent that: 'The Office is, and ever has been, so very undefined as to deprive the Representative of the Crown of the Authority necessary for the administration of Public Business'. Arthur himself was one of the officers most active in the attempt to extend his authority. Among the powers gradually assumed by the Superintendent was that of issuing proclamations, of summoning the Public Meeting, of nominating the Magistrates and other officials and of exercising control over finance.

The vexed question of the right to issue proclamations was one which was not settled for many years. Neither the Superintendent's Commission nor his Instructions authorized him to issue proclamations, but most Superintendents seem to have made use of this instrument of legislative authority from time to time. It was only when Superintendent Arthur began to use proclamations to introduce new policies or to apply imperial policy to the settlement that objections were raised. In 1817 he declared by means of proclamation that in future no land was to be occupied without the consent of the Superintendent; in another proclamation he declared the consolidated slave law of Jamaica to be in force, while a third set up a Board to enquire into the wrongful detention of certain Indians in slavery. In issuing proclamations of this type Arthur certainly exceeded his authority as some of the leading settlers were quick to observe. Archibald Colquhoun, a Magistrate who was engaged in a lengthy dispute with the Superintendent, went so far as to make a public statement that the proclamations issued by Arthur had no binding force. As a result he was arbitrarily dismissed from the Bench of Magistrates. Another of his opponents, Dr Young, wrote directly to the Secretary of State complaining of Arthur's use of proclamations. No action was taken although the Law Officers stated emphatically in connection with the introduction of the Jamaican slave laws that 'the Superintendent possesses no authority to form or introduce laws for the government of the Settlement'. Arthur defended himself privately by pointing out the difference between the settlement and colonies with regular assemblies and law courts. He asserted that the use of proclamations was necessary to preserve peace. There the matter seems to have rested until 1840 when the Superintendent's use of proclamations was again queried during a major constitutional crisis. Colonel Macdonald, a man of impulse, set up an Executive Council and issued a proclamation declaring the laws of the settlement null and void and replacing them by English law. His action aroused a good deal of opposition not only in Honduras but among the officials of the Colonial Office who strongly contested his right to do any such thing. Lord John Russell was Colonial Secretary at the time and he decided to seek the advice of the experienced Governor of Jamaica, Sir Charles Metcalfe. After a detailed investigation into the circumstances Metcalfe advised a moderate course: he suggested that as the proclamation which had caused the furore made very few actual changes it should be recognized as a *fait accompli*. No rules were laid down about the use of proclamations but as the machinery of government grew more complex more regular methods of passing laws came into use.

The Governors of the West Indian and other colonies traditionally had the right to summon the representative assemblies
and to make public appointments. In Honduras both these privileges were retained by the Magistrates, a fact which successive
Superintendents found hard to accept; several of them felt it
necessary to assert their authority by assuming these powers. Sir
Richard Basset met the Magistrates in a head-on collision on the
first issue: he insisted that the written permission of the Superintendent was necessary before a Public Meeting could be held.
The Magistrates, on the other hand, asserted that 'the right of
calling the Public Meeting has always been inherent in the Magistrates'. An account of the dispute was sent to London and no
Public Meeting was held for a year. Once again no fixed procedure
was adopted for the summoning of the assembly but it seems to
have become customary for the Magistrates to consult the Superintendent. Later officers were more tactful than Basset, and when
difficulties arose they usually gave retrospective permission for a
Meeting. Both Colonel Smyth and Colonel Arthur continued to
maintain that Public Meetings held without their consent were
illegal. In 1820 when new regulations concerning the Public
Meeting were drawn up it was agreed that it should meet on the
Monday after the closure of the Supreme Court. The Superintendent was to be informed when the Public Meeting had assembled
and in practice the Meeting was often convened at his request.

The initiation of legislation was an issue which caused further
difficulty. In 1808 a rule was made that three months' notice had
normally to be given before a motion could be put forward at the
Meeting. It seems unlikely that this rule was enforced for long.
Any member of the Public Meeting could put forward a motion
for discussion, but the Superintendent could bring any matter he
wished to the attention of the Meeting during the course of his
opening address. In 1830, however, a drastic change in procedure
was introduced on the appointment of a new Superintendent. This
time the initiative came from the Colonial Office itself. In drawing
up the customary instructions for Colonel Cockburn the complaints
of previous Superintendents about the unruly nature of the Public
Meeting had been considered more carefully than usual. Cockburn,
who had made his own investigation into the history of the settlement, was told that constitutional reform was contemplated but the
treaties with Spain could not be queried at that time. Meanwhile

the people were to be told tactfully that measures for discussion had to receive the Superintendent's assent first since 'it seems indispensable that the power of initiating all Laws, which are to be debated and enacted at Meetings should be vested in H.M.'s Superintendent'. The Superintendent was directed to exercise great forbearance in prohibiting subjects for discussion but this was without doubt a revolutionary step. Its significance was emphasized by the further instruction that in future all laws passed by the Public Meeting were to be sent for approval and were not to be regarded as final until they had received His Majesty's sanction. This was certainly a reversal of the policy of ignoring the affairs of the settlement so long as they did not interfere with imperial policy. No doubt the increased concern felt over the position of slaves and coloured people throughout the West Indies was responsible for this change in policy. But it was not to be imagined that the settlers would treat this new attack on their cherished privileges lightly. At the Public Meeting the innovations were condemned on the ground that the settlers had enjoyed the privilege of initiating legislation for more than sixty-five years. The proceedings were sent to the Colonial Office for consideration, but a note scribbled on the back of the papers by an unknown official said that it was pointless to consider such details until the whole constitution could be reformed. It is a matter for doubt whether the new regulation was ever strictly enforced, but it was not until 1848 that the privilege of initiating motions was officially restored to the Public Meeting. It is equally unlikely that the Colonial Office made any serious attempts to control the enactments of the Public Meeting. In 1839 James Stephen told Lord John Russell that none of the laws of the settlement had been confirmed or disallowed within his memory: memory played him slightly false, for certain taxes had been disallowed from time to time.

Some holders of the office

The personality of the different Superintendents obviously played an important part in their success or failure in handling the settlers. It is not easy to assess the characters of these men from official despatches and records: only in the case of Colonel Arthur do private letters survive which enable us to discover something of his attitude to his life and office in Honduras. We learn that he accepted the post of Superintendent in order to gain promotion to the rank of Lieutenant-Colonel, but once having accepted the post he performed his duties with zeal. His religious faith meant a good deal to him and his policies were informed by a practical humanitarianism which had a lasting effect on the settlement. Arthur was the only Superintendent of the settlement in this period to achieve any wider distinction in the field of colonial administration. From Honduras he went to Tasmania, later to Canada and finally to India. When ill-health compelled him to retire from the public service he was on the point of being made Governor-General of India, an honour which would have made a fitting end to his career. Before his death in 1854 Arthur had received a baronetcy, been made Lieutenant-General and a Privy Councillor and had been given an honorary degree by the University of Oxford. Like Arthur, the other Superintendents in this period were all military men seconded from their regiments to supervise the settlement. Their tenure of office was usually two or three years, Arthur's eight years being the longest period of continuous rule. Chance comments do little more than reveal tantalizing snippets of information about the various Superintendents. Thus Major-General Codd, who held office from 1823–9, lost control of affairs to such an extent that the leading settlers split into factions and he left the settlement suffering from mental ill-health.

In 1837 Colonel Alexander Macdonald was appointed; he had already held the post in a temporary capacity in 1829 when he made a very unfavourable impression on Henry Taylor, the person most concerned with Honduras affairs in the Colonial Office. A private letter from Taylor to a friend comments bitterly on the decision to make Macdonald Superintendent for a second time. He wrote that his only merit was 'an exterior which would no doubt have recommended him very strongly to Catherine of Russia or to a recruiting Serjeant, and his proper place would be on the back of a great black horse under one of the Archways at the Horse Guards'. Taylor went on to say that he had warned the Colonial Secretary against Macdonald, but

> Lord Glenelg has the face to say that he saw him and that he talked very sensibly about education. *He*, this Horse Guard, talked sensibly about education. I turned extremely sick when I heard of it . . . and I swore in my sickness that if I recovered I would never do another stroke of work in Honduras affairs

until some instrument shall be given me which I can make use of, instead of this Colonel Macdonald who is so conspicuously and dramatically thick headed and who never did and never could talk sense and never was and never could be educated.

Taylor's opinion, strong as it was, seems to have been justified, for Macdonald certainly caused the British Government much embarrassment by his high-handed behaviour both within the settlement and in relation to other Central American states. His successor, Colonel St John Fancourt, wrote a *History of Yucatán* on his retirement, but on the whole the Honduras administrators were not men of note.

When the settlement officially became a colony in 1862 the office of Superintendent was the only element in the constitution which had survived intact; the Magistracy and Public Meeting had changed beyond recognition. Anomalous as it was in many ways, the post of Superintendent had been strengthened to such an extent that it closely resembled the office of Lieutenant-Governor in the other small colonies and which it was now to become in the colony of British Honduras. This development was mainly due to the increased backing given by the Colonial Office from 1830 onwards. But in one respect the position of the Superintendent had been seriously weakened. The result of Macdonald's arbitrary actions in 1840 was to emphasize his subordination to the Governor of Jamaica. After 1841 all correspondence to the Secretary of State had to be transmitted via Jamaica where the Governor was instructed to deal with all petty disputes himself. Few of the Jamaican Governors had much interest in the affairs of the settlement and this subordination was greatly resented by the inhabitants. However it was not until 1884 that British Honduras was finally released from its humiliating dependence on Jamaica.

The Magistrates

The rôle of the Superintendent has been considered in some detail, but the part played by the Magistrates in the simple constitution was even more complicated for they fulfilled the dual rôle of acting as the executive, in increasing cooperation with the Superintendent, and as the judiciary. The office of Magistrate preceded that of Superintendent possibly by as much as fifty years: it was certainly acknowledged and confirmed by the Burnaby Code in 1765. The Code gave the Magistrates authority to hold courts for the settling of minor disputes and also a part to play in the task of enacting new laws.

Election and qualification

In 1800 the Public Meeting laid down some new regulations concerning the election of Magistrates: there were to be seven, one of whom was to be chosen as Police Magistrate by his fellows and paid £300 a year. No man could be forced to act as Magistrate for two years in succession, but refusal to accept his election for one year or his re-election at a later date would mean a fine of £100. The appointment of a paid Police Magistrate was regarded as an innovation by Superintendent Basset and was abolished after only a few months. As the Magistrates were unpaid a considerable burden was imposed on the mahogany cutters who were forced to be absent from their work for long periods, and although they rarely refused to serve the penalty of a fine was occasionally imposed. In June 1800 two men were fined for deleting their names from the poll book and another person for refusing to take the oath of office after he had been duly elected. Again, in 1820 two men, Messrs Wall and Gentle, who had previously held office refused to serve. Superintendent Arthur felt that they should have been given an opportunity to explain their reasons before being summarily fined.

At first there were no definite qualifications for election to the Bench. The office was confined to whites by custom rather than by law, and in a small community where there were perhaps only one hundred white men at the turn of the century it was natural that a few wealthy merchants and woodcutters should control affairs. There was no objection to foreigners holding office, but in 1799 a man of unknown nationality who had been resident in the settlement for fourteen years was excluded from the Bench because he refused to take the oath of office. In 1809 the Public Meeting passed a resolution which introduced two important qualifications for election to the Magistracy. In future all Magistrates were to be residents, white and British born and, in addition, they were to own at least £500 in visible property. This seems to have been an attempt to make the Magistracy a more respectable institution, but, if we are to believe the Superintendents, it was not a very successful

innovation. Colonel Smyth described them as 'superlatively
ignorant and totally unqualified for so great a trust', while nine
years later Colonel Arthur told a friend 'you can form no idea of
the depravity of some of the Inhabitants who are raised to the
Magistrates Seat'. There were no schools in the settlement until 1807,
and though a few white children may have been sent to Jamaica or
even to England for their education it was probably felt that the
life of the woodcutters required no formal schooling.

Magisterial duties

The duties of the Magistrates were onerous. In their executive
capacity they seem to have met almost daily as a miniature Executive Council. It has already been seen that there was no clear-cut
distinction between the Superintendent as chief executive officer
and the Magistrates; for the most part the daily administrative
decisions were discussed with the Superintendent. The Magistrates
were usually responsible for the initiation of legislation in the
Public Meeting and they had the important duty of allocating the
public money voted by the Meeting. They corresponded with the
London agent and other merchants interested in the settlement and,
in cases of dispute with the Superintendent, they drew up petitions
to inform the Governor of Jamaica and the Secretary of State of
their feelings and attitudes. At the beginning of the nineteenth
century their powers were almost unlimited and, although they
performed a formidable amount of public work in addition to their
own private business, some of them held office for many years.
Marshall Bennett, one of the most important men in the settlement
at this period, sat on the Bench for twenty-two of the thirty years
between 1798 and 1828. The Magistrates were always unpaid and
their only reward seems to have been their opportunity to influence
the Superintendent and the British Government in their own
interests. However, these interests were usually those of the other
free men in Honduras and if there was a clash of opinion and
interest then the remedy lay to hand in the practice of free annual
elections. This democratic practice stopped the Bench from
becoming an irremovable oligarchy.

The abolition of an elected magistracy

Relations between the Bench and the Public Meeting were
normally harmonious until after 1832 when the practice of free

elections was abolished and Magistrates began to be appointed by the Superintendent. This was the most serious assault on the privileges of the settlers yet made and, although it was not a deliberately conceived act of policy on the part of the Colonial Office, it was part of the growing tendency to deprive the Honduras settlers of their unique constitution and to replace it by more conventional colonial institutions. This change was announced in the course of a lengthy despatch by Secretary of State Goderich who stated that he hoped shortly to introduce a Bill to put an end to current anomalies. Meanwhile the Government could no longer consent to practices 'subversive of the first principles of good government'. Among these he regarded the practice of the public appointment of officers of justice 'a right which is not exercised or claimed by His Subjects in any other part of his Dominions'. Superintendent Cockburn was quick to interpret this despatch to his own advantage and to use it as an excuse to take the action he had long favoured. Having consulted the Commissioners of the Supreme Court he issued a proclamation stating that in future the Magistrates would be nominated by the Executive. A few weeks later he reported to Goderich that although he had anticipated trouble from this announcement it had passed off smoothly and he had appointed the Bench for 1833 without any protest. That the settlers should accept this drastic curtailment of their long-cherished rights is the more surprising in view of their attitude to the appointment of minor public officials.

Responsibility for public appointments

These appointments were traditionally in the hands of the Magistrates or the Public Meeting. In 1806, for instance, appointment to the important post of Public Treasurer was removed from the Public Meeting and vested in the Magistrates with the proviso that the Treasurer himself was not to be a Magistrate. Six years later the Public Meeting regained its control over this appointment. Other minor officials such as the Clerk of the Market and the High Constable seem to have been chosen by the Magistrates. These officials usually received payment from fees gained in the performance of their duties rather than salaries. In 1817 Superintendent Arthur reported to London that there was a strong likelihood of an unsuitable person becoming Treasurer. To Arthur's pleasure Lord Bathurst wrote back that in all British colonies the nomination of public officials lay with the Crown and therefore Arthur could appoint a more suitable person until the will of the Crown was known. Two years later Arthur became involved in a dispute with the Public Meeting on the question of appointing a translator and Clerk of the Courts. The Public Meeting and Magistrates argued that the instructions in Bathurst's despatch had referred only to the appointment of Treasurer, while Arthur maintained they were equally applicable to all other appointments. The only way of settling the controversy was for Arthur to refer the whole dispute to Lord Bathurst. He was very gratified to receive full approval for his actions and, in particular, to be told, 'I am to instruct you in no case to recognize or admit any person in any public capacity whose actual nomination or appointment shall not have originated with yourself'. On receipt of this despatch the Magistrates had no choice except to apologize and to ask the Superintendent to confirm all the existing appointments. In this way the traditional rights of the people were gradually whittled away. The Government's insistence on Crown appointments was technically illogical for it gave some validity to a constitution which, on other occasions, was described as totally without legal foundation.

In 1823 a circular despatch reached the settlement stating that in future the Colonial Office was to be notified of all vacancies; the information obtained was not used, but ten years later the whole question of public appointments was revived. This time the inhabitants of Honduras were to realize that there were worse evils than the Superintendent's right to nominate officials. A lengthy dispute involving the dismissal of the Keeper of the Records by an acting Superintendent and his reinstatement by the Colonial Secretary, Goderich, eventually led to the latter's decision to make the settlement at Honduras conform with other British possessions. Henceforward appointments were to be made direct from England. He informed Colonel Cockburn that 'I have considered it indispensable that H.M.'s authority should be practically vindicated at once, by sending out individuals from this country to be invested with the Offices of Clerk of the Courts and Provost Marshal'. He argued that Lord Bathurst's instructions to Arthur had not been intended to vest all power of appointment in the hands of the Superintendent; the object had been 'an exclusion as against the Settlers not as against the Crown'. The new policy was bitterly resented: the Chairman of the Public Meeting went so far as to say that the intention was to plant 'in our Councils a nest of hired and official anti-slavery spies'. An examination of appointments made during the next twenty years or so suggests that in practice these were usually made by the Superintendent and then approved by the Governor of Jamaica. Occasional requests were made to England for the appointment of a particular officer, notably when qualified legal officials were first required during the 1840s. Another difficulty concerned the Superintendent's authority to dismiss officials. The power to do so had long been exercised without serious objections; but it was not until 1854 that additional Instructions under the Royal Sign Manual were given empowering the Superintendent to suspend an officer.

The decline of the magistracy

As the power of the Superintendent grew, so that of the Magistrates decreased. In 1839 Colonel Macdonald seized on the suggestion that a small council should be appointed to help him deal with the question of land grants and drew up plans for a formal Executive Council. He explained to the Secretary of State that the Council should 'supersede entirely in a legislative point of view the present Public Meeting which had long since ceased to be of any utility—and to relieve the Magistracy from the administration of and control over the Public Funds'. By the time this despatch reached England Lord John Russell had taken over the Colonial Office from Lord Normanby and he immediately pointed out that his predecessor had had no intention of authorizing such sweeping changes. However he went on to give Macdonald permission to set up a council to assist him provided this did not supersede the Magistracy or the Public Meeting. It was to consist of only six or eight men whose names were first to be submitted to the Governor of Jamaica for approval. In this way the Executive Council came into being, more as an acknowledgement of a *fait accompli* than as a deliberate act of policy by the British Government, as stated by most historians of British Honduras.

The ensuing conflict between the new Council and the old-established Public Meeting was largely the result of Macdonald's tactlessness. The Council met for the first time early in 1841 and at once the *Honduras Observer* expressed its disapproval at the Council's proceedings. A few days later the Public Meeting itself drew up a resolution protesting at the Council's assumption of legislative and financial powers. Feelings in the settlement ran high and it is by no means easy to disentangle the truth from the accusations made on all sides. It was at this point that the officials in the Colonial Office wearied of these petty disputes and instructed the Superintendent to communicate through the Governor of Jamaica. Matters reached such a crisis that eventually the Public Meeting refused to transact any business at all; Sir Charles Metcalfe in Jamaica advised Macdonald to conciliate the Meeting and act with moderation, but in London it was realized that Macdonald must be replaced. When Colonel Fancourt was appointed in 1843 Henry Taylor said that no additional instructions were necessary since the restoration of harmony would depend on the Superintendent's character and not on any specific orders.

Colonel Fancourt had not been in the settlement long before he too was recommending constitutional changes. He pointed out that the attempt of Macdonald to deprive the Magistrates of their administrative powers and the Public Meeting of its legislative authority was a failure since the new Council had no control over public funds. He felt that the real cause of all the trouble in the past had been the 'independent Executive authority assumed by the Magistrates which is calculated to occasion serious embarrassment to the Superintendent'. He believed that if the nominated Magistrates were appointed *ex officio* as the Superintendent's Council, most of the difficulties would disappear. He went on to suggest that if his proposal were approved all supplies could be granted to the Superintendent-in-Council so that the Magistrates would reach no administrative decisions without the Superintendent but would simply retain their independence in all judicial matters. The Permanent Under-Secretary, Stephen, doubted whether the scheme was practicable: he thought that the Magistrates would at once see that 'they are to exchange substantial Authority for mere titular distinction'. However, the Secretary of State, Lord Stanley, thought that Fancourt should be given permission to put the scheme into operation if he felt this could be done without disturbance. In July 1844 Fancourt reported that the old Executive Council had been abolished and the Magistrates appointed as the new one. A few months later he wrote that the Public Meeting had expressed great satisfaction with the new Council. This satisfaction did not last for long. On 3 March 1846 the Public Meeting passed an act finally abolishing the unpaid Magistracy and substituting paid Police Magistrates instead. The records are silent about events leading up to this change. In a private letter to Lord Elgin, then Governor of Jamaica, Fancourt wrote, 'a little revolution has been created—that we have now a responsible Police Magistrate and an Executive Government composed in a manner more calculated to command respect; now that the prize of the Magistracy will no longer be a subject of contest betwixt the merchants, we shall go on I think much smoother'. But only two years later the Public Meeting was complaining that all public confidence in the Council was lacking now that it was composed merely of public officials and the Superintendent. In the next few years the main centre of constitutional interest in the settlement shifted to the Public Meeting and the various schemes of reform which led, in 1854, to the creation of the Legislative Assembly in its stead.

The Public Meeting

The Public Meeting was a unique institution in the history of British overseas possessions; its history was sometimes stormy but its miniature democracy typifies the independence of the early Baymen. The Public Meeting grew out of the practice of holding informal meetings during the long years of insecurity in the eighteenth century. As in the case of the Magistrates the practice was strengthened by the Burnaby Code which stated that all new regulations had to be approved by a majority voice of the inhabitants. Gradually meetings became more regular and occurred after each session of the quarterly courts. In time the Public Meeting, as it was now called, acquired the characteristics of a Legislative Assembly.

Qualifications for membership

At first no special qualifications were required for membership but the Meeting gradually introduced its own rules. In 1805 a resolution was passed which authorized the Magistrates and an unnamed committee to decide on the eligibility of members. Three years later some more precise regulations were framed. In future all voters at the Public Meeting and all electors of the Bench of Magistrates were to be British subjects. White men had to prove a year's residence in the settlement and to own £100 in visible property. The rules for the free coloured were more stringent; they were obliged to show residence of five years standing and to own property of £200. However, the fact that the free coloured population was admitted to the Public Meeting on whatever terms showed a degree of enlightenment on the part of the Baymen not seen anywhere else in the West Indies at that time. This liberal tendency was remarked on by all visitors to the Bay of Honduras and deplored by all Superintendents, who saw in it the explanation of much disorderly behaviour at the Meetings. Colonel Arthur described to Lord Bathurst the disorder at the Court House but went on to say 'this disgraceful exhibition is harmony itself in comparison with the proceedings of the Public Meetings . . .' He believed that the free coloured had complete control through sheer force of numbers. Yet if this were true, is it likely that the coloured population would have agreed to their exclusion from the Magistracy or from juries? Even worse in Arthur's eyes was the attempt made to introduce free blacks and Caribs to the Public Meeting. At the end of his period of office Arthur's attitude to the coloured population had undergone a dramatic change. By 1822 he considered them the most stable and responsible section of the community. But he never changed his attitude to the Public Meeting and its irresponsible influence over the affairs of the settlement. His views were echoed many times by successive officials during the next thirty years.

The qualifications introduced in 1808 seem to have done little to ensure a respectable legislative body for the settlement. Men were made members for life, with the result that they did not lose their place by subsequent bankruptcy, perjury or criminal convictions. Each Superintendent in turn reported in shocked tones on the ignorant and often criminal characters of members of the Public Meeting. By 1820 steps had to be taken to reform its composition. On 24 July the Public Meeting met to consider the recommendations of a committee which had been set up to revise the constitution. It was agreed that in future white British subjects had to have one year's residence and to own property worth £500 while coloured men had to be born in the settlement and own £1,000 in property. Fifteen members were to constitute a quorum; the Meeting was to assemble after every meeting of the Supreme Court and members in Belize or nearby who failed to attend could be fined £10 unless they were ill. The following day a more drastic scheme was presented to the Superintendent whereby all legislative power would be placed in the hands of an elected body of fifteen men known as the General Assembly. Over the years harassed Superintendents devised similar schemes but, in every case, the officials at the Colonial Office agreed that the abolition of the Public Meeting would create as many difficulties as it might solve, despite the insecure and illegal basis of its foundation. This general attitude was succinctly expressed by Goderich, the Colonial Secretary, in 1832 when he told Superintendent Cockburn: 'If His Majesty's Government are disposed to acquiesce in the system which has hitherto prevailed, that acquiescence must not be construed into approbation of it; still less into an acknowledgement that it rests upon any legal basis'. Ten years later it was argued that one reason for not informing the Colonial Office in detail of the acts of the Public Meeting was the inconvenience of asking the Queen to give or withhold assent to measures passed by an illegally constituted assembly. Henry Taylor even suggested that this very unsettled state of affairs was an advantage since the 'Public Meeting does not feel itself strong and can at any time be told that it has no legitimate existence'.

Responsibility for public finance

It seems unlikely that the settlers themselves were greatly concerned by such legal technicalities. While the Public Meeting continued to hold the purse strings their position was one of considerable strength. Any attempt to encroach on this power was resented and resisted. The right to exercise some control over governmental expenditure had long been one of the most cherished privileges of British subjects, and the Honduras settlers were as jealous of their rights as the American colonists. Burnaby's Code provided for the imposition of taxes by two of the Magistrates and five elected inhabitants; this method seems to have continued for some years. The taxes imposed were mainly on transient traders and the ships arriving in the settlement. By 1795 the Public Meeting had taken over the functions of this committee and a Public Treasurer was appointed. In spite of this the settlement's finances seem to have been rather chaotic and there was usually a heavy public debt. The procedure for raising revenue and controlling expenditure was by no means consistent; on some occasions the Superintendent made suggestions which were adopted but at other times any such interference was resisted. The Public Meeting and Magistrates usually allied themselves against the Superintendent, but in 1813 the Public Meeting found itself unexpectedly accusing the Magistrates of gross disrespect to the representative of the Crown because of a poll tax which they had recently voted. As a result of this disagreement the Public Meeting cancelled all the new taxes. When Colonel Arthur took office the following year he made a very powerful speech to the Public Meeting deploring the disorder in the assembly and on the Magistrates' Bench. He went on to accuse the settlers of resisting every proposal to raise public money for essential services, commenting that the bridge across the River Belize, the gaol and the Church were all in a state of decay. He had no wish to compel the people to pay a particular tax which they seemed to dislike as much as the poll tax, but he regarded it as being one of the fairest taxes. His speech must have been very persuasive for the tax was reimposed for two years along with other taxes on molasses and spirits. Arthur seems to have exercised considerable influence in financial matters without causing resentment; in 1816 for instance he was present at a meeting of the Magistrates to discuss ways of liquidating the public debt. He was able to use some influence in Parliament on behalf of the settlers in questions concerning the taxes on timber; this was much appreciated. His advice was frequently sought on financial and economic matters and after five years in the settlement he was able to write with satisfaction that, during his superintendency, the public debt had been liquidated and Government House built, together with a new bridge and Court House. A large sum had also been spent on the Church and the enclosure of the burial ground. Nevertheless the treasury actually possessed a balance of £2,000. Much of this was obviously due to Arthur's good sense and guidance; he treated the expenditure of public money as though it were his own. But, as he himself was quick to point out, the return to peacetime conditions had brought about a great increase in trade. Naturally there was not always perfect harmony between Arthur and the public on questions of money; before he retired from the settlement he had come to the conclusion that it was time for the whole question of the administration of public funds to be discussed with the Government. He told the Magistrates that in other colonies, funds of the type raised in British Honduras would be applied solely to government expenditure and 'the various disbursements to which the Revenue is chiefly applied here, are met in the Colonies by a Rate or some other internal Tax'. However it was another ten years before the Government began to interfere seriously in the financial affairs of the settlement.

It has already been shown how Superintendent Cockburn, with the support of the Secretary of State, gradually gained control over official appointments and the conduct of the business of the Public Meeting. In the same way he acquired some control over taxation. On his arrival in 1830 he found the settlement was encumbered by a public debt of £20,000 largely due to mismanagement, and even corruption, since Arthur had left the settlement. Trade was also in a depressed state, and he found both Government House and the barracks in urgent need of repair. The Public Meeting offered to repair his residence and provide £2,000 for furniture, but Cockburn's pleasant surprise soon turned to annoyance when the Meeting refused to vote the necessary funds for the repair of the barracks. It was suggested at first that the troops might be withdrawn if the repairs were not carried out, but then Goderich made the even stronger threat that an enquiry should be made into the way in which all duties were levied. He gave Cockburn permission to tell the Masters of all vessels that the Magistrates had no powers to levy import duties. This dire threat, coupled with Cockburn's tactful handling, produced an immediate vote of £3,000 with the promise of another £1,000 for the next three years. When the same problem arose three years later Cockburn had to threaten the withdrawal of troops, and it was much to everyone's relief that in 1838 the British Government made the Ordnance Department responsible for the barracks.

Attempts to control public expenditure

The money voted by the Public Meeting for specific purposes was in practice allocated by the Magistrates. So long as the Bench continued to be elective there was little criticism of the Magistrates' management of finance, but as soon as they were nominated by the Superintendent the position changed. A special enquiry in 1829 concluded that certain public undertakings had been unnecessarily expensive and in future tenders were to be submitted for projects costing more than £50. A quarterly estimate of revenue and expenditure was also to be put before the Public Meeting. In spite of these measures a critical attitude towards the Bench persisted and the conflict came to a head in 1836 when it was resolved to withdraw the management of public finances from the Magistrates. The Bench was extremely angry at the proposal to examine the expenditure for the last three years but, despite the eloquent explanations of Mr Coffin on behalf of the Bench, it was agreed that an enquiry should be held. When the proceedings were reported to London Henry Taylor commented that Coffin was a merchant with a direct interest in the case; it was apparent that there had been irregularities and that the sum of £10,000, agreed in 1829 as sufficient for annual expenditure, had been exceeded so much that by 1835 it had soared to over £23,000. The rule about public tenders had also been ignored and there were cases of gross overspending, as in the cost of £600 for a dinner to a visiting Vice-Admiral. In spite of the obvious irregularities the enquiry bore little fruit, the only positive suggestion coming at a Public Meeting later in the year when it was suggested that the fees for public officers should be abolished and replaced by salaries. But in the event this important act was not passed until 1842 when it was generally welcomed and contributed to the smoother running of public business. For the time being no specific changes were introduced in the handling of public money, and this was one of the most pressing matters behind the Superintendents' attempts to gain more control through the use of an Executive Council.

Changes in the Public Meeting

From the time Colonel Fancourt became Superintendent in 1843 he was highly critical of the members and conduct of the Public Meeting and, during the next ten years, much of his correspondence with Jamaica and London, and that of his successors, was concerned with the proposed constitutional changes which led to the creation of the Legislative Assembly in 1854. In one of his early reports Fancourt pointed out that of 41 members only 16 of them were liable to pay direct taxes and in 1843 the taxes paid by those men amounted to half of the entire revenue. He listed another seven men who were entitled to sit and who paid taxes but these men refused to 'be mixed up with the numerous disreputable persons who are members of the Meeting'. He also cited nine foreigners who, though they were responsible taxpaying residents, were deprived of the privilege because they were not British born. In November 1843 the Meeting passed an Act which redefined the qualifications for voters. Until this Act any man with the right qualifications could be a member of the Public Meeting for life; the introduction of voting is not commented on in the available records and were it not for a despatch from the Superintendent written in 1848 it would be difficult to understand how the new system worked. However Colonel Fancourt explained to the Governor of Jamaica that anyone with the right qualifications— i.e. a British born resident with property worth £300—who wished to be considered would inform a member. He in turn would ask the Provost Marshal to open a poll for seven days and if at the end of that time twenty-five registered voters recorded their vote for him he was duly elected. Before taking his seat he had to swear that he was suitably qualified to sit: he would then be a member for life. A recent regulation had been made which required each member to swear every three years before the Grand Court that he owned £60. If they had lost their money since being elected they were still allowed to remain a member but deprived of their voting rights. He went on to say that out of the 64 members—there was no limit on the numbers of members—only 33 were qualified to vote at that time. Fancourt himself thought that the old system was preferable to the present system which had produced an oligarchy. 'The real governing body,' he wrote, 'consists of 5 or 6 Mahogany Houses in Belize whose operations are almost entirely dependent on certain other Houses in London'.

Progress towards a Legislative Assembly

In 1850 the growing desire to regularize the position of the settlement led to a petition for colonial status. Fancourt was advised that this should be accompanied by proposals for the creation of a more orthodox legislative assembly based on similar institutions in other British possessions. Accordingly a scheme was drawn up by the Public Meeting for a number of changes in the constitution which, it was envisaged, would be made at the time when the settlement became a colony. The scheme included a proposal for an elected Legislative Assembly and a partly elected Legislative Council. But the qualifications suggested for members of the Assembly and for the electors were so high that Fancourt thought there would only be seventeen men eligible for election.

His successor who took over in April 1851 agreed about the qualifications but thought that one legislative body would be sufficient. He also maintained that Fancourt's scheme to divide the whole of the Honduras settlement into electoral districts would be completely impracticable. The various proposals went first to Jamaica where the Governor, Charles Grey, added his own suggestions before forwarding them to London. By December Henry Taylor, confronted with three different schemes, was writing: 'If we are to apply ourselves to invent constitutions, no two persons will invent the same, and the more projects the more perplexing'. The papers circulated in the Colonial Office for almost a year; there was general agreement that the new Superintendent, Wodehouse, was right in thinking that a single chamber was best for Honduras, but the number of members to be officially nominated was the subject of some argument. However, by the end of 1853, after a number of modifications, the Act 'To amend the system of Government of British Honduras' received the royal assent and elections took place under the new system.

The Legislative Assembly which met for the first time in January 1854 had 21 members of whom 18 were elected, and 3 officials nominated by the Superintendent. The members had to be British born or naturalized subjects, over 21 years old and owning property worth £400; their electors either had to own a small amount of property or earn £100 a year. Every member had to declare in writing, before taking his seat, that he was legally qualified to do so. The Assembly was to elect one of its members as Speaker and this election would be subject to the Superintendent's confirmation. The Chairman of the last Public Meeting, Mr W. H. Coffin, became the first Speaker in the new Assembly. The Assembly was to last for four years, but the Superintendent had the power to prorogue or dissolve it at any time; he was required to summon it every January. In addition he could originate bills, as could the Assembly, and he could give or withhold consent to those bills or reserve them for the Crown's pleasure.

After the Legislative Assembly had been functioning for a year the Superintendent reported to Jamaica that he had opened the Assembly with more ceremony than had been the custom as he wished to give the new body greater importance. He thought that 'the result has been a more systematic and parliamentary mode of conducting the public business than was ever previously observed in this Settlement'. The general satisfaction with the new constitution was widespread, the only remaining problem being the long promised elevation to colonial status. This will be discussed in more detail later, but it is interesting to notice that a year before the new constitution came into effect the Governor of Jamaica was suggesting to Superintendent Wodehouse that 'the general tone and language of the acts of the Public Meeting and the Superintendent on this occasion should be an assumption that British Honduras has for some time been in fact a Colony rather than any announcement and declaration of its being now suddenly and all at once erected into one'—with this the settlement had to be content until 1862.

The Judicial System

The many administrative difficulties created by the Spanish treaties of 1783 and 1786 were increased by the lack of an adequate judiciary. The elected Magistrates had long been accustomed to administering rough and ready justice and their position had been strengthened by the Burnaby Code. Only a few simple regulations were framed and it was laid down that any crime not mentioned in the Code was to 'be punished according to the Custom of the Bay in like cases'. This somewhat meaningless phrase was widely quoted and used by the settlers almost as a Bill of Rights. They would have been mortified had they been informed of the ruling made by the Law Officers of the Crown, in response to a query by the Secretary of State in 1812, on the competence of the Honduras courts. The firm statement was issued that: 'We cannot trace the authority of the Magistrates at Honduras, or the Laws by which their decisions are governed, to any legal origin, and therefore we do not conceive that such decisions can be legally enforced'.

The settlers had some justification for believing that their courts had been sanctioned by the Government: the Governor of Jamaica had pardoned a man sentenced in a Honduras court and, more recently in 1810, it had been decided that appeals concerning actions of over £700 could be made to England. Nevertheless the Colonial Office continued to insist that legal tribunals could only be established with the authority of Parliament or the Crown and not by agreement among the inhabitants.

The use of Courts Martial

In the early years of the century many of the Superintendents resorted to the use of the unpopular Court Martial in criminal cases. When Lord Bathurst took over the Colonial department in 1812 he examined the anomalous judicial situation and posed the question whether offences committed in Honduras could come within the jurisdiction of the Admiralty Court. Once again the Law Officers answered in the negative. When a slave murdered his master the following year he was tried by a Court Martial and sentenced to death. Superintendent Smyth reported that this method of dealing with a dangerous situation had given general satisfaction. The gravity of this case must have done much to alter the attitude of the settlers to the use of Courts Martial. Colonel Arthur and Bathurst between them did much to improve the position although they frequently had to contend with the rigid position adopted by the Law Officers. Arthur speedily recognized that the Magistrates' lack of effective authority was bringing the Bench into grave disrepute despite their apparent power. Certainly the Magistrates performed many functions in their legal capacity: they sat as Judges in the various courts, they issued warrants and assessed damages but they were rarely impartial. This last complaint was common throughout the West Indies and applied equally to the juries.

Powers of the civil courts

In 1815 Lord Bathurst issued a directive stating that while the ancient laws of the settlement were to be enforced the powers of the civil courts were to be restricted. In future criminals were to be punished only by fines, imprisonment or transportation; the question of punishing murders and other crimes subject to the death penalty was left unresolved. Nor were the civil authorities to have any power over military or naval personnel in civil or criminal cases. This did help to clarify the situation, but it was not long before another murder was committed and the whole question was raised again. This time the accused was a female slave and Arthur reported that she had been tried before the civil court and found guilty, but punishment had been deferred until he received definite instructions. The Law Officers suggested that the accused should be tried by the Spanish tribunals in the Bay—apparently unaware that the settlement had never been occupied or administered by Spain. Bathurst forwarded this decision with the suggestion that the offender and witnesses should be sent to England for trial. Arthur was astonished at the increasing impracticality of the suggestions made, but for the time being the matter rested there. Offenders were kept in prison without trial, a possible course since the writ of Habeas Corpus was not introduced to the settlement until as late as 1853.

In 1818 the Public Meeting drew up a lengthy petition addressed to the Prince Regent lamenting that they were compelled to draw public attention to the fact that 'there is no Authority by which the hand of the Assassin can be legally stayed'. Their petition was supported by Arthur who asked one of his friends to call for its publication in Parliament if the Government ignored it. Bathurst seems to have realized that some action was at last inevitable. He told Arthur that application would be made to Spain to establish legal tribunals. In fact this never seems to have been done.

Establishment of a Supreme Court

In 1819 it was decided to legislate for Honduras without further formality and this momentous step was taken without producing any reaction from Spain. The 'Act for the Punishment of Certain Offences in the Bay of Honduras' was placed on the statute book in June, apparently without debate: the Act provided for the establishment of a Supreme Court consisting of four or more persons issued with a Commission from the King. The offences punishable under the new Act were confined to murders, manslaughters, rapes, robberies and burglaries. Arthur's reception of the Act was rather critical for he foresaw that difficulties were bound to arise from the lack of legally trained Commissioners. However he appointed an army officer to act as King's Advocate while asking Bathurst to appoint a legal adviser. To his friend Gascoyne and the Magistrates he was less critical, maintaining that much had been achieved simply by legislating exclusively for Honduras in the English Parliament. The Supreme Court was set up in June 1820 and it solved some of the more urgent judicial problems, but the limited nature of its jurisdiction left many others unresolved. For instance, although cases of attempted murder came within the spirit of the Act it was not one of the named offences which could be tried by the Supreme Court. Yet this Court remained the only legally established tribunal until after Honduras became a colony in 1862. Soon afterwards an attempt was made to put the civil courts on a more legal footing. James Stephen, at that time Legal Counsellor to the Colonial Office, drafted a Bill to deal with civil cases. When the proposals were sent out to the Bay it was found that Stephen had decided that trial by jury was unsuitable. The objections raised by Superintendent Codd and the leading settlers must have carried some weight, for though a second Bill was drafted no attempt was made to implement the proposals. It was agreed to leave the matter in abeyance until the Commission of Legal Enquiry which had been appointed to enquire into the administration of justice in the West Indies had made its report.

The Commission of Legal Enquiry, 1825–1829

The Commission visited Honduras in 1825, but its report was not presented to Parliament until four years later. This report provides a useful summary of the courts existing in the settlement at that time and the laws which they administered. It appears that there were three courts in addition to the Supreme Court. The Grand Court dealt with criminal offences not within the jurisdiction of the Supreme Court and also all civil cases involving sums of money over £10. The Summary Court took care of cases involving smaller sums as well as minor assaults, while a separate Slave Court existed for the punishment of non-felonious offences committed by slaves. The Summary Court sat once a month with one Magistrate as Judge and a jury of three men for civil cases and twelve for criminal ones. The jury in the Slave Court was composed of seven men. The Commission observed that on the whole the law administered was the same as English law with a few adaptations to suit local conditions. It was found that only one appeal from the settlement to the King-in-Council had ever been made. The Commission felt that despite the irregular basis of the courts the proceedings were conducted with as much dignity as elsewhere in the colonies. Only a few recommendations were made and the Commission seems to have regarded the judicial system of Honduras in a much rosier light than the Superintendents and other observers. Several curious legal discrepancies seem to have gone altogether unremarked. Perhaps the most controversial of these was the practice in the lower courts of the settlement whereby the jury not only decided the verdict but also awarded the punishment.

This naturally led to friction between the Magistrates and the juries; the matter came to a head during the superintendency of Colonel Arthur. He took the situation in hand and issued a proclamation to the effect that in future English law was to be observed in this respect and the jury was to confine itself to delivering the verdict. Bathurst approved Arthur's action and instructed him to make the ruling permanent.

Judicial reforms

From time to time suggestions for reforming the courts were made but nothing was done. In 1840 Macdonald's proclamation declaring the laws of England to be the laws of British Honduras created much consternation. However, when the Governor of Jamaica pointed out that in practice it made very little difference it was agreed to accept the situation. Sir Charles Metcalfe also recommended that a Judge should be appointed to preside over the courts. It was not until 1843 that Robert Temple became the first Chief Justice of British Honduras, an appointment which was to create many new problems during the next twenty years largely owing to his ungovernable temper and undue sense of his own importance. Temple's attempts to introduce English legal practices into the settlement were thwarted by the Magistrates and the Public Meeting, who were supported by Superintendent Fancourt. Less than a year after his arrival the Public Meeting was congratulating the Magistrates on their defence of long established customs. In March 1845 an Act was passed to define the powers vested in the Chief Justice; Temple was indignant but the Act was upheld by the Secretary of State who approved the claim of the Public Meeting to make rules of court as was the practice in other colonies. Unfortunately a number of serious disagreements took place and many charges were voiced about Temple's behaviour. But the officials of the Colonial Office made no attempt either to remove him from office or to pacify the settlers, believing that inaction was the best solution. Henry Taylor summed up the situation in a note written in 1848: 'unfortunately Mr Temple turned out to be a perfect representative of the rigour of the law in a place where there was no law'. He was inclined to think that Temple should be removed, but this step was not finally taken until as late as 1861. In the meantime several important changes were made.

In 1847 a bill was passed to enable an Attorney-General to practise in the settlement with the proviso that he was only to act on behalf of the Crown or the public in criminal cases. Five years later the writ of Habeas Corpus was at last applied so that prisoners could no longer languish in prison without trial. In 1855 the jurisdiction of the Supreme Court was enlarged, and the criminal law of the country was stated to be identical with English law. But there were still minor variations in civil law and no legally established civil court.

It is true to say that most of the difficulties in administering the law of the settlement were the result of the rigid attitude and the ignorance of the Law Officers of the Crown. On every occasion on which their professional advice was called for by the Colonial Office they tended to dismiss the courts in the settlement as illegal and to deny that any change could be made without breaking the agreements with Spain. The one important exception was the creation of the Supreme Court in 1819. The more general policy of avoiding mediating or interfering except in the most urgent cases meant that in the judicial sphere, as in everything else, too much depended on the character of the Superintendent.

The development of both the constitution and the judicial system in the period between 1798 and 1862 was very much a matter of piecemeal improvements. Changes were made at the instigation of the Superintendent and then given the stamp of approval only when there seemed to be no alternative. The *laissez-faire* attitude of the Colonial Office towards the Honduras settlement can be seen in a large number of memoranda which usually advised the Secretary of State to ignore the issue at hand and to avoid any sort of statement which might commit the government in its attitude. This very unsatisfactory state of affairs was always attributed either to the Spanish treaties or to the unbending views of the Law Officers. But by 1851 even these rigid upholders of the *status quo* were prepared to view the status of the settlement in a more positive light. When asked their advice in a case of piracy before the courts they said: 'we are disposed to think that at present it has become a part of the Dominions of Her Majesty', and certainly by this date this was the tacitly held view of the situation although some years remained before the necessary legal steps were taken.

8

Timber, Trade and Land

Timber

For almost two hundred years the exploitation of the forests of
Belize was the only reason for the existence of a British settlement
in Central America. Timber alone was the basis of the economy
and without the resources of the tropical forest there was nothing
to attract men to the swampy and fly-invested land which today is
rapidly developing as a modern agricultural country. The growth
of the timber industry and the corresponding failure of agriculture
to expand until recent times are an important aspect of Belize's
history and essential to its understanding.

Developments in mahogany felling

It has already been seen that logwood first lured the buccaneers
to the shores of Yucatán, and that after the establishment of
settlements, first in Campeche and then around the Belize River,
mahogany ousted logwood as the primary object of trade during
the eighteenth century. Whereas logwood grows prolifically along
river banks and presents few problems in cutting or transportation,
the extraction of mahogany is altogether more difficult. The
mahogany tree does not grow in stands but is scattered throughout
the forests and so surrounded by many other trees and dense
undergrowth that it has to be searched out by specially skilled
'huntsmen'. Moreover the full-grown tree takes many years to
reach maturity; consequently its ruthless exploitation without any

replanting led to gradually diminishing returns. Perhaps the most striking feature in the history of the mahogany industry is how little the methods of felling or transportation changed between its early beginnings and the introduction of mechanization in the present century. Until the advent of tractors, sawmills, a road system and logging railways, the only major development was the use of oxen to haul the logs to the river banks. This came about at the beginning of the last century, in 1805, and enabled the mahogany cutters to extend the scope of their logging operations. As long as they were dependent on human labour to haul the timber, these operations were necessarily limited. In the early years mahogany was cut wherever it could be readily found in the coastal forests and immediately beside the river banks. As all communication was by water the cutters gradually went further and further upriver in search of timber. The rivers of the country drain in an easterly or north-easterly direction towards the Caribbean Sea, and as the most accessible timber was exhausted in the area for cutting granted by the Spanish treaties, the Baymen moved south by sea and then inland up the Monkey River, Río Grande, the Moho and the Sarstoon. But the scale of cutting operations on these southerly rivers was limited by the difficulty of transporting the timber along their fast-flowing and often unnavigable waters. With the introduction of oxen it became possible to move away from the river and trees were cut five miles, and in some cases even as much as ten miles, away from the water.

Description of mahogany felling

Climatic factors made the industry largely seasonal. About August the mahogany gangs were assembled, each numbering anything from ten to fifty men led by a Captain and huntsman. The latter was sent ahead of the gang to explore the land from the river bank. Travel was by means of pitpan or dorey, and a keen and practised eye was required to spy out the mahogany trees. Once having selected the best trees for felling the huntsman had to lead his men to the area while concealing their tracks from rival gangs; this was necessary as the regulations concerning ownership of mahogany works could not be enforced. After the trees had been located and the camps built, the work of felling began towards the end of the rainy season in November. The gangs returned to Belize for the Christmas season which was usually a prolonged period of celebration preceding the period of really hard work. In the first place roads had to be cut from the trees to the river banks, and then once the weather was dry, the task of trucking began. The oxen hauled the mahogany with simple two-wheeled carts; because of the great heat this work was carried out at night by the light of huge pine torches. Contemporary descriptions present an enjoyable picture of the scene. Colonel Cockburn described trucking operations with great enthusiasm: '. . . a more enlivening scene cannot be imagined . . . the Cattle are of the finest description, the men in the highest spirits and the whole scene most brilliantly illumined by the numerous Pitch Pine Torches with which it is accompanied . . .' Once they reached the river banks, or landings as they were known, the logs which had already been cut from the trees after felling, were roughly squared off, marked with the owner's name and lashed together. Then, when the heavy rain came in June, the logs were floated down the rivers to the 'boom' at the mouth of the river where they were sorted out at the owners' wharves and prepared for shipping.

Problems of the industry

Honduras mahogany was generally of good quality; buoyant and durable, it could resist changes in temperature and in the first half of the nineteenth century was much in demand for ship-building and cabinet making. But the quality and size of the timber varied and new regulations were constantly being enacted about the size of the mahogany which could be exported. It is obvious that the industry was very dependent on the weather. In years when the floods proved too heavy many of the logs were washed out to sea, while in years when the rains were lighter some of the logs could not be floated down river at all and were left to rot in the forests. An examination of the export figures for mahogany and logwood compiled by the Forestry Department reveals an interesting pattern of alternating high and low exports which gives a very good indication of the economic state of the settlement in any given year. This was determined not only by internal factors such as the weather but also by demand from the world market. The mahogany industry seems to have reached a peak in the years 1845-6 when the railway boom in Europe was at its height and mahogany was needed for building carriages. Thereafter the quantity exported seems to have declined fairly steadily. The following table shows the quantity of mahogany exported for selected years; the amount is expressed in square feet, not to be confused with amounts expressed in cubic feet. The tables show the extremely fluctuating nature of the mahogany trade.

Exports of Mahogany from British Honduras: Forestry Dept. File No. 54/36

1803	4,500,000 sq. ft.
1805	6,500,000 ,,
1810	7,250,000 ,,
1820	3,000,000 ,,
1837	8,500,000 ,,
1845	10,000,000 ,,
1858	6,275,374 ,,
1868	3,006,619 ,,
1878	3,146,582 ,,
1884	7,527,879 ,,
1896	2,769,676 ,,
1906	11,037,480 ,,

Logwood had not completely ceased to be exported and towards the end of the nineteenth century the trade underwent a revival until it was entirely superseded by synthetic dyes. The following table shows the quantity of logwood exported in tons.

Exports of Logwood from British Honduras (Various sources)

1756	18,000 tons
1783	7,000 ,,
1805	1,270 ,,
1846	4,314 ,,
1862	7,802 ,,
1883	18,082 ,,
1889	21,978 ,,
1907	6,663 ,,

The seasonal nature of the timber industry had a lasting effect on several other aspects of life in the settlement. As the men who worked in the mahogany gangs were usually the strongest slaves and could relax for lengthy periods in Belize out of the mahogany cutting season, this helped to induce an attitude of condescension towards weaker men toiling in the fields throughout the year. Even today some of this feeling survives and over the years it has certainly contributed to the slow development of agriculture. In the first half of the nineteenth century there was general compliance with the terms of the Anglo-Spanish treaties which forbade the development of plantations and prohibited the growth of food-stuffs except for subsistence.

The reluctance of the Colonial Office to see any constitutional or judicial developments within the Honduras settlement during the first half of the nineteenth century was paralleled by its refusal to sanction the development of agriculture. In 1818 Superintendent Arthur was trying to find work for some disbanded negro soldiers settling in Honduras. He proposed a scheme for growing cotton sponsored by Marshall Bennett, but the Board of Trade rejected it as an infringement of the 1786 Treaty. At this time raw cotton was much in demand and its growth was being encouraged throughout the West Indies, a fact which makes this refusal even more striking. Even the independence of the former Spanish colonies could not change the attitude of the British Government. In 1833 the Public Meeting itself proposed that cotton, tobacco, coffee, rice and other tropical produce could be cultivated, but this was also turned down with the explanation that it was not a suitable moment for discussions with Spain. Later petitions were equally unsuccessful and similar restrictions were applied to attempts to develop a shipbuilding industry.

Restrictions on shipbuilding

At first the Board of Trade was adamant that ships built in the settlement could not be given the privilege of registering as British-built ships. On this occasion the excuse used was that such a step would be contrary to the Navigation Acts, but by this time these Acts were no longer applied to Honduras. Colonel Arthur was convinced that the registration of ships would be so beneficial to the development of the settlement that he persisted with his requests and persuaded his friend Gascoyne, the Member of Parliament for Liverpool, to act on behalf of the settlers. In June 1820 an Act was passed which Gascoyne felt was very favourable to the settlement. The privileges of British-built ships were granted to all vessels built in Malta, Gibraltar and Heligoland, while ships built in the Bay of Honduras could be regarded as British provided they were owned by British subjects and confined in their use to the direct trade between Honduras and the United Kingdom. Arthur was very disappointed with these concessions. He explained in a letter to Gascoyne that the settlers really wanted to build small vessels suitable for the coastal trade between Honduras, Jamaica and the Spanish ports. This trade was carried on by North American ships and Arthur felt that the Board of Trade was throwing away a great opportunity. Five years later the agent for the settlement was still trying to obtain an extension of these privileges, but there was no response from the Board of Trade.

The effect of timber duties

Arthur was able to call upon the services of Gascoyne in another matter which was of fundamental importance to the prosperity of the Honduras settlement—the complex question of timber duties. This question must be seen in relation to British policy towards Baltic and North American timber. For centuries naval supplies had been regarded as one of the most important British imports and the Baltic was the traditional source of supply. The various Navigation Acts had done something to encourage supplies of colonial timber, but it was a bulky cargo and the cost of freighting it from North America gave the more durable Baltic timber the advantage. It was not until the 1807 alliance between Napoleon and Alexander I of Russia that a dramatic change in policy was brought about. The alliance closed the Baltic to British shipping and the price of timber rocketed. At a time when British strength depended on a navy of wooden ships the situation was critical. As a result new rates of duty were imposed on foreign timber while colonial timber for naval purposes was to be admitted duty free. Although this ruling did not at first apply to Honduras, for it was not a colony, the imposition of heavy duties on foreign timber did benefit the settlement. Moreover the Admiralty was seeking new types of timber and for this purpose a Captain Wright was sent to Honduras. Samples of mahogany were sent to the naval dockyards with the recommendation that cedar and santa maria wood could be used, but it was some time before this suggestion was adopted. In 1818 it was agreed to admit santa maria duty free for naval purposes, for as long as the same concession was applied to Canadian timber. For his part in this achievement Gascoyne was voted a sum of money by the Public Meeting.

After the Napoleonic wars the general depression affected the European demand for mahogany and the settlers felt that large-scale imports of mahogany from St Domingo were adversely affecting their trade. Arthur supported their case, stating that it was impossible to compete on equal terms with the cheap labour supplies from St Domingo and asking for increased duties on foreign timber. The Board of Trade agreed with the analysis but declined to act on the ground that Honduras timber already enjoyed an advantage. This decision was not surprising as at the time there was a general reaction against old-established trading principles and a desire to sweep away many of the restrictions imposed by the Navigation Acts. Reform was in the air in England and select committees were set up to examine these issues. Pamphlets were written and heated debates took place in Parliament. General Gascoyne presented several petitions from Liverpool to the effect that any reduction in the duties on foreign timber, despite the obvious advantages to be gained from a renewal of supplies from the Baltic, would prove highly detrimental to the colonies. It was argued that much capital had been invested in North America and those colonies had been deliberately encouraged to promote their timber industry. Not only would they lose if a change were made, but much British shipping was likely to be thrown out of employment. At no time was the timber from Honduras mentioned in the debate. News of the proposed changes brought much despondency to Honduras so that it was with some satisfaction that Arthur was able to tell the Magistrates towards the end of 1820 that for the time being the Board of Trade had abandoned its intention of removing the heavy duties on foreign timber. The following year an Act was passed which did reduce the duty on Baltic timber and introduce a small duty on Canadian, but mahogany was not affected by these changes and the duty continued at the existing rates. Mahogany from Honduras was imported into Great Britain at the rate of £3.16.0 per ton as against £5.0.0 from St Domingo, Cuba and Jamaica and the very high rate of £11.17.6 from other places.

One of the main problems of the mahogany cutters was the natural exhaustion of supplies, which led to the cutting and purchase of mahogany from Spanish soil. In 1818 a local law imposed a heavy duty of £25 per 1,000 feet on all mahogany cut outside the settlement; the boundaries were not defined for the purpose of the Act but it was usually applied to timber cut north of the Rio Hondo. An attempt to export mahogany from the Mosquito Shore, at the same favourable rate as locally cut timber, was strenuously resisted by the Superintendent and the Public

Meeting. But a few years later it became apparent that foreign mahogany was being shipped in considerable quantities as British. Superintendent Cockburn issued two proclamations to stop this violation of the local and United Kingdom laws. In 1833, after some discussion at the Public Meeting, the prohibited tax against foreign mahogany was repealed. Meanwhile the British customs duties had been amended so that mahogany from Honduras was paying £1.10.0 per ton as against £4 on all other mahogany. When Cockburn raised the question whether this lower rate of duty could be applied to all mahogany shipped from Honduras the reply was favourable.

The decline of the industry

This changing attitude towards trade was not always welcomed by the woodcutters. The gradual reduction of duties on foreign mahogany caused much alarm and distress in the settlement but it was an essential part in the move towards free trade which was overturning all the old economic principles in England during the 1840s. The decline in the value of mahogany was having disastrous results, as a petition drawn up by the Public Meeting stated early in 1841: 'Mahogany, which in 1835–6, was sold here at a price equal to £18 and £20 sterling will not bring more on the spot than £9–£12; and when shipped to British markets netts only from £4–£7 per 1000 feet.' Later that year the Tory party was returned to office under the leadership of Sir Robert Peel, who was determined to reform the fiscal system. In a series of budgets free trade in most raw materials was introduced and the old colonial preferences swept away. The duty on foreign timber was progressively reduced until by 1846 it stood at only 15/-.

Although the Honduras woodcutters lamented the new policy, 1846 marked a high point in the export of mahogany despite the complaints about exhaustion of resources. A book published in 1850 stated that the effect of the change in duty had been so beneficial that in the years 1842–5 the import of mahogany into the port of Liverpool alone had trebled. It is impossible to know how much of this mahogany was shipped from Honduras. According to the ever-increasing complaints of the Baymen their timber was being rapidly exhausted and the abolition of the favourable differential duties had caused great hardship. One such complaint came from the firm of Hyde and Company in

November 1847. Addressing the Secretary of State they declared
that mahogany from Cuba, where slave labour was still employed,
was their chief competitor. They complained that there had been
such an unprecedented increase in public taxation in the last few
years that the small population of ten thousand was quite unable
to bear the burden. The reply from the Colonial Office was not at
all sympathetic to the problems of the woodcutters. It pointed out
that the rate of duty on many articles had been reduced and the
increase in revenue indicated that the wealth of the community
was growing. It went on to say that the increase in taxation was in
response to the demand for expenditure on certain public works
made by the Public Meeting. In 1849 and again in 1860 the Superintendent reported years of great depression in the mahogany
trade, but the general commercial position showed signs of improvement. In 1856 the Superintendent was able to state that the
annual exports now amounted to over half a million pounds in
value, while imports were worth less than half this. The 1850s
was a period of rapid expansion as the northern part of the country
around Corozal and Orange Walk was occupied by immigrants
from Yucatán fleeing from the Caste War. In 1841 the total population was under 9,000, but by 1857 it was estimated that it had
increased to 19,000. The majority of these new inhabitants were
Indians practising agriculture in the northern districts. At last it
seemed possible to hope for the development of a stable agriculture. Some of the settlement's increased prosperity was due to the
trade with Central America, the importance of which must now
be examined.

Trade

The economy of the country was based on timber, but her
prosperity also depended on the general trade which was carried
on in Belize, since the bulk of the revenue came from import and
export duties. In the period of the Spanish colonial empire Spain
jealously guarded the trade between her colonies in the New World
and her ports in Europe. But towards the end of the eighteenth
century a breach had been made in this monopolistic system with
the growth of free ports in certain parts of the Caribbean. The
guarda costas who patrolled the area were unable to prevent

Spanish colonists from carrying their goods to the new free ports at such places as Jamaica and Grenada. The British merchants who engaged in this trade exchanged the raw materials from the Spanish colonies for manufactured goods, rum and negro slaves. During the eighteenth century Belize seems to have played little part in this profitable trade but during the first half of the nineteenth century she came into her own as an entrepôt of considerable importance. In times of peace the Honduras settlers traded their imported manufactured goods for essential cattle and foodstuffs at the Spanish ports of Omoa and Trujillo. Whenever this trade was closed, as in time of war, or on the appointment of a more officious Spanish Commander, the settlers were forced to turn to North America for their supplies. This was responsible for much hardship and distress in the settlement. As the Spanish colonies freed themselves from the stranglehold of Spain in the first quarter of the nineteenth century, it was natural that Great Britain should take the place of Spain as a source of the manufactured goods needed in the new republics and as a market for their raw materials. A profitable contraband trade between Jamaica and the former colonies had long been carried on and this was gradually transferred to Belize, which was more accessible for the merchants of Guatemala and the other Central American states. In time Belize became the channel for a legal trade between Great Britain and Central America but this was, perhaps, in spite of rather than because of any positive encouragement on the part of the British Government.

Trade with former Spanish colonies

British manufacturers and merchants were understandably eager to establish trade relations with the newly emerging countries of Latin America and it has been estimated that by 1825 over £20,000,000 of British capital had been invested in these countries. It is clear that commercial relations preceded political negotiations and the British Government showed itself somewhat slow to accept the full implications of these developments. Although Britain lent moral support to the colonies in their struggle against Spain and declared that her navy would prevent any interference by any other European nation, she did little to give early recognition to them. It was not until December 1824 that Secretary George Canning persuaded the Cabinet to give recognition to

Mexico, Colombia and Buenos Aires and even this was granted in the form of commercial rather than political treaties. By this time the United States had proclaimed the Monroe Doctrine and recognized the new republics. Canning's policy of encouragement towards these new states was tempered by the fear that the old monarchies of Europe might be confronted by an alliance of the vigorous young republics of the New World. Nevertheless British Consuls were appointed for several of the new states and special commissioners were sent out to study the prospects for trade. In 1825 Consul O'Reilly became the first British official in Guatemala. There were a number of disagreements between Guatemala and Britain and it soon became clear that Guatemala intended to use the smuggling which went on between there and Belize as a pretext for diplomatic argument and threats. Soon after his appointment the new Consul reported home a conversation with the President of Guatemala in which he had pointed out that, in accordance with his instructions to discourage smuggling, he had made some enquiries at Belize on his journey out. He went on to say that he had told the President that 'in nineteen cases out of twenty the merchants of this country went to Belize with hard dollars, indigo or other produce and bought or bartered with the merchants for British goods. Therefore that their own citizens were the smugglers and the only remedies for smuggling were low duties, good roads and honest Customs House Officers . . .'

The Consul's sound advice was not taken. The time was not ripe for these reforms in Central America. The commercial relations of the country were bound up with the political situation, which was not at all stable at the time. Early in 1826 M. Zebadúa was sent to London as an envoy from the Central American Republic with the responsibility of negotiating a commercial treaty, but the civil war which broke out between the rival political parties in his absence brought the discussions to an end for the time being. The following year the Guatemalan Assembly imposed a ban on all foreign and coasting trade. But, although a schooner was stationed in the Bay of Honduras, the contraband trade continued to flourish. At the same time forced loans were levied on the few British merchants in Guatemala; O'Reilly advised them to pay this money to avoid all trade by foreigners being stopped.

In January 1828 the British Consul in Guatemala was murdered and it was over two years before a new British representative arrived in the country. Marshall Bennett, one of the leading mahogany cutters and merchants of Belize now resident in Guatemala, had failed to be appointed to this coveted post. He was the most important British merchant in Guatemala until his death in 1839 and was interested in many aspects of the economy apart from timber. He had an interest in mining, owned several ships and was even an agent for Lloyd's. In 1830 when Charles Dashwood arrived as Consul, the Liberales party, which was now in power, promised to protect British merchants in Central America: later a renewed attempt was made by Zebadúa to obtain commercial recognition. But in 1831 he was recalled and by the following year civil strife prevailed and the Federation of the Central American states was in danger of imminent collapse. It was during this unsettled state of affairs that a new British figure arrived in Guatemala.

The appointment of Frederick Chatfield

Frederick Chatfield was a junior consular official appointed by Palmerston and for nearly twenty years, with only one brief interruption, he represented Britain in Central America. Unfortunately for relations between the two countries he was not ideally suited for this task. He was an ambitious young man and his main object was to promote British commercial interests; his interest in local politics was always subordinate to his first aim and he was not above changing his support from Galvez and the Liberales to Morazán and the Serviles as he saw which way the wind was blowing. Moreover he was a somewhat self-righteous man, conscious of his own superiority as a white Protestant in a country of coloured Catholics. He was consistently anxious to negotiate a commercial treaty and took a previously prepared draft with him, but his task was made unenviable by the insistence of the British Government that the question of the sovereignty of the Honduras settlement and its boundaries was not to be discussed with any country but Spain. Since the Morazán government had already declared the British tenure of the settlement as an usurpation of Central American territory Chatfield was bound to encounter great difficulties. The Serviles were more tolerant towards Belize, and Chatfield opened negotiations with Zebadúa, who was now the Foreign Minister. However he insisted on an immediate British abandonment of the claim to the Mosquito Shore, the Bay Islands and the limitation of the Honduras boundaries to those laid down in 1786. The result was naturally a complete stalemate. The British Government decided to re-open discussions with Spain and Chatfield was forced to sit and wait for an opportunity to begin again. Meanwhile the internal political situation deteriorated rapidly and in 1839 Costa Rica, Nicaragua and Honduras seceded from the Federation and by the following year it had completely collapsed.

Relations with Guatemala

During this period of turmoil Guatemalan claims against British subjects had grown ever more demanding: in 1835 Superintendent Cockburn was informed that unless the settlers confined themselves to the area between the Hondo and Sibún Rivers, as laid down by treaty, a 20% tax on all British imports would be charged. The British Superintendent asked for permission to retaliate with a tax of 25% but neither of these new rates of duty seems to have been imposed. However, between 1840 and 1847 the outlook for British trade in the area was bleak; not only were conditions very unstable but the five newly independent states enforced different regulations. There were never many British merchants resident in Central America (in 1838 no more than 31) but those who did live there were subjected to such irritations as forced loans and military service. Lord Palmerston never tolerated the harassment of British subjects in any part of the world and, by June 1840, he and Lord Russell, the Colonial Secretary, had decided to protect British subjects in Central America by using naval units stationed in the West Indies and the Pacific and demanding compensation for injuries. Chatfield was pleased with this show of support and endeavoured to use it as a constant threat in his dealing with the separate states. Central American reaction to the presence of British warships off its coastlines was one of hostility, and possibly helped the increasing spread of United States influence during this period. By 1847 it certainly represented a definite challenge to British interests in the area and by the time permission was granted for a renewed approach to negotiations for a treaty, Chatfield's policy had undergone a considerable change. At first he had maintained, with the British Foreign Office, that the Federal constitution was binding until all the states repealed it together. He had therefore refused to recognize the sovereignty of individual states, which caused much resentment. Now, however, he realized that it was essential for Britain to assert her interest in Central America and to proclaim it in a practical way if she were not to be outdone by the United States and lose excellent trading opportunities. So in June 1847, after Guatemalan independence had been declared, he concluded a treaty of amity and commerce without waiting for further instructions. This was approved the following year and Costa Rica also joined in. The three remaining states had less interest in commercial relations with Britain and stayed aloof for the time being. Meanwhile the United States representative in Central America, Ephraim Squier, and Chatfield were engaged in a personal feud and clashed over the British occupation of the island of Tigre in the Gulf of Fonseca. But in 1850 the Clayton–Bulwer treaty was arranged between Great Britain and the United States, bringing about a reconciliation of interest and a more cooperative attitude between the two powers in the Central American area. Two years later Chatfield returned to England.

Belize as an entrepôt

It is by no means easy to discover the details of the trade which was carried on between Central America and Britain via Belize. Much of the trade continued to be illegal and so no records were kept. Moreover many of the goods exported were treated for customs purposes as though they were produced in the settlement and therefore obtained preferential treatment. It has been estimated that during the 1820s four-fifths of Central American trade went through Belize. In the next decade the proportion was still three-quarters but by the 1840s the direct trade with Europe was almost as high as that through Belize. When Dashwood became Consul in 1830 he reported to the Foreign Office that, since the setting up of Commission Houses in Belize in 1824, trade with Central America had greatly increased. He thought that the value of exports through Belize to Central America and certain Mexican ports would amount to nearly £260,000 annually in the years 1825–8. This was no small amount. The goods imported by Central America were chiefly cotton textiles, dry goods and hardware in return for cochineal, indigo and bullion. Both indigo and cochineal were much in demand for dyeing in the English cotton industry but, by 1845, Central American indigo had been replaced by East Indian, and the mines were so depleted that specie or bullion could not be exported. Instead, coffee from Costa Rica was rapidly developing and formed an important trading commodity. Other goods which changed hands in Belize were such natural produce as sarsaparilla, balsa wood and tortoiseshell.

On the whole the old-established merchant oligarchy of Belize showed little appreciation of the opportunities in the developing trade. The Commission Houses mentioned by Dashwood were usually set up by British commercial companies with the specific object of trading with Central America. There was soon open hostility between the old residents and the new arrivals, and when Superintendent Cockburn deprived the old guard of their political privileges many of them left for England or became junior partners in British companies. Only a very few went to Central America and Chatfield was highly critical of the lack of enterprise shown by the Belize citizens. For the most part the trade was carried on by the Central Americans who bought their goods in Belize and shipped them to Izabal, then transported them overland to Guatemala. The Belize merchants were often heard to complain of the dishonesty shown in these transactions, but they themselves were much to blame for their reckless extension of credit without any form of security.

Problems of communication

Not only were the merchants of Belize lacking in initiative but, despite the apparent desire of the British Government to share in the profits of a lucrative trade, no positive encouragement towards this objective was given. Not only was diplomatic recognition withheld long after France and the United States had recognized the new republics, but no official steps were taken to invest British capital in the area. Moreover the trade was made more difficult by the lack of any efficient system of communications. The residents of Belize had long complained that they were dependent on an irregular sailing packet from Jamaica. It was not until 1836 that a regular mail service between Belize and Guatemala was set up. In 1839 the first steam packet between Britain and the Caribbean was introduced but Belize still had to depend on a monthly sailing ship from Jamaica. Not until as late as 1851 were new steam packet routes arranged which included Greytown and Belize. But in spite of these difficulties the advantages of trade through Belize were so great for the Central American merchants that the trade prospered throughout the first half of the nineteenth century. It was not until after 1850 that direct links with Europe and with America were established so that the role of Belize as an entrepôt suffered some decline. Britain could not be relied upon to give any support for the building of roads, warehouses or ports but she continued to dominate foreign trade largely because of her experience and effective monetary and banking system. Belize prospered as a direct result of this expertise, but this was due to the efforts of individuals and not the British Government. It was only on rare occasions that the latter was prepared to lend support and insist on compensation for damage to people and property. To a historian of Central America this attitude may seem surprising, but it was consistent with the general attitude of the government towards British Honduras throughout the first half of the last century. In 1839 James Stephen, by then Under-Secretary and possessing a wide knowledge of the settlement's history, could seriously write: 'it carries on a very large and valuable smuggling trade with Central America. This constitutes the real value of the place'.

Land Tenure

During the early history of the Honduras settlement the provisions regarding land tenure were extremely rudimentary. There was an attempt to make some regulations immediately after the adoption of the Burnaby Code in 1766. A meeting of the inhabitants decided that the action of building a hut in an unoccupied logwood area would give a man the right of ownership for a thousand yards on each side of the hut. It was also agreed that no one was to own two logwood works on one river at the same time. The following year the new rule was repeated and clarified so that 'the method of measuring logwood works shall be a straight line of two thousand yards or paces to be begun and ended at the River Side . . .'; it was laid down that no logwood work would be considered evacuated unless the owner either left the settlement or occupied another work on the same river at the same time. No further measures regulating mahogany sites were enacted for another 20 years and no system was devised for registering ownership of the different works. It was inevitable that under such a loosely defined scheme of landownership disputes should and did arise. Sometimes these led to violence but more often to prolonged litigation which could not be satisfactorily settled in the courts of the settlement. It was therefore natural that Colonel Arthur in his desire to achieve efficiency in the administrative affairs of the settlement should introduce a system of registration of land.

The introduction of land registration

Arthur explained to Lord Bathurst that such a scheme would achieve two desirable objects at the same time: firstly it would make it more difficult for the woodcutters to ignore the boundaries laid down by Spain, and secondly it would lead to fewer disputes among the woodcutters. Having received permission from the Colonial Office to proceed, Arthur issued a proclamation in 1817 which compelled all landowners to register their property within six months. After that date no tenure could be considered valid unless it were duly registered. The Superintendent's next action was to set up a Commission to report on land tenure in the settlement. The object was to discover how much vacant land was available which could be used to settle some needy pensioners. Eleven men were appointed to serve on the Commission but they showed an extreme reluctance to act. It was not until Arthur threatened to appoint a military board to take their place that they took action. Even so their report on land tenure was not produced until 1820. It described the early regulations defining logwood works and stated that in 1787 it had been laid down that three miles in a straight line was to delimit a mahogany works. The report pointed out that since 1796 the settlers had taken what they needed for provision grounds despite the Spanish restrictions. The only constructive proposal made by the Commission was that provision grounds which had not been cultivated for the previous five years should be forfeited to those in need of the land. Specific recommendations were made by which old settlers were to receive 10 acres for the head of the family and 5 for the other members of the family: new settlers were to receive a piece of land 100 by 300 yards. The Commission emphasized that all the land held was regarded as freehold property and recognized as such by the local courts. When Arthur forwarded the report to the Colonial Secretary for consideration he pointed out that there was apparently no mahogany land left vacant and that, although the old rules had stated that no man was to hold more than two works on one river, it was well known that some men held as many as eight or ten works. The government took no further action at that time and it was not until the 1830s when the question of the sale of Crown lands in other colonies was occupying government attention that the question was again raised.

In a prolonged and bitter legal case between two mahogany cutters the whole question of land tenure was again brought to the attention of the Colonial Office. It seemed that the acting Superintendent Macdonald had promised George Hyde a mahogany works on the River Hondo. Colonel Cockburn dealt with the application in the usual way and was much surprised when, almost a year later, a Mr Craig demanded that the grant to Hyde should be cancelled on the ground that he had himself held the land in question since 1814. Cockburn insisted that he had no power to cancel grants once made and therefore Craig summoned Hyde to the Grand Court for the sum of £6,000. Superintendent Cockburn regarded this as outright defiance of his authority, but this view was not supported by the Colonial Office; it was felt in London that Cockburn had been in the wrong in attempting to interfere in a judicial process. The case was therefore allowed to proceed but the difference of opinion between the Magistrates was such that three of them actually withdrew. Cockburn complained that he had been libelled in the matter and when the case was put to the jury they were locked up for four days and nights without being able to reach a decision. The case dragged on for five years at the end of which Craig reluctantly abandoned his claim to the works in dispute.

The sale of Crown lands

It was not until 1838 when a circular despatch was addressed to all the West Indian colonies requiring the payment of £1 per acre for every grant made that the matter was again ventilated. By this time Macdonald was Superintendent and he protested that the new rule could not be applied to the settlement without making it even more difficult to encourage the development of agriculture. But this time the authorities in London were determined to adopt one policy on the matter and it was explained to the Superintendent that the wholesale alienation of Crown lands had only led to laziness and not to development of the land. Henry Taylor was very sceptical as to the wisdom of allowing the settlers a fixed property in the soil of Honduras as he foresaw nothing but troubles from a turbulent assembly and the settlement's neighbours. Nevertheless the decision was taken to authorize land grants. It was in fact this decision which brought into being the controversial Executive Council: in authorizing the Superintendent to sell land for cultivation, provided that an adequate survey was carried out first, the Secretary of State suggested that a Council might be appointed to dispose of the revenues accruing from the sale of land. Macdonald not only used the land question to obtain his long desired Council but he failed to carry out the instructions of the Colonial Office in disposing of Crown lands. In 1842 he issued two notices which allowed certain individuals to hold land in fee in cases where they had occupied it before the Crown grants were made. Macdonald's notices were disallowed by the Secretary of State. Four years later Superintendent Fancourt had to issue a proclamation to prevent certain people from cutting young wood on ungranted lands—a direct result of Macdonald's irresponsible policy. No longer was it possible for a mahogany cutter to choose his work and to exploit the mahogany there without first paying for the land. Twenty years later, in 1867, the first tax on land and property was introduced as a major contribution to the flagging revenues of the country.

9

Society and Slavery

The Condition of the Slaves

The state of slavery, in its ultimate form, can best be defined as the subordination of one man to another in such a way that the former has no freedom of action or any personal rights whatsoever: he is, in other words, neither more nor less than one of the goods and chattels of his master. The institution of slavery is by no means modern: it was practised in ancient Greece. Even today there are parts of the world where it has not been completely eradicated. The Europeans who discovered and colonized the American continent and the West Indian islands from the sixteenth to the eighteenth centuries needed labour to exploit the riches of their new colonies. This applied equally to the silver mines of Peru, the agricultural acres of North America and the sugar plantations of the West Indies. It also inevitably applied to the mahogany forests of Belize. Native labour, Indian and Carib, was inadequate both in numbers and strength; as European labour was expensive to import and could not stand up to hard work in a tropical climate, negroes from the West Coast of Africa provided the answer. So, for over three hundred years, negroes were shipped across the Atlantic in their thousands, to a life of slavery in a new world.

The Triangular Trade

This traffic in slaves formed part of an extremely profitable triangular trade which brought riches to many merchants and adventurers. Manufactured goods such as cloths and tools were carried from London, Liverpool, Bristol, the northern French ports and those of Portugal to the Gold and Guinea coasts of Africa, where they were exchanged for healthy negroes who were then carried westwards in the most deplorable conditions. On arrival in the West Indies or the Americas the sea captains, with little concern for the despair of separated families, sold those who had survived the journey. The sailing vessels were then cleaned out and reloaded with colonial produce for sale in Europe.

Occasionally conscience was pricked and isolated individuals could be heard denouncing the nature of the slave trade; but, generally speaking, it was not until the last years of the eighteenth century that opposition became widespread. Meetings were then held throughout England and sermons preached against the iniquities of the slave trade, but it was not until 1807 that the work of Wilberforce, Clarkson and others was rewarded by the passing of an Act for the Abolition of the Slave Trade.[1]

Abolition brings recognition to the settlers

The Abolition Act made it illegal for all British subjects to carry on the African slave trade and all dealings in slaves were to be punished by fines. While the Act forbade the removal of slaves from Africa or any place in the West Indies or America which was not a British possession, it did not forbid the transportation of slaves from one British colony to another. Unfortunately the trade was so profitable that the small fines imposed did not prevent smuggling and in 1811 another Act was passed which introduced more severe penalties for carrying on the trade. The anomalous status of the Honduras settlement led to a good deal of uncertainty as to whether the Abolition Act was applicable there or not. It was not until a specific case of importing slaves was brought to the attention of the Superintendent in 1814 that the export of slaves between Jamaica and Honduras was declared illegal. Colonel Arthur's proclamation of 1815 was based on the opinion of the Jamaican Attorney-General that, even if the Honduras settlement

1. Eric Williams has argued that abolition was only possible because British economic interest no longer required the slave trade and that economic rather than humanitarian motives were responsible for abolition. This interpretation has now been challenged and a more convincing argument suggests that abolition became possible in 1807 because of the changing political climate in Britain and the formation of a government more favourable to reform.

could be regarded as a British colony, it was not within the West Indies and therefore did not come within the meaning of the Act. This decision presented the Superintendent with certain difficulties. The slave traffic between Jamaica and the settlement might be illegal but, as there was no Customs official at Belize, who could be authorized to seize any offenders? There was some confusion between seizures in the case of ordinary contraband and slaves, before Arthur was informed that he must take responsibility for the latter himself—since the Abolition Act applied to 'British subjects alike in a British Colony or in a Foreign Country'. Thus at last the settlers of Honduras were officially recognized as British subjects. The Abolition Acts did not put an end to traffic in slaves. Many continued to be carried between colonies in the guise of domestic servants, a practice which was allowed until a licensing system was introduced in 1824. It is not possible to discover how many slaves entered Honduras in this way; the demand for labour was high and it is probable that many more than those licensed were brought in before the abolition of slavery in 1833.

The import of slaves to the Honduras settlement

Compulsory registration of slaves was never the custom in Honduras, a fact which makes it difficult to be precise about the numbers in the settlement or the type of work in which they were employed. It is very unlikely that negroes were imported before about 1720. A Spanish missionary stated in 1724 that the community consisted of about 300 Englishmen and some negroes who had recently been introduced from Jamaica and Bermuda. There was no direct slave trade between the settlement and Africa; the negroes were usually purchased in Jamaica or perhaps intercepted en route to the Spanish colonies of Central America. By the end of the eighteenth century, after the influx of the Mosquito Shore people, the slaves in the settlement totalled 2,132 out of a population of 2,915. It is therefore clear that the economy, and indeed the very existence of the settlement, was dependent on slave labour. It is curious that a myth has pervaded the whole social history of British Honduras that slavery never existed there, or, if it did, it was slavery in name alone. The evidence will lead us to a very different conclusion.

The Reverend John Armstrong, who was Chaplain to the settlement for twelve years from 1812, had ample opportunity to reflect on the state of slavery. In a pamphlet which he wrote to refute the charges made against Colonel Arthur by some of the leading mahogany cutters, Armstrong admitted that on the whole the slaves in Honduras were physically well-treated and given generous food and clothing allowances. Some of the slave-owners were even prepared to encourage the religious education of their slaves. He then explained why it was so difficult to regulate the relations between slave and master by legislation. 'The grand doctrine of most, perhaps all, slave colonies,' he declared, 'is that, to a certain extent, the power of the master over his slave is absolute, and that all interference in this respect produces insubordination; the consequence is, that not only every measure for the melioration of slavery is viewed with jealousy and opposed with violence, but the necessary means of protecting slaves from oppression and cruelty are withheld, and every attempt to shield them from barbarous usage is considered an invasion of the rights of the owner; and, to such an extent is this carried, that even in cases of the most flagrant abuse and injustice, it is almost impossible to convict a master of cruelty, or recover for the injured slave either right or remuneration.' Armstrong was clearly writing from experience and he went on to illustrate his assertions by specific examples. When we discuss the institution of slavery in the British settlement of Honduras, we must therefore take into consideration not only the daily work and lives of the slaves, but the opportunities they had to improve their position and their status in law.

The records of slavery

Slavery in the West Indies can be studied from a variety of historical material. During the eighteenth and early nineteenth centuries travellers visiting the West Indian islands wrote down their impressions of life and society in letters, diaries and memoirs. Reports were compiled by missionaries and agents of the Anti-Slavery Society for their patrons in London; the laws passed in the local assemblies were carefully scrutinized and then commented upon by the Colonial Office; court cases were recorded and reports of several Commissions of Enquiry published. Furthermore, as the anti-slavery agitation increased, the attention of both Houses of Parliament was focused on the Caribbean and much information was collected and printed for Parliament in the form of

estimates of population, returns of baptism, marriages and punishments awarded. Little of this vast body of material relates to
Honduras. Few travellers visited the Bay, and those who did saw
little of life in the mahogany camps outside Belize. Occasionally
the returns called for by the House of Commons were sent to the
settlement, filled in and forwarded to London. The Commission of
Legal Enquiry did visit Belize in 1825, but on the whole the historian has to work from general impressions rather than carefully
compiled statistics and reports. Perhaps it is this limitation which
has led so many observers to believe that slavery as practised in
Honduras barely existed. Or is it perhaps that contemporaries who
arrived from Jamaica found the situation so different from that
prevailing throughout the West Indies that they could not fail to
be favourably impressed? Even so practised an observer as Colonel
Arthur wrote to the Secretary of State after two years in Belize:
'Although I came to the West Indies . . . a perfect Wilberforce as
to Slavery, I must now confess, that I have in no part of the world
seen the labouring class of people possessing anything like the
comforts and advantages of the Slave population of Honduras.'
How different was Arthur's attitude to the slave-owners when he
left the settlement six years later.

Slave conditions peculiar to Honduras

There were several factors which might account for a milder
form of slavery in Honduras than in the British West Indian islands.
In the first place the Honduras settlers were men who regarded
the place as their home; they lived and worked there and few of
them had any regular contact with England. In this respect they
were like the French and Spanish colonists who made their colonies
their home and were not always looking towards the mother
country. The English sugar planters in Jamaica and Barbados, on
the other hand, stayed in the West Indies only long enough to earn
sufficient money to employ an attorney to manage their estates
and then they became absentee landlords. Apart from infrequent
visits to their plantations they had no personal contact with their
slaves and were accordingly usually uninterested in their welfare.
The proximity of Honduras to the Spanish colonies was also bound
to have an effect on the settlers' treatment of their slaves simply
because the possibility of escape was always open to them. During
the eighteenth century Spanish slavery was regulated by a strict

series of edicts for the benefit of the slaves. The cruelties perpetrated in nineteenth-century Cuba showed that Spanish colonists were no more humanitarian than any other when economic interests were at stake. Nevertheless the Spanish attitude to their slaves in Mexico and Guatemala made the Honduran woodcutters very aware that their slave property was too valuable to lose to the inducements held out by their neighbours. Finally, the very nature of their employment gave the slaves in Honduras a much greater degree of liberty than was possible or ever contemplated on the sugar plantations, from which any escape was out of the question. It was this which made so great an impression on casual visitors and which made them ignore the lot of the ordinary domestic slaves.

Population figures for Honduras are notoriously unreliable but one observer stated that in 1806 there were 1,270 male slaves in the settlement of whom perhaps 1,000 were employed in the mahogany and logwood industries. But a return of inhabitants made to the Colonial Office that year gives a total of 2,527 slaves and, as there were always more males than females in Honduras, as in other slave societies, it seems likely that this figure of 1,270 was somewhat low. It probably comprised only the number of employable males, excluding boys and old men. Those not working in the forests were engaged as domestic servants, porters on the wharves, or in fishing and shipbuilding. Almost nothing is known about this section of the population as observers were primarily interested in the timber industry. In the latter, the formation of the slaves into mahogany gangs was followed by the period of exploration and setting up camp. The masters joined the men in the camps and there was said to be a congenial atmosphere in the camps, which were established further away from Belize every year. The slaves were armed with machetes for cutting their way through the dense undergrowth, with axes for felling the trees and with guns for shooting game. In these circumstances relations between master and slave could hardly fail to be amicable, as slaves far outnumbered the white men. Occasional accidents took place after a drinking bout, but the murder of master by slaves was a rare occurrence. The slaves on the sugar plantations were driven to work with whips; and overseers were always on the watch for laggards and defaulters. The practice of whipping was unknown in the mahogany works, though naturally offences could be punished by the Magistrates later.

The mahogany cutters seem to have been generous in their supply of provisions to their slaves. Captain Henderson, writing about his visit to the settlement in 1809, estimated that each slave cost his master £36 a year. This sum provided the slave with food, clothing, rum, tobacco and medical attention. It is not clear whether the quantities of food and clothing were a matter of local custom or of law, but they do seem to have been more liberal than elsewhere. However these reports may not be always reliable. The Reverend John Armstrong was highly critical of an article published by a Captain Maclean in the *Jamaica Royal Gazette* of March 1824. This account painted an extremely favourable picture of the condition of the slaves; it stated that he had visited several properties and found the slaves so contented that there were never desertions, and that not only did the slaves have their usual allowances but were supplied with tobacco and rum. The Chaplain alleged that in fact Maclean had only dined with a few of the richer men, had not visited their properties, that 39 slaves had absconded the previous year and that rations of rum and tobacco were never issued as a regular measure. However, one unusual feature of the life of the slaves in the mahogany camps deserves notice: they worked for only five days and if they were willing to work on Saturdays they were paid at the rate of 3/4d per day. Sundays were always quite free.

Rebellion and desertion

Occasional slave risings and the recurrent problem of slaves fleeing to the Spanish colonies show that all was not quite as harmonious as the wood-cutters would have liked. The first detailed information about a rebellion in the settlement concerns the killing of two white men up the Belize River in May 1773. An English naval captain had been sent from Jamaica by Admiral Rodney to investigate the theft of a cargo of indigo from the Spanish schooner *Thetis*, wrecked on the Northern Triangles. While pursuing his enquiries Captain Davey was asked for help in quelling the rebellion. He reported that before his men could catch up with the slaves they 'had taken five settlements and murthered six white men and were join'd by several others the whole about fifty armed with sixteen Musquets, Cutlasses etc.' The next day fourteen of the rebels gave themselves up, but Davey felt it would be difficult to recapture the others, especially as the inhabitants were short of arms and ammunition. Some of the slaves escaped to

Spanish territory beyond the Hondo and in August another naval captain was sent to persuade the Yucatán authorities to hand over the murderers. It was not until November that the rebellion was said to have been completely suppressed, but complaints against the Spaniards for receiving runaway slaves continued unabated.

In 1795 a Summary Court imposed a sentence of flogging and transportation on two slaves merely on suspicion that they intended to escape to Spanish territory. In May 1820 a similar situation attracted some publicity since the Superintendent himself decided to tour the mahogany camps to discover the causes of the rising. This decision took the settlers by surprise for they had always attributed the elopement of their slaves to Spanish influence, and were afraid that Arthur might find other influences at work. The Superintendent first issued a proclamation offering a free pardon to those slaves who surrendered and also threatened martial law. Two detachments of troops were sent up the Belize and Sibún Rivers with instructions to avoid all shooting. Then Arthur himself followed, accompanied by one of the Magistrates. In his report on the situation to London he spoke of 'the poor deluded people' whom he hoped to help without the use of force. He was therefore surprised to find that some of the slaves had 'been treated with very unnecessary harshness by their owner, and had certainly good grounds for complaint'. Little damage had been done apart from the killing of a few cattle, and the slaves were soon persuaded to return to work. But a month later twenty still remained at large. When an expedition proved unsuccessful in its search for the missing slaves, it was assumed that they had escaped. Colonel Arthur expressed the hope that the settlers would treat their slaves with more kindness after this episode. Whether Arthur was now more aware of acts of cruelty or whether the settlers' attitudes to their slaves hardened after this rising it is difficult to say, but later in the same year Arthur reported that acts of cruelty towards negroes were on the increase. By 1825 the inducement of freedom held out by the Central American republics was causing widespread desertions and the leading mahogany cutters were extremely concerned.

Cruelties imposed on domestic slaves

Although whippings and cruelty were not part of the daily lot of the slaves working in the mahogany camps as they were on

the sugar plantations of Jamaica and Barbados, the women working as domestics were often subject to much ill-treatment. There
were very few white women in the settlement and the coloured
women who lived in concubinage with leading inhabitants often
made hard task-mistresses. The records show that the majority
of cases of cruelty reported were inflicted on women. In 1816 a
man called Michael Carty was convicted in the courts of terrible
cruelty to a female slave, but his only punishment was a fine of
£50 and the withdrawal of his licence to sell liquor. Four years
later Colonel Arthur was very shocked by the case of Duncanette
Campbell. She was a free coloured woman who lived with one of
the Magistrates and she was brought to court on the charge of
inflicting severe injuries on her slave, Kitty. Although there were
visible marks of cruelty on the body of her slave, the prisoner was
acquitted in less than five minutes on the ground that every owner
was entitled to give their slave up to thirty-nine lashes with a whip.
The only question for the jury was therefore to decide whether
this punishment had been exceeded. But more frequent than the
case of slave-owners appearing on charges of cruelty were the
punishments ordered by the Summary Courts of the settlement for
very minor offences. Few of these cases appear in the printed
histories of the country but they are available for all to read in the
court records kept in the Registry. In August 1817, for instance, a
slave, Lizzy, was brought before a Summary Court accused of
acting with 'insolence and bad conduct' to her mistress Elizabeth
Potts. Lizzy was found guilty and sentenced to be lashed 100 times
on her bare back and then led round the town 'at the cart's tail'.
In October a slave found guilty of stealing was sentenced to 250
lashes and then to be dragged round the town. Dreadful as these
punishments now seem it must not be forgotten that at that period
a child could be hanged in England for stealing a loaf of bread.
Nevertheless it is absurd to claim that there was no cruelty in
Honduras and that all slaves were uniformly treated with great
kindness by their owners.

The Status of the Slaves

It is clear that there was very little legal protection for the
slaves in Honduras; but it is not always easy to ascertain their

status in law for this seems to have varied over the years. In 1803 Superintendent Barrow reported that the Consolidated Slave Law of Jamaica 'is adopted so far as the local situation thereof will admit', but this assertion was later challenged by Colonel Arthur. Barrow reported in the same despatch that Slave Courts with two Magistrates and five jurors tried petty offences, while more serious cases were tried by Special Courts with three Magistrates. The Commission of Legal Enquiry published its report in 1829 and it contained a good deal of information about the legal position of the slaves. But the Commission formed such a favourable impression of a judicial system about which successive Superintendents complained so bitterly that some of its conclusions should be viewed with a certain degree of scepticism. This is especially the case with regard to the legal position of the slaves, since here most of the information was obtained from biased sources.

The Supreme Court which had been set up in 1819 dealt with five serious criminal offences while lesser crimes were tried in Slave Courts by Magistrates with a seven man jury. The accused slave had the right to choose someone to defend him but in practice this was usually his owner. It was still generally believed that an owner had the right to inflict thirty-nine lashes on his slave or to imprison him for petty offences without a warrant. The Commission recommended that practices so open to abuse should be stopped. In some respects the Report does show that the Honduras slave-owners were more enlightened than was usually the case in the islands. For instance the slaves in Honduras were entitled to own property and also, through their owners, to sue in the courts. The older colonies strongly resisted the right of slaves to own property when the Colonial Office tried to introduce this reform in 1824. Another controversial question was the admission of slave evidence in the courts. The British Government had been pressing the various legislative assemblies to make slave evidence admissible for some time, and in 1827 Superintendent Codd suggested to the Public Meeting that it would be a pity if the settlement were to lag behind the islands on this matter. He was unable to convince the Public Meeting and it was not until two years later (when the use of a slave's evidence was the only method of obtaining a conviction) that it was permitted in the Grand Court.

The Report is remarkably silent on the type of punishments

awarded in the courts, but it does make the point that there was no difference between the treatment of slaves and free persons. In fact it suggested that there was a tendency to favour the slaves on account of their 'low intellect'. This is borne out by a case reported in the *Honduras Gazette* in 1827. Tom Dixon, a slave who was found guilty of assaulting a free negro, was recommended to mercy on the ground that he had been provoked by the taunt that he was 'a damned negro slave'. The presiding Magistrate, Marshall Bennett, felt Dixon should have appealed to the Bench for help, but said: 'The Magistrates would never allow even in the most remote degree, abusive and contemptuous language to be used towards slaves, particularly by a class of persons who differed from them only in having the good fortune to obtain their manumission. It was quite misfortune enough for a person to be a slave without being taunted with it, or it being made a term of reproach, particularly by one of their own class'.

One of the most serious allegations made by the Abolitionists against the slave-owners was their lack of respect for all family ties. Not only did they actively discourage marriage, but when slaves were sold in cases of debt, or on the death of the owner, families of common-law marriages were separated regardless of their feelings. The Commissioners stated that this never happened in Honduras but there was no law to prevent it. Slaves were sold for debt as in other colonies; in the five years between 1821 and 1826 ninety-four slaves were sold for this reason, a figure which does not include children.

Manumission

The ease with which slaves were able to obtain their freedom, or manumission, is a useful guide to the attitude of the community towards its slaves. The incidence of manumission and the methods by which it could be achieved varied from colony to colony. In the Spanish colonies manumission was common and the process of obtaining it uniform. In Honduras the incidence of manumission was by no means as great as in the Spanish colonies but it was a good deal more so than in the British West Indies. The comparative figures for the years 1821–5 show that in Barbados 408 slaves were manumitted, in Demerara 142, in the Bahamas 176, with a total of 141 for Honduras. Since its slave population was much smaller than the other colonies this was a respectable figure. In the last few years of slavery the rate of manumission accelerated; in the fifteen years between 1808 and 1823, 376 slaves were manumitted in Honduras, while in the four years from 1826–30 the figure was 169. There was one significant difference between the position of the slaves in Honduras and those in Jamaica. If a disputed case of manumission were brought before the courts it was always assumed in Honduras that the slave was free unless it could be proved otherwise. But, in Jamaica, it was the slave who had the more difficult task of proving his freedom. This was a great advantage to the negroes in Honduras as the Legal Commission pointed out. The latter also emphasized that, in the settlement, information on manumissions was registered and fully accessible to the former slaves. It was therefore impossible to defeat the benevolent intentions of an owner who freed his slaves in his will.

Manumission by will was only one of the ways in which a slave could obtain his freedom. There was also the practice of selling slaves for their freedom; if a reasonable price were offered it was said that the owner never refused to sell, but freedom could sometimes be postponed: for example in 1821 Superintendent Arthur paid £77 for the freedom of a male and female slave to become effective after an interval of one year. Perhaps the most usual method was the slave's purchase of his own freedom. The cost of manumission varied enormously; the records of wills and contracts for the year 1792–3 show that many slaves were manumitted for as little as five shillings. Often these were cases of children born by slave women to their masters, but adult manumissions could cost as much as £300. Although no tax was imposed on manumissions in the settlement except for a short period between 1805–8, a charge of two-and-a-half dollars was made for recording the manumission. There is little doubt that the Commission of Enquiry was correct in its view that few obstacles were placed in the way of slaves obtaining their freedom. One case which came before the Grand Court in 1823 lends support to this view. A slave called Priscilla had been manumitted by the will of Edward Meighan who died insolvent in 1816. His widow maintained that the insolvency of her husband made the manumission invalid, but the court found for the plaintiff, Priscilla, and made a statement of principle that 'by the custom of this court, the question of freedom has ever taken precedence over matters of debt'.

In 1828 the *Honduras Gazette* stated that whereas in the settlement one slave out of every 100 was manumitted annually, the comparative figure for Demerara was only one in 2,800.

Conflicting attitudes towards slaves

Although the ease of manumission in Honduras favoured the settlers' claim of humanity towards the slaves, two incidents which cast considerable doubt on these claims occurred towards the end of Colonel Arthur's period of office. They did much to create the feelings of bitterness between Arthur and the settlers which followed him from Honduras to Tasmania. In the first case Arthur discovered that the Police Officer had been instructed to punish four slaves without any trial. The Magistrates attempted to pass the matter off, but the Superintendent insisted that their action was illegal. He then instituted proceedings which resulted in a Mr Bowen being sent for trial, but the Bench expressed itself unable to prosecute and the jury would not find Bowen guilty, although he had handcuffed and whipped a female slave and left her lying naked for three weeks. Arthur was afraid that Bowen's acquittal would lead to a disturbance among the slaves and he decided to proclaim the Consolidated Slave Law of Jamaica in operation until new laws could be passed. At the same time he sent a strong letter to the Magistrates in which he commented that he much regretted that he had been forced to proclaim that the slaves were completely unprotected by law. Threats were exchanged on both sides but Arthur was now determined 'to prosecute with increased zeal my enquiries into the grievances and situation of the slaves'. Arthur was not a man of idle words and when Bowen's name appeared as a candidate for the Bench he objected. His policy was approved by the Secretary of State although the Law Officers later said that the Superintendent had no power to introduce laws without the consent of the settlers. By that time, however, Arthur had left the settlement and this opinion does not seem to have been sent to his successor.

The second and even more serious incident arose from the first. During the course of Bowen's trial it appeared that a number of Indians had been illegally kept in slavery. Rather than antagonize the slave-owners further Arthur submitted the question of the Indian slaves to Jamaica for legal advice. On receiving a favourable reply he issued a proclamation in 1822 declaring the right of the

Indians and their families to freedom and he set up a Board of Commissioners to examine the resulting claims. But the matter could not be dealt with so simply and the controversy which followed was not finally settled until 1830. It appeared that as long ago as 1775 the then Governor of Jamaica had expressly forbidden the enslavement of the native Indians on the Mosquito Shore. In spite of this they had been carried to Honduras when the Shore was evacuated in 1786 and kept in slavery. The work of the Board in investigating the claims was progressing smoothly when one of the owners discovered that an earlier Jamaican Act of 1741 permitted the enslavement of Indians provided that they were registered by their owners. This gave the owners of Indian slaves the opportunity they had been seeking to resist the threat to their property and they were not slow to seize it. Arthur reported to Jamaica that 'the Proprietors . . . now determined not to give up the reputed Indians however clearly their descent might be proved'. Their resentment was so great that several complaints were heard of cruelty to the Indians, and when the Commissioners informed Arthur that their powers were insufficient to protect the Indian slaves he placed them under the care of the Provost Marshal, much to the indignation of their owners. They claimed that there was a general spirit of anarchy which had spread to the African slaves as a result of Arthur's action. The Board came to the decision that the Indians whose descent had been proved should be freed, but that as their owners had been ignorant of the illegality of owning them they should not be penalized. The settlers were not content with this decision and petitioned the Governor of Jamaica so that Arthur was forced to put the whole matter in the hands of the Colonial Secretary. Shortly after this he left the settlement but the matter was not allowed to rest. Proceedings were very slow but eventually the Commission of Legal Enquiry was called upon to give its advice. The Commissioners' views as to the rights and wrongs of the case differed from that of the Board but they agreed that, since the slaves had for all practical purposes been freed, they should not be returned to slavery but their owners should be compensated. Twenty-two owners claimed nearly £20,000 for about ninety slaves; the amount finally awarded was £8,000 to be provided from funds in the Admiralty Court.

The case of the Indian slaves shows that when their property was at stake the mahogany cutters of Honduras could prove as obstinate and cunning as the sugar planters of Jamaica. It also demonstrates that Arthur was a man whose principles could not be swayed by the most determined opposition. When the correspondence between the Superintendent and the Secretary of State was published the settlers were bitterly resentful; and after their country had been held up to Members of Parliaments as 'the most detestable spot on the face of the globe' they were incensed. A small group of the leading men combined together to publish *A Defence of the Settlers of Honduras against the Unjust and Undefended Representations of Colonel George Arthur*. This pamphlet sought not only to give the settlers' attitude to the Indian question, but also to condemn the whole administration of Colonel Arthur. The language used was so intemperate and the views expressed so directly opposed to those they had earlier held towards their Superintendent that it did little to improve their case. Arthur's policies had upset the vested interests of a small but wealthy section of the community who were then determined to blacken his reputation.

Missions and Schools

No discussion of slavery would be complete without a reference to the provisions made for the spiritual welfare of the slaves and indeed for the entire population of this small British settlement. The Reverend Mathew Newport, Armstrong's successor as Chaplain, regarded the place as a bastion of the Protestant faith, being 'the only Protestant settlement between the boundaries of the United States and Cape Horn'. Newport was not the first person to appreciate this importance and Colonel Arthur, a very devout man himself, had done a great deal to encourage the spread of religion and of education. He had taken a personal and active interest in the building of St John's Church, although it was not actually consecrated until 1826. He had also corresponded with various churchmen in England and had been largely responsible for securing the appointment of the first missionaries to Honduras.

The role of the church

Although the Bishop of London was interested in sending teachers and chaplains to the Bay the Anglican Church gave little active support to the encouragement of religion; this was largely left to the Baptist and Wesleyan Missionary Societies. Yet even before the arrival of the missionaries baptism into the Church of England was growing steadily; between 1812 and 1823, 1,800 people were baptized. Slave marriages on the other hand were still unusual. Armstrong reported that he had never married a slave couple as permission had always been refused by the owners. The leading white men usually lived with coloured women and did not marry them, but by 1830 the *Honduras Almanack* reported that marriage was definitely on the increase. The settlers claimed that marriage and baptism fees were never exacted from slaves; but the Colonial Office insisted that all such fees should be finally abolished and the Public Meeting passed the necessary law in 1829.

In 1824 Honduras was incorporated into the Jamaican Diocese and the new relationship was emphasized two years later when the Bishop of Jamaica visited Belize to consecrate St John's Church. Visits by the Bishop were very infrequent and the Anglican Church lost much ground to the Nonconformist missionaries and to the Roman Catholics who had many converts among the Yucatecan immigrants in the Corozal area. By 1856 the Catholics were second in strength to the Anglican Church as the following list of denominations taken from the Blue Book for that year shows. This list is apparently limited to the population in the city of Belize itself:

Presbyterians	240
Baptists	500
Wesleyans	500
Roman Catholics	1,000
Church of England	2,500
Others	2,260
Total	7,000

The coming of the missionaries

The first Baptist missionary arrived in the settlement in 1822 and despite some initial opposition from the Acting Superintendent his mission prospered. He was followed three years later by the first Wesleyan, who had high hopes of cooperating in the mission work with the Baptist, Mr Bourne. Unfortunately this cooperation was not forthcoming and Mr Wilkinson was obliged to carry on alone. He had been instructed to take the Gospel to the slaves in the mahogany camps away from Belize, but he decided that this was not financially possible and instead acquired some property in Belize which he intended to use as a centre for his congregation. By the end of three months he had a regular congregation of thirty and, like the Baptists, had set up a Sunday school. As many of the missionaries succumbed easily to the climate and tropical diseases in the early years there was little continuity in mission work. Although there was some hostility from a few individuals, the missionaries in Honduras escaped the persecution which those in the West Indian islands faced. In Jamaica and the other islands the missionaries were vilified and blamed for all the unrest among the negroes during the 1820s and savage Acts were passed against them. This was unknown in the settlement, where the missionaries were normally given permission to preach on their arrival.

The only question which created much difficulty was the performance of the marriage service. The Wesleyan, Thomas Johnston, confirmed the statement made by the Anglican Chaplain that many of the slaves had been refused permission to marry by their owners. One marriage which had been solemnized by the Reverend James Bourne had been declared illegal by the Magistrates. Johnston stated that he himself would baptize negroes but not marry them, but one of his successors was less careful, with the result that the Chaplain complained that illegal marriages were being performed. Superintendent Cockburn was not very tolerant towards the Dissenters and he reported to the Secretary of State that he had declared all marriages null and void unless solemnized by the Church of England. Goderich, the Colonial Secretary, agreed with this step but insisted that the missionaries should be treated with tolerance in all other respects. He felt that there should be no legal restrictions on their freedom to preach and he also objected to the interference of the Magistrates in ecclesiastical matters: he informed the Superintendent that 'His Majesty entirely disallows the claim they make to act as a Court of Ordinary'. In reply the Magistrates stated that their right to act in this way had long been recognized, and in fact it continued until 1846 when the Magistrates were abolished and their duties vested in the Superintendent. They also pointed out that there was no law on the question of missionaries preaching, but it was customary for them to present their credentials on arrival, whereupon the Bench gave them permission to take up residence in the settlement and to preach: since 1820 a local law had required all newcomers to obtain permission from the Superintendent to remain.

In 1836 the English Marriage Act which allowed Dissenters to perform marriages was passed and the West Indian colonies were urged to adopt a similar act. This was done in the case of the Crown Colonies but no such act was passed in Honduras until 1852. Only a year earlier the Public Meeting passed an act allowing the Wesleyan, Baptist and Presbyterian Ministers to officiate at the funerals of members of their own congregations at the burial ground. Similar permission was extended to the Catholics in the next year. One other matter which caused some difficulty was the refusal of certain Dissenters to take an oath in the law courts. Two leading Baptists, Alexander Henderson and Frederick Crowe, author of *The Gospel in Central America*, were imprisoned for contempt of court. The Colonial Office, through the Governor of Jamaica, consistently asked the Superintendent that some form of affirmation should be introduced to replace the oath, but the Public Meeting declined to pass an act to this effect. He also urged that amends should be made to the two Baptists, as Crowe's five months' imprisonment for contempt of court was quite unprecedented. In spite of continued pressure by the Government it was not until 1863 that an act was passed to allow an affirmation to be made instead of the swearing of an oath.

The beginning of formal education

It was in the field of education that both the established churches and the missionary societies performed their most important work. It was also this which aroused the deepest suspicion on the part of the slave-owners throughout the West Indies. Just as the nineteenth-century English factory owners saw no need for their employees to learn to read, so the sugar planters feared the effects of education on their slaves. The woodcutters in Honduras seem to have been rather more enlightened; at least they did not positively prevent the education of their slaves, however little they may have done to encourage it. In fact the foundation of the free school for ten poor children in 1807 was an admirable gesture on the part of the Public Meeting. Colonel Arthur showed a great interest in the school and by 1833 there were said to be between 90 and 120 boys attending the school, while the Superintendent's wife was holding classes for girls. At the same time the missionaries were starting their own educational establishments: the Methodists were particularly successful in setting up schools and establishing their mission stations outside Belize. They enjoyed considerable success among the Caribs in the Stann Creek area, where in 1834 the local people built both a Chapel and a school. By the end of 1838 fifty Caribs were said to be regularly attending school, while ten years later the Methodists had four chapels for 400 full church members and five teachers.

As the time for emancipation of the slaves approached, the need for educational facilities was realized but government support was totally inadequate. In 1835 it was stated that there were 218 pupils at the free school, but the buildings were much too small. A Parliamentary grant for negro education was made in 1836, but although an inspector visited Honduras none of the money ever found its way there. In 1843 the Superintendent and Chaplain requested that some of these funds should be made available, and stated that the four rural schools would benefit greatly from the comparatively modest sum of £300. Stanley replied that the settlement could have the miserly sum of £39 which was all that remained of the grant. In the same year a report made by the committee for the Honduras free school drew attention to its deficiencies. Although there were 211 boys on the register, daily attendance was only between 130 and 140. It felt that parents had no authority over their children and suggested that some way must be found to make the truants attend school. It was also suggested that public reward was a powerful incentive to scholarship and prizes should therefore be publicly awarded. There was a great shortage of suitable books at the school. Matters were even worse at the girls' school where, from a register of 130, only 60 girls attended. They were taught only reading and writing and few of the girls were very proficient even in these subjects. In 1850 a local act was passed to provide for more schools and to make new regulations. A Board of Education, nominated by the Superintendent, was to consist of five members, each with a salary; but education was to continue to run on denominational lines.

The settlers' attitude towards slavery

It does seem that some of the claims made on behalf of the settlers of Honduras were justified. They were perhaps more inclined to treat their slaves as human beings and less as chattels than elsewhere in the West Indies, but it is important to remember that the slaves in the settlement had virtually no legal protection and were entirely dependent on the whims of their masters. It was maintained in the *Defence of the Settlers of Honduras* that, because of Spanish inducements to desertion, slaves could be kept only if treated with kindness and affection. But the records and disputes concerning fugitive slaves over the years show that many of them believed they would be treated with more kindness in the Spanish colonies or republics than in the Honduras settlement. It is impossible to assess the numbers of those who sought their freedom in this way but it must have been quite considerable and it proves that there were many who found the Honduras woodcutters hard, and even cruel, taskmasters. It is also important to remember that most of the available evidence relates to the nineteenth century when conditions were generally improving throughout the slave colonies. To claim that in Honduras 'slavery existed in name only' is a distortion of the facts. To say as Superintendent Macdonald did in 1839, only one year after the complete abolition of slavery, 'that for a great length of time slavery has existed in Honduras only in name; the very remembrance of it seems now certainly forgotten' is absurd.

10

Emancipation and Free Labour

The Position of the Coloured People in Honduras

The abolition of the slave trade in 1807 was only the first stage in the struggle to end slavery throughout the British Empire. It was followed by the slow improvement of conditions in the slave colonies, while in England the movement for the complete abolition of slavery gathered momentum amidst a blaze of publicity and conflict. This slow process was accompanied by the efforts of the free coloured population of the West Indies to secure for themselves the same privileges and position in society as those held by free white men. By 1833 the disabilities under which the coloured community had long lived had been removed; the way was now open for the final stage of the campaign for complete abolition and its replacement by a system of free labour.

In the 1820s the coloured people[1] of Honduras formed a large and rapidly increasing section of the community. By 1829 the combined population of free coloured and free negroes in the settlement had risen to 2,266 compared with 1,422 six years earlier. According to the admittedly unreliable figures there were at this time 2,127 slaves and only 250 whites. Never subjected to the indignities suffered by their counterparts in the West Indies, the coloured people's liberty as British subjects was nevertheless restricted in certain specific and irksome ways. In the British West

1. 'Coloured people' is used in its historical sense to denote the half-caste or mulatto children of white and negro unions.

Indian colonies the mestizos, fourth in line of descent, were considered white in law, but in the Honduras settlement the possession of white blood never automatically conferred freedom. Some early charters of the West Indian colonies gave the children of white men by black or mulatto women all the privileges of white subjects; but discriminatory legislation against the coloured inhabitants had gradually been introduced during the eighteenth century. They were debarred from serving on juries, holding commissions in the militia, giving evidence in court against whites and holding certain posts. Everywhere except in Barbados they far outnumbered the white population and despite legal obstacles were gradually assuming a position of economic importance through their control of secondary industries such as coffee, ginger and pimento.

On his arrival in Honduras in 1814 Colonel Arthur was astounded and dismayed by the prominent position of the coloured people in society. He felt that the presence of the free coloured at the Public Meeting was the thin end of a wedge which would inevitably lead to the admission of free negroes into the legislature and to growing unrest throughout the West Indies. His proposals for reforming the Public Meeting, which included the exclusion of the coloured population, were however disregarded in London. Indeed the policy adopted in the settlement never influenced the other Caribbean colonies where, in fact, the coloured people achieved their citizenship earlier than in Honduras. Arthur's attitude was clearly expressed in a despatch to Lord Bathurst which accompanied a petition from Mr Usher claiming the full rights of a British subject. 'The People of Colour,' Arthur wrote, 'have already privileges far beyond what are granted in any other part of the West Indies and our security certainly requires that they should be curtailed rather than extended'.

He went on to explain that the only disability suffered by the coloured in Honduras was that they were debarred from acting as Magistrates or jurors. But there were other limitations on their rights as citizens which Arthur ignored. During the struggle with Spain coloured men had held commissions in the militia but this privilege had since lapsed with the unfortunate result that a wealthy coloured employer might find himself under the authority of one of his junior clerks in the militia. The Public Meeting was certainly open to coloured residents but their qualifications for membership were twice as onerous as those for whites. Although there were no serious economic restrictions on the activities of the coloured population, a law had been passed in 1805 which required a coloured person to own at least four male slaves before he could locate a logwood works. It was in such simple ways that a coloured man was made to feel that his position in society was an inferior one. Lord Bathurst's reply to Mr Usher's petition gave little satisfaction, either to the Superintendent or to the coloured people, for he suggested that the Jamaican laws should be adopted in the settlement. Nothing came of this suggestion, which would have made life even more irksome for the coloured.

By the time Colonel Arthur left Honduras in 1822 his views had undergone a radical change, for he had come to recognize the importance of the coloured section of society as the most stable and orderly element in the community. He felt that Government should protect them against the 'unjust and over-reaching conduct of the white population' and that they had borne their disabilities with great patience. During the next few years the demands of the coloured population throughout the West Indies were voiced more loudly. In Parliament their cause was championed by Dr Stephen Lushington who received an ever-increasing number of petitions on the subject. In Jamaica the bitterness of the coloured people was strengthened in 1826 when the very demands they were making were granted to the Jews on the island. Meanwhile one of the leading coloured men in Honduras, George Hyde, sent a petition to the Colonial Secretary pointing out that he had been educated in England and was now a successful merchant but, on his return to Honduras, he would be penalized 'on the sole ground of his mother being a woman of colour'. As a result he would be 'excluded from sitting as a Juror, serving as a Magistrate, from holding a Commission in the Militia or from filling any Public Office of Trust or Honour'. Hyde received the reply that the Secretary of State could not interfere in a matter of local custom, but that he had advised the Superintendent to offer commissions in the militia to coloured men. Dissatisfied with this answer, Hyde prepared a petition to Parliament which was among those presented by Lushington on 12 June 1827. During his speech Lushington drew attention to the rising importance of the coloured class throughout the West Indies and condemned the attitude of the Jamaican Assembly. He made no allusion to the position of the coloured people in Honduras but a few months later sent a detailed report on the latter to James Stephen at the Colonial Office; he concluded by suggesting that Honduras should be used as an example to the other colonies. He felt that there was so little prejudice against coloured people in Honduras that if the Government set an example by appointing one or two coloured men to vacancies in the Supreme Court there would be very little opposition from the Public Meeting. Lushington also recommended that the legislature should be advised that the Government would look with favour upon all measures designed to improve the position of the coloured community. Stephen agreed with these proposals, but before a letter to that effect could reach Honduras, a committee was appointed by the Public Meeting to consider the whole question.

Superintendent Codd proposed that the laws of Jamaica should be adopted in the settlement, but this was clearly a retrograde step and was severely criticized in the pages of the *Honduras Gazette*. In a letter to the newspaper on 17 March 1827 it was pointed out that 'the people of colour in this Colony, have ever enjoyed many of those Civil Rights, that have never been allowed in any of the Islands. . . . It is a most pleasing fact and does great honour to our white population, that in this respect they have always treated the Gentlemen of colour as themselves, and the only difference has been, in the Civil Government and the situations in the Militia'. Nevertheless, after the committee had made its report a year later, an Act was passed similar to that in Jamaica, requiring coloured persons to petition the assembly individually for extensions of their privileges. In future this was to be the only way by which a coloured man could become a member of the Public Meeting. Although this decision was in direct contradiction to the benevolent intentions of the Colonial Office, Superintendent Codd reported with satisfaction that the Government's wishes had been carried out. But the measure was only in force for a year. After a heated debate the clause concerning membership of the Public Meeting was repealed in July 1829. In that same year the coloured people in the Crown Colonies of Trinidad and St Lucia were relieved of all their disabilities and in 1830 Jamaica followed this example. It was not until July 1831 that a similar Act was passed by the Public Meeting in the settlement: an attempt to extend the same privileges to all free negroes failed. Lushington's other suggestion—that coloured people should be appointed to the

Supreme Court—was supported by Colonel Cockburn when he became Superintendent in 1830, but the constant postponement of judicial reforms delayed the matter until 1838 by which time the coloured people were full citizens in Honduras.

Abolition and Apprenticeship

During the 1820s, while the coloured population of the West Indies struggled to obtain equality and civil privileges, the slaves and their supporters were becoming progressively more dissatisfied. When a Whig government was at last returned to office in England in the autumn of 1830, Buxton and his fellow anti-slavery supporters realized that the moment was opportune for the complete abolition of slavery. While the Government tackled the task of reforming Parliament itself, plans were laid to bring pressure to bear for abolition. There was much disagreement within both the Cabinet and Parliament as to how this could be best carried out, the main points at issue being the speed with which slavery should be terminated and the compensation allowed to the slave-owners. The Abolition Act, finally passed in June 1833, was largely devised by James Stephen in the course of a weekend after Lord Stanley's own plan had been severely criticized. The main intention of the Act was to bring about emancipation as smoothly as possible and to treat the slave-owners with sympathy and generosity.

Terms of the Abolition Act, 1833

In pursuit of this aim the Act introduced a system of apprenticeship and empowered the Treasury to raise twenty million pounds as compensation for the slave-owners. The new scheme was to operate from 1 August 1834 when all registered slaves over six years of age were to become apprenticed labourers. The apprentices were to be classified in different groups according to the type of work they performed; the first group was to obtain complete freedom after four years apprenticeship, to be followed in turn by the other two groups two years later. The scheme was to be enforced by Special Magistrates who would be sent to each colony and who would settle all disputes which arose between masters and apprentices. Each colony could make local laws regarding the details of the system, provided that these improved on the Imperial Act and were approved by the King-in-Council. Without this approval no colony would be entitled to its share of the compensation. Clause 62 of the Act made it applicable to the settlement of Honduras, while ignoring all questions of sovereignty, as in the case of the Act setting up the Supreme Court in 1819.

News of the Government's proposals was sent to the West Indies and the other colonies in a series of circular despatches during 1833. Some anxiety was aroused in Honduras until it was learned that a specific clause had been included to make the Act applicable there. In October the Bill was read at a Public Meeting and great willingness to cooperate was expressed. It was hoped that the high price of labour and the liberal attitude of the wood-cutters to their slaves would be taken into consideration when the compensation figures were assessed. A memorandum was drawn up to show the customary generosity of the settlers with regard to provisions, but it was feared that any attempt to alter the regulations concerning the hours of labour performed in the mahogany camps would be very detrimental. It was with some relief that the actual Act was received, together with the news that local improvements could be made. Several of the leading settlers viewed the provisions for Special Magistrates with scepticism. They felt that the dispersal of the mahogany works throughout the country would make the task of these officials impossible and that the existing system of courts in Belize would be adequate to protect the former slaves. The Superintendent, while acknowledging the generally good treatment of the slaves, felt that the appointment of independent Magistrates was vital to the success of the whole scheme.

The first step towards implementing the Act was the registration of all the slaves in the settlement. An Order-in-Council for this purpose reached Honduras in March 1834 and one of the Magistrates was appointed to act as Registrar. Two months were allowed for the completion of the work. The Abolition Act was also to be put into effect by means of an Order-in-Council. An Order was drafted for Trinidad: and as in the other Crown Colonies the Governor was to enforce it strictly. This Order was sent as a model to those colonies with Legislative Assemblies; and on this occasion they had to adopt the Order as it stood or improve it under the penalty of losing all compensation. Although there was thus little room for manœuvre by the Assemblies, their differing attitudes were reflected by the way in which the apprenticeship system worked in each colony. In Antigua and Bermuda the planters decided to dispense with apprenticeship from the first, with the result that all the slaves in those colonies became free on 1 August 1834. Since the amount of compensation for each colony was to be assessed, not on the basis of number but on the industrial value of the slaves, the newer and less developed colonies would benefit more than the older ones. As a result the planters of Trinidad and British Guiana were more prepared to cooperate during the period of apprenticeship than the slave-owners in Jamaica and Barbados, who were determined to extract the maximum amount of labour from their apprentices.

The Act applied to Honduras

The Order-in-Council, with a covering letter expressing understanding of the peculiar problems of adapting it for the settlement, did not arrive in Honduras until July 1834, by which time the Superintendent had already had some discussions with a committee of slave-owners about the best way of introducing apprenticeship. Cockburn took only three weeks to revise the Order-in-Council and return it for formal approval. The elaborate administrative and judicial structure of Trinidad necessarily made the Order far too complicated for the small settlement of Honduras but, as far as possible, Cockburn tried to keep to the original. The Supreme Court was to act in place of the Chief Justice of Trinidad and the clauses relating to the Special Magistrates were adhered to quite closely. The Trinidad Order laid down that the Magistrate was to visit every plantation in his district once a fortnight: this was clearly impossible in the settlement. The Special Magistrates were to reside in Belize but had to be prepared to visit any mahogany works on the request of the Superintendent, the owner or an apprentice. The specific amounts of food and clothing provided for in the Trinidad Order were ignored as irrelevant, as the Superintendent claimed that the slaves already received more than the amounts specified for the apprentices. Cockburn's accompanying letter was received with satisfaction in the Colonial Office and Lord Aberdeen, the new Colonial Secretary, remarked with approval that 'The form, although very unusual, is recommended by so much practical convenience, and is at once so simple and so intelligible, that an Act of far more artificial structure would probably have answered the purpose much less effectually'. This opinion was not shared by the Anti-Slavery Society. The measures adopted in Honduras were strongly criticized by the Society on the grounds that all the restrictive provisions of the Trinidad Order-in-Council had been retained, while the protective ones had been abandoned as unnecessary. The 'mutilated' Trinidad Order was condemned in a scathing critique which concluded by saying 'If, under such a system, the Negroes enjoy a comfortable servitude it certainly can be attributed to no legislative precaution on their behalf but will be owing probably to the neighbourhood of the Republics whose proximity produces at least one salutary influence in their favour'. These criticisms were justified to the extent that the welfare of the negroes continued to depend on custom rather than law and on the honesty and generosity of the employers.

As the great day approached it became increasingly obvious that the success or failure of the apprenticeship system would depend to a very large extent on the efficiency and character of the Special Magistrates. By the summer of 1834 the Honduras settlers had revised their opinion that Special Magistrates would be unnecessary and had begun to view 'with dismay and consternation' the prospect of the changeover without the arrival of the new officials. Here, as throughout the West Indies, the preparatory measures were quite inadequate; the number of Magistrates required had been under-estimated and very few had actually been appointed. Superintendent Cockburn announced his intention of appointing local men until the new Magistrates arrived. He was clearly concerned with the problem of controlling, rather than protecting the apprentices, for he felt it essential that they should be subject to inspections at the mahogany works to prevent 'idleness, profligacy and insubordination'.

The appointment of Special Magistrates

Little is known about the men who were appointed to perform the difficult task of supervising the transitional period. At first an attempt was made to choose impartial men, who consequently lacked knowledge of colonial conditions. Many were unable to adapt to the tropical climate and died from disease and overwork, while others found it difficult to understand the speech of the apprentices. Those who favoured the apprentices were liable to find themselves without food and lodgings, which were usually supplied by the employers. Often the men selected were half-pay officers inclined to severity. Some of the civilians were more dubious characters who had chosen the post as a means of escaping their responsibilities in England. Yet some of the Special Magistrates did perform their difficult task with skill and sympathy for very little reward.

Two local Magistrates, William Coffin and William Maskall, were appointed by Cockburn to act as Special Magistrates in Honduras, but these appointments were never sanctioned by the Colonial Office, which stated that only one Special Magistrate was required. There seems to have been some misunderstanding, for after Lieutenant Grigg arrived at Belize in April 1835 the Superintendent still retained the services of Mr Maskall. A circular despatch in June conveyed the ruling that no one who owned an apprentice could act as Special Magistrate. Although Cockburn expressed disbelief that the ruling could be applied to Maskall the Government insisted, as it wanted to establish a general principle. Meanwhile Grigg had died after only a few months in the settlement and was replaced by a resident who owned no apprentices. The appointment was confirmed and later a second man, Gow, arrived from England.

Despite the monthly reports made by the Special Magistrates, their work is very difficult to assess. It is almost impossible to tell whether they were subservient to the employers or whether they were prepared to defend the apprentices against injustice. Certainly their salaries were very low—£300 in the first instance—so it seems unlikely that men of high calibre were recruited. Only three months after emancipation the Governor of Jamaica considerably increased the salary of the Special Magistrates without permission. In Honduras the Superintendent was very worried by the lack of arrangements for paying the police and Magistrates. He had established two police gangs, consisting of five men and a sergeant, and after repeated requests for money to the Colonial Office he was forced to pay them from the Military Chest. He was told that the salary and provisions for the police had to be defrayed from revenue as in other colonies; and it may have been this despatch which prompted the reduction of the police gang in each district from six to three men. In some colonies extra provision was made for the Special Magistrates by the local Assemblies, but the meagre revenues of Honduras made these payments impossible. However, in 1837, the Public Meeting voted £50 to each Magistrate for extra work in connection with some liberated Africans who were landed in the settlement.

Apprenticeship in operation

In spite of the initial difficulties in preparing for the period of transition and the bewilderment of the slaves when they found, as one observer put it, that 'the cart was put before the horse, the negro was first made a freeman and then condemned to modified slavery', the actual changeover from slavery to the apprenticeship system passed off quietly without any disturbances. In June 1835 one of the Special Magistrates was able to report, after a three-week tour of mahogany camps, 'I have never witnessed more peace, good order and quietude . . .' Yet, in spite of such favourable reports, it appears that in the first year of apprenticeship no fewer than 117 apprentices were punished by the Special Magistrates. Although over half of the offenders were women accused of disobedience and other minor offences, the figure seems remarkably high. Some doubts were raised by the Colonial Office about the number of hours of work performed by the Honduras apprentices. According to the Order-in-Council these should have been restricted to 45 hours a week, an instruction clearly disregarded since the hours of work in the towns were from 6 am to 6 pm with a two-hour break for lunch. Similarly, the alterations authorized because of the peculiar nature of the timber industry should not have been extended to the domestic and town workers; but nothing was done to stop this flagrant abuse. Contrary to the terms of the 1833 Act, these shortcomings did not have any effect on the compensation awards which were assessed during the apprenticeship period.

Compensation claims

The Honduras slaves had always had a high value placed on them by their owners; even before abolition a skilled male negro was valued at the high sum of £200–£300. The reasons are not hard to find. The extra cost of transporting the slaves from Jamaica, the need for healthy and strong slaves for forestry and the generally more humane treatment accorded them, all tended to give them a high value. When the compensation claims were filed the price paid for slaves in Honduras turned out to be higher than for any other British colony. The only comparable prices were those paid in the mainland territory of British Guiana. The following table of the average prices paid for slaves sold between 1822 and 1829 compared with the average amount of compensation actually awarded illustrates this point very clearly.

Colony	Average of sale of slaves 1822–9	Rate of compensation per slave
Bermuda	£27. 4.11¾	£12.10.5
Jamaica	£44.15. 2¼	£19. 5.4¾
Barbados	£47. 1. 3½	£20.13.8¼
Trinidad	£105. 4. 5¼	£50. 1.1¼
British Guiana	£114.11. 5¾	£51.17.1½
Honduras	£120. 4. 7½	£53. 6.9½

Preparations for Freedom

As the time approached for the liberation of the first groups of apprentices some fears were expressed that this might disturb those who still had two years of apprenticeship to complete. On 29 June 1838 the Public Meeting passed an Act to liberate all apprentices on 1 August. Soon afterwards it was decided that the apprenticeship period should be terminated on the same day throughout the British Empire. As the fateful day drew nearer some preparations were made for what was expected to be a great upheaval in society. In Honduras these preparations were more concerned with legal questions than economic problems. A series of circular despatches from the Colonial Office assisted the preparations and the replies to these provide us with useful information. It appears that although by 1838 coloured men were acting as Magistrates and jurors, free blacks were still excluded from these privileges. On the other hand the obligation to serve in the militia now applied to all males except apprentices. There were no restrictions on employment, all trades being open to whoever wished to practise them. Employment contracts were usually made out for a term of six to twelve months in the presence of a Magistrate. However, although the employer could obtain redress by imprisonment and whipping for a breach of contract, no such redress was available to the employee.

A law to settle disputes between masters and servants was passed by the Public Meeting in March 1838, but it failed to gain the approval of the Superintendent, who protested that the most valuable part of the Act for the protection of the workers had been mutilated. A few months later Macdonald persuaded the Meeting to accept an Act which enabled the employees to bring complaints against their masters before three Magistrates empowered to fine them. It was also agreed that in future labourers were to be hired in writing; the agreement was then to be registered for a fee of 1s. 8d. at the Clerk of Court's Office. In this way it was hoped to avoid the possibility of a man hiring himself to several masters and then making off with his advance wages.

Poor relief

Another important matter which came to light in the preparations for the liberation of the apprentices was the fact that there was no poor law in the settlement. The Keeper of the Records, Patrick Walker, whose task it was to draw up a detailed schedule of information for the Secretary of State, pointed out that because of the constant demand for labour and the high price paid for it in the settlement, there was no pauper class. The old and infirm had traditionally been cared for by their masters and small pensions had been granted from the public treasury to the needy; there were 16 pensioners on the books in 1838. It was clear that something more definite was needed when a large number of men were to be thrown on to the labour market at once, and in November an Act was passed which gave the Magistrates authority to dispense poor relief. A sum of £100 was allocated for the next four months and a committee set up to examine the problem in greater detail.

Labour problems after Emancipation

Once these preliminary preparations had been made, 1 August 1838 was awaited with eagerness by the apprentices, and trepidation by the employers. The date was celebrated as a public holiday throughout the West Indies. In Honduras, after church services, all assembled in front of Government House to listen to an address by the Superintendent. Feasting and rejoicing occupied the remainder of the great day which was also celebrated by a general amnesty releasing all the prisoners in the settlement. The following morning everyone returned peacefully to his daily work and great satisfaction was expressed at the way in which so momentous an occasion had passed off peacefully.

The principal anxiety still felt by the settlers was the possible shortage of labour now the apprentices were freed. For some time the problem had been under discussion, and as early as 1834 a decision was taken at a Public Meeting to apply for 1,800 Africans captured from slaving ships who were at the disposal of a special Commission in Cuba. Although these proposals were supported by the Superintendent, and approved in principle by the Colonial Office, certain objections were raised which proved insuperable at that time. The mahogany cutters were demanding a term of apprenticeship of eight to sixteen years which was considered to be far too long. Renewed efforts were made by Superintendent Cockburn on behalf of the settlers, and in July 1836 the Commission finally sent a cargo of 193 liberated Africans to the settlement. In December another 203 arrived, 45 of these being recruited for the 2nd West India Regiment. Disagreements occurred concerning the proportion of men to women as well as over the question of whether the Bench of Magistrates or Special Magistrates should be responsible for disputes concerning these Africans. These led to so many difficulties that by December 1837 only 357 had been imported into Honduras. When apprenticeship came to an end it was also decided to end the indenture system for captured Africans. The settlers objected, with the result that the Commission at Cuba received instructions from London not to send any more Africans to the settlement. The acute labour shortage which had been predicted did not, in fact, materialize and no further attempts were made to recruit labour in this way. Nevertheless, with the growing realization that agriculture would have to play an important part in the future development of the colony (as it was soon to become) an increased labour supply became a matter of some urgency.

The encouragement of immigration

A number of schemes were devised to attract immigrants, and especially agricultural labourers, to the settlement, but the influx of East Indian coolie labour was never encouraged in Honduras as it was in Trinidad and British Guiana. During the 1860s an attempt was made to obtain Chinese labour under an indenture system, but this does not seem to have been very successful. The Colonial Office was critical of the first scheme proposed and disallowed the bill. In 1865, 474 Chinese finally arrived, but three years later 263 of these had either died or fled the colony. In the early days as a fully fledged British colony great hopes were held for its future agricultural prosperity, but the expected thousands of immigrants from the Southern states of the United States failed to arrive and only small and somewhat isolated projects were begun, such as the Toledo settlement in the south. The need for sufficient labour to develop the agricultural resources of the country to their full is still today, a hundred years later, one of the country's most serious problems.

But if the second half of the nineteenth century was to be beset by economic difficulties, at least the social problems presented by the complete abolition of slavery were less evident in Honduras than in America and the West Indies. Soon after apprenticeship was brought to an end the Superintendent testified to the prevailing harmony and commended 'the orderly and well behaved conduct of the apprentices'. In 1839 the distinguished American traveller and writer, John Stephens, commented after a brief visit to Belize: 'before I had been an hour in Belize, I learned that the great work of practical amalgamation, the subject of so much angry controversy at home, had been going on quietly for generations; that colour was considered mere matter of taste'. Here at least was a good augury for the future of the country.

Kinich Ahau, Maya Sun God. Jade carving found in a tomb of c. A.D.600, at Altun Ha.

Plaza at Altun Ha, before and after excavation.

Temple of the Masonry Altars, Altun Ha, as it would have appeared c. A.D. 600–650.

Maya artefacts found at Altun Ha.

a. Jade necklace from Sun God's tomb of c. A.D. 600.

b. Painted ceremonial pottery vessel, c. A.D. 600–700.

c. Two-piece censer, for burning copal, c. A.D. 500–550.

Maya artefacts.

a. Figurines of c. A.D. 700, found at Lubaantun.

b. Stela showing a standing Maya ruler, c. A.D. 700, from Xunantunich.

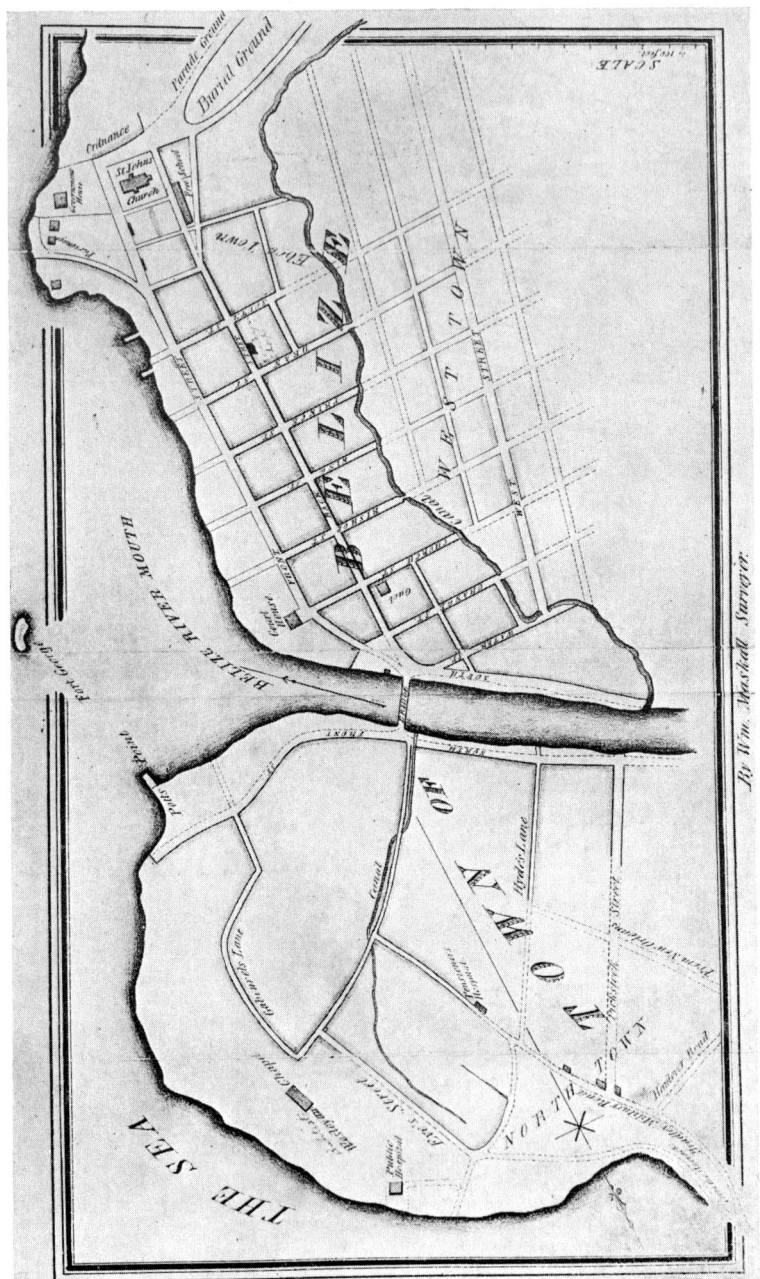

Plan of Belize, taken from Honduras Almanack of 1829.

6

Print of Belize, early nineteenth century, with soldiers from the West India Regiment on duty.

St John's Cathedral, Belize, founded 1812—the first Protestant church in Central America.

Wall plaques to commemorate its foundation and consecration, in 1826.

Government House, Belize, dating also from the early nineteenth century.

Rail-mounted crane of the timber trade today.

Cutting a mahogany tree before the introduction of mechanical methods.

Sugar-cane crusher of about 1870, Seven Hills, Toledo District.

Belize Sugar Industries factory at Tower Hill—the most modern in Central America.

The Courthouse, Belize: the elegant new building of 1923–26 was modelled on the nineteenth century one (*above*), which was destroyed by fire in 1918.

Hurricane Hattie, 1961 : aerial view of Belize showing widespread destruction.

Some faces from present-day Belize.

Creole

Lebanese

Mopan Indian

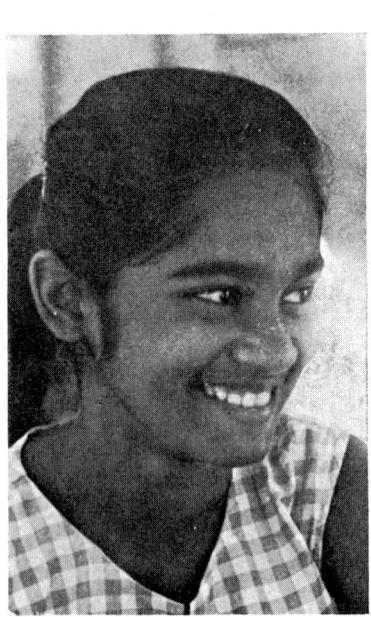

East Indian

Kekchi Indian

Mestizo

Black Carib

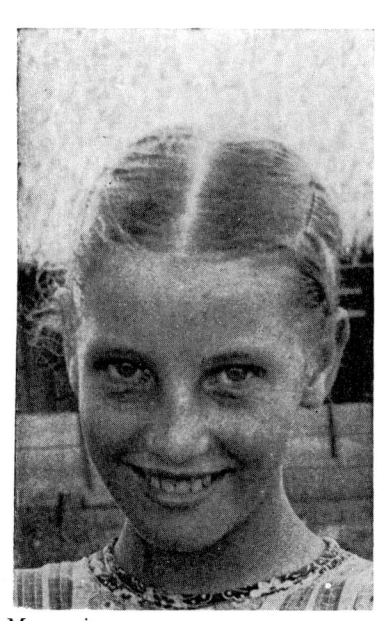

Mennonite

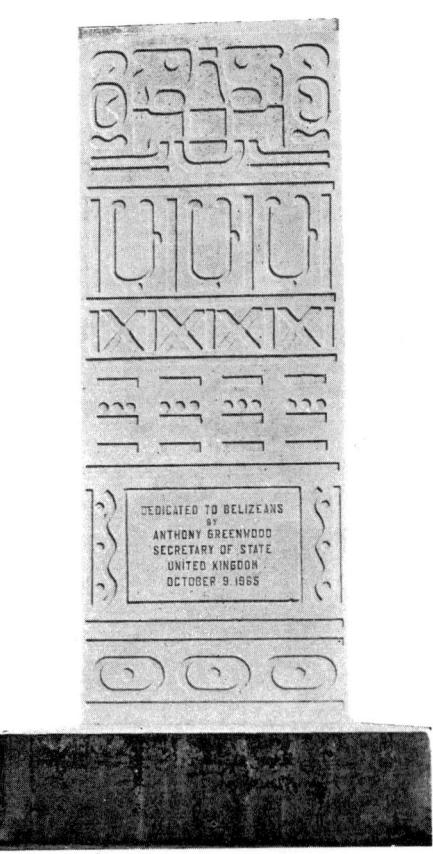

Belmopan—the new capital of Belize. Both the main Government buildings and the commemorative stela are based on traditional Maya forms.

11

Boundaries and Sovereignty: A Colony Defined

The New Central American States

The dispute between Great Britain and Guatemala over British Honduras has dominated international attitudes to the country ever since the signing of the 1859 Anglo-Guatemalan Treaty. This controversy has tended to obscure relations between British Honduras and other countries and, indeed, many other aspects of British Honduras history. But that history is more complicated and interesting than the usual simplifications suggest. No country can live in isolation from its neighbours: from its earliest days the settlement traded with the Spanish colonies to the north, south and west despite the efforts of Spanish officials to prevent such trade. Later, as these colonies freed themselves from the shackles of colonial rule and became independent republics, commercial relations assumed a greater importance. As a British settlement and, after 1862, a colony, it followed that relations between British Honduras and other countries were controlled by British policy formulated in London. A special relationship with the British West Indian islands was inevitable and between 1841 and 1884 the colony was subjected to the direct supervision of the Governor of Jamaica. In the middle of the nineteenth century the United States also played a part in the affairs of British Honduras. The American acquisition of California, resulting from the Mexican war of 1846–8, intensified the efforts of her government to find a suitable route for a canal from the Atlantic to the Pacific coast. For some years therefore, the United States showed a keen interest in Central American politics. Moreover her government was determined to maintain the policy inspired by the Monroe Doctrine[1] and to prevent the expansion of British interest in the region.

The collapse of the Spanish Empire

The collapse of Spanish authority throughout Latin America, together with the emergence of the new Central American republics during the second decade of the nineteenth century, inevitably introduced a new phase in the history of British Honduras. A mere fifteen years elapsed between the first stirrings of revolt in Mexico and the principal cities of South America in 1808–10, and the final collapse of the Spanish Empire on the mainland. This rapid disintegration of a once great empire was the result of many local and spontaneous revolts; there was no preconceived plan and little cooperation between the different regions, but certain factors were common to all areas. During the latter half of the eighteenth century the Bourbon rulers of Spain introduced many economic and administrative reforms to their empire. It was divided into provinces under the control of a peninsula-born *intendente*; while this led to an increase in administrative efficiency it also aggravated the existing differences between the *peninsulares* and the locally born *criollos*. Long overdue reforms in the commercial system were introduced, entitling the colonies to trade with each other and with certain ports in Spain. The vast increase in trade which followed this more liberal policy brought about a spirit of regionalism and, at the same time, the door was opened to the spread of enlightened European ideas. The increased prosperity of the 1770s and '80s was brought to an abrupt halt by the Napoleonic wars and the interruption of trade between Spain and her colonies by the English navy. The discontented *criollos* were more than ready for some form of self-government and although, at first, they were not revolutionaries, Napoleon's invasion of Spain in 1808 gave them the necessary stimulus. At first the *criollos* were loyal to their deposed king, Ferdinand VII, but their early opposition to French control of Spain soon turned to hostility towards Spanish control of South and Central America.

1. The Monroe Doctrine expounded by President Monroe in 1823 declared that the newly independent states were not to be regarded as subjects for colonization by any European nation.

The heroes of the wars of independence were idealists such as Bolívar in Venezuela and San Martín in Argentina and Peru, but their long struggle for independence from Spain finally ended in disillusion and the knowledge that only despotism could replace Spanish authority. In Central America the first attempts to gain independence were made in El Salvador in 1811, followed by plots and intrigues in Nicaragua. But it was not until 1821 that Mexico achieved independence under Iturbide and gained temporary control over the whole of the former kingdom of Guatemala. Iturbide's rule was short-lived, and on his fall the provinces which had made up the kingdom declared their complete independence as the United Provinces of Central America (1823). Throughout the existence of this Central American Federation it was racked by internal dissension and civil strife and was never more than a weak political unit. Recognized by the United States in 1824, it never obtained recognition from either Spain or Great Britain. Like the visionary leaders of South America, those of Central America were unable to fulfil their hopes for the unity and prosperity of their independent states.

At the time when the Spanish colonies became independent the boundaries between the British settlement of Honduras and her neighbours had not been clearly defined; they remained, at least in theory, as they were described in the Anglo-Spanish Treaties of 1783 and 1786. In practice they were, by 1821, very different and in any case the settlers had always protested that the maps used by the English and Spanish plenipotentiaries were inaccurate. The British Government made matters more complicated by consistently refusing to discuss the boundaries of the settlement with any country but Spain. The maintenance of the fiction that Spanish sovereignty still extended over the settlement meant not only, as has been seen, a good deal of administrative inconvenience, but so linked the boundary question with the issue of sovereignty that the frontiers were not settled for another forty years. The reluctance of successive British Governments to give offence to Spain was the sole reason for this delay: although the matter was raised from time to time the only serious attempt to settle the question with Spain took place in 1835. When the efforts of the British Ambassador in Madrid failed no further approach was made. The whole question was once again allowed to lapse until, in the late 1850s, international interest in the area made the settlement of frontiers a matter of urgency.

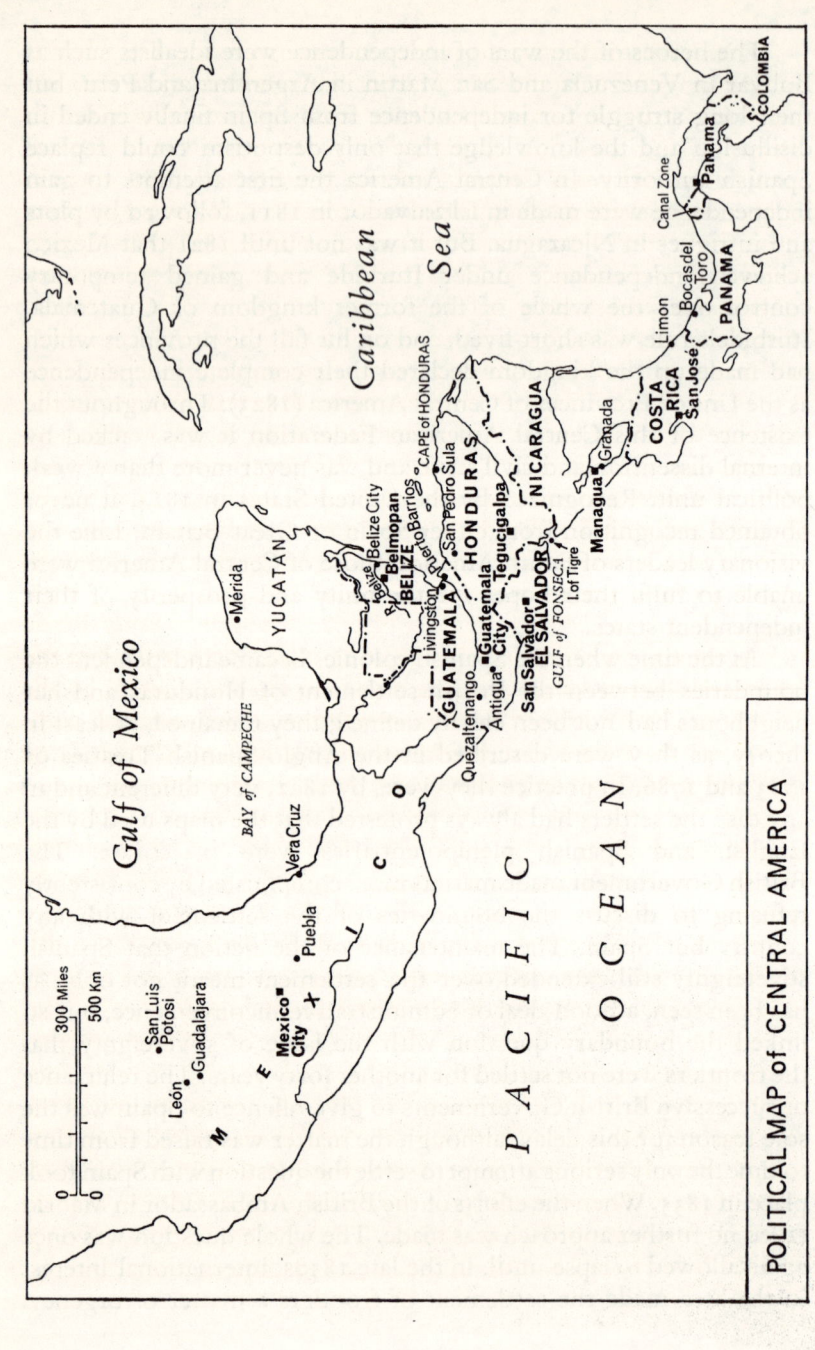

POLITICAL MAP of CENTRAL AMERICA

Throughout the period British influence in Latin America was of paramount importance. This is not difficult to explain, for Britain's prosperity as the world's leading industrial and imperial power gave her a position of unparalleled supremacy in international diplomacy. Her naval strength was a decisive factor in the successful revolts of the Spanish American colonies, for the revolutionaries were confident that the British navy would not be used against them. From 1821 onwards the newly independent states sought her diplomatic recognition and her commercial favour. Canning, British Foreign Secretary from 1822 to 1827, preferred to grant recognition by means of commercial treaties wherever possible. He also insisted that any country requesting recognition should abolish the slave trade. Both Mexico and the Central American Federation went further than was strictly necessary and by 1829 had completely abolished all slavery in their territory. This created some difficulties for the British authorities at Belize. There had already been minor embarrassments during the period of the colonial uprisings while Britain sought to maintain a position of strict neutrality between Spain and her insurgent colonies. Since Belize was a neutral port, facilities for refitting were occasionally granted to the rebels; this led to some protests and retaliatory steps by the Spanish commanders in Trujillo and Omoa. When Spanish authority came to an end relations between Belize and the neighbouring ports were normally amicable.

Boundaries of settlement in 1821

It is important, in view of later arguments, to ascertain the position of the British settlers in 1821, the year in which both Mexico and Guatemala achieved independence from Spain. Legally at this date the settlers only had a usufructuary right[1] to cut wood between the River Hondo and the River Sibún as arranged in 1783. But the reality was far different: as early as 1814, the settlers declared that Spanish hostility in the north had forced them to abandon their works on the Hondo and move southwards to the Moho River. By 1821 there is no doubt that the settlers were cutting mahogany as far south as the River Sarstoon and had done so for several years. When the attempt to settle the boundaries with Spain was made in 1835, it was declared at a meeting of the Superintendent and the

1. The right to use and enjoy the advantages of another's property short of destruction or waste.

Magistrates that when Central America became independent in 1821, the settlement had consisted of all the land between the Rivers Hondo and Sarstoon. The western boundary was then, and still is, an imaginary line running due north and south from Garbutt's Falls on the Belize River. Although some mahogany cutters may well have extended their activities beyond these lines, especially into the Petén district of Guatemala, these are the boundaries consistently claimed by Britain. Had the British Government been less careful of Spanish susceptibility, and more alive to the views of the settlers and their administrators, the question of boundaries and sovereignty could doubtless have been resolved in the early days of the new republics. As Colonel Arthur pointed out on his return to England in 1822: 'It is certainly of the last importance that some negotiations should be entered into, so that our Limits may be confined to the extent we have occupied during the last sixteen years—if this is not done now we shall hereafter be in endless Litigation with the Independent Governments'.

Results of the Anglo-Mexican Treaty 1826

The accuracy of this prophecy was soon to be revealed by the Mexican attitude towards the settlement. The independence of Mexico was recognized by the United States in 1822 and three years later a treaty was signed with Great Britain. But this treaty, which was signed in Mexico City, contained a clause which might be construed to give Mexico sovereignty over the British settlement of Honduras. For that reason the treaty was not ratified by the British Government and it was not until December 1826 that a treaty, which omitted the objectionable clause, was ratified. However Article XIV did make some concession to Mexican opinion by admitting the validity of the 1786 Convention with Spain. The Article guaranteed British subjects peaceable possession of the area which they had occupied by agreement with Spain, that is between the Hondo and Sibún Rivers. Although the right to make further arrangements at a later date was reserved, the clause was strongly criticized in the Mexican Senate for not firmly stating Mexican sovereignty over the settlement; in Belize the clause was naturally regarded as offensive since it detracted from the settlers' claim to hold the territory between the Sibún and Sarstoon Rivers by right of conquest.

Once Mexico had obtained official recognition from the United

States and Britain her claims became somewhat bolder. In 1827 two men were appointed to make a report on the boundaries between Mexico, Guatemala and the British settlement. Superintendent Codd was alarmed and wrote to the Colonial Office that 'now Mexico has been recognized by Great Britain she is becoming ambitious to extend her dominion'. In fact the Commissioners did not show much interest in the British boundaries, which remained those roughly marked out after the 1783 treaty. When Spain finally recognized Mexico in 1836 the British Minister at Madrid asked that no mention should be made of the British settlement in the treaty. The result was an ambiguous situation. Mexico could, and later did, assert that she had inherited all Spanish rights in the area, while the British could point to the fact that as the Honduras settlement had not been mentioned, Mexico had no claims to it. During the next thirty years there were minor disagreements about the northern boundary of the British settlement which the British took to be the River Hondo. The Mexicans tried to show that the more southerly tributaries of the Hondo—Booth's River or Bravo Creek—were in fact the boundary, but all attempts to settle the question came to nothing. The attitude of the British Government was that since no treaty had been made with Central America and since the boundaries between that republic and Mexico had not been fixed, it was impossible to settle the matter. The disturbances caused by the Indian rising against the Mexican Government during the Caste war in Yucatán prevented any further assessment of the situation during the 1840s and '50s.

Guatemala and her Claims

More involved than the dispute with Mexico was that between the Honduras settlement and Guatemala, or the United Provinces of Central America, as the Federation was known (1823–39). This protracted story is still not concluded: the arguments have been revived from time to time by Guatemala, often for reasons of internal politics. But, even in the days of Spanish rule, there was friction between the British settlement and the kingdom of Guatemala because the mahogany cutters claimed that the Spaniards deliberately enticed their slaves away from them. The land which is now called Belize was never occupied by Spain, nor was there a clear boundary between the territory under the jurisdiction of the Captain-General of Yucatán and that under the Governor of Guatemala. It was generally believed that at least the area between the Hondo River and the Sibún came under the authority of Yucatán. Certainly it was from Yucatán, and not from Guatemala, that Commissioners were appointed to inspect the settlement in accordance with the terms of the Anglo-Spanish Treaties; and it was from Yucatán that the principal attacks on the British were launched during the eighteenth century. These facts must be taken into account when considering Guatemala's claim to the whole territory of Belize.

Claims and counter-claims

The Guatemalan case was, and still is, based on the doctrine known as *uti possidetis* which, although it has been accepted by certain Latin American states, has never been adopted as a principle of international law. The doctrine states that a province which successfully revolts against a colonial power inherits all the rights of that power in that province and its boundaries become those claimed by the colonial power at the time of independence. Applied to the case of Guatemala and Mexico this would mean that either one or both of the new states would inherit Spanish sovereignty over Honduras according to where the provincial boundaries were claimed to lie in 1821. The counter-doctrine to *uti possidetis* was formulated in the 1840s by Lord Palmerston, who maintained that the state which had revolted could inherit rights only over the land it actually occupied at the time of independence and not over an area which it did not occupy. As the British woodcutters and administrators were in unquestioned occupation of British Honduras in the 1820s, Palmerston's doctrine would clearly exclude any claim either by Mexico or Guatemala to inherit the sovereign rights of Spain.

Of more importance than the theories and legal doctrines underlying Guatemala's claim to sovereignty are its consequences for both people and historians of Belize. When Spanish rule was rejected Mexico became a huge, but fairly stable state, which, as we have seen, was soon recognized by the United States, Britain and Spain itself. Central America, on the other hand, after a period of short-lived rule by Mexico, became an unwieldy and unstable federation composed of the five states of El Salvador, Honduras,

Nicaragua, Costa Rica and Guatemala. But not the whole Captaincy-General of Guatemala was incorporated into the new Federation: Chiapas preferred to be part of Mexico and so it remained despite a long and bitter argument between the two countries. When the Federation was dissolved in 1839, Guatemala declared that she inherited its rights to the British settlement which had once formed part (so it was alleged) of the Petén district of Guatemala. The Federation had been anxious to obtain recognition from Great Britain and it is possible that if the British Government had acted promptly the matter could have been settled as early as 1824 by a simple definition of boundaries in exchange for British recognition of the new state. As it was the Federation soon showed that it was prepared to assert itself and claim sovereignty over the British settlement. In a number of minor but irritating ways threats were made to the British inhabitants.

In 1823 two British Honduran settlers who happened to be in Guatemala on business attended a meeting of the National Assembly where they heard a statement to the effect that British rights to the Honduras settlement had lapsed with the relinquishment of Spanish authority. Two years later the more practical issue of fugitive slaves came before the Assembly. Slavery had been abolished throughout the Central American Republic the previous year, and both the authorities at Belize and the Vice-Consul in Guatemala believed this would lead to the abandonment of the settlement by the negroes and its ultimate ruin. This was thought to be the deliberate objective of the Central American Government. The Senate refused to agree to any restitution of deserting slaves but, in February 1826, the President of the Federation told Consul O'Reilly that he was prepared to negotiate with Britain over the two issues of the slaves and the sovereignty of the settlement. Nevertheless no serious attempt was made to negotiate a treaty for several years, although Marcial Zebadúa was sent as an emissary from Central America to London where he arrived in May 1826. Canning had already stated that the time had come to make treaties with the new American states which bordered on British possessions, and, in December the same year, such a treaty was signed with Mexico. However the British Government required that any state requesting formal recognition must be able to show that it could keep the peace at home and carry out its obligations abroad. There was no evidence at all that Guatemala was anything but the centre of civil strife.

Moreover the treaty it proposed was similar to the first one put forward by Mexico which had been turned down by the British Foreign Office. Finally the political situation changed so rapidly in Central America that Zebadúa kept receiving contradictory instructions. After his recall in 1831 the negotiations lapsed.

Meanwhile the first of several incidents had occurred in 1827 when Guatemala used the excuse of the contraband trade to station guarda costas off the coast of the settlement. The Captain of one of these vessels went so far as to state that he intended to prevent British ships trading south of the River Sibun since 'Central America had a right and control over that Territory as the inheritor of what formerly belonged to Spain'. The *Honduras Gazette*, in commenting on this incident, made a definite claim that the settlement was held by right of conquest and it raised the question of whether Central America was foolish enough to claim territory 'which even Spain in the zenith of her Power did not dare to contest, well knowing that its tenure was that of conquest'. This viewpoint was not shared by the British Government. A memorandum prepared by Henry Taylor in 1829 for the information of the newly appointed Superintendent, Lieutenant-Colonel Cockburn, stated that there was no question of holding the land between the Sibún and Sarstoon Rivers by right of conquest; nor could long possession of the area confer a right which was prohibited by the treaty of 1786. On the other hand Spain was no longer in a position to confine the woodcutters to the original area granted by the treaty and, since the area never had been occupied by Spain, Guatemala could have no claim to it. He went on to state that the new countries of America had been recognized on the simple grounds of possession and explained: 'We have recognized them as Sovereigns of what they have got, *because* they have got it, and because they are in a condition to keep it'. Taylor was fully aware that the problem was to persuade Spain to abandon her rights under the old treaties or to let them lapse. He felt that the most advantageous course would be to assume sovereignty silently and so avoid all definition of boundaries but, much as the British Government would have liked to adopt this proposal, it eventually became impossible to postpone the boundary issue.

For the time being relations between Guatemala and the settlement improved and there were only minor incidents to disturb the harmony. But in 1832 the Central American Congress was told that the 'settlement at Belize represented a manifest usurpation of Guatemalan territory'. Colonel Cockburn reported to the Colonial Secretary that the disturbed state of Central America had led to renewed protests against the settlers. Among the complaints was the accusation that the British authorities at Belize had helped the rebels by giving some of them protection and shelter. A map published the same year was the first of many drawn to show that the British settlers had invaded the land to the west of the original treaty lines and to the south of the Sibún River. The Superintendent reported to London that the settlers had given no recent cause for complaint but he acknowledged, 'the encroachment of the British has long, very long, been the subject of complaint'. In a despatch written a few days later Colonel Cockburn suggested that the only satisfactory solution would be to arrange a treaty with Guatemala which would recognize the boundaries of the British settlement.

The problems of Consul Chatfield

Shortly after this Frederick Chatfield was appointed Consul at Guatemala with powers to negotiate a treaty of amity and commerce. The Colonial Office took the opportunity to ask the Foreign Office to incorporate three main points in the treaty provided that this could be done without offending Spain. The boundaries of the settlement were to be defined with the Sarstoon as the southern limit; the Central American Government should abandon any claim to sovereignty and the heavy tax on goods imported from Belize was to be repealed. Unfortunately for the settlers, Lord Palmerston, then Foreign Secretary, took the definite line that any discussion on sovereignty should be reserved for future discussions with Spain. In his opinion it would be inexpedient to give Guatemala any reason to believe that her recognition was necessary to establish British rights to a settlement which had been so long occupied by British subjects. Chatfield was therefore given instructions to negotiate the treaty without discussing British rights to the settlement. Marcial Zebadúa was now Foreign Minister and, when Chatfield showed him the proposed treaty of friendship, the Central American Minister asked that it should include a clause similar to the Article XIV of the 1826 Anglo-Mexican treaty. This Chatfield refused and so arrangements were made to send a special emissary from the Central American Government to London.

The man chosen to represent the Central American Government

was a Colonel Galindo. Irish by birth, but claiming Guatemalan citizenship, he was an unprincipled adventurer seeking only to advance his own and his family's fortune. His ruthless exploitation of the tension between Guatemala and Britain for his own personal ends is an unsavoury chapter in the history of Anglo-Guatemalan relations. At Galindo's instigation the Guatemalan Government in 1834 made two grants of land in areas which were at least partially occupied and claimed by British woodcutters in the Honduras settlement. One of these grants was made to a London Company calling itself the Eastern Coast of Central America Commercial and Agricultural Company, a company of somewhat dubious origins. Among those involved in the company was Marshal Bennett, one of the leading Belize settlers, who had long had interests in Guatemala. The land granted to the company included fourteen million acres in the Vera Paz region and the whole of the area between the Sibún and Sarstoon Rivers. The only condition imposed by the Government was that one thousand families were to be settled in the area within ten years. The second grant, made in March 1834, was to Galindo himself. In August the Colonel published a notice to the people of Belize stating that he had been granted land between the River Hondo and its tributary, the Blue Creek. He was proposing to sell the land in lots of one hundred and sixty acres at a public auction, but meanwhile no mahogany was to be cut in the area. Superintendent Cockburn protested vigorously to Consul Chatfield and to the Colonial Office and requested immediate naval protection. Although the concessions made never seem to have become effective the petty annoyances continued. In the Central American Almanack for 1835 Colonel Cockburn was listed as a foreign agent. Only the determination of Consul Chatfield prevented the introduction by Guatemala of very heavy discriminatory duties against goods from Belize.

Negotiations with Spain, 1835

By the spring of 1835 Superintendent Cockburn had decided that the only way to settle the endless disputes with Guatemala was to obtain the complete cession of sovereignty from Spain. In a despatch to Lord Aberdeen, then Colonial Secretary, he pointed out that discussion with Central America was useless and went on to say: 'The affair of Boundary once settled with Spain, its limits should be notified to Central America, and the sooner the better, as those which Great Britain is prepared and determined to maintain'. In the meantime the British Government had reached the same conclusion independently, for Spain had announced that she was preparing to recognize the independence of her former colonies. This news was considered of sufficient importance for the Foreign Office to disregard its previous policy towards Spain, namely, to support the more liberal party under the Queen Regent and not to aggravate the difficulties of a former ally. At the request of the Foreign Office, the Colonial Office had a long memorandum drawn up by Henry Taylor which outlined the history of the British occupation of the Bay settlement and suggested that the boundaries of the settlement should be those agreed by the resolution of the Magistrates in November 1834. Taylor's line of argument now moved from his previous rigid adherence to the Anglo-Spanish treaties towards an enlarged interpretation previously advanced by the King's Advocate in 1825. Sir Christopher Robinson did not dispute the validity of the original treaties but declared that long, undisturbed possession had changed the situation. He believed that 'the substantial ground of claim must be rested on the right to *assume* the perfect title of sovereignty when it shall have ceased to be available to Spain', and Henry Taylor thought that this moment had now arrived. Further information was provided by Thomas Miller, the Clerk of the Courts and Keeper of the Public Records in Belize, and he was actually sent to Madrid to support the British Ambassador.

By this time Sir Robert Peel was in office with the result that it was the Duke of Wellington who, as Foreign Secretary in place of Lord Palmerston, drafted the final instructions to the Minister in Madrid. George Villiers, later Lord Clarendon, was a skilled diplomat. He took the line that it was time to clarify the whole matter of the British settlement at Honduras since Spain was about to recognize her former colonies and there might be some confusion with regard to the definition of boundaries. He told the Spanish Minister that 'the actual Sovereignty of Great Britain over this Settlement is an improbable matter of dispute—the Country has long been and will doubtless long remain under British sway: it can answer the purpose of no Country to question its tenure, but Spain is in a situation to accord an additional satisfaction in the possession of it'. In these circumstances Britain was asking Spain, as a mark of respect to an old ally, to cede any right of sovereignty which could still be considered to rest in the Spanish Crown. At the same time he defined the proposed boundaries of the settlement and included with them the Cays and islands including the Bay Islands of Bonacca and Ruatan. This Note was presented on 5 April 1835; the Spanish Minister replied that he could not foresee any difficulty and would give a formal reply shortly, but two months later he resigned and there the matter rested for the time being. Privately Villiers had already told the Foreign Under-Secretary that had he been in charge of the Colonial Office he would have legislated for Honduras without any reference to Spain. In February of the following year he managed to obtain a verbal promise that the boundary of the British settlement would not be discussed by Spain in her negotiations with Mexico. Later the same year he again tried to press for an answer from Spain, but no reply was received; this was the last time that Spain was approached on the matter—but not the last time that her rights were considered.

Colonel Galindo's activities

Meanwhile Colonel Galindo had arrived in London in August 1835 with authority from the Central American Government to act on its behalf in the struggle against the Belize settlers. He had failed to enlist the support of the United States for his mission and he found that Lord Palmerston was not prepared to receive him as an official envoy. Palmerston had been forewarned by Consul Chatfield who had described Galindo's commission as 'highly irregular', and he therefore declined to treat with a British subject who had a personal interest in the matter under discussion. This rebuff hardly dismayed Galindo, who managed to obtain an interview with Palmerston as a private person and then sent misleading reports back to Guatemala. He also published notices describing British aggression in Central America and tried to persuade a Dutch Company to colonize the land which had been granted to himself. The British Government countered with a direct approach to the Dutch and, on his return to Central America in 1837, Galindo found that he had lost his position of influence with the Federal Government. These failures did not stop Galindo from concocting further schemes of colonization, this time in the Boca del Toro region, but these were no more successful than his earlier ventures and in 1840 he was killed in battle. His career had done nothing but harm both to his adopted country and the relationship between it and Great Britain.

In 1838 his last intrigues had resulted in an outrageous gesture by Guatemala. It summoned a Constituent Assembly to revise the State constitution and invited the residents of Belize 'as inhabitants of that state' to send a deputy to the Assembly. Chatfield protested to the Federal Government, which disclaimed all knowledge of the Guatemalan action. Moreover Palmerston informed his Consul that the invitation must be withdrawn or it would be treated as an act of hostility justifying any action the Crown saw fit to take. In reporting that the decree had been repealed and an apology duly made in August 1839 Chatfield said: 'I hope that the pretensions of persons in Guatemala respecting Belize are now for ever silenced'. Happily for Chatfield he could not foresee the events of the next hundred years.

It was at this juncture that the Central American Federation fragmented into its constituent states; it had not succeeded in obtaining recognition from either Spain or Great Britain and had been so continually overrun by civil war that any real government was impossible. In April 1838 Nicaragua left the Federation and during the next eighteen months its lead was followed by the other republics. El Salvador, under the leadership of the former Federal President, Morazán, tried to keep control and even captured Guatemala City. However this victory was very short-lived for soon afterwards Rafael Carrera recaptured the town and was virtual ruler of Guatemala for the next fifteen years.

The Anglo-Guatemalan Commercial Treaty, 1849

The newly independent states naturally sought recognition and commercial treaties, but it was not until as late as 1863 that Spain recognized Guatemala. An approach was made to Britain by the President of Guatemala as early as 1841, but Palmerston decided that in the circumstances it would be more sensible to test the stability of the new state. A few years later Chatfield reported that impending changes in Mexico and the growing interest of the United States in Central America made it desirable to conclude a commercial treaty with Guatemala. He reported that President Carrera had restored order since the breakdown of the Federation and had made great efforts to improve trade and roads. Chatfield had therefore signed a treaty in 1847 based on his original draft of 1834. In a despatch sent a month later Chatfield enclosed a note from the Guatemalan Minister to the effect that he wished it placed on record that 'the Rights of this Republic with regard to the boundary and concessions in Belize' were not affected by the treaty. In particular he denied that Mexico had any rights in Belize as implied by the Anglo-Mexican treaty of 1826. But this treaty was not ratified because the Board of Trade considered that certain modifications had to be made to bring it into line with recent British commercial legislation. No objection to the alterations was raised by Guatemala and the new treaty was signed and ratified in 1849 when Chatfield, to his great satisfaction, was given the rank of Chargé d'Affaires. Meanwhile Guatemala appointed Consuls both to Great Britain and to Belize. At this time relations between the two countries were so friendly that the Guatemalan Government even considered asking Britain to guarantee her independence and was prepared to place herself under British protection. It is most unlikely that such a suggestion would have met with any response from Britain who had already rejected a similar proposal from Costa Rica.

The Bay Islands and the Mosquito Shore

Britain's reluctance to acquire any further responsibilities in the New World was a fact not always recognized by her representatives on the spot. Frederick Chatfield was only one of the Englishmen in Central America who had ambitious designs for the extension of British rule from the River Hondo as far south as San Juan (Greytown) or even Boca del Toro. His attempts to take over some islands in the Gulf of Fonseca off the Pacific coast were disavowed by Palmerston; but as a result of Chatfield's actions Britain was often regarded as an aggressor in Central America. Superintendent Macdonald, appointed to Belize in 1837, contributed to these suspicions. His high-handed actions in proclaiming English law, founding an Executive Council and making land grants outside the original limits of the settlement have already been noticed. His equally aggressive behaviour in the diplomatic sphere was to cause even greater embarrassment.

The Bay Islands of Bonacca and Ruatan occupied a position of strategic importance between the British settlement and the Mosquito Shore. Formerly occupied by Britain, they were evacuated after the 1783 treaty but the majority of the inhabitants still regarded themselves as British. In the 1830s some British immigrants from the Cayman islands had taken up residence there and in 1838 they complained to Colonel Macdonald that the Commandant of Trujillo had raised the Central American flag on the island. Angered by this action Macdonald sailed to the island in a British warship, took down the flag, and asserted British authority. This somewhat high-handed action was supported both by the Colonial Office and the Foreign Office and was lent some substance by the occasional appointment of Magistrates from Belize. In 1852 Ruatan and the neighbouring islands became the short-lived British colony known as the Bay Islands.

British relations with the Mosquito Indians

The situation with regard to the Mosquito Shore was more confused. Soon after taking up his appointment Macdonald received a letter from King Robert Charles Frederick of the Mosquitos complaining that the Belize woodcutters to whom he had made grants were being threatened by Central America, now laying claim to part of the coast near the San Juan River. When the news reached Palmerston he asked for a full account of British relations with the Mosquito Shore from the Colonial Office and he then decided that the old custom of making occasional presents to the Mosquito chiefs should be resumed. Macdonald paid a visit to the Shore for this purpose and made a demonstration of British goodwill to the Indians. But he went further still; in 1840, at the request of the invalid Mosquito King, he nominated a board of commissioners to govern in the King's name. In the opinion of the Colonial Office this was nothing more or less than a declaration of British sovereignty over the Mosquito Shore and it led to a far-ranging review of policy.

Unfortunately the Colonial Office had for some years held different views from the Foreign Office about British responsibilities in the region. Lord Palmerston at the Foreign Office was always ready to sympathize with measures enhancing Britain's prestige. But the Colonial Office, first under Glenelg, then under Lord John Russell, strongly opposed any increase in British influence. Henry Taylor pointed out that there were two alternative policies, either to throw off as much responsibility in the region as possible, or to strengthen Britain's position in case of a threat from the United States. James Stephen endorsed these views, pointing out that 'we cannot surround the Globe with a chain of Colonial Settlements without opening to an Enemy in almost every quarter points of attack'. The Colonial Secretary, faced with the problem of whether or not to approve Macdonald's actions, asked for further details. The Superintendent justified himself by explaining that the board had been set up to repel foreign aggression rather than to interfere with the internal government of the Mosquito Shore. Russell insisted that the board should be disbanded, but as Palmerston had no wish to see the old alliance with the Indian Chiefs dissolved, Macdonald's instructions were modified so that the King would not be insulted.

In August 1841 the enterprising Superintendent visited the King, who himself set up a commission with almost the same members as before and again headed by Macdonald. The British officer then accompanied the King on an inspection of the coast in an effort to ascertain the limits of the King's authority. The party progressed from Gracias a Dios to Boca del Toro, and at the port of San Juan, once a Spanish post, they deported the Nicaraguan customs officer to the disapproval of the new Colonial and Foreign Secretaries, Lords Stanley and Aberdeen. The following year the Mosquito King died, leaving the administration of the kingdom and the education of his children to Macdonald and the other commissioners. There was so much confusion on the Shore and so many rival claims by neighbouring states that the British subjects in the region complained of lack of protection. After some indecision on the part of the British Government, and at the suggestion of Macdonald who had returned to England in 1843, it was finally decided to send a British Resident to the Shore. The choice fell on Macdonald's former secretary at Belize, Patrick Walker. From 1844 until his death four years later, Walker ruled the kingdom with vigour in the interests of the Indians rather than the British residents, to whom he showed little favour. The young King was crowned at Belize in 1845 and was given an excellent education in Walker's own household.

Once again, as before its evacuation in 1786, the Mosquito Shore was under British protection. An announcement to this effect was made in 1847 when the territory was called Mosquitia and said to extend from Cape Honduras to the San Juan River. This decision was taken only after two years of debate, a debate which hardly considered the wider realms of strategy but was primarily concerned with the protection of the Mosquito Indians —not the position of Britain in Central America. Despite the innumerable memoranda produced in the Foreign and Colonial Offices on British relations with the Mosquito Shore, British policy was in no way coherent but should be regarded as a series of piecemeal actions devised to meet each new situation as it arose. The announcement that Britain was not prepared to see any encroachment on the Mosquito King's territory was followed by the personal intervention of Walker in the company of the young King. After a prior warning to the Nicaraguan authorities at San Juan, the party landed there on 1 January 1848 and replaced the Nicaraguan flag with that of Mosquitia. A brief attempt at resistance was foiled by the arrival of two British vessels and soon afterwards San Juan was renamed Greytown in honour of the Governor of Jamaica.

The Rôle of the United States of America

The gradual extension of British influence in Central America, however erratic, could not indefinitely pass unremarked by the United States. During the 1840s her own expansionist policy had been at its height, leading to the annexation of Texas in 1845 and the war with Mexico (1845–8) which resulted in New Mexico, Arizona and California coming under the American flag. Although there had been interest in the possibility of a trans-isthmian canal for some time, it was the opening up of California and the discovery of gold there in 1848 which prompted United States interest in the Central American region. The American Government had appointed a Consul to Belize in 1847 and had ignored events on the Mosquito Shore and the Bay Islands; but she could not be expected to accept the fact that Britain appeared to be establishing herself right along the Caribbean coast of Central America and, in particular, around the mouth of the San Juan River—the most likely terminal point on the Atlantic for a canal. In June 1849 the second of two American agents, E. G. Squier, arrived in Nicaragua with instructions to frustrate British designs and to start negotiations with Nicaragua for the construction of a canal. A private company had already been formed for this purpose and had signed a contract with the Nicaraguan Government, only to be opposed by Chatfield who announced that since San Juan belonged to Mosquitia it was under British protection. Squier and Chatfield proved formidable adversaries and soon became engaged in a diplomatic trial of strength involving negotiations with Nicaragua and Honduras and the seizure of the island of Tigre. Both men were rebuked by their respective governments and Squier was withdrawn. Neither the United States nor Great Britain wished to be drawn into war by the over-hasty actions of their Central American representatives. The American Secretary of State, John Clayton, was well aware that British cooperation and finance would be essential in the construction of a canal. On the other hand Palmerston, who was again Foreign Secretary, had no desire to monopolize a canal or to do anything more than carry out the commitments which already existed.

The Clayton–Bulwer Treaty, 1850

It was with these considerations in mind that the famous Clayton–Bulwer Treaty was signed on 19 April 1850 between the United States and Great Britain. The object of the treaty was to reconcile British and American interests in Central America, but its compromise terms were phrased in such ambiguous language that it created more difficulties than it resolved. It did succeed in permanently restricting both British and American territorial ambitions in Central America and in ensuring that both countries would support the construction of an inter-oceanic canal. Further than this it was unable to go. In Article 1 of the treaty the two countries undertook not to obtain exclusive control of any canal and not to 'fortify, or colonize, or assume, or exercise any dominion over Nicaragua, Costa Rica, the Mosquito Coast, or any part of Central America'. But this wording was vague in the extreme. It did not define what was meant by Central America, it did not mention British Honduras and it was not clear whether it was intended to apply to the British occupation of the Bay Islands and the Mosquito Protectorate. It soon became only too clear that there was room for differing interpretations on these matters. Some of these doubts were raised in the United States Senate when the treaty was laid before it for ratification. Once ratified, Palmerston took care to instruct the British negotiator, Sir Henry Bulwer, to obtain a statement excluding British Honduras from the terms of the treaty. Clayton made a declaration to the effect that the British settlement in Honduras and the small islands which were its dependencies were not included in the treaty. Palmerston himself seems to have felt sure that among the latter were the Bay Islands; even before the treaty was signed he told Bulwer that 'the Island of Ruatan and also the Island called Bonacca are not only British *de jure* but are actually occupied by British settlers who are governed by a British Magistrate appointed by the Superintendent at Belize'. At the end of May, in approving the signing of the treaty, he made known his views on the question of the Mosquito Protectorate. He felt that provided security was obtained for the Indians its boundaries could be defined by a series of treaties with its neighbours in cooperation with the United States. The importance of Greytown as a terminal port for the canal would demand special arrangements. He later suggested that it should become a free port under Costa Rica, but he finally agreed to the American suggestion that, like the Pacific terminal, it should belong to Nicaragua.

Anglo-U.S. relations deteriorate

Unfortunately, just as it seemed that a new era of tranquil relations in Central America lay ahead, two events happened to disturb the harmony. The Bay Islands were formally made a British colony without adequate consultation between the Foreign Office and the Colonial Office. Meanwhile, in the United States, the Whig administration which had signed the Clayton–Bulwer Treaty was defeated by the Democrats in 1853. This party had already shown signs of hostility to the treaty, which it regarded as a violation of the Monroe Doctrine. The creation of the Bay Islands colony added further fuel to the flames and the new American Government took the line that British Honduras belonged to Guatemala and that Britain had only limited rights in the areas originally granted by Spain. In July 1853 the new Minister in London, James Buchanan, was instructed to persuade Britain to withdraw from Central America and British Honduras if possible.

Buchanan was a very distinguished diplomat who had already served as Secretary of State during the expansionist era of President Polk (1845–9); after leaving London he was to become President of the United States. Although his views and instructions were clear, he seems at first to have been on amicable terms with the new British Foreign Minister, Lord Clarendon. The latter reported to the British Ambassador in Washington on 6 January 1854: 'he [Buchanan] appears fully and firmly convinced that the Clayton–Bulwer Treaty meant that we were to turn out bag and baggage from South America [*sic*], and what's more he declared that until he heard the Doctrine from me, he had not a notion that it was prospective only and did not apply to all our possessions!' However, the opinions which Buchanan expressed on paper were much more forceful than in his interview with Lord Clarendon; they produced strong reactions from diplomatic officials and members of the Government. Palmerston wrote to Clarendon, 'I have seldom read a paper more full of false assertions and bad arguments than those of Buchanan'. Although opinions in the British Cabinet varied as to the validity of Buchanan's lengthy arguments, no one was prepared to abandon the Mosquito Indians entirely. The place might be of 'no earthly advantage', but nevertheless Britain had assumed certain obligations which she could not lightly throw aside. On the other hand she did offer to make Greytown a neutral port provided there were suitable safeguards for the Indians. The Bay Islands colony was even more questionable. Lord Aberdeen told Clarendon that its establishment was 'an imprudent act, and that our right was at best very questionable'. It appeared to be the one area in which the Americans could accuse Britain of violating the Clayton–Bulwer Treaty. No matter how much Palmerston asserted that 'Ruatan has from ancient times been held to be a dependency of Belize and occupied as such', he was definitely on weak ground. There was never any intention to yield to America on the question of the boundaries of British Honduras. Lord Aberdeen still maintained in 1854 in spite of everything that 'our tenure of Belize reserves the rights of Spain'. Palmerston insisted that 'these Yankees are most astute bullies and are always trying how far they can go', but just as it seemed that Britain might be prepared to make sweeping concessions a new crisis occurred. The international situation was already inflamed; but while the British people were quite ready to fight the Russians in the Crimea they were not prepared to go to war against the United States over questions of diplomatic niceties in remote parts of Central America.

While discussions were in progress in London and in Washington events in Central America moved swiftly. The controversial American E. G. Squier was again in the region and it was reported from Washington that 'he stakes all his hopes of future success in life on the prospect of annihilating all vestige of British influence in Central America'. More seriously, Greytown, which was still in British and Mosquito hands, was bombarded and destroyed by an American warship in July 1854. Even though a section of American opinion was outraged by this unprecedented act the Administration declined either to disown it or to compensate the victims. The following year Central America became the scene of virtual anarchy with expeditions by American filibusters. The most notorious, William Walker, attacked Nicaragua which was already engaged in civil war and set up a provisional government at Granada which was even recognized by the United States Government. The Central American Republics were now so unnerved that suggestions were made for Britain and France to protect them. Buchanan was again demanding British withdrawal from Mosquitia, the Bay Islands and British Honduras south of the River Sibún. After the outrages committed by the filibusters, the British Government, having already made an offer to submit the interpretation of the Clayton–Bulwer Treaty to an independent court, was even less prepared to yield. Lord Clarendon was well aware, as he told the British Minister in Washington, Crampton, that 'we wouldn't get much support at home if we quarrel with the United States' and he was relying on the offer of arbitration. But a few days later he added that Buchanan had denied that such an offer had ever been made. Fortunately good sense prevailed and renewed diplomatic efforts to obtain a compromise agreement were made.

Reconciliation and settlement

In October 1856 the Dallas–Clarendon Treaty was signed. By its terms the Mosquito Protectorate was to become part of Nicaragua with an Indian reserve; the Bay Islands were to be part of Honduras; British Honduras was declared to be unaffected by the Clayton–Bulwer Treaty and its southern limit was acknowledged as the Sarstoon River. The hope was expressed that if possible the western limits with Guatemala should be fixed within two years, after which time the boundaries were not to be extended. Britain had thus won a major diplomatic victory as regards her oldest possession in Central America; but the treaty failed when Buchanan, now President of the United States, refused to ratify it because of a technicality affecting the government of the Bay Islands. At no time, however, did the United States Senate question the clauses relating to British Honduras.

Palmerston, who had become Prime Minister in 1855, profoundly distrusted Buchanan, and the breakdown of the Dallas–

Clarendon Treaty seemed to place Anglo-American relations in the melting-pot once again. There were suggestions in both countries that the Clayton–Bulwer Treaty should be abrogated, but once the British Government moved towards this view the American Government seemed to withdraw. It was felt that the abrogation of the treaty would allow Britain to retain too much territory in Central America. The new British Minister in Washington, Lord Napier, suggested that the wisest course would be to carry out the spirit of the treaty by entering into direct negotiations with the countries immediately concerned. Palmerston accepted the suggestion and the task was entrusted to Sir William Gore Ouseley, who arrived in Washington late in 1857 to inform the United States Government of his mission. Ouseley's discussions in Washington took longer than expected and soon after he reached Central America it was realized that he was not competent to complete the task. Accordingly Chatfield's successor in Guatemala, Charles Lennox Wyke, was instructed to take over. During 1859 and 1860 it was he who arranged the treaties with Nicaragua, Honduras and Guatemala which met with the approval of the American Administration. The Anglo-Nicaraguan Treaty, signed in January 1860, gave Nicaragua sovereignty over most of the Mosquito Coast but safeguarded the position of the Indians and made Greytown a free port. The treaty which was signed with the Republic of Honduras in November 1859 gave Honduras the Bay Islands, despite the wishes of the inhabitants, and also part of the Mosquito Shore. Finally the Anglo-Guatemalan Treaty of 30 April 1859 defined the boundaries of British Honduras along the lines which had been suggested as early as 1825.

The Anglo-Guatemalan Treaty of 1859

In the hundred years since the Anglo-Guatemalan Treaty of 1859 was signed and ratified it has perhaps been more thoroughly discussed and debated than any other international treaty. This document has been responsible for the prolonged dispute between Great Britain and Guatemala which still seems far from a solution today. Since its chief concern was with the territory of British Honduras, or Belize as it is now called, it has inevitably had unfortunate repercussions there. In 1859 when the treaty was actually signed neither of the plenipotentiaries of the two nations concerned could have foreseen the consequences of their work. Many learned books and articles have been written by legal experts and historians to explain how the 1859 treaty came into being and to interpret its meaning and results. But it is still necessary for us to outline the main arguments and to consider the political background to the treaty.

It has already been seen that the Anglo-Guatemalan Treaty was drawn up as part of a general series of treaties to settle Britain's position in Central America to the satisfaction of the countries immediately concerned and—of more importance as far as Great Britain was concerned—to restore amicable relations with the United States. During the 1850s both Mexico and Guatemala had shown a renewed interest in settling the outstanding boundary questions with Britain, but for different reasons. While Mexico had been prompted by the internal difficulties of continuing raids and war by the Indian tribes, Guatemala had shown increasing concern at the activities of the American filibusters in Central America. In 1853 Wyke, who had succeeded Chatfield in Guatemala, was told by the Guatemalan chief minister that until the boundaries with British Honduras were settled, America would always have an excuse to interfere. In order to avoid further American interference his government was ready to conclude a secret treaty which would settle the matter for ever. This proposal seemed to the English Foreign Secretary, Lord Clarendon, fraught with danger and it was ignored.

Draft proposals for a boundary treaty, 1857

Two years later a proposal was made that Britain and France should jointly take Guatemala under their protection. This was also ignored, but in 1856 the Guatemalan Minister in Paris was instructed to proceed to London to negotiate a boundary treaty and at the same time to obtain some compensation in the form of protection against filibusters for the territory guaranteed by the treaty. When Francisco Martín arrived in London in May 1857 to try to carry out these instructions he found that William Stevenson, until recently Superintendent of the British settlement, was already there and preparing to discuss the proposed treaty. Their conversations were followed by the drawing up of two draft treaties defining the boundaries. The only difference between them lay in the Guatemalan mention of a renunciation of sovereignty over British Honduras for which the British Government should offer some indemnity. It was suggested that this might be financial, but Guatemala preferred some form of guarantee against the threats from filibusters. Naturally, no such question of indemnity appeared in the English version of the draft treaty. Stevenson himself was convinced that unless a similar treaty with Mexico were arranged there could be no satisfactory solution of the boundary question. Lord Clarendon agreed, and it was hoped that the Mexican Minister in London would be given power to conclude such a treaty, but he was withdrawn before this could be done. When Sir William Gore Ouseley was entrusted with the task of settling all the outstanding problems in Central America in the autumn of 1857 the London negotiations lapsed. Martín had already returned to Paris believing that the British Government would never consider the question of compensation.

Martín's beliefs were fully borne out by the Instructions which were sent to Charles Lennox Wyke when he replaced Ouseley in February 1859. The new British negotiator was explicitly told that he must not agree to anything which could possibly be interpreted as a cession on the part of Guatemala in case the United States should regard this as an infraction of the 1850 Clayton–Bulwer Treaty. The treaty was to be a simple 'definition of a boundary long existing, but not hitherto ascertained'. Apart from the delicate question of the Clayton–Bulwer Treaty two other important factors were raised by the negotiations with Guatemala. The first was that there had been no treaty definition of the boundaries since the Anglo-Spanish Treaty of 1786, although the British authorities in Belize had declared the limits of the settlement during the 1830s and had made land grants within those limits. The other factor was that in spite of continued appeals by the settlers, and the stated opinion of the Law Officers of 1851 that the settlement had become by long possession part of the dominions of the Crown, no definite assertion of sovereignty had been made and the British Government had declined to alter the status of the territory from a settlement to a colony.

The terms of the 1859 Treaty

It was with these factors in mind that Wyke began the negotiations in Guatemala with Pedro de Aycinena. The Convention which was signed by the two men on 30 April 1859 was exactly the same as the draft given to Wyke by the Foreign Office except for the addition of the vital Article 7. The first clause was merely a declaratory one which stated the boundaries of the British Settlement to be those which existed before and on 1 January 1850. These were said to be from the mouth of the Sarstoon River, up the river until the Gracias a Dios Falls were reached, from whence a line should be drawn in a northerly direction to Garbutt's Falls on the Belize River and thence due north until the Mexican border was reached. Provision was made in the later Articles for the appointment of commissioners to mark out these boundaries, and another Article provided for the free navigation of ships in the boundary channels. There was, however, no attempt to negotiate a commercial treaty at the same time as had once been suggested. The additional and controversial Article 7 was introduced on the sole responsibility of Wyke and it was framed in such an ambiguous way that it has been the subject of argument ever since. This Article proposed that the two contracting parties should arrange for a road to be built between the Atlantic coast near the settlement of Belize and Guatemala City. This road would add to the prosperity of both England and Guatemala by increasing trade, and, since it would divert some trade from the Pacific ports, it would also restore some of the former prosperity of the Belize settlement.

On the day the treaty was signed Wyke wrote to the Foreign Secretary explaining his action. He said that he had encountered much more opposition in drawing up the treaty than he had anticipated as President Carrera refused to agree to an unconditional surrender of what he called his country's rights. Wyke himself seems to have been unduly influenced by Carrera's views or to have had insufficient briefing from the Foreign Office on England's position for he stated: 'As in point of fact we have no legal right beyond that of actual possession to the tract of Country between the rivers Sibun and Sarstoon which formerly belonged to the ancient kingdom of Guatemala, this opposition was the more difficult to overcome, without agreeing to give them some compensation'. Wyke's view was quite contrary to that always maintained by the Colonial Office and at once expressed by Henry Taylor on reading Wyke's despatch. Taylor pointed out that since the land in question had been occupied by British settlers before the revolt of the Spanish colonies the only country which might have questioned it was Spain. 'But,' Taylor continued, 'it is not occupied in violation of any rights possessed by Guatemala, because our recognition of the South American Republics and their rights proceeded upon the *de facto* principle, and we and not they were at the time of that recognition *de facto* in possession of the tract between the Sibun and the Sarstoon'. Taylor urged that this should be put into writing and Wyke's opinions disavowed to avoid any later objections.

Apart from this criticism the treaty at first met with general approval although, as later events were to show, the Foreign Office officials were extremely hazy as to the actual commitment made on their behalf by Wyke. An objection to the treaty was raised by the American Minister in Guatemala, but this was done without the authority of the United States Government which hastened to rebuke him for his lack of understanding of the situation. Aycinena also rejected the protest on behalf of the Guatemalan Government, stating that Guatemala was not concerned with the Clayton–Bulwer Treaty but simply with bringing about a general understanding in the area. But Aycinena had to deal with opposition to the treaty at home, both in the Council of State and in the Chamber of Representatives. The treaty was ratified by the Council with a small majority and when it was put before the Chamber Aycinena expounded at some length the advantages of coming to an understanding with the powerful British Government. The Guatemalan Foreign Minister pointed out that although Guatemala had inherited Spanish rights she had never occupied or exercised sovereignty over the lands occupied by the British. Even if Britain were to abandon responsibility for the settlement, Guatemala would be incapable of governing it and instead of having 'a great and powerful nation' for neighbour there would be 'an association of adventurers and irresponsible pirates, lords of the Gulf of Honduras'. Apart from overcoming these disadvantages Guatemala, by the treaty, had secured the cooperation of Great Britain in constructing a road which could do nothing but benefit Guatemalan trade and agriculture. Aycinena's justification of the Anglo-Guatemalan Convention won the approval of the Chamber of Representatives which urged that the road should be built as soon as possible.

Controversy about Article 7

It was at this point that the misunderstandings began. It soon became clear that not only did the two negotiators, Wyke and Aycinena, hold different interpretations as to the wording of Article 7 but that there had also been verbal agreements between them which had not been fully conveyed to the British Government. Thus, in 1860, the Foreign Office was not fully informed of its commitments and its view of the treaty differed substantially from that of the Colonial Office. The officials in that department were extremely sceptical about the value of the proposed road and held that since the road would not pass through British territory it was no concern of the Colonial Office. Wyke wrote to the Foreign Secretary, Lord John Russell, that: 'it is impossible to help smiling at the naïveté of this declaration which expresses in set phrases the desire of eating the kernel of the nut without taking the trouble to break the shell which contains it'. It is permissible to suggest that had there been more cooperation between the Foreign Office and the Colonial Office the long drawn out dispute with Guatemala might have been avoided altogether.

The extent of the Foreign Office's ignorance of the understanding reached by the two negotiators soon became clear. In December 1859 Lord John Russell informed Hall, the acting Consul-General at Guatemala, that Captain Wray of the Royal Engineers had been sent to mark out the boundary line between British Honduras and Guatemala and to survey the proposed route for a road. But Hall was told to make certain that the Guatemalan Government did not expect 'H.M.G. to incur any expense whatever in the actual construction of the road'. Hall received the letter as the treaty was being debated and both he and Wyke feared that if its contents were made known Britain might be accused of lack of good faith and the treaty might be cancelled. Wyke at once told Russell that his understanding had involved more than paying for a survey. He explained 'we thought that a roughly made and practical cart road would be established by the two Governments conjointly, Guatemala furnishing the materials, we the scientific direction of the works and both parties equally paying the labourers who are to construct it'. A memorandum which Wyke drew up a year later enlarged on this explanation and said that he and Aycinena had estimated the total cost to be at most £100,000. Wyke always insisted that the engineer's estimates were far too high and based on proposals for a much more elaborate road than he and Aycinena had ever envisaged. On receiving Wyke's letter of explanation Lord John Russell again wrote to Hall in terms which showed no sign of wishing to evade the obligations entered into on behalf of the British Government. On the contrary, he told Hall to point out that although the clause concerning the road was an unusual one, the treaty had been ratified and the British Government would fulfil its obligations.

Meanwhile Captain Wray had arrived in Guatemala and begun his task of carrying out a survey for a road. The work took him until November 1860, by which time he had worked out a route between Guatemala City and the port of Izabal. The road would be 157 miles in length and he estimated that it would take four years to build at a cost of some £145,000. When he sent his report to the Foreign Office Wray also sent a very depressing account of the situation. He felt that the road would be of no benefit to the British settlement of Honduras and that the Guatemalan Government could not be relied upon to carry out its obligations and he thought that it should not be entrusted with any money for the work. By the time the Foreign Office received Wray's discouraging report it had already become aware of the disadvantages in Article 7. It had been deceived as to the whereabouts of the proposed road, about its cost and about its value to British Honduras. Already in the summer of 1860 Russell had raised the question of whether the Government could discharge its obligations by the payment of a lump sum. The Colonial Office under the Duke of Newcastle was convinced of the futility of the road and even suggested that the trade through Belize might be injured by it.

When Wray's report arrived it was thoroughly discussed by Russell, the Colonial Office, Prime Minister Palmerston, Wyke and Superintendent Seymour. Only the last two men believed that the road could be of any positive benefit to British Honduras; doubts were expressed as to whether Parliament would vote the necessary money but no one at this stage attempted to deny the moral obligations incurred by Wyke on behalf of the British Government. Gladstone, as Chancellor of the Exchequer, suggested that the only sensible course would be to clarify both Article 7 and the verbal understanding between Wyke and Aycinena as well as to check the estimates for the road so that proposals could be put before Parliament. This should be done in the form of a supplementary convention and after some delay the Cabinet agreed on this course in September 1861. The Colonial Office stated there was no advantage in the 1859 treaty and was prepared to see it cancelled, but this course was regarded as most inadvisable by Russell. In a private letter to Gladstone he pointed out that it would be wrong to give anyone the chance of accusing Britain of bad faith and he thought 'we ought to fulfil the engagements of the Crown, even if it should cost £100,000'. Moreover the treaty had brought to an end a lengthy dispute and a source of trouble with America which it would be foolish to ignore.

The new negotiations dragged on for two years, first in Guatemala then in London. By this time certain of the advantages which Guatemala had sought to gain from the original treaty had already been obtained. The American filibuster, Walker, had been captured by British naval forces and the threat of American intervention in Central America had receded. The Guatemalan Government was therefore in a much stronger position and ready to make fresh demands on the British Government, as its representative George Mathew soon found out. Mathew was informed in June 1862 that while Britain was now completely disinterested in the building of the road she was perfectly prepared to carry out her obligations provided that Guatemala did the same. If Guatemala herself made the suggestion that the road should be abandoned Britain would be happy to agree. Mathew soon discovered that Wyke's and Aycinena's views of their agreement were materially different and that Guatemala claimed that Britain should not only provide the engineers and scientific expertise but that she should also pay for all the labour used, not half the cost of labour as understood by Wyke. Mathew protested that Guatemala's demands were exorbitant and the discussions were prolonged by letter and interview. A series of alternative proposals were made and rejected by both sides. However, early in 1863 Aycinena for the first time formally stated that by signing the Convention of 1859, Guatemala had made a definite sacrifice of 'the rights which she had reserved to the territory of Belize'. At the same time Aycinena said it was clear from the wording of the original Article that Britain was to pay a greater share of the cost than Guatemala, since each country was to employ 'their best means' to build the road and naturally British means were greater. In fact these words do not appear in the Article, which said that the two countries should 'use their

best efforts, by taking adequate means' to carry out the proposals.
Aycinena also said then, as has been stated many times since, that
Article 7 was included by Wyke as compensation by Britain to
Guatemala. The wording had been deliberately vague in order to
prevent any challenge by the United States on the grounds that
Britain had acquired new territory and so infringed the Clayton–
Bulwer Treaty. The weakness of this argument lay in the fact that
British Honduras had been specifically excluded from the terms of
the 1850 Treaty. Moreover, by the unratified Dallas–Clarendon
Treaty of 1856, the United States had already recognized the
southern boundary of the British settlement as the River Sarstoon.

The Additional Convention, 1863

At this stage the discussions were transferred to London and
finally in August 1863 agreement was reached and an Additional
Convention signed. By this Convention the British Government
bound itself to ask Parliament for £50,000 to be paid in instalments
to Guatemala for a road which was to be finished in four years.
Guatemala was to accept this sum as a full discharge of British
obligations under Article 7 and final ratifications were to be exchanged within six months. But this was where the arrangements
for the proposed road came to a halt. Guatemala was at war with
El Salvador and no steps were taken to ratify the Convention,
although Russell was asked in April 1864 whether the ratification
could be postponed for one year. The Foreign Secretary replied
that because Guatemala had failed to complete the ratifications
within six months the Convention 'fell to the ground'. In private
Russell seems to have given the Guatemalan Minister the impression that the time could be extended if Guatemala eventually ratified the Convention. This was in fact done in 1865 with minor
changes of wording, and in May 1866 Martín wrote from Paris
to Lord Clarendon who had succeeded Russell at the Foreign
Office. He stated that the Additional Convention had now been
ratified by Guatemala and he hoped that ratifications could be
exchanged as in his verbal agreement with Russell. But at this
point the Ministry fell and Lord Stanley, who took over the Foreign
Office, agreed with the Treasury and the Colonial Office that the
whole question should be allowed to lapse. He therefore informed
Martín that the British Government considered that Guatemala's
failure to ratify the Convention within the specified time, together

with her wish to add new declarations to the Convention, made it impossible for the British Government to accede to her request to ratify.

During the correspondence which followed it appeared that at least the Permanent Under-Secretary at the Foreign Office had his doubts. Hammond felt that if Article 7 of the 1859 treaty were set aside, Guatemala would be justified in holding that the whole treaty fell to the ground, thus re-opening the boundary question. In December 1866 an official letter from Guatemala declared that Article 7 had been included as compensation to Guatemala 'expressed in a decorous form, for the abandonment of the territorial rights to Belize' and suggested that a new Convention could be signed by Martín. Lord Stanley at once denied Guatemala's claims to have made any cession to Britain and added that the 1863 Convention had merely engaged the Government to ask Parliament for £50,000. There had been no guarantee that this would have been granted in 1864 and there was still less reason to suppose that it would in 1867. This somewhat extraordinary statement by the Foreign Secretary will not bear close examination, although it remained the official view for seventeen years. It was clear that the British Government had contracted a moral obligation by accepting Article 7 of the 1859 treaty and that she had not thoroughly tried to implement its conditions. Moreover, although the treaty was not, and never could be, regarded as a treaty of cession by the British Government, it was understood in this light by Guatemala and the British negotiator certainly regarded Article 7 as the inducement which persuaded Guatemala to sign it.

By 1869 the Guatemalan Government had raised a loan which it was prepared to use for her share of the construction of the road and the question was once more reopened. Wyke insisted that the Additional Convention had not been ratified because Guatemala had never had the necessary funds or the intention of carrying out its obligations and that Guatemala was in a weak position. The Foreign Office refused to move from the position adopted by Lord Stanley and in November 1869 it repeated that the Convention had failed through the fault of Guatemala alone. Once again Guatemala's claim to territorial rights over Belize was firmly denied and, for the time being, the matter rested there, however unhappily. It was briefly revived in the 1880s, but not seriously raised again for another fifty years.

The Achievement of Colonial Status

In the decade between the signing of the Anglo-Guatemalan Treaty and the lapse of the Additional Convention another important step had been taken to regularize the position of British Honduras. In 1862 it was formally created a British colony with its own Lieutenant-Governor under the authority of the Governor of Jamaica. It has sometimes been suggested that there was a direct connection between the creation of the colony and the signing of the treaty with Guatemala which defined its boundaries. But the discussions which preceded the acquisition of colonial status by British Honduras, as conducted between the Foreign Office, the Colonial Office, Jamaica and Belize, made no reference at all to Guatemala. It has already been seen that the whole question had been a matter for prolonged discussion for at least thirty years. The application to Spain of 1835 had failed, a similar proposal in 1841 had been thwarted by a change of government in London and when the matter was raised again in 1848 yet another point of view was put forward. Earl Grey was Colonial Secretary at that time and he suggested that the time had come to ignore Spanish claims and to assume 'for the Public Meeting the authority to legislate on matters which have hitherto been considered as beyond its control—considering it as a *de facto* established legislature'. Henry Taylor was asked to comment on this proposal and his usual distrust of independent colonial legislatures was revealed in his reply. He could foresee no possible objection from Spain but he thought it should be considered whether or not it was expedient to legitimize the Public Meeting. He did not feel convinced 'that the Public Meeting of Honduras is a Body which could be expected to work as well as it does if it were uncontrolled'.

Two years later a petition requesting colonial status was forwarded from Belize. Taylor again showed an unwillingness to change his attitude on this point although perfectly ready to devise a new constitution. He stated quite firmly: 'In my own view of the case the British Crown has all the Sovereignty it has occasion for, and as to the neighbouring Republics, it is impossible they can seriously regard as an usurpation on them, an occupancy which existed before their independence existed'. In spite of Taylor's opinions Lord Palmerston decided to settle the question of Spanish rights permanently by declaring that the British Government intended to make changes in the constitution of British Honduras.

He told the Ambassador at Madrid that if any objection were raised it was to be stated that Britain had held the settlement by right of conquest since 1798 and that Spain no longer had any rights on the American continent. But once again the more hesitant policy of the Colonial Office intervened and, at the suggestion of Earl Grey, Palmerston agreed not to communicate with Spain but to wait and see if she made any objections to the constitutional changes. The new Legislative Assembly came into being without any comment from Spain and the hand of the settlers was strengthened in 1851 when the Law Officers expressed the opinion that Honduras 'has become a part of the dominions of Her Majesty'. No public announcement was made at the time but this view did show a striking change in the attitude of the legal advisers to the Crown. Memoranda passed backwards and forwards between the Foreign Office and the Colonial Office throughout 1855 and 1856 but no further action was taken until the inhabitants of British Honduras renewed their pleas in 1861.

The petition prepared by the Legislative Assembly in March 1861 acknowledged that reasons of state policy had formerly prevented Honduras being raised to the status of a colony. But, the petition argued, it could no longer be denied that British sovereignty over the settlement was complete. It went on to list the ways in which sovereignty was exercised and the list included the granting of lands, the legislative powers of the Superintendent and Assembly and the full powers over life and property of the Courts. The marking out of the boundaries of the settlement was further proof of British sovereignty. The petition concluded: 'That your Petitioners humbly submit to your Majesty, that the time has now arrived when British Honduras should be in name, what it really is in fact, a 'Colony' . . . and when the supervision of the Governor of Jamaica over our affairs should also cease.'

This time no objections were raised by any government department but, on the advice of Superintendent Seymour, it was decided to retain the link with Jamaica. Accordingly the necessary Letters Patent were framed and on 12 May 1862 Frederick Seymour became Lieutenant-Governor of the colony of British Honduras subject to the authority of the Governor of Jamaica. Thus at last the territory, which had been occupied by British subjects for about two hundred years, became an acknowledged British colony with boundaries defined by international treaties.

Part III
From Colony to
Nation, 1862-1970

12

Belize and her Neighbours

During the last century the history of the colony of British Honduras, soon to become the independent nation of Belize, has necessarily become more complex. Nor has the story been one of unimpeded progress and development towards nationhood: indeed, the latter part of the nineteenth century seems to have been a period of some stagnation. Attempts to promote the economic development of the country by encouraging immigration, by agriculture and by building a railway or roads to open up the interior were frustrated either through lack of resources and imagination on the part of the imperial government and colonial authorities, or because of the vested interests of opposing groups within the colony. Constitutional development was equally disappointing. Although it is true that the colony was freed from its restrictive connection with Jamaica in 1884, a retrograde step was taken in 1871 when the Legislative Assembly voted its own demise, and with it representative government, in exchange for a Legislative Council and a Crown Colony form of government. The subsequent constitutional history of British Honduras was largely concerned with the struggle to reverse that fateful step and to obtain an unofficial majority on the Legislative Council, as a prelude to the restoration of the elective principle, later leading to the gradual introduction of political parties and finally to self-government. As the population increased the machinery of government was expanded to meet new needs. Economic problems were no longer simple questions of trade but became bound up with the general political situation. It is no longer possible to distinguish cause from effect or to separate British Honduran constitutional history from that of its economy. The close interlocking of such themes is very evident when one turns to the question of British Honduran relations with other nations, the wider context within which the country evolved her own sense of identity.

Mexico and the Northern Frontier

Throughout the second half of the nineteenth century relations between British Honduras and her northern neighbour, Mexico, were complicated by what were loosely termed the Indian wars. Mexico, already weakened by her loss of territory to the United States during the war of 1846–8, was further disrupted by the terrible Caste War which almost halved the population of Yucatán between 1847–55. But, even when that war was officially over, the Maya continued their struggle against the white Yucatecan authorities; the different tribes fought each other and also threatened the security of the British mahogany cutters and the northern part of the colony. The British colonists were by no means blameless for the disorder which took place on the northern frontier: until the end of the century, they continued to supply the Santa Cruz Indians with arms while complaining bitterly of the activities of the Chichanha or Icaiché tribe. The southern part of Yucatán was not pacified until the turn of the century, by which time Mexico and Great Britain had at last concluded a peace treaty.

Mexican claims to British Honduras

Mexico's internal disorders were not confined to the Yucatán peninsula. She was wracked by almost constant civil war and subject to intervention by the European powers. When the War of Reform finished in 1861 France, Spain and Britain intervened in order to collect outstanding debts; this intervention resulted in the temporary establishment of an empire under the French puppet, Maximilian of Austria, in 1864. Despite internal strife the new government was soon putting forward new and far-reaching claims to territory which involved an entirely new attitude towards British Honduras. A decree published in September 1864 and signed by the Imperial Commissioner for Yucatán declared that the province's boundaries extended to the Sarstoon River in the south, and to the River Usumacinta in the west. This river lay deep in the Guatemalan province of Petén, while the Sarstoon had never at any time come within the jurisdiction of Yucatán. It is hardly surprising that the publication of the decree caused considerable agitation in British Honduras, especially since it increased the threatening attitude of the neighbouring Indian tribes. The Icaiché, led by Marcos Canul who described himself as 'General' with the authority of the Mexican government, claimed rents from those individuals and companies who cut wood within the disputed area between the Blue Creek and the Río Bravo. The decree had so confused the Indians that the Santa Cruz, a tribe who resisted all Mexican authority, believed that the British colony was about to pass into Mexican hands and were therefore prepared to attack. Lieutenant-Governor Austin insisted that Mexico must renounce all claim to sovereignty over British Honduras, and, at the same time, must annul any commission which had been granted to Canul.

The British Government was prepared to take a calmer view of the situation and to believe that a mistake had been made. The British Minister in Mexico, Campbell Scarlett, presented a Note stating that Mexico could have no claim to any part of British Honduras. He was assured that no such claim had been made and the mistake would be corrected, but, three days previously, the Imperial Government itself had published a decree which supported the claims put forward by the Yucatán Commissioner. Scarlett's immediate protest was followed in July 1865 by a stronger Note demanding a public denial of all claims to British territory and the removal of Canul's commission. Since the Imperial decree had mentioned the possibility of boundary negotiations between Mexico and Guatemala, the Foreign Office seized the opportunity to suggest that Britain was ready to settle the boundary question between Mexico and the British colony, but would not acknowledge that Mexico had any rights in the matter except those of mutual convenience. It was also stated that the treaty of 1826 had been a temporary arrangement which had not admitted that Mexico inherited any rights from Spain.

During the years between 1865 and 1867, after which the execution of the Emperor Maximilian ended diplomatic relations between Mexico and Great Britain, Scarlett was engaged in a futile diplomatic correspondence. His efforts to obtain a renunciation of the Imperial decree and Canul's commission were in vain. Further protests against a map drawn in support of that decree were equally useless. While Mexico continued to assert that she had inherited all the rights of the Captaincy-General of Yucatán, as recognized by the treaty with Spain in 1836, the British Government denied that Mexico had any claim to any part of the British colony and maintained that the only point to be settled between the two countries was the boundary line along the Rio Hondo. Mexico even went so far as to assert that Britain and Guatemala had no right to conclude the 1859 Treaty since it affected territory to which Mexico had a claim. Eventually, in March 1866, Campbell Scarlett was given authority to negotiate a boundary treaty which would not discuss the question of sovereignty in relation to British Honduras, nor would it commit Britain to any joint expedition against the Indians. After lengthy discussion in the Colonial Office it was agreed that the boundary line should be the Rio Hondo with its northernmost tributary the Snosha, or alternatively, if that proved unacceptable, the more southerly branch of the river, Blue Creek. But despite a personal interview with the Emperor in September, Scarlett was unable to make any progress with the treaty; the empire was on the verge of collapse and Scarlett's hope of obtaining a permanent settlement with Mexico disappeared with it. A Treaty of Friendship and Commerce, signed in October, agreed to consider the problem of British Honduras in a separate treaty, but it was never ratified. The triumphant return to power of President Juárez on the defeat of Maximilian led to the withdrawal of the British Minister from Mexico and a break in diplomatic relations until 1884.

Indian raids, 1866

Meanwhile, in May 1866, the Icaiché Indians, who were doubtless encouraged by the Mexican claim to British soil, had made a serious attack on a mahogany camp at Qualm Hill on the Rio Bravo. A force of one hundred and twenty-five Indians under Marcos Canul killed two men and took seventy-nine prisoners, including a number of women and children. The manager of the British Honduras Company immediately demanded military or police protection and three weeks later the Legislative Assembly resolved to ask for men and money from the British Government to protect the colony and to pay for the expenses involved in rescuing the captives. Lieutenant-Governor Austin was inclined to blame the mahogany cutters for their difficulties: he accused them of cutting outside the limits and avoiding payments which they had agreed with the Indians. The Indians themselves were outside the law and subject to control neither from the Yucatán authorities nor from Mexico City: their claims were often little more than a form of blackmail. In the case of the Qualm Hill outrage they demanded ransom money of 12,000 dollars for their prisoners. Austin commissioned one of the leading citizens, a former Prussian officer, to undertake their rescue. It was not until 1 July that Mr Von Ohlafen was able to report that all the prisoners had been handed over to him at Corozalito and that he had been able to beat the Icaiché down from their original demand to 3,000 dollars. The Secretary of State, Lord Carnarvon, condemned the incident in a despatch to the Governor of Jamaica on 13 October 1866. He considered it outrageous that the ransom money should be paid by the public rather than by the manager or the company he represented. He also deplored the Legislative Assembly's rejection of the offer of a share in an armed steamer to protect the colony, which H.M. Government thought to be the only possible hope of restoring order on the northern boundary. In view of this refusal no further offers of help would be made for, as Lord Carnarvon pointed out, it was in Britain's interest to *restrict* and not to extend interests in the north of the colony, and there could be no question of further expansion there either by land purchase or by payment of tribute to the Indians.

Later the same year another and more disgraceful episode took place. Some of the refugees from Yucatán had established themselves in the western part of British Honduras and founded small settlements there. San Pedro, situated between Yalbac Creek and the Belize River, was the most important of these villages. The local Chief and Alcalde, Ascension Ek, had been asking for arms and ammunition to defend the village since 1863. Only after the attack on Qualm Hill was approval given and arms supplied to Ek at the beginning of August 1866. The military force in the north was also strengthened—an additional eighty men were stationed at Orange Walk in September. A month later rumours that Ek was playing false led to a reconnaissance visit to San Pedro by Captain Delamere with a small patrol. The rumours proved correct, for Canul was marching towards San Pedro and the guns supplied to

Ek for the defence of the village were to be used in alliance with the Icaiché. In this situation Delamere's small force was helpless and so he retired to Orange Walk. At the end of December a larger expedition under the command of Major MacKay, and accompanied by the Civil Commissioner, Mr Rhys, was sent to drive Canul and his men from San Pedro. A short distance from the village the troop was ambushed by waiting Indians and after a short fight the signal was given to retire. The reports by Major MacKay and other men involved naturally try to justify this withdrawal: MacKay stated that the men were already exhausted by a long and arduous march from Orange Walk and that the dense bush enabled 400–500 Indians to surround them. Five men were killed and sixteen wounded before it was decided to sound the retreat. Perhaps the worst feature of this encounter was that Mr Rhys did not return with the troop and he appears to have been abandoned, along with certain equipment and ammunition, amidst the confusion. A Court of Enquiry held in Jamaica into Major MacKay's conduct found that although he had lacked judgement and firmness he had not shown any want of courage, nor had Mr Rhys been deliberately abandoned. Lieutenant-Governor Austin had evidently criticized officers and men in scathing terms for it was stated that 'the men behaved throughout in a most creditable manner' and Austin's criticism had been 'unnecessarily severe'.

The first weeks of 1867 saw a period of considerable panic in the colony; appeals for assistance against the Indians were sent to Cuba and to Jamaica; a Civic Guard was raised in Corozal and, towards the end of January, the Governor of Jamaica himself arrived to assess the situation. Sir John Grant was accompanied by Lieutenant-Colonel Harley with reinforcements for the garrison. Harley himself was soon in action with a force of over 300 men; the Indians seized the village of Indian Church but on 9 February Harley responded with an all-out attack on San Pedro. A rocket tube which could launch incendiary missiles was used successfully there and at other villages such as San Jose. The Indians suffered a great deal for their complicity in Ek's schemes. Ek himself left letters demanding rent not only for the disputed areas along the Hondo, but also for Orange Walk and even Belize itself. But by April the Lieutenant-Governor was able to withdraw the martial law which had been imposed in the disturbed districts, and the militia force was discharged.

The Guatemalan–Mexican Treaty, 1882

One of the recommendations made by Governor Grant was that the frontier line which had been partially marked out by Captain Wray in 1861 should be completed, and that the work of demarcation of boundaries be brought to a conclusion by the drawing of an east–west line from the Garbutt's Falls meridian to the Blue Creek. The second part of this proposal was approved by the British Government and in April 1867 the work was carried out by Lieutenant Abbs. However, there was no communication with the Mexican Government on the subject, and as neither the British Government nor the Legislative Assembly of British Honduras seemed prepared to pay for the completion of Wray's line due north to meet that marked by Abbs, the western frontier remained incomplete. It was almost twenty years before the boundary lines were finally completed and then only after the signing of a treaty between Guatemala and Mexico in 1882. The appointment of commissioners to settle the boundaries between the two neighbouring countries encouraged the British authorities to finish the demarcation of the western frontier. It was thought that unless this were done the Guatemalan and Mexican commissioners might encroach on British soil in ignorance of the true boundaries. There was no objection from Guatemala, but certain Indians were on their guard lest the line should be carried too far north. The work was carried out by Assistant Surveyor Miller in spite of extreme heat and shortage of food and water; on finishing the task in February 1887 he reported that stones or wooden stumps had been set up every half mile.

Resumption of the Indian raids

Any hope that the demarcation of the frontier would put an end to the Indian raids was soon disappointed. The Maya of San Pedro had been subdued, but Canul remained a threat. In October 1867 Mr John Carmichael of Corozal, lately Captain of the Militia, travelled to the village of Chan Santa Cruz to seek the support of that tribe against the Icaiché. The Santa Cruz promised help and even asked whether they might become British subjects in return for surrendering their conquered territory and laying down their arms. They also asked for permission to pursue the Icaiché on to British soil. But despite these offers of help the Icaiché continued to disturb the Northern District and make occasional raids to terrorize the people of Corozal and Orange Walk. No sooner had the frontier force been withdrawn in April 1870 than Canul, at the head of 116 men, marched into Corozal to shouts of 'Mexico forever'. He occupied the town but there was no fighting as neither the white Yucatecan refugees nor the Maya who lived there were inclined to fight. They did, however, use the occasion to demand enormous sums of money as compensation from the authorities at Belize who had failed to protect them. Canul, for his part, maintained that he had merely been searching for the Santa Cruz and had withdrawn as soon as he realized they were not in the colony.

Canul's final raid was perhaps the most famous episode in the long drawn—out drama between the colonists and their Indian neighbours. On 31 August 1872 Canul led a band of about 150 armed men across the Rio Hondo near Corosalito; the following day they advanced on Orange Walk where a small garrison of the West Indian regiment succeeded in barricading itself in the one-room barracks. The Indians opened fire from nearby buildings and also used piles of logwood as cover. The officer in command, Lieutenant Smith, was wounded early in the action but insisted on retaining his command until compelled to delegate responsibility to Sergeant Belazario. When Canul found that he was unable to dislodge the garrison an attempt was made to fire the building—the kitchen which stood only a few yards away was completely burnt out. Accounts of the latter part of the engagement vary. The official report states that after about six hours the Indians began to retire, whereupon Belazario led an immediate assault killing and wounding many Indians. Other sources record that the garrison was rescued by a group of ex-Confederate Americans who attacked the Indians from the rear. All accounts agree that the Indians lost at least fifteen men while many more were wounded; two of the British garrison were killed and fifteen wounded. Canul himself was so seriously wounded that he only lived long enough to be dragged across the Hondo. His position as Chief was taken over by Rafael Chan, who wrote to the British Lieutenant-Governor shortly afterwards asking for peace and pardon.

New defence measures

This was the last serious attack on the colony although alarms and threats continued throughout the 1870s and '80s. Repeated British complaints to Mexico were completely ineffectual and were countered with charges that the British supply of arms to the Santa Cruz was responsible for the unrest on the border. A British Note of protest sent in 1873 asserted that the Mexicans, despite their denials, were in contact with the Icaiché: unless Mexico restored order on her side of the Hondo, Britain would insist on her right to pursue and arrest felons on Mexican soil. Meanwhile the Commanding Officer in the West Indies had made a personal tour of the colony and produced certain recommendations for its defence. Corozal was to become the headquarters for the troops in place of Belize; Orange Walk was to be organized as a second garrison with at least three officers and fifty men. By February 1874 new barracks and defence works had been erected at Orange Walk, and Fort Cairns was completed two years later. During 1878 Volunteer Corps were raised at Corozal and Belize, but when a Bill was passed the following year to raise a regular militia in the colony the unofficial members in the Legislative Council objected. Throughout the period there was a general unwillingness on the part of the leading citizens to defend their own interests; the British Treasury was equally unwilling to finance extra troops and military assistance, so the defence of the colony continued on an *ad hoc* basis.

In 1879 a group of Icaiché kidnapped several inhabitants, but their own Chief, Santiago Pech, was seized as hostage. Three years later Lieutenant-Governor Barlee issued a proclamation forbidding all trade with the Icaiché as they were threatening to make war on the colony. A small volunteer force under Major Fowler was sent to the Cayo District where it was rumoured that the Icaiché were making trouble. However, according to a later report in the *Colonial Guardian*, the local people had known nothing of these disturbances: Major Fowler was accused of using the expedition to protect his own agent in a dispute with local tenants—at a cost to the colony of nearly two thousand dollars.

Negotiations lead to agreement

Meanwhile, in the absence of diplomatic representatives, communications between the British and Mexican Governments had been carried on directly between the two Foreign Secretaries. The long controversy culminated in 1878 with a polemical 400-page Note in which Mexico recounted the entire history of the British Honduras question. Lord Salisbury again stated that Britain was not prepared to discuss the question of sovereignty: despite tentative proposals to renew diplomatic relations in 1880 and 1881, this remained a stumbling block for several years. When relations were finally resumed in 1884 no reservation of rights was made by Mexico. Almost immediately discussions were begun to settle the outstanding differences between the two countries. Britain had always maintained that only a simple boundary question was at stake, but by 1886 this position was clearly untenable. The arms trade between Belize and the Santa Cruz Indians could not be ignored and although the Foreign Office had been prepared for some time to link the boundary negotiations with an embargo on arms, the Colonial Office continued to hold out on behalf of the colonists and the Santa Cruz. The authorities in Belize were anxious to see order restored in the vicinity of the Rio Hondo, but they preferred to see the Mexican Government accomplish this by peaceful means. After all, the Santa Cruz had been their allies against the Icaiché for many years; moreover there were still merchants who found the arms trade very profitable. It was feared that any punitive measures adopted by Mexico against the Indians would either bring down their wrath on the colony or, at the least, lead to a mass immigration by the Santa Cruz seeking refuge in the colony. Both of these possibilities alarmed the people of British Honduras and the Colonial Office.

In April 1887 the Mexican Foreign Minister, Mariscal, finally put forward definite proposals for a treaty to the British Minister, Spenser St John. It is possible that the Mexican Government was influenced by the news of a meeting which had taken place at Corozal where the Chief of the Santa Cruz again offered to give up land in return for the Queen's protection. On this occasion Henry Fowler, the Administrator of the colony, asked for advice and was told to persuade the Indians to make peace with Mexico. The proposed treaty was discussed secretly lest it should excite any jealousy from the United States. The Rio Hondo and Blue Creek were to form the frontier between Mexico and British Honduras; both Governments were to ban the supply of all arms to the Indians and were to make every effort to stop Indian raids. Although these clauses were substantially the same as those finally signed in 1893, a long delay was caused mainly by Mexican hesitation and fear of public opinion. Mariscal said that his Government preferred to wait until it could mount an effective expedition against the Santa Cruz. There was also some panic in the colony lest the

Indians should try to take arms and ammunition by force. The officials at the Foreign Office tried to quieten these fears by pointing out that they were not pressing for immediate ratification of the treaty.

During the subsequent delay the British carried out a careful survey of the Blue Creek which revealed that the main stream ran slightly to the south of Lieutenant Abb's line. When the treaty was signed this modification to the line of frontier was included, but otherwise there was little alteration to the original proposals. However, despite the anxiety of both governments to secure ratification, opposition in the Mexican Senate on patriotic grounds delayed this for yet another four years. The Yucatán authorities pressed for settlement but it was only when Mariscal obtained an Additional Article guaranteeing free navigation to merchant vessels between Ambergris Cay and the mainland, that the treaty was ratified. The export of arms and ammunition from the colony was immediately prohibited, but the difficulties of enforcing such an embargo were recognized. Mexico stationed a floating barge at the mouth of the Hondo with a small group of armed customs men. The British Government was not perturbed by this action although some of the Belize citizens complained. Britain still hoped to see a peaceful solution to the pacification of Yucatán, but the Santa Cruz themselves resisted all attempts at mediation and by 1900 a military expedition had become the only answer to Mexico's problems in her southern territory. Late in 1900 General Bravo began a devastating two-pronged attack on the Santa Cruz who were forced to yield to the inexorable new methods adopted by the Mexican Government. Two years later, amid strong protests from the citizens of Yucatán, the new state of Quintana Roo was created.

The Anglo-Mexican Treaty which was signed in 1893 and ratified in 1897 brought to an end the long-standing dispute between the two countries without any definition of sovereignty over British Honduras. Opposition in the Mexican Senate centred on the argument that Mexican claims were being abandoned without any compensation but, to the Yucatán authorities and the Mexican Government, British cooperation in the pacification of the Indians seemed an adequate recompense. Since the treaty, relations between Mexico and Great Britain have been peaceful; large sums of British capital were invested in Mexico at the beginning of this century. No claim against Britain has ever been put forward, but

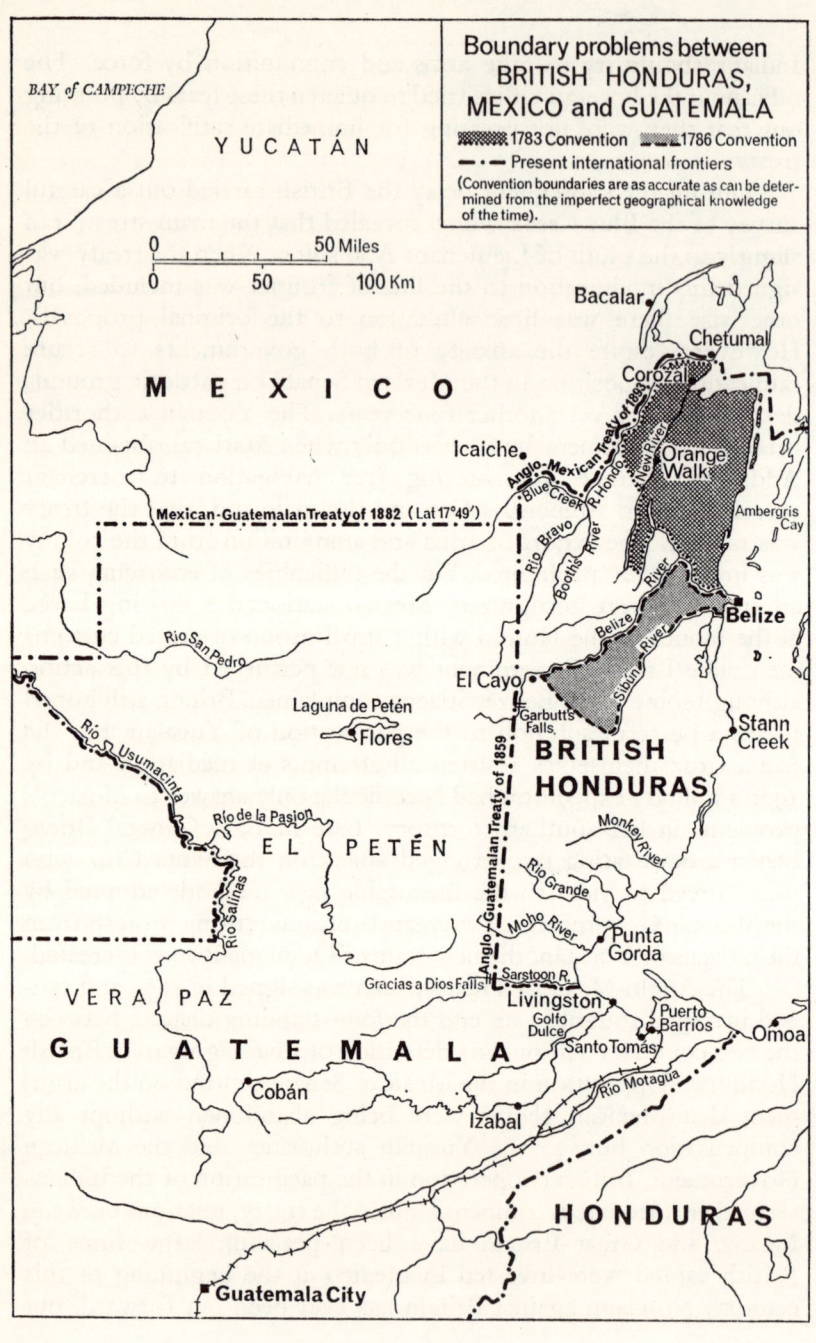

Boundary problems between
BRITISH HONDURAS,
MEXICO and GUATEMALA

▨ 1783 Convention ▨ 1786 Convention
— · — · Present international frontiers
(Convention boundaries are as accurate as can be determined from the imperfect geographical knowledge
of the time).

BAY of CAMPECHE

YUCATÁN

0   50 Miles
0   50   100 Km

M E X I C O

Bacalar
Chetumal
Corozal
Icaiche
Orange Walk
Ambergris Cay
Blue Creek
Rio Bravo
Booth's River
New River
R. Hondo
Anglo-Mexican Treaty of 1893

Mexican-Guatemalan Treaty of 1882 (Lat 17°49')

Rio San Pedro

Laguna de Petén
Flores

El Cayo
Garbutt's Falls
Belize River
Sibún River
Belize

Rio S. Usumacinta

Río de la Pasión

EL PETÉN

Rio Salinas

BRITISH
HONDURAS

Stann Creek

Monkey River
Rio Grande

VERA PAZ

Anglo-Guatemalan Treaty of 1859

Moho River
Punta Gorda

Gracias a Dios Falls
Sarstoon R.

G U A T E M A L A

Cobán

Izabal

Livingston
Golfo Dulce
Santo Tomás
Puerto Barrios
Omoa
Rio Motagua

H O N D U R A S

Guatemala City

on several occasions during the last forty years when Guatemala has laid claim to British Honduras, Mexico has made statements reserving her rights should any change in the status of the colony take place. Mexico has rightly asserted that Guatemala has no possible claim to any land north of the Sibún River, and that if Guatemala were to obtain any rights in British Honduras Mexico would expect to obtain the northern half of the country. Mexico has pressed these arguments in a series of pamphlets addressed to Guatemala, but, it must be emphasized, she has never tried to revive any claim against Britain.

The Anglo-Guatemalan Dispute, 1870–1900

In 1867 and again in 1869 the British Government had taken a definite stand against Guatemalan protests at the non-fulfilment of the 1859 Treaty. According to Lord Stanley, in an opinion later confirmed by Lord Clarendon, the failure of the Guatemalan Government to ratify the Additional Convention of 1863 released the British Government from all obligations. Throughout the 1870s Britain did not move from this position despite one or two half-hearted attempts by Guatemala to re-open the whole question. In 1879 the Guatemalan Minister in Paris, Crisanto Medina, was appointed to the London Embassy as well. He was an extremely able diplomat and at once devoted himself to a close study of relations between Guatemala and Britain. In July 1880, as a result of his investigations, he asked Foreign Secretary Granville whether the British Government would agree to submit the dispute to an independent arbitrator. He pointed out that not only had Britain failed to implement the controversial Article 7, but that Article 2 which provided for the completion of the boundary line between Guatemala and British Honduras had also been ignored. Lord Granville rejected Medina's suggestion of arbitration and Guatemala made no further representation for four years.

Revival of Guatemalan protests, 1884
However, the Guatemalan claims were soon revived because of a new departure in the policy of the United States of America. By 1880 American anxiety to obtain direct control over the proposed trans-isthmian canal was so great that she was prepared to ignore

the Clayton–Bulwer Treaty of 1850. As her suggestion that it should be modified was not accepted by the British Government, the American Secretary of State tried to prove that Britain had violated the treaty which consequently the United States need no longer regard as valid. The accusation turned on the question of British Honduras and the encroachment by her citizens on neighbouring territory, as well as on the recognition of her status as a British colony. Lord Granville seems to have emerged the victor in the heated correspondence which took place with Secretary Frelinghuysen during 1882–3. But Medina used the publication of the letters to make a new and stronger protest to the British Government against the increasing occupation of an 'integral part of Guatemalan territory'. He pointed out in a letter dated 5 April 1884 that Guatemala had done everything possible by diplomatic means to make the 1859 Treaty effective. Britain on the other hand had suspended the work of the boundary commissioners, made no effort to build a road, declared the Additional Convention of 1863 invalid, declined all discussion on the subject and had finally refused arbitration. In these circumstances Guatemala had decided that either the 1859 Treaty in its entirety must be considered to be in force and the relevant compensatory clauses should be carried out: alternatively the treaty should be regarded as null and void, so that Guatemala was not bound to recognize her boundary with British Honduras. Although this protest was not a definite repudiation of the Anglo-Guatemalan Treaty it marked a new phase in the long story of Anglo-Guatemalan relations. For the remainder of the nineteenth century the Foreign Office tried to resolve the problem in a way which would satisfy both Guatemala and the Colonial Office, but her efforts were constantly thwarted by the Treasury.

By 1884 the importance of British Honduras as a British foothold in Central America had been greatly reduced in the eyes of the Foreign Office. The mid-century competition with the United States for control of the proposed trans-isthmian canal had disappeared with the building of the Panama railway and the series of treaties negotiated by Britain in 1859–60. The commercial importance of the British colony had also gradually decreased with the opening up of new trade routes, but the colonists themselves looked forward to a great revival in trade and commerce if only the Home Government could be persuaded to finance the building of a railway. During the last two decades of the century innumerable schemes were put forward both by individual sponsors and by the authorities in British Honduras, and, from 1884, the Colonial Office tried to link the obligations under Article 7 of the 1859 Treaty with the need for a railway.

Medina had chosen a good time to register his protest. United States preoccupation with the possibility of an inter-American railway had renewed her interest in Central American boundaries. Moreover such interest increased local pressure in British Honduras for construction of a railway which, it was supposed, would lead to an immediate rise in land values. Furthermore the Commercial Treaty which Chatfield had negotiated as long ago as 1849 had now expired and the British Government was anxious to renew it; this Guatemala refused to do until the 1884 protest was answered. It was against this background that the Foreign Office appealed to the Law Officers for their opinion on the 1859 Treaty and asked in particular whether its main clauses were rendered invalid by the failure to comply with Article 7. At first the Law Officers seemed inclined to regard Article 7 as independent from the main part of the Treaty, and said that by using its 'best efforts' to obtain £50,000 from Parliament the British Government had discharged all obligations. However, Guatemala might still insist that there was some obligation and the Law Officers therefore thought it important to know why Article 2 providing for the joint boundary survey had not been fulfilled. When it was learned that Britain had stopped the survey in order to avoid complications with Mexico the Law Officers took a more serious view of Britain's position. Having reconsidered the question and Wyke's explanation that he could not have obtained Guatemalan consent to the boundary treaty without the addition of some compensatory clause, they concluded that there was at least a moral obligation to give effect to Article 7. Thus by the end of 1884 the British Government, or more accurately, the Foreign Office, had withdrawn from the stand taken seventeen years earlier and was prepared to seek a solution to the problem.

Railway projects

The Colonial Secretary was then Lord Derby who, as Foreign Secretary Stanley, had repudiated all British obligations in 1867. He was certainly not disposed to re-open the question but felt that if the Foreign Office insisted, the Board of Trade should also be consulted. The trade experts saw little point in building a road between Guatemala City and Puerto Barrios on the Atlantic coast; a railway which would open up a route between British Honduras and the forests of the Petén would prove more profitable to the colony and, at the same time, fulfil the obligations incurred in Article 7. Under President Barrios (1873-85) Guatemala had begun the process of modernization; by 1884 the capital was already connected to the Pacific port of San José by rail and it was hoped to extend this route to the Atlantic port of Puerto Barrios. Surveys, concessions and contracts were prepared but shortage of money was to delay the completion of this project until 1908. In March 1886 the British Minister in Guatemala, Harriss Gastrell, suggested that if Britain were prepared to pay £50,000 towards this railway she would free herself from her obligations to Guatemala, settle the boundary question and be in a position to obtain the commercial treaty she wanted. Four months later, according to Gastrell, the Guatemalan Government had changed its mind and was no longer interested in his proposal. She now wanted Britain to offer more money or to cooperate in building the railway as an investment.

The Governor of British Honduras had added his authority to the arguments in favour of the building of a railway from Belize to the Petén so that by the summer of 1886 there were two possibilities to be considered by the Cabinet. The matter was further delayed until the spring of 1887 when a definite decision was taken to ask Parliament for a grant of £10,000 a year for five years in order to build a railway from Belize to Guatemala City. This new proposal made by the Colonial Office and supported by the Foreign Office met with an absolute refusal from the Treasury. The Lords of the Treasury replied that 'in the present condition of the finances of the country, they would not be justified in recommending to Parliament the grant of £10,000 a year'. So the long discussions were to no avail: for the time being nothing more could be done at Westminister. In British Honduras, however, some progress towards the construction of a railway was being made. Proposals made by the Legislative Council encouraged the Governor to invite tenders and in 1888 a draft contract was issued. The plan was for the contractor himself to negotiate a concession with the Guatemalan Government to extend the railway beyond the frontier into Guatemala; but the tenders proved unsatisfactory and Guatemala refused to move from her existing position—that she would neither grant concessions nor make a commercial treaty until the road and boundary questions were finally settled.

In January 1891 the Colonial Office once again raised the question of applying to Parliament for money. The failure of private schemes had prompted the Legislative Assembly of British Honduras to offer £60,000 towards building the railway from Belize to the Petén. The appointment of Audley Gosling as the new Minister to Guatemala provided the opportunity for a joint Foreign and Colonial Office conference. It was agreed that Gosling should open discussions in Guatemala with a view to giving direct financial help to complete the line between the Petén and Guatemala, on the basis of mutual help and a desire to 'settle all outstanding questions'. Cabinet discussion on this new scheme led nowhere for, as Lord Salisbury noted on a minute, there was 'no money to be had'. Gosling was simply instructed to receive any Guatemalan proposals in a conciliatory spirit, but the Guatemalan Government made no overtures at all. Two years later Gosling suggested that a submarine cable between Guatemala and Jamaica via Belize might be a suitable alternative to the road or railway, but once again the Foreign Office decided that there was no point in asking for money.

Chamberlain seeks a solution, 1895–1901

The stalemate continued until Joseph Chamberlain became Colonial Secretary in 1895. With his vigorous approach to the problems of the colonies it at last seemed possible that the Anglo-Guatemalan dispute might be resolved. He at once decided that a railway from Belize to the Guatemalan border would be the most profitable way of using the £50,000 which he felt Britain was morally obliged to spend. But he had to know whether Guatemala would regard this expenditure as a discharge of all obligation and whether she would grant a timber-cutting concession to the promoters of the railway. Discussions proceeded on these lines, but the Guatemalan President preferred to leave aside the money offer and to regard the railroad as a business concession. Gosling explained that this apparent generosity was determined by the President's desire to amass a personal fortune which he could more easily do by means of timber concessions. Negotiations were prolonged, and early in 1898 the President was assassinated. Gosling warned that Guate-

malan finances were so insecure that no railroad would be completed
except by British finance. The Colonial Office now proposed that a
loan be made to enable the colony to arrange with a private company to build the railway. The loan would have to be accepted by
the Guatemalan Government as fulfilment of British obligations.
The Treasury remained firmly convinced that Article 7 had been
rendered obsolete by the lapse of time and that Britain was under
no obligation to Guatemala. Moreover it doubted that the proposed
railway would be of any value to British Honduras; the railway being
built by Guatemala to Puerto Barrios would achieve all that had
been desired in the 1859 Treaty. The Colonial Office was quite
unable to obtain a change of heart from the Lords of the Treasury.
A final attempt was made to obtain concessions from Guatemala
for private contractors, but by 1901 all negotiations had ceased. The
Guatemalan protest of 1884 remained unanswered, but by the end
of the century it hardly seemed likely that the question of Article 7
would be raised again, even though both the Foreign Office and
Colonial Office admitted that there was a moral obligation to
Guatemala. The Treasury, on the other hand, denied any such
obligation and by 1900 it appeared that the Anglo-Guatemalan
dispute would die a natural death.

The Anglo-Guatemalan Dispute, 1900–1970

For the first thirty years of the twentieth century the Anglo-
Guatemalan controversy remained dormant, and was only revived
when the outstanding issue of the western boundary of British
Honduras was raised in 1931–2. The frontier with Guatemala, which
had been partially marked out by Captain Wray in 1861 and completed by Mr Miller in 1887, only ran from Garbutt's Falls in a
northerly line to the Mexican–Guatemalan border. The southern
section to Gracias a Dios on the Sarstoon had never been surveyed,
although a mark had been placed at the boundary. In 1929 the
original boundary markers were inspected by joint commissioners
and replaced by concrete monuments. Two years later in August
1931 notes were exchanged by the two Governments which agreed
that 'these monuments, thus determined, form part of the boundary
line between British Honduras and the Republic of Guatemala'.
Notwithstanding this agreement British efforts to obtain a joint

survey of the southern section of the line failed, although Guatemala agreed that the British Honduras Government could carry out the work unilaterally. This was done at the sole expense of the colony in 1933, and when the line was opened Guatemalan officials were present and signed reports to the effect that the boundary had been correctly marked.

Revival of Guatemalan claims, 1933

However the main effect of the boundary survey seems to have been to re-awaken Guatemalan claims to the territory of British Honduras. In 1933 the Republic reminded Britain of her obligations under Article 7 of the 1859 Treaty and declared that unless Britain fulfilled these obligations she herself would be unable to complete the boundary arrangements. The British Government expressed its willingness to cooperate but considered that the completion of the railway line to Puerto Barrios had fulfilled the requirements of Article 7 and that therefore any new line of communication would have to benefit both countries. The Guatemalan reply claimed that the fairest way to settle the matter would be for Britain to pay part of the cost of this railway. The British Government naturally refused since it had not given prior approval to such a scheme; the railway was not the road specified in the Treaty and it was of no commercial benefit to Britain or the colony of British Honduras. A number of alternative proposals were made culminating in 1936 with the British offer of an outright payment of £50,000. Guatemala not only rejected this offer but increased her demands in 1937 to a sum of £400,000 or, somewhat surprisingly, the complete cession of British Honduras for a payment of the same sum by Guatemala. The abortive discussions which followed President Ubisco's unrealistic demands led to the Guatemalan suggestion that the dispute should be referred to President Roosevelt of the United States. Britain thereupon expressed willingness to place the whole matter before the International Court of Justice at the Hague. The British Government considered the dispute as essentially a legal matter which could well be determined by a court of international law. Guatemala, however, has never been willing to submit her case to such a court since she has insisted that the question is one of equity.[1]

---

1. Equity may be described as the use of principles of justice to supplement statute law.

The publication by Guatemala of a lengthy and tendentious White Book in 1938 did little to improve her case in the eyes of reputable international lawyers. The White Book presents Guatemala's claims to the territory of British Honduras in as favourable a light as possible, but the inaccuracies, contradictions and omissions are very noticeable. For instance, the British Government is blamed for the non-ratification of the Additional Convention of 1863, although it was Guatemala who refused to ratify at the appointed time, and who, when she later wished to ratify, tried to add 'clarifications' to the Convention. Moreover it was explicitly stated in the White Book that because the 1863 Convention had not been ratified the Treaty of 1859 remained in force; but only one year later (1939) Guatemala asserted for the first time that she no longer regarded that treaty as valid. If Guatemala held that the treaty had lapsed it was illogical for her to claim, as she had done in 1933, that Article 7 had never been fulfilled.

The contradiction in Guatemala's position has always been evident, and it is clear that by the 1930s her real desire was for territory. The declaration that the treaty was no longer in force gave her the opportunity to assert that she could 'recover' the land which she had 'ceded' in 1859. This contention brought the argument back full circle to Wyke's controversial Article. Guatemala has long maintained that Article 7 was an integral part of the treaty which was included as compensation for the cession of territory by Guatemala. Britain, on the other hand, has consistently stated that the treaty was nothing more than a boundary treaty, that Article 7 was included as an inducement to sign, and that if Guatemala was yielding anything, it was merely a vague claim to territory. Thus, if it were decided by a Court that the Convention of 1859 had lapsed for whatever reason, there would simply be a return to the pre-1859 position when there was no question of Guatemala exercising sovereignty over British Honduras.

British attempts to settle the dispute

In 1940 Britain made a further effort to have the dispute with Guatemala settled once and for all. In spite of the belief that an International Court was the correct place for arbitration of international disputes the British Government now agreed (29 January 1940) that the argument could be considered by a tribunal with a chairman nominated by the United States. In March 1940 it was further agreed that if the International Court were to try the case considerations of equity could be introduced. These offers were both major concessions for which Guatemala had been pressing, but they were now rejected and the President declared that he would leave the matter in abeyance for the duration of the Second World War. In spite of this statement Guatemalan propaganda continued and in 1945 her new constitution included 'Belice', i.e. British Honduras, as part of Guatemalan national territory.

When the war came to an end in 1945 the new United Nations established its own International Court of Justice. In 1946 the British Foreign Secretary made a declaration accepting the jurisdiction of that Court in the legal dispute concerning the boundaries of British Honduras. The declaration was later renewed for a further five years. This declaration empowered the Court to consider two distinct claims put forward by Guatemala: firstly, her argument first made in 1939 and renewed at the end of the war, that Britain's failure to fulfil her obligations under Article 7 had rendered the 1859 Treaty void; secondly, that as a result Guatemala was entitled to recover the territory of British Honduras which she had ceded by that treaty and which she now asserted Britain held illegally. The following year Guatemala made a declaration to the effect that the case would only be submitted to the International Court if it could be decided on an equitable basis. The reason for this move is not too difficult to find. Even if the Court were to decide that Guatemala was entitled to revoke the treaty, a question of some legal complexity, it would be unlikely to support Guatemala's claim to the territory of British Honduras which she based on *uti possidetis* or inheritance from Spain. Since this doctrine is unrecognized in international law, Guatemala's claim was most unlikely to succeed and her only hope of acquiring land or of prolonging the dispute was to insist on an equitable decision. This would allow extra-legal points to be considered by the Court so that, for example, Guatemala could win sympathy by presenting Britain as a great imperial power which had browbeaten a relatively small and inexperienced republic in 1859.

Guatemalan interest in the disputed territory

Guatemala's comparatively recent interest in obtaining territory can be attributed to two factors. The first is the question of national pride which has been invoked in the dispute; the second is the old and genuine need to exploit the resources of the Petén district. The department is cut off from the rest of Guatemala by mountains and her route to the sea is blocked by Belize; the Petén therefore remains undeveloped and sparsely populated despite its natural forest resources and the possibility of mineral deposits. It has also been suggested that Guatemala would find the acquisition of new territory a financial embarrassment, and that her only interest in prolonging the controversy has been to divert attention from certain internal difficulties. Whatever her motives Guatemala never submitted her case to the International Court, but instead introduced the matter at various Inter-American conferences.[1] In 1948–9 a number of diplomatic exchanges took place after British warships had been sent to Belize in response to threats of invasion. Mounting excitement in Guatemala and the temporary closing of the frontier brought the dispute no nearer solution. When Guatemala's declaration expired in 1958 she made no attempt to renew it, possibly because a case could now be made out that Britain's long possession of her colony gave her too good a claim to an 'equitable interest' in Belize. An appeal to equity was perhaps now less likely to help the Guatemalan cause.

Moves towards self-determination

As Guatemala and Great Britain were unable to reach any agreement as to how their long-standing dispute should be determined, another factor in the situation gradually assumed importance —the attitude of the people most affected by the controversy, the inhabitants of British Honduras or Belize. It was not until the postwar period that their wishes were even mentioned, but, in 1948, the Legislative Council passed a resolution of loyalty to the British Crown and declared the wish of the colony to remain in the Commonwealth. This naturally strengthened the position of the British Government since it brought the prominent question of human rights to the fore, and enabled it to state that territory could not be relinquished against the wishes of its inhabitants unless legal judgements made this imperative. Since Guatemala could not ignore this line of argument, she gradually began to enlist sympathy from within the colony.

The time was opportune: the rise of nationalist groups throughout the few remaining territories of the British Empire

1. e.g. 1947 Rio de Janeiro, 1948 Bogotá.

created an anti-colonial atmosphere to which Belize was no exception. From 1950 onwards the People's United Party gradually assumed a dominant political role in the country. It strenuously opposed proposals for joining the West Indies Federation and appeared to favour links with a Central American Federation. After the split in the party which occurred in 1956, Mr George Price became its leader. In the following year he was alleged to be involved in secret discussions with Guatemala, discussions which were brought to public notice in November 1957 when he was found to be considering Guatemalan proposals at the time he was in London as a member of a delegation to discuss economic aid for Belize. The talks were at once broken off and Mr Price was dismissed from his position as Minister for Natural Resources. Shortly afterwards the London talks were resumed without the P.U.P. leader, who was at pains to make his own views clear during 1958. In a number of speeches and press releases he emphasized that his main objective was independence for Belize and that he had no intention of subjecting the country to Guatemalan political rule. Some form of economic association with the Central American states was clearly desirable and he thought it possible that an independent Belize could become a member of the Organization of Central American States (ODECA).

It soon became apparent that the P.U.P.'s plans for the future of their country had little in common with the policy of the new Guatemalan President, Ydigoras Fuentes. Soon after becoming President in 1958 he had tried to enter Belize, but was turned back at Benque Viejo on the orders of the Governor. His policy appears to have been to assert Guatemalan claims and inflame public opinion without any consideration of legal problems. His assertions that 'Belice will be ours by right or might' and Guatemala would take Belice 'by reason or force' merely weakened the Guatemalan position. In 1960 the British Government and delegates from Belize were able to agree on the steps to be taken towards self-government and declarations were made that Belize would remain within the Commonwealth after independence and that Guatemala had no rights in the country. Mr Price has consistently associated himself with these declarations and in an important speech in August 1962 he summarized his attitudes towards independence within the Commonwealth and Belize's relations with her neighbours. Since the views of the first Premier of the country are so significant, it is worth quoting them. The theme of the speech was the building of a new nation without any second-class citizens and he went on to say:

'Let every citizen be assured that we do not intend to be integrated, re-incorporated, assimilated or taken over by any country. The whole world knows that our political aims are self-government within the Commonwealth and independence. We can fulfil these aims without launching a competition in armaments in this part of the world. We do not propose to launch such a competition because we cannot at this time afford the heavy financial burden it involves.

'Yet we do not expose our citizens to military adventure from anywhere. We have ample guarantees for our peace and security. As a member of the Commonwealth we can rely on their military protection. As a sovereign, independent nation, there is the peacekeeping machinery of the United Nations and the Organisation of American States.

'While we shall not surrender even one square centimetre of our national territory, we do not propose to spew insults or recriminations against our neighbours. Because of our steadfastness, our demeanour, our willingness to meet our neighbours at the conference table, we expect in time that they will acknowledge our right to freely exercise the principle of self-determination.'

Unfortunately for the people of Belize Mr Price's hopes are still unfulfilled and Guatemalan ambitions remain unsatisfied. In April 1962 Britain held talks at Puerto Rico with representatives from the Belize Government and from Guatemala in an effort to reduce tension. It was agreed to promote economic and social development between the peoples of Guatemala and Belize and to find ways of improving political and commercial relations between Guatemala and Britain. At the same time it was agreed to raise the diplomatic missions in Guatemala City and London to the rank of embassies. In spite of this apparent improvement in relations the Guatemalan President resumed his bellicose attitude the following year. At a conference of Central American Presidents he appealed to President Kennedy for help in recovering territory. He followed this step by using the London constitutional conference of July 1963 as an opportunity to break off diplomatic relations with Britain. At the conference a date for the internal self-government of Belize was agreed; the Guatemalan Government then asserted that the uni-lateral policy of the British Government made the maintenance of diplomatic relations between the two countries impossible and they were consequently broken off. Nevertheless, in December talks were held in Washington and it was stated that the two countries wanted to resume diplomatic relations and settle the long-standing dispute over Belize. In fact no formal talks have taken place since that time.

American mediation rejected, 1968

Two years later President Johnson of the United States made an attempt to reconcile the differences between Guatemala and Britain by appointing an international lawyer to act as mediator with the approval of all the countries concerned. Bethuel Webster spent three years preparing his report which was presented in the form of a draft treaty to be negotiated between Great Britain and Guatemala. Webster recommended that British Honduras should become the fully independent nation of Belize no later than Decem-ber 1970 and that a Joint Authority of seven members from Guate-mala and Belize should then be established in Belize. The Authority would be responsible for carrying out Webster's other recom-mendations on trade, travel, communications and so on. The two countries would be required to consult on questions of foreign affairs and Guatemala would be bound to assist in the defence of Belize. She would also support Belize's entry into such Central American organizations as the Central American Common Market.

The announcement of these proposals was greeted with con-siderable panic in Belize and the Mediator's report was speedily rejected by both political parties, by the Belize Government, by Guatemala and by Britain. The grounds for rejection by Belize were straightforward. As the Premier asserted in a speech to the nation in May 1968: 'The proposals of the Mediator, of course, do not meet the People's United Party's mandate to lead Belize to independence within the Commonwealth and under the protection of the United Nations. They in effect deny full sovereign rights of the new Belize'. There was disappointment on all sides that the long-sought mediation had failed, that the dispute between Britain and Guate-mala remained unsettled and that the future of Belize was still closely linked with the need to find a solution to the difficulty.

Only when Belize becomes fully independent will she enter into diplomatic relations with foreign powers. Until that time her links with the United States, Canada, the West Indies and Central American states will remain principally economic and cultural rather than political and diplomatic.

13

The Making of a People

The Population Problem

The one problem which has attracted the attention of every commentator on Belizean affairs during the last hundred years or more has been the size of the population. Virtually every book, pamphlet and report published about the country has pointed to the small population as the most serious obstacle to economic progress. Innumerable plans to attract immigrants have been devised, plans which in the later decades of the nineteenth century were eagerly promoted by the leading newspapers. But, on the whole, the colonial authorities took little active part in the promotion of such schemes and, with a few exceptions, they were mainly unsuccessful. However within the last twenty years the rate of population growth has accelerated so rapidly that if it continues to expand at the same rate there should be no need for an immigration policy in the future.[1]

From the point of view of the historian it is more important to examine how and why people of so many races have come from so many different countries to make their home in Belize and to work together to build a new, independent nation. In 1835, shortly before the slaves were emancipated, the total population of British Honduras was still under four thousand. When the first detailed census was taken in 1861 the population had risen to 25,365 owing

1. In fact in 1963 a United Nations Mission rejected the concept of large-scale immigration and this was accepted in the 1964-70 Development Plan.

to the influx of Yucatecan refugees from the Caste War. This enormous increase in the population naturally played an important part in the growing prosperity of the colony in the mid-nineteenth century and was responsible for the introduction of an agricultural element into the population. By the time of the general census a hundred years later in 1960 the population had more than trebled, reaching the figure of 90,505. However, the most striking feature of this expansion is that although the population had continued to increase steadily throughout the period, the annual average rate of increase had been less than 1% until after 1946 when it rose to 3%, one of the highest rates in the world. According to the provisional figures for the 1970 census this rate of increase has become even more pronounced, rising to 3·28% per annum in the period 1960–1970 making a total population of 119,645. Improved medical and public health facilities have undoubtedly contributed to the increase in population by lowering the death-rates and especially by the startling reduction in infant-mortality rates revealed by the following table:

Birth-rates and death-rates

	Average 1935–8	Average 1948–57	Average 1958–65	Average 1966
Birth-rate per 1,000	34·9	41·0	45·5	43·6
Death-rate per 1,000	19·0	11·5	7·7	6·9
Infant-mortality rate per 1,000	190·0	93·0	61·6	50·0

Yet, in spite of this high growth rate, Belize remains a sparsely populated country. The low overall density of the population was clearly illustrated by the 1960 census which gave a figure of 10·2 per square mile. The geographical distribution of the population in that year was more remarkable. No less than one-third of the total lived in Belize City itself, while another 12,000 or so lived in the six principal towns.[1] The remainder of the population was divided between about a hundred villages the majority of which lie between Orange Walk and Corozal in the north, and in the Toledo district in the south. By 1967 the density of population to the square mile had risen to 13, but this figure is still very low

---

1. The provisional figures for 1970 show that this proportion has been maintained with a population of 39,257 in Belize City although this figure will be reduced by the rapid growth of the new capital.

compared with the neighbouring Central American republics or the West Indian islands. Comparable figures show that the density per square mile in Guatemala was 106, in Salvador 390, while in Jamaica it was 431 and in the very over-populated island of Barbados, it was as high as 1,480. These figures help to explain why immigration has been seen as an answer to the country's economic problems since the 1860s and, at the same time, a possible answer to the overcrowding of the West Indian islands. This, in fact, was the main concern of the 1948 Settlement Commission for British Guiana and British Honduras.

Efforts to increase immigration

Although the mahogany cutters of British Honduras had survived the effects of emancipation without resorting to any large-scale immigration of labour, the attempts to encourage agricultural schemes from the 1860s onwards was accompanied by the realization that an increased supply of labour would be an essential ingredient of success. The Legislative Assembly took certain steps, such as abolishing an annual tax on foreigners, to encourage the immigration of agricultural labourers, but the price of Crown lands remained too high to attract buyers until Lieutenant-Governor Barlee reduced the price to one dollar per acre and established a standard survey fee of six dollars during his vigorous administration (1877–82)..

The American Civil War presented the merchants of Belize with a splendid opportunity to benefit from the profits of a contraband trade with the Southern Confederate states and at the same time efforts were made to attract both white capitalist emigrés and negro labourers from the south. In 1861 the American Federal Government declared a blockade of over three thousand miles of Confederate coastline in an attempt to abolish the South's cotton trade. But contraband centres grew up around the Gulf of Mexico, notably at Matamaros on the Mexican side of the Rio Grande. Belize was the nearest British port and her merchants were quick to seize the chances presented to them. Washington was not slow to see the danger of the situation and in 1861 a commercial agent, George Raymond, was appointed to Belize in an attempt to control the smugglers. But Raymond was unequal to the task and though he soon reported that arms and ammunition were being transported from Belize to the South he was quite unable to put a stop to the traffic. The following year a more efficient expert in consular affairs replaced Raymond and set about breaking the contraband trade. Dr Leas was well aware that the majority of Belize citizens favoured the Southern cause and he was at pains to make a good impression on the authorities. Lieutenant-Governor Seymour welcomed Leas to the colony effusively—his predecessor had made himself *persona non grata* at Government House—and at their first meeting made it clear that the colony would welcome American immigrants. Leas' first concern, however, was with the contraband trade and by the summer of 1863 he was able to report to Washington that his vigorous measures had effectively stopped the traffic from Belize. Lincoln's policy of emancipating the slaves freed by the Northern army encouraged hopes that some of the freed labourers could be attracted to the colony. But Dr Leas' reports tended to frustrate these hopes. He pointed out that such immigration would not be in the interest of the negroes who would simply be used as tillers of the soil without any prospect of improving their situation. The British Honduras Company made direct efforts to procure negroes under the leadership of its manager John Hodge, who visited both London and Washington in an attempt to obtain approval for his scheme. But Leas found the Company's proposals so unsatisfactory that he himself drew up a list of requirements for a scheme which would guarantee land, housing and education to the immigrant families. Yet despite a good deal of preparatory work the proposals were turned down by the Federal Government.

The effect of land prices

The desire to encourage Confederate emigrés to settle in British Honduras was as great as the desire for the freed men. Leas felt that Confederates who wished to seek refuge in the colony should be allowed to do so and as the Confederate cause weakened a growing number of emigrés arrived in Belize. Many of them went on to seek land in Guatemala or Honduras, but quite a few attempted to settle. Yet, despite the recognition that an influx of American capital and labour might prove the economic salvation of the colony in a time of increasing commercial distress, little or no effort was made to welcome the prospective settlers. When the Southerners found that not only private land but the less accessible Crown lands were five dollars an acre they soon moved elsewhere. In the years immediately after the end of the Civil War all the

Latin American countries were eager to obtain Southern immigrants and Brazil was even offering land free. As the Editor of *The Colonist* pointed out: 'It is also simply absurd to talk of Colonial advancement and improvement without first doing our best to augment our present population'. It seems clear that the large landowners combined with the authorities in London in such a way that the officials on the spot found their hands tied. Thus, when Lieutenant-Governor Austin arranged a grant of 300,000 acres of land at a nominal fee to a group of Southern Americans, the transaction was cancelled from London and shortly afterwards he was recalled. The United States Consul reported that this had caused consternation among the Americans in the colony, many of whom now planned to leave for the Central American Republic. Austin's departure and the arrival of the new Governor in November 1867 was welcomed as the beginning of a new era. The American Consul informed his State Department that 'the fortunes and the prosperity of the Colony have been steadily declining for many years', but never had matters reached such a desperate state as under Austin. His attempts to reduce the price on Crown lands and remedy the financial situation had proved a failure in the face of a declining mahogany trade. The sugar industry, though full of promise for the future, had not yet justified the heavy expenditure of capital; and the Southern immigrants had been disappointed to find that cotton was an unsuitable crop for the colony. But the greatest obstacle to agricultural expansion, in the view of the American Consul, was the high price of land. Yet within a few months of this depressing despatch a change of attitude seems to have occurred on the part of the landowners, for, in January 1868, it was reported that a Mr J. C. McRae was looking for a tract of land on which to settle a group of people from Alabama. He was said to be wealthy and to be on intimate terms with some of the leading commercial men in the colony. When he eventually made his purchase of eighteen square miles up the Belize River he was reported to have paid only thirty cents per acre through the medium of the British Honduras Company.

The Toledo settlement

Since relatively little is known about the purchases made in this period the history of the Toledo settlement is especially interesting. This venture originated in 1867–8 when many of the larger landowners were beginning to sell land to speculators. Extensive advertising again brought Southerners to the colony in search of their fortunes; few arrived with sufficient means or the necessary aptitudes for self-discipline and hard work. By the summer of 1869 Consul Prindle was reporting that the trend of the last two years which had brought an average of fifty discontented Southerners per month to Belize had been reversed and many were now returning to the United States. He commented that 'Some of the emigrants return wiser, but all of them return sadder and poorer than when they left their homes'. One exception to this gloomy account was the Toledo settlement.

In 1867 a group of Methodists from Mississippi under the leadership of the Reverend Levi Pearce acquired some land a short distance from Punta Gorda. Young, Toledo and Company sold the land on favourable terms and took some pains to attract these settlers, even going to the expense of erecting simple 'bush houses' at Cattle Landing for the new arrivals. Within a year twelve families had taken up tracts of land of about 160 acres, two or three miles inland. The life of the settlers was by no means easy; the virgin forest had to be cleared and few families had sufficient food or money to survive for a year until the first crops could be harvested. The cholera epidemic of 1868 killed several Americans and discouraged others but, in 1870, a new group arrived to reinforce the settlement. It was soon realized that crops cultivated in the state of Mississippi could not be successfully produced in the colony; although bananas thrived, the distance from the market made them unsuitable as a cash crop. From 1870 onwards sugar proved to be the most successful commodity and within a short time twelve sugar estates were established, each with its own mill.

Twenty years later about 600 acres were under cultivation and the settlers were employing about three hundred labourers. But 1890 proved the high point in the fortunes of the Toledo settlement. A determination to succeed, evident from the beginning of their enterprise, could not enable the Methodists to prevail against adverse social and economic factors. In the first place theirs was a closed community which opposed complete integration with the community; once they reached adolescence the children were sent back to the United States for their education. In this way any question of miscegenation was avoided. But not only did the group regard itself as an exclusive community from the social point of view, it was equally unwilling to employ outside labour. As the sugar estates prospered the settlers had to change their minds on this point, but on one issue they would not be moved. This was the important question of the manufacture and sale of alcohol. As the price of sugar in Europe dropped and the competition from sugar beet grew it became imperative for colonial producers to distil spirits. At the Toledo settlement rigid Methodist attitudes made it impossible to accept the necessity for this step and, rather than yield, molasses were fed to the cattle or poured in the river. Economic ruin was preferable to the evils of alcohol and when one member of the community did resort to distilling, his own brother refused to help transport the casks of rum. But the collapse of sugar prices on the European market meant the inevitable end of the settlement's prosperity and only those families who turned their attention to the mahogany industry survived. After 1910 there was a steady drift back to the United States, and the Toledo settlement virtually ceased to exist. Nevertheless this group of American Methodists had shown that it was possible for white men to lead a normal working life in the tropics and to build up a prosperous estate without dependence on coloured labour.

The Yucatán refugees

The story of immigration from the Southern States of America has been examined in some detail both because it engendered such high hopes among the colonists, and because its very failure ought to have led to a more constructive policy to obtain immigrants. However the most important addition to the population during the nineteenth century had undoubtedly resulted from the Caste War of Yucatán which broke out in 1847. The refugees who fled from the horrors of that war were mainly Spanish and mestizos, but later they were followed by Indians seeking escape from the revenge of the Yucatecan authorities. The majority of these refugees were Roman Catholics seeking peace and agricultural land. Consequently the need for a Magistrate and police constables was felt in the Northern District as early as 1850; seven years later the Superintendent reported that the new town of Corozal had a population of 4,500. The following year he announced in the Legislative Assembly that the total population of the Corozal District had risen to about 8,000. By the time the official census of 1861 was prepared the number of people living in the northern part of the colony was more than twice that of the inhabitants of Belize. The same census figures showed that while 10,937 inhabitants of British Honduras were born in the colony, almost as many (9,817) were born in Yucatán and over 2,000 in Central America. It is impossible to place too much reliance on these figures, for any census of the time was hampered by the lack of communications. Although some figures were doubtless mere estimates while others were falsified by language difficulties, they do serve to show the importance of the 'Spanish' element in the population. The table opposite reveals the very diverse settlement pattern of the country by recording the place of birth of the population at ten-yearly intervals.

The diversity of races

This table vividly demonstrates how people have come from many different parts of the world to form the nation of Belize. During the 1860s a group of Chinese were brought to the colony as indentured labourers, but this venture was not very successful. Some died from disease while others deserted to the Indians in Yucatán: few had any practical experience of farming and by 1871 only 133 of the colony's residents had been born in China. About this time several landowners made a request for East Indian labourers to be imported as they had been successful in Trinidad and British Guiana. But only a very small number were brought to the colony. Some of the East Indians were employed on the Toledo estates and their descendants still grow rice in the Toledo district while the remainder live in the Corozal area. Other small groups of settlers during the nineteenth century included 450 Italians who arrived from Guatemala in a distressed state and were settled on Crown land near the Manatee River. A group of Germans applied for land and in 1882 about fifty to sixty of these families settled at Stann Creek. Few of these ventures proved to be a success; they were hampered by unsuitable farming techniques, poor organization and often by lack of transport facilities.

Among other groups of people who made their home in the country were some from the West Indian islands of Jamaica and Barbados. The greatest number, about 1,200, seem to have arrived between 1880 and 1890, attracted by the growing prosperity of the banana plantations in the Stann Creek area. Some West Indian labourers were employed in the building of the

Place of birth of the population of British Honduras as given in the censuses from 1861–1946

	1861	1871	1881	1891	1901	1911	1921	1931	1946
British Honduras	10,937	14,623	18,811	22,712	28,505	32,805	38,317	44,454	53,538
United Kingdom	173	191	186	193	177	184	279	216	107
Jamaica	—	426	834	1,015	864	673	640	738	856
Barbados	179	230	204	264	229	144	150	111	52
Other British Colonies	443	240	267	221	211	86	80	57	177
East Indies	12	10	175	291	190	104	74	50	26
United States of America	55	105	125	118	178	159	170	185	120
Central America	2,346	1,943	1,975	3,786	4,789	4,523	4,027	3,850	3,315
Yucatán	9,817	6,069	4,088	2,233	1,712	1,276	1,351	1,233	725
Spain	29	8	26	14	11	17	27	20	15
Germany	34	26	46	50	37	50	21	24	37
France	31	9	16	11	6	8	16	10	39
Italy	—	3	22	13	2	6	5	4	—
Africa	894	628	394	236	110	46	16	7	—
China	1	133	68	52	27	27	12	59	42
Other places	314	66	215	262	431	350	132	329	171
Total	25,635	24,710	27,452	31,471	37,479	40,458	45,317	51,347	59,220

From the British Guiana and British Honduras Settlement Commission's Report 1948.

railway from Middlesex to Stann Creek at the beginning of this century, but West Indians have never been very welcome in Belize. The fact that outsiders from the islands were often appointed to fill the more important posts in the public service and commerce may have been responsible for feelings of resentment. Certainly this attitude to West Indians played its part in the anti-federation movement of the 1950s.

Community Groupings

It is clear that there are many distinctive groups of people in this small country. These communities are by no means segregated from other communities and it would be possible to divide people into groups on several different lines. Thus for instance occupation, religion or language could be taken as the decisive factor, but more usually the communities are based on racial differences. The Creoles form the largest group of people but include those of negro descent, coloured and a small number of whites born in the country. Among the other communities are the Caribs, the Mennonites, the Syrians and other Asian groups.

The Maya Indians

Perhaps the most isolated of the various communities are the Maya Indians or Amerindians as some authorities prefer to call them. In fact the modern Maya comprise several distinct groups, although faulty census returns and the isolation of their villages make it difficult to be precise about their numbers and provenance. Most of the villages in the Cayo district and along the western frontier were founded by Maya from the Petén seeking asylum from forced labour and heavy taxes in Guatemala. The Mopan Maya of the western parts of the country have much in common with the Yucatecan Indians from the north. Most of them live in large villages and play an important rôle in the social and economic life of their own communities and the country as a whole; by contrast the Mopan Maya and Kekchi of the Toledo District tend to lead far more isolated lives. At the time of the 1861 census there were already between 4–5,000 Maya in the country and this number had at least doubled by 1946. Their tendency to wander at will across national frontiers in search of fresh land for their *milpas* and peace in which to cultivate them is well illustrated by the history of San Antonio. Today a thriving village of perhaps 1,300 people, it was founded about 1884 by a small group of Maya Indians from San Luis in Guatemala. At first the community failed to prosper and was hampered by illness and poor crops. In search of a remedy for their misfortunes, the Indians decided to make a raid on their old village to 'rescue' their *santos* from the church. The men collected what ammunition they could and returned in an armed band to San Luis: they then removed the precious *santos* and the bells from the church. Fearful that retaliatory measures would be taken against them, the San Antonio villagers appealed to the authorities for the means to defend themselves, as they were in danger of attack 'for some unknown reason'. Their story was evidently believed for they were supplied with some old rifles. When a party from San Luis did arrive the women of San Antonio were alone, the men being in Punta Gorda that day. But the resourceful women were able to defend themselves until the men returned. Forty of the San Luis party were captured and taken before the District Magistrate. In due course he reported to the Governor that they had been released on their promise that they would never cross the frontier again. The restoration of the *santos* appeared to bring peace and prosperity to the village for since that time traditional farming has been successfully carried on by the Maya of the San Antonio area. They produce corn, beans and rice and also rear hogs. The building of the twenty miles of road to Punta Gorda has brought the people of San Antonio into closer contact with a wider community and many of them are forsaking the traditional subsistence farming for work in the citrus orchards.

The Kekchi Indians on the other hand still cling to their unsophisticated way of life. They too live in the Toledo District, in villages of not more than 500 people and all within a radius of about forty miles of each other. The Kekchi migrated from the Vera Paz region of Guatemala, some of these migrations being very recent. They tend to be a self-sufficient people growing corn and rearing pigs; they continue the traditional practice of community or group work and still lead lives insulated from modern civilization. Nevertheless the building of roads and the acquisition of radios are bringing changes so that in time the Kekchi too will play a more important part in the life of the country. For the present the principal external influences come from the primary schools and the missions run by American Jesuits. The Kekchi tend to be a religious people who retain some of their own pagan practices alongside the Christian ones. Each village has its own Alcalde (Mayor) who is elected by the villagers but whose appointment is officially recognized. They have kept their own language and few have benefited sufficiently from their schooling to speak English or Spanish correctly. In fact the Kekchis do not even understand Mopan Maya, although as some of them are beginning to inter-marry with their neighbours this may also change in time.

European and Asian immigrants

The census figures for the twentieth century reveal that immigration has played a very minor part in the recent expansion of the population. By 1960 only 7,570 out of a total population of 90,000 were born outside the country. Nevertheless there have been small but significant groups of immigrants in recent years. Some of the most successful business men in the community are the Syrians or Lebanese who have now lived in the country for two or three generations. In 1946 there were only 128 Syrians and 50 Chinese, but although few in number these people have fulfilled an important economic rôle.

A more recent and perhaps more controversial body of immigrants has been the Mennonite community. Originally from Germany, the Mennonites have led a migratory existence in an attempt to win complete freedom for themselves. Many of them settled in the United States and Canada, but the Canadian Government's insistence that their children should attend state schools drove them to northern Mexico. It was from Chihuaha that, for similar reasons, they left for Belize in 1958. They signed a special agreement with the Belize Government which guaranteed them complete freedom to practise their own distinctive form of Protestantism and to farm within their closed communities. Under this agreement they were to pay all their own expenses and they purchased their land outright at an average price of three Belize dollars per acre. This land would cost perhaps four times as much today; they hold nearly 150,000 acres but only a small proportion of this has as yet been cleared and cultivated. As part of the agreement the Mennonites were exempted from military service and from paying contributions to compulsory insurance and other welfare schemes, but they were liable for all other taxes. There are now four separate communities; one is at Spanish Lookout about forty miles west from Belize City, while the others are at Blue Creek on the northern border and in the Orange Walk district. The Mennonites are a distinctive community within the state; in appearance they still look like blond German farmers, speaking a German patois and wearing traditional clothes. The children are not educated beyond primary school and at present all work on their farms. They are totally disinterested in politics and have no wish to take public office or even to use their right to vote. There is naturally some criticism of so exclusive a community, but the Mennonites have shown how hard work and agricultural skill can transform bush into fertile land. Their knowledge of dairy farming has had a marked effect on the economy, and the distribution of their fresh milk and eggs through the Mennonite Centre in Belize City has already made a big change in the eating habits of the people. It will be interesting to see whether the Mennonites are able to retain their separate existence as their communities expand from the present figure of 3,300, and whether they will play a more public part in Belize's affairs.

The Caribs

The two other most important communities are the Creoles and the Caribs. Both lived in the country long before the question of encouraging immigrants was raised: indeed the Creoles, some of whom are descended from the original Baymen and their slaves, tend to think of themselves as the only genuine British Hondurans or Belizeans.

The Caribs are descended from the original Red Carib Amerindians who occupied many of the West Indian islands when they were discovered by Columbus. Carib resistance to European domination earned for them a reputation as ferocious savages, but it was only by their determined self-defence that they survived at all. By the end of the eighteenth century they were confined to the islands of Dominica and St Vincent, where the aboriginal Caribs had been joined by fugitive slaves and other negroes from wrecked ships. The union of the Caribs with the negroes produced the typical Black Carib of Belize and the neighbouring republics. They arrived on the mainland of Central America soon after 1797, the year in which five thousand of them had been deported by the

British to Ruatan after a violent rebellion. From Ruatan they gradually dispersed and established coastal settlements along the northern coast of Honduras to the Livingston area of Guatemala and the south coast of Belize. About 150 of them had already been admitted to the country by 1802, but at first they were regarded with the greatest suspicion and had to be registered. They gradually established that they were hardworking and peaceful and built up their communities in Stann Creek, Punta Gorda and the villages of Hopkins and Seine Beight.

The Caribs have retained their separate identity in spite of the fact that physically they differ little from the Creoles. Few of them have chosen to marry outside their race or to leave the coastal settlements where the majority make their living from fishing and farming. Although they have retained their own language, the majority of Caribs speak English as well. They are an industrious people and those with ambition have been successful in such professions as teaching and the law. Many of the rural schools are staffed entirely by Caribs, who seem to have a facility for acquiring languages and have therefore formed a useful link with the Amerindians of the Toledo District. Yet despite their many gifts the Caribs have failed to win complete social acceptance for themselves and are regarded as different by some Creoles with a consequent lack of self-esteem among some Caribs. In 1946 when the last attempt to classify the population by race was made, the Caribs formed about 7% of the total, but quite a large proportion of these were recent immigrants from the neighbouring republics.

The Creoles

The term 'Creole' as applied to the largest group of people has a somewhat specialized meaning. In the French colonies the word, itself French in origin, is applied only to those of French descent born in the colonies. The word 'criollo' is used in the same sense in the Spanish-speaking areas. But in Belize it signifies those with some African blood and, in a very few cases, some locally born whites. The Creoles form almost 60% of the total population and of these perhaps two-thirds are negro and one-third coloured. The Creoles are centred around Belize City where more than half of them live; English is their language but the less educated speak a Creole dialect which is difficult for outsiders to understand. The Creoles are the main supporters of the Protestant Churches although about a third of them now form a strong Catholic group. They pursue urban occupations and are sometimes resented for their dominance of the administration of the country. By tradition the Creoles have provided the labour for the forestry industry and in the season they are to be found wherever logging is being carried on. Some Creoles carry on small-scale subsistence farming when not engaged in forestry, but there are only a few permanent settlements of Creole farmers, mostly along the Belize River and the western and nothern roads out of Belize City.

Even a brief survey of some of the factors involved in the pattern of settlement and the distribution of population reveals a number of interesting features. As far as the population structure is concerned the most striking feature is the low overall density and the rapid rate of expansion in the last two decades. Another interesting conclusion to emerge is the even distribution of the rural population, a reflection of the growing importance of agriculture. At the same time it should be pointed out that several areas of the country are almost uninhabited, or at least without any permanent settlement. Unusual mobility among the labour force may be the natural result of the traditional methods of employment in the forestry and chicle industries. But it still seems surprising to find that many workers may live at San Ignacio and çommute to work at Central Farm or Augustine: in some cases men may go even further afield and return to their homes only at weekends.

To the visitor the most obvious and interesting fact is the mingling of so many races, within such a small community. This feature has been remarked from the early nineteenth century onwards when travellers such as John L. Stephens commented favourably on the racial inter-mixture. Today there are few families of entirely pure descent in any racial group, but as has been seen, this does not mean that there are not separate groups. It is the task of the government to find means of unifying these groups or communities and giving them all a common sense of identity and nationality as citizens of Belize. The task is by no means easy and is hampered by language problems, traditional habits of isolation and self-sufficiency and not least by prejudice, which though not necessarily based on colour, is equally insidious to eradicate. An important start has been made but it will be a slow process, for no one today would wish to enforce an unnatural uniformity which might lead to the withering away of all the minority languages, customs and arts.

14

The Diversification of the Economy

The population problem of Belize is only one aspect of a broader theme which has dominated the history of the last hundred years. That theme has been the need to diversify the economy, to deliberately bring about a transition from the traditional forest industries to agriculture. Although forestry would never be abandoned altogether, it would no longer provide the sole base for the country's economy. This change in emphasis was apparent as early as 1860 and was given additional impetus by the agricultural success of the Yucatecan refugees in the northern part of the colony. Unfortunately the larger landowners were somewhat sceptical and in any event unwilling to promote large-scale agricultural schemes lest they should lose their skilled forestry labourers to the land. Moreover the men themselves seemed to prefer the irregular life of the mahogany camps and showed little desire to turn to farming with its more settled way of life. This attitude has persisted to the present day among the Creole community and since farming has remained a relatively unattractive occupation this has added to the difficulties of obtaining suitable labour.

The cause of agriculture was promoted by several of the more far-sighted colonial administrators such as Lieutenant-Governor Barlee and by certain individuals such as Frederick Gahné, Editor of the *Colonial Guardian*. But it was obvious that the promotion of agriculture alone was not the answer to the colony's problems, for agriculture itself created new demands. It demanded a larger population to cultivate the land and better communications with the interior. There was little advantage in planting rice, or bananas, or any other perishable commodity, if the journey to market had to be made by slow river transport. The last quarter of the nineteenth century saw continued public debate as to the best routes for the proposed railway from the Atlantic coast to the Guatemalan border and for the most essential roads. In a very real sense these basic requirements—agricultural development, an expanding population and better communications—have contributed to all discussion and economic planning for the last hundred years and today are still the most important factors in economic development. Considerable progress has been made in all these spheres although it has been rather uneven: there have been dramatic spurts followed by severe setbacks, just as in the early years a boom year in mahogany exports seemed to be followed by a slump. Some of these setbacks may have been the result of human failure, but, generally speaking, they have been caused by such external factors as a depression on the world market or natural disasters like a hurricane.

The Declining Rôle of Forestry

As we have seen, the timber trade of British Honduras had always fluctuated; but as the nineteenth century drew to a close without the benefit to the mahogany cutters of any improvements in transport or felling methods, there seemed every prospect that all the timber within the colony would soon be exhausted. This had not yet happened because such a large proportion of the wood was inaccessible to animal haulage. Consequently a relatively small quantity of the total volume of timber had been cut by the beginning of the present century. Nevertheless the threat of timber exhaustion was constantly being cited by officials who argued for the encouragement of agriculture. In his speech to the Legislative Council in January 1872 the Administrator, R. W. Harley, made this very clear when he said: 'I have much pleasure in noticing that Mahogany, the old staple of the Colony, has become so enhanced in value, as to give encouragement to the wood-cutting interest of the Colony, but I cannot impress too strongly upon all, that however valuable the natural productions of the Country may be, the cultivation of the soil must be the main source from which its future wealth and prosperity will flow'. Thus, although there were years in which mahogany did well—there was even a small boom around 1900 in response to a sudden demand from the United States—it was already evident that the years of ruthless exploitation of the forests had taken their toll. The largest and best trees had been cut without any thought of replanting and since natural regeneration is not only slow but a very wasteful process there was little prospect of further prosperity from timber.

Nevertheless at the end of the First World War (1918) important changes occurred which transformed the forest industry. Until that time the traditional methods of cutting, uncontrolled exploitation and animal haulage were in use, so that there are still old men alive today who can tell stories about felling huge trees with axes, hauling them to the river with the aid of oxen and floating them down to the boom at the river mouth. But in 1918 the situation appeared so grave that an experienced forestry officer was asked to make a report on the future of the industry. As a direct result of Hummel's report the first Forest Department was set up in 1922. From this date a definite attempt was made to introduce intensive forest management aimed at a policy of conservation and sustained yield in contrast to the old unchecked methods.

The introduction of mechanization

The second revolutionary feature of the 1920s was the introduction of tractors. These rapidly transformed logging operations since timber, which had hitherto been too far from the rivers to bring out by oxen, could now be reached, and an attempt was made to extract wood from hilly and rougher terrain. Skidding equipment and huge log-wagons were also brought into use. The logs were skidded to assembly points in the forest, loaded onto a train of four or six wagons and then hauled by tractor to the river, which was normally about twenty miles away, but could sometimes be as far as forty miles. The old dependence on river transport was therefore perpetuated with the result that no permanent roads were built and logging operations were still confined to the dry season. The few roads and railway tracks that were built extended only from the centre of logging operations to the nearest river. Nevertheless the use of tractors did boost the failing industry by opening up new areas. However, it was not for another twenty years that the real revolution in transport came with the introduction of huge trucks and heavy road-building machinery such as bull-dozers.

This enabled the Forest Department to build all-weather roads which could be used to transport the timber from the forests rapidly and economically throughout the year. Moreover, these innovations made it possible to exploit the relatively virgin forests in the south. The largest private timber concern, the Belize Estate and Produce Company, successor of the old British Honduras Company, is still heavily dependent on water transport.

The development of road transport has been of great importance in the post-war forest industry. The construction of a road from the Western Highway into the Chiquibul Forest has brought about the exploitation of valuable cedar and mahogany forest; at the same time it serves the large pine forest in the Mountain Pine Ridge area and is also used for the transport of chicle. Today the Belize River no longer carries floating logs; the boom has been dismantled and the great trucking camions use the Western Highway to bring logs from Guatemala to Belize City.

Felling by mechanical means has also been introduced with great effect. The use of mechanical saws and other modern techniques enables timber to be extracted more rapidly using a much smaller labour force. The inevitable result of this increased exploitation has been the rapid depletion of forest resources. In order to counteract this trend the Forest Department has taken various steps to enforce more systematic forest management, but, as it was not until 1944 that legislation was introduced, it was almost too late to control felling on private land. However this legislation together with the example set by the Department has now begun to have a beneficial effect.

Forestry control

In the early years of its existence the Forest Department only had sufficient resources to collect information about the forest stocks and to begin small-scale restocking procedures on Crown lands. In 1933 a detailed assessment was made of the measures needed for the regeneration of the forests; the recommendations made then formed the basis of policy for the next few years. The main tasks of the Department were seen as the creation of forest reserves, the enumeration of resources, the enforcement of sustained yield management and the control of felling on private land. One example of this policy is the scheme drawn up for the Chiquibul Forest Reserve based on controlled felling under licence for ten years. Under this scheme each licensee has to cut all the mahogany and cedar trees included in the annual *coupe* over 7 feet 6 inches in girth; he is also obliged to cut a certain volume of secondary hardwoods annually, and to build a specified mileage of permanent roads. This policy is beginning to show good results, but in the northern forests mahogany had already been felled to such a low girth that there was little prospect of natural regeneration. The smaller private owners have been particularly reckless both in this way and in selective felling of the best trees without any regard for the future.

The B.E.P.C. Sawmill, 1933

The twentieth century has seen not only revolutionary changes in transport, felling techniques and forestry control, but also in the nature of the end product. The real revolution in this respect came as early as 1933 with the opening of the Belize Estate Company's sawmill. This was in itself something of a controversial undertaking as the Company, like every other firm and indeed individual in the colony, had been hard hit by the disastrous hurricane of 1931. Two months after the hurricane the Company approached the Royal Bank of Canada for a substantial loan but, despite government support, the loan was refused. The Bank's Manager, Mr Beattie, maintained that the Company was being mismanaged and if it had to sell out the colony would benefit. The Company therefore appealed directly to the Government for financial aid. The Hurricane Loan Ordinance, authorized by the British Government, provided for 100,000 dollars to be made available to the Company out of the total loan of 1,100,000 dollars. Still not satisfied with this offer and despite the objections of some members of the Legislative Council, the Company asked that the amount should be doubled. In a Message to the Legislative Council the Governor recommended that this request should be granted 'if Honourable Members accept the premise that it would be disadvantageous to the Colony for the Company to close down its operation'. The British Government clearly regarded the Company's continued existence as essential to the colony's economic recovery, for not only was the additional loan granted but financed out of that part of the loan originally assigned for agricultural development.

Part of this Government loan was used to open the first sawmill in the country. Until the mill opened in 1933 all mahogany and cedar was exported in the form of logs, but the quantity of sawn lumber now increased rapidly. Several smaller portable sawmills were gradually brought into use and by 1965 there were twenty-six mills in operation although the primary purpose of some of these was to clear land for agricultural use. Additional help was given to the Belize Estate Company shortly after the first mill began operations by the removal of the export tax on sawn mahogany. The tax on mahogany logs remained at 2.50 dollars per one thousand feet.

Pine and chicle

Another striking development during the last twenty-five years has been the exploitation of timber other than first grade hardwoods. Pine forest covers about 12–15% of the total area of country but, until 1940, pine for building was imported from the United States. Since then the general shortage of softwoods, combined with the purely local demand for suitable constructional timber, has led to large-scale pine felling. Pine grows on the coastal lowlands and more compactly in the Maya Mountains. The peak of production was probably reached about 1955, but the excellent natural regeneration of pine (a tree reaches maturity in twenty-five years), together with the careful policy of the Forest Department should ensure a steady supply in the future. The most serious problem is the susceptibility of the young tree to fire, so that in the Pine Ridge forests the main concern has been the establishment of fire protection procedures. A series of fire lines has been constructed around Augustine and these measures have been reasonably successful.

Pine extraction requires local mills to make production profitable. Therefore, once all the timber has been extracted from a particular area, the local mill has to be closed with consequent disruption of employment. Although there is an insufficient supply of pine to make pulp or paper mills profitable, two unsuccessful attempts have been made to start resin extraction mills. An American company opened a resin mill at Mango Creek in 1963, but was forced to move to Nicaragua after only two years because of the inadequacy of the preparatory survey and alleged labour difficulties. Nor has the promotion of such secondary hardwoods as santa maria and ziricote yet proved very successful; the lack of world demand is especially unfortunate in this case as the extraction of these woods from the forest would help the regeneration of mahogany.

Chicle is the other forest product which at one time played a considerable rôle in the economy. Chicle is obtained by bleeding the sapodilla tree for its latex which is then boiled until hard blocks can be made and exported to the manufacturers of chewing gum in the United States. Since the Second World War competition from synthetic substitutes and other varieties of chicle has coincided with a decline in demand: there has consequently been a substantial drop in the amount of chicle produced and exported.

The forest industry has therefore declined in the absolute sense: for the long-term depletion of the forests' resources has at last caught up with its exploiters. Only time and skill can restock the exhausted areas. In a more relative sense, forestry has declined in relation to other parts of the national economy. Until 1945 forest produce amounted to about 90% of the country's total exports, but this figure has now declined to somewhere between 25 and 30%. In 1959 the combined output of sugar and citrus exceeded timber for the first time; this trend has continued to the present day. Between 1960 and 1964 the decline of timber and chicle in relation to the rise in sugar and citrus is illustrated by the following table of domestic exports:

B.H. $ million

	1960	1961	1962	1963	1964
Domestic Exports	10.164	11.186	8.252	15.430	17.903
Sugar	2.206	4.021	3.853	5.125	6.242
Citrus	3.128	3.507	1.428	3.812	4.489
Timber	3.521	2.153	1.837	2.687	2.856
Chicle	0.493	0.434	0.392	0.236	0.247

From the Report of Tripartite Economic Survey of British Honduras, 1966.

This transformation of the whole basis of the economy is emphasized by the change in occupation figures. From 1946 to 1960 the number of workers engaged in agriculture rose by over 4,000 while those employed in forest industries dropped by 700. This trend has continued and has doubtless been accelerated by the Government's changed policy towards forestry as outlined in its 1964–70 Development Plan.

The 1964–1970 Development Plan

The early intensive exploitation of forest resources was an appropriate activity for a country with a small population and very limited labour force. But the population explosion which is now taking place has brought with it the need to expand agriculture in order to feed the people and to cut down on the traditional but expensive import of foodstuffs. Thus, although large areas of Belize are more suited to forestry than agriculture, land is increasingly being cleared for farming. When there is competition for land the swifter return on capital obtained by agriculture always ensures that it will triumph. The 1964–70 Development Plan argues that 'A country with limited resources and a desire for higher production as early as possible must use its resources in quicker yielding investment projects'. It also points out that, despite the declining importance to the economy of forest products, expenditure on forestry has always been high. Government policy should therefore aim to lower these costs by reducing the level of forest activity. Only a minimal amount of reafforestation work should be carried out although the natural regeneration of pine ought to be encouraged. Forest legislation should be enforced and fire protection continued in the forest reserves. On the other hand the Plan brought the Forest Department's road-building programme to a halt and led to a drastic reduction in the number of staff. This serious revision in the work of the Forest Department did not altogether meet with the approval of the Tripartite Economic Mission in 1966. The Mission's report pointed out that a large proportion of the country would always be covered by forest which could still make a valuable contribution to the economy.

The Development of Agriculture

The impetus given to agriculture by the immigration of small farmers from Yucatán was, at first, largely confined to the production of sugar and rum in the northern part of the colony. In 1862 the first attempt to export sugar was made and during the next five years the amount of sugar manufactured rose from 397,176 lbs in 1862 to 1,336,496 lbs in 1866. In 1867 over 50,000 gallons of rum were produced, of which 5,000 gallons were exported. The success of these operations encouraged other groups of immigrants to experiment with crops such as coffee and cacao, but few of these experiments met with success. During the 1870s there was a period of general stagnation and gloom in the colony which was all the more striking in view of the prosperous banana trade carried on between the Central American republics and New Orleans.

Sir Frederick Barlee became Governor in 1877. He was an outstandingly energetic man who was not afraid to adopt controversial measures to ensure the prosperity of the colony under his charge. Barlee's first step was to make an unprecedented tour of inspection which enabled him to see for himself many of the problems at first hand. He then instituted a series of reforms designed to develop the economy. Perhaps the most important of these was to change the mail subsidy from Jamaica to the New Orleans route since this opened up the possibility of exporting bananas to the American market. As neither the commercial nor passenger traffic from Belize was sufficient to support a regular scheduled service a government subsidy was essential. The route had already been changed several times but Barlee's action was intended to stimulate agriculture as well as to pay for the mail service. The immediate result was heavy investment in banana production and within a few years the trade was extremely prosperous until over-production brought the usual penalty of depression.

Another important measure taken by Barlee was the abolition of the excise tax on sugar and the more efficient collection of taxes on rum. The excise duty had tended to discourage the production of sugar on the small cane plots in the north, and its abolition encouraged both the growth of cane and the production of rum. With the stricter enforcement of the distillery tax there was an immediate gain to the colony's revenues. Despite these measures, changes in world market conditions brought about a steady decline in exports of sugar and rum from Belize in the last few years of the nineteenth century. Competition from sugar-beet had already put paid to the efforts of the pioneer Americans in the Toledo settlement. It was not until just before the Second World War that there was a revival of interest in sugar production.

Attempts to introduce new crops

Meanwhile a number of different crops including coffee, cocoa and cotton, had been tried out on small estates. Daniel Morris, Curator of the Jamaica Botanical Gardens, visited British Honduras in 1882 and wrote a vivid account of the agriculture of the time. But ten years later many of the estates visited by Morris had closed down. Faulty management, difficulties in transporting produce to the coast and uncertainty on world markets had all to some extent contributed to this lack of progress. Where management was more efficient, as in the German-run Kramer estates, coffee and cocoa were successfully produced; in 1890 the total coffee requirements of the colony were grown internally as well as a small surplus for export. Cocoa was grown by the same management on the Sittee and Sarstoon Rivers. At the turn of the century a variety of grasses and fodder crops were beginning to be grown to feed the oxen needed for logging work and also the beef cattle for the local market.

At this date the most popular cash crop produced by the small farmers after they had grown their own supplies of corn was without doubt bananas and plantains. Not only were these sold on the Belize market, but large estates began to plant bananas for export to the United States. In 1891 half a million stems were exported and the industry continued to expand. Banana production required only a small but permanent labour force. This was more satisfactory to the large producers than a seasonal labour force inclined to disappear to the forests and not return for harvesting. But, after the rapid development of banana cultivation in the Stann Creek Valley, there was an equally rapid decline with the onset of Panama disease, attack from rats and the difficulties caused by the use of poor soils and the shifting *milpa* type of cultivation. By 1906 the export of bananas had declined to only 750,000 stems. However, although the large-scale producers cut their losses and withdrew from banana production, this remained a popular concern with many smallholders. Even dwindling markets and the development of leaf-spot and Panama disease did not deter peasant farmers, who ignored government warnings to such an extent that in 1937 there was a shortage of corn and cassava in the Toledo and Stann Creek districts. Among other crops successfully exported over a period of years were coconuts. Like cocoa the latter are particularly susceptible to hurricane damage and small farmers are now reluctant to grow either crop on a sufficiently large basis to make their export worth while.

The establishment of an Agriculture Department, 1928

The organization of agriculture was left to private individuals and at first the government played little active part, its only positive action was to set up an Agricultural Board in 1879. The Board was to supply the growers and exporters of fruits with information and to offer various bonuses for successful exports. When a Department of Agriculture was eventually established in 1928 the old Board became redundant. For the first twenty years of its existence the Agricultural Department had only a small budget and staff: as late as 1948 it consisted of only three senior and twelve junior members. The essential work of agricultural research and demonstration was therefore limited but was nevertheless the beginning of a more scientific approach to agriculture. In 1933 district agricultural stations were set up in order to provide demonstration centres for the small farmers but this policy was abandoned when Central Farm was set up in 1948. At Central Farm research is carried out and practical demonstrations made of the use of fertilizers, cover crops and approved methods of cultivation. The need for local agricultural stations has again been recognized and these have been revived. At the same time attempts are being made to encourage an interest in agriculture at the primary school level. The aim of the most recent Development Plan for the country in this field was stated to be 'the teaching of the rudiments of scientific agriculture in all rural schools, the development of Lynam College and of the School of Agriculture at Central Farm to produce farmers, farm supervisors and agricultural administrators'.

Today agriculture is the most vital sector of the economy and its continued development is essential to the future prosperity of the country. Agriculture in Belize falls into two distinct groups: the first covers the export sector, mainly citrus and sugar; the second is the domestic sector which provides fruit, vegetables, dairy produce and meat for the home market. The success of the domestic sector is as important as the first since only by its expansion can the country's traditional reliance on imported foodstuffs be ended. The tendency is for the production of the export groups to be concentrated on the larger more productive farms, while the domestic sector is supplied by the less efficient peasant type of farming. It was calculated in 1964 that of 10,000 people engaged in agriculture some 75% were working in small farming units. Since the one great advantage the country possesses is its large area of agricultural land in relation to the available man-power it is essential to increase each man's productivity.

The sugar industry

The expansion of both sugar and citrus has been a comparatively recent development. Sugar continued to be produced for the local market but the export market declined steadily from the turn of the century until, in 1937, a mill was installed near Corozal capable of producing 3,000 tons of sugar a year. In fact only a third of this total was achieved at first. The colony was given an export quota of 1,000 tons of sugar a year in the International Sugar Agreement of 1937, but this was rendered inoperative by the outbreak of war in 1939. At first the cane for the mill was grown by small planters and the yield was very low, only twelve tons per acre as against forty tons from scientific planting. But the sugar content was high and after the war the industry expanded very rapidly. Belize was given an export quota of 5,000 tons in 1953 and by 1961 over 27,000 tons of sugar were exported to Britain. The mill was enlarged and in 1964 was taken over by Messrs Tate and Lyle Ltd. This company is now known in Belize as the Belize Sugar Industries Ltd. Under the new management a thorough overhaul of plant and methods has been undertaken and in 1970 nearly 67,000 tons of sugar were produced. Nevertheless the yield per acre remains low and the current Development Plan provides for instruction to the small producers on the use of fertilizers and the need to plant new canes more regularly. The new sugar company plants about half the cane it uses on its own land; it also leases land to planters and buys cane from small producers.

The industry is no longer confined entirely to the Corozal area. In 1965-6 a new mill was built at Tower Hill, near Orange Walk; with over 9,000 acres of land under cane it is expected to increase the sugar output considerably. The process of mechanization has begun and machines are now being used to harvest the cane. One machine tended by three men will cut 250 tons of cane in a day, while a good labourer using his machete could only hope to cut four tons at the most. At the factories the crushed cane has the molasses driven out of it by force; the end product is clean brown sugar which is then sent to Liverpool for refining at the Tate & Lyle refinery. Government measures have greatly assisted the cane planters by regulating the industry, by appointing a cane farming officer and setting up a Sugar Board. Improved techniques have all had a good effect and the fact that a large part of the sugar produced is sold under a negotiated price protects the industry to some extent from the problem of fluctuating prices on the world market.

Citrus growing

Citrus production, on the other hand, suffers severely from price vicissitudes, although, in some respects, it shares marked similarities with the sugar industry. Citrus growing is also localized largely in the Stann Creek Valley where it is produced mainly on big estates. As in the case of sugar there has been a rapid expansion since 1945, but a small export trade of good quality fruit began as early as 1925. Indeed the quality of the fruit was so outstanding that it won medals in several Imperial Fruit Shows. In 1928 the Governor spoke to the members of the Legislative Council of the importance of the newly developing industry and urged growers to take advantage of the experience of the newly appointed Agricultural Officer in selecting stock and combating disease. He went on to point out the importance of the new industry and advised that the colony's best hope of success lay in quality rather than quantity. This is still the case today when world markets are threatened with a glut in citrus. The industry is now in the hands of two large firms. The original Jamaican firm of Sharpe Brothers has been incorporated into the Citrus Company of British Honduras Ltd and produces tinned orange juice. The Canadian firm of Salada Foods has 3,000 acres in the Stann Creek District and its plant can handle up to half a million boxes of oranges each year, producing the frozen concentrate so popular on the North American markets. The current Development Plan provided for the expansion of acreage under citrus from 7,000 to 10,000 acres by 1970 and proposed to help the small citrus growers to increase their yield.

As sugar and citrus have replaced timber's rôle as the most important export commodity their production has been considered in some detail. But there are now a plentiful variety of other crops which are being grown for domestic use such as tobacco, beans, rice, coffee and corn. Not only livestock farming but the fishing industry has an important contribution to make to the economy. Recently a thriving export trade in lobster tails has been established. Unlike most of the other industries fishing is entirely controlled by Belizeans themselves, often through the use of Co-operatives. In the future other commodities may turn out to be as successful and profitable to the country as sugar and citrus have proved in the recent past.

Land Tenure and Taxation

The haphazard nature of land registration in the early history of the colony has already been noticed. It was not until 1859 that a Lands Title Registry was set up so that every parcel of land registered bestowed an indefeasible right on the owner. Thirteen years later legislation was enacted to ensure that Crown lands were regulated and in that same year the Governor announced the appointment of the first qualified Surveyor-General.

The early alienation of the land in large blocks at high prices had two very damaging consequences which are still evident in the existing land structure. The first was that only wealthy men could afford to buy land so neither local small farmers nor prospective immigrants could take up farming on their own account. As Governor Barlee discovered when he tried to change the land tenure system, he was powerless against the opposition of the wealthy landowners. He was able to reduce the price of Crown lands to as little as one dollar per acre and to institute a standard survey fee, but he could do nothing about the privately held lands in the Northern District where the landowners would neither sell their land, nor compensate their tenants for improvements. The *Colonial Guardian* fulminated against the iniquities of a feudal system of land tenure which favoured the powerful landowning classes and drove the small farmers to despair, but it was not until the introduction of the location ticket system in 1915 that a genuine attempt was made to assist small farmers to own their land.

The second unfortunate result of land tenure arrangements which had developed in such piecemeal fashion was the poor utilization of the land available for agriculture. Only recently has it been realized that the large amount of cultivable land in relation to the population is a potentially favourable factor in the developing economy. Increasing mechanization will enable larger areas of land to be placed under crops and the productivity per acre increased. In the past, division of the land into large estates, often owned by absentee landlords, meant that much of the suitable agricultural land was simply not cultivated. A careful survey of land use was made in 1959 which showed that of over two million acres of land suitable for cultivation (38% of the total acreage) only about 5% was at that time being exploited.

Introduction of a land utilization tax

In order to put an end to this absurd situation the present Government introduced the Rural Land Utilization Tax in 1966 which was designed to stop large-scale land speculation and at the same time to encourage the settlement of rural land. In introducing the Bill to the House of Representatives the Minister of Natural Resources, Mr Hunter, described how certain land speculators had been making huge profits by the sale of large estates. Government was determined that the land should be made available to the small farmers who wished to put it to productive use, and the Bill therefore proposed to introduce a tax from which small holdings under one hundred acres and land which had been permanently improved would be exempt. The tax would vary according to the land's distance from the nearest road, but its effect would be to induce owners to cultivate or sell their land at the current market price. The Minister pointed out that altogether only 365 persons held land in excess of one hundred acres, and of these the 181 who were not Belize nationals held by far the greatest quantity of land. He concluded his important speech by saying: 'We shall demand from those in possession of our land a contribution to the national welfare commensurate with the privilege which they enjoy. It is an act of economic emancipation marking a watershed in our history'. It is still too early to say whether the new tax will realize all the hopes placed on it, but a start has been made in encouraging the development of all suitable land and together with other government measures positive benefits should soon be visible.

Land holding and taxation

In the late nineteenth century several large agricultural estates were beginning to be planted with sugar, bananas or cocoa but most of the farming was carried on either by small-holders or by tenant farmers. The small-holdings tended either to be situated along the rivers, usually Creole, or in coastal settlements, usually Carib. The tenant farmers were almost all Indians renting land on an annual basis on the large private estates in the north. An attempt had been made about 1880 to settle the Indians in the Cayo District on small allotments, but these generally proved too small and the Indians continued their traditional pattern of shifting *milpa* cultivation. Until the introduction of the location system in 1915 few farmers could afford to cultivate their land throughout the year and many worked in the forests during the logging season, only attending to their farms in intervals between employment. This pattern of cultivation still survives to some extent; many of the Maya from the Toledo District seek work on the citrus plantations leaving their *milpas* in the temporary care of other members of the family.

The system of location tickets can only be applied to Crown lands. The applicant for land is given a ticket which makes him a tenant-at-will without further rights. The purchase price for the land has to be paid in ten semi-annual instalments; the applicant then has to plant at least half of the total area with permanent crops within five years. The system was commended in a report prepared for the International Bank in 1954 as 'an admirable one for encouraging farmers to settle permanently on the land'. Another method by which small farmers have been helped in the past is the reservation of certain areas of land, often conveyed to the Crown in lieu of taxes, for renting by small-holders. The average size of such holdings is about fifteen acres. A different type of reserve has been created for Maya Indians in the Toledo District. On payment of five dollars a year (1948 figure) any Maya between the ages of 18 and 80 can occupy as much land as he needs for cultivating in the reserve. In practice this usually amounts to about ten acres cultivated on a rotation basis. There are no Indian reserves in the other districts: and many Maya now work for wages, particularly on the large sugar estates in the Corozal and Orange Walk Districts.

When the first land taxes were introduced in 1871 they were based on the old system of the mahogany works. The tax was eight dollars for every mile or part of a mile of the base line of a timber works on a navigable river. The amount was increased but the system itself continued until 1907 when land was taxed at a rate of half a cent per acre. This amount was gradually increased to one-and-a-half cents until in 1931 it was raised to two-and-a-half cents per acre, of which one cent was set aside for developing agriculture and roads. Although the rate of taxation was still very low the large landowners, including the Belize Estate Company, objected so much to the increase from one-and-a-half cents to two-and-a-half cents that for four years they refused to pay the tax. In 1935 the Government was obliged to give way on this point and the rate was once more reduced to one-and-a-half cents with retrospective effect from 1931.

In the days of the government railway in the Stann Creek Valley (1908–37) a special tax was levied on all land which lay within two miles of the line. At first this was at the rate of ten cents per acre, but by 1935 it was as high as fifty cents an acre on all land within one mile of the railway. Exemptions were granted to land that was properly developed, as was usually true of small holdings, but several large estates were surrendered to the Crown in default of payment. When the railway was removed and the track made into a road it was decided that it was no longer fair to tax landowners in the Stann Creek Valley at a different rate from those in other areas of the colony, and the tax reverted to the general one of one-and-a-half cents per acre. The non-payment of the tax has led to quite large areas of land being returned to Crown use although it was often the less valuable land that was surrendered. In recent years the general land tax has been altered so that it can be adjusted to the type of land and its proximity to roads, but even this graduated tax is no more than a revenue measure. During the last ten years most official reports on the economy of Belize have recommended that land taxation should be used as an instrument in the policy of developing the agricultural economy and, at the same time, as a social measure which could secure greater justice for the small farmers.

Currency and Banking

The history of the currency used in Belize is of some interest and is itself an integral part of the country's economic history. In the early days of the settlement Jamaican currency was in occasional use but the more regular form of exchange was by means of logwood and later mahogany. At a meeting held at St George's Cay in May 1766 it was agreed that 'all debts contracted in the Bay of Honduras shall be payable in logwood unless there shall be a special agreement made between the parties in writing to the contrary'. At the same meeting certain penalties were imposed for various named offences which were to be payable in 'Bay currency' —presumably this meant in logwood. In 1784 the local regulations were altered so that in future all business was to be transacted in Jamaican currency. Mahogany was now given the fixed price of £15 per thousand feet; by expressing the price of mahogany in sterling a link was made with the Jamaican currency which was to continue for some time.

In 1825 the British Government tried to introduce British silver coins throughout her colonies and the circular despatch to the Superintendent of Honduras stated that one Spanish dollar was to be regarded as the equivalent of 4s. 4d. But both in Jamaica and Honduras the official rating was rejected and the shilling was re-named a 'maccaroni' or quarter dollar. During the first half of the nineteenth century the important entrepôt trade from Belize to Central America meant that Spanish American coins such as pesos and reales were the dominant currency in circulation. The Californian gold rush and the increasing influence of the United States brought American gold dollars into circulation so that it became imperative to clarify the confused currency situation. In 1855 the Legislative Assembly passed an Act which laid down that all public accounts were to be kept in dollars and reales, a dollar was to be equivalent to four shillings sterling. The reale was to be one-eighth of this sum, but shortly afterwards reales were abolished and henceforth local currency was expressed in dollars and cents.

Unfortunately the measures of the 1850s were inadequate to deal with the confused state of the currency. Mr Dieseldorff, one of the leading merchants of British Honduras, wrote in 1860 to the Superintendent about the proposal that the amount of silver currency in use should be limited as legal tender. He described the existing confusion and explained why there was such a preference for silver coins: 'There being no Bank in the Colony and no kind of paper money, the currency is purely metallic, consisting of British gold and silver chiefly, of Spanish doubloons and parts, Spanish silver and foreign gold and silver coins, all having a current value established by custom. There is a constant exportation of the precious metals to the United States of America and England. The merchants on that coast (i.e. neighbouring republics) have made us their Bankers, and send here their Bills, chiefly on the U.S. for negotiations and returns in specie—and so great is the preference of silver over gold for this purpose, that these transactions have lately been coupled with the one universal request, "send us, if you can, all silver money".' Dieseldorff went on to say that the limitation of silver would be an unmitigated evil in these circumstances.

So wide a variety of coins continued to circulate in the colony that, in his address to the Legislative Council in November 1884, Governor Goldsworthy actually said that not only was the currency question of urgent importance but that the present position was a disgrace to a British colony. The merchants tried to remedy the situation from time to time by declaring that certain coins would be received at stated rates. In this way it was agreed that the Mexican dollar should be equivalent to 100 local cents, but the Guatemalan and Chilean dollars only 87½ cents. In 1887 the position was simplified by a proclamation which made the silver peso or Guatemalan dollar the legal unit in the colony and introduced bronze cent pieces. This solution did not survive for long. By 1894 the colony's trade with the United States, through New Orleans, had expanded greatly at the expense of the Central American trade. As a result it was decided to adopt the gold standard and the United States dollar took the place of the Guatemalan; local money was linked with sterling but the British Honduras dollar followed the American in its exchange rates with sterling. This system lasted until 1950 when the B.H. dollar was devalued three months after the pound sterling. From 31 December 1949 the rate of exchange became 4 B.H. dollars = £1 sterling; from this date the link with the U.S. dollar ceased to exist and British Honduras joined the sterling exchange system. Accordingly the B.H. dollar was again devalued by 14·3% in November 1967 shortly after the British devaluation of that year.

For over two hundred years the leading merchants had acted as bankers in a private capacity. It was not until 1904 that a group of local men founded the Bank of British Honduras and began to issue notes which were legally linked with dollars and an exact equivalent in value. Eight years later in 1912 the Royal Bank of Canada bought out this first bank and continued to exercise a note-issuing function until 1937 when the Currency Commission was founded. The Commission took over the task of providing currency, but it has no control over the amount of local currency in circulation. It issues currency against sterling lodged in London and redeems it at a fixed rate. Until recently the local currency had to be backed by 100% or even 110% sterling, but since 1954 the Currency Board has been allowed to issue up to 800,000 dollars backed by local securities, so introducing more flexibility into the system. In 1949 Barclay's established a bank in Belize City and both Barclay's and the Royal Bank now have branches in several of the principal towns. In 1968 the Bank of Nova Scotia was opened and a fourth bank, the Atlantic, opened its doors in August 1971. In addition to these commercial banks there is an important Government Savings Bank which operates from Belize as well as a Credit Union system which is distributed throughout the country and which plays an important rôle in mobilizing the savings of the small farmers and in helping with emergency loans to members. The many local Co-operatives also play an important part in the developing economy.

Public Works and Expenditure

The first Surveyor of Public Works was appointed in 1852 after a period in which the local government had already made various attempts to improve living conditions in Belize and to provide certain amenities. From that year British Honduras had a Department with the specific task of supervising public works. In the 1858 Blue Book, to take one example, it was reported that the Department had completed the new gaol, some school buildings and made improvements to the city streets. During the closing decades of the nineteenth century various schemes to improve the quality of life for the inhabitants of the colony were discussed. At the same time plans to assist economic development were under consideration. These schemes were not necessarily the responsibility of the Public Works Department, but they came into the category of work for the public good. They had two main objectives: the improvement of the water supplies, sewage and harbour facilities in the town of Belize, and the opening of a railway from the capital to some part of Guatemala.

The Siccama Plan, 1880

A comprehensive plan of municipal improvements was devised by an experienced engineer, Baron Siccama, during Governor Barlee's administration. The plan, as first published in 1880, proposed to improve sanitary conditions by dredging the south and north side canals, filling in low-lying town lots, increasing water storage facilities and building a pier. The estimated cost of the scheme was 150,000 dollars which was far beyond the capacity of the local treasury. The Secretary of State, Lord Kimberly, authorized work to begin on one part of the scheme and it was agreed to begin by increasing the water supply for Belize. Barlee told the Legislative Council that although the whole of Siccama's plan had met with approval in London, no further steps were to be taken until, as the Secretary of State insisted, 'the Council have agreed to some well considered scheme under which the outlay will be eventually borne by the town, the inhabitants of which are more particularly interested in the matter'. A local committee was therefore formed to see how the necessary funds could be raised.

When Governor Goldsworthy took up his post in Belize in 1884 he ignored the recommendations made by this committee and awarded the contracts for dredging the canals to a Mr C. T. Hunter. He also made Hunter's brother the Colonial Surgeon and generally showed great favour towards the family. The scandal which ensued not only led to violent antipathy towards Goldsworthy, but produced a constitutional crisis in the colony and effectively ended the hopes of implementing Siccama's plan as a whole. Briefly, Hunter was given *carte blanche* to dredge the canals with complete disregard for the sanitary requirements previously announced. Instead of carrying out the work in the cool, wet season, the sewage was dredged in the heat of summer and piled on the canal banks rather than being sunk at sea. Although Dr Alexander Hunter had at first been most emphatic that strict precautions should be taken, he changed his opinion when his brother was awarded the contract, as did Governor Goldsworthy. The predictable result was an outbreak of yellow fever and a disease described as 'canal fever'. Since the regular labourers refused to do the work prisoners were set to work at one-third the usual wage and were issued with special boots at the public expense.

In the autumn of 1886 after two years of Goldsworthy's maladministration the colony rejoiced at his departure for London.

The surplus funds which had been so carefully amassed by Governor Barlee had been squandered and the colony was heavily in debt; it was little wonder that the day of the Governor's departure was treated as a public holiday. Unfortunately for British Honduras Goldsworthy was sent back to Belize after a short leave. As Administrator in the interval, Henry Fowler was able to carry out a number of popular measures which included the cancellation of one of Hunter's contracts and the seizure of his dredging equipment. As a result Hunter sued the colonial government for damages and a complicated lawsuit took place which was partly settled in Belize and partly in London. It was the ramifications of this case which brought about demands for constitutional reform which will be considered in the next chapter.

Railway projects

The plans for a railway attracted much public attention during the 1880s and '90s but were little more successful. It was not simply a question of choosing the most desirable route and interesting investors in the construction of a railway; the whole question was entangled with diplomatic considerations relating to the Guatemalan road. Agitation for the construction of a railway had been widespread in Belize for a number of years. The desired immigration of capital and labour which had been hoped for after the American Civil War had failed to materialize, and it was widely believed that the lack of communications with the fertile lands of the interior was responsible. Build a railway line, ran the argument, and immigrants would pour in to seek their fortunes and colonize the country at the same time. The expansion of railways in Central America during the 1870s only lent added support to these arguments.

The main point at issue was the route to be selected. Should the line follow the Belize and Sibún Rivers westwards to the Cayo district and across the frontier to the rich forests of the Petén? Or should it take a more southerly direction to Cobán in the Guatemalan province of Alta Vera Paz? The advantage of the second route was that it might eventually connect up with the existing line from San José on the Pacific to Guatemala City, while the economic advantages of exploiting the timber of the Petén needed no emphasizing.

In 1884 a public meeting of about 800 persons took place in

Belize to consider railway proposals laid before the government by an American promoter, Walter Regan. The local merchants evidently felt the need to bring pressure to bear on the government for they summoned the meeting in order to appeal to the working classes for their help. Regan's railway would take the south-westerly direction towards Cobán which would pass through Crown lands and open up some of the healthy hilly regions of the colony. The Regan proposals were ignored by Governor Goldsworthy; the *Colonial Guardian* which supported them alleged that Fowler, then Colonial Secretary, had blocked the Regan plan from self-interested motives. Fowler owned a large area of land in the Cayo region which would be enhanced in value by a railroad to the Petén and it seems that there must have been some truth in these serious charges since Fowler took no legal action against the newspaper.

Meanwhile an independent assessment of the various railroad proposals had been made by a distinguished scholar, archaeologist and traveller, Sir Alfred Maudslay. In the course of his journeys through Central America in search of Mayan ruins, Maudslay had an unrivalled opportunity to observe the possible effects of building a railway. He felt that the matter was of such importance that he decided to submit a memorandum to the Foreign Office on the subject. His reasoned arguments came out in support of a railway from Belize to the Petén provided this could be built as a government measure in lieu of the proposed cart road of the 1859 Guatemalan Treaty. Maudslay thought that to be financially viable the line must be extended into the Petén with the consent of the Guatemalan Government. He commented in favour of such a railway as follows:

1. The facility it would afford for the transport of timber which cannot profitably be hauled to the river banks.
2. The immense increase in the facility for the transport of logwood.
3. The opening up of a large district suitable to fruit culture.
4. The increase of trade with Petén.
5. The access given to some of the most promising land in the colony around the edges of the great southern Pine ridge, and to the south of it, land which must otherwise remain valueless.

This memorandum was forwarded to Lord Salisbury late in 1887 along with some relevant maps, but for some reason the document never reached the officials for whom it was intended until 1890 when it came to light again and was used as the basis of discussions with Guatemala during the 1890s. In London the question of a railway for British Honduras was never of great concern to the officials in the Colonial Office who had far more weighty problems to deal with during this period. Nevertheless some attempt was made to argue the case for the colonists after the mass public demonstration of 1884. The Foreign Office still hoped for the final settlement of the boundary question; and both in Guatemala and Belize it was felt that all the problems could be settled by building a railway. But, as was so often the case, the Treasury had the last word and no subsidy for a railway was forthcoming.

In 1892 a light railway was opened by Governor Moloney from Stann Creek to Melinda; it had been built privately with the specific object of developing the growing fruit industry and it was never regarded as an answer to the more general problems of agricultural development. It did, however, have a beneficial effect on the fruit industry. In 1896 Moloney himself wrote a memorandum which favoured a railway from Belize to the Petén and which he saw as the answer to the colony's desperate economic situation in the face of the collapsing logwood market. At the same time Moloney pointed out that the railway should be used to settle the road and boundary question with Guatemala and so satisfy everyone concerned. But the question of a railway was destined to the same limbo as all the discussions on the Guatemalan boundary. Unlike that thorny problem it was never to be seriously revived.

Recent developments in communications

Although a railway has therefore never been built, the twentieth century has seen the gradual expansion of communications: in the last ten years or so rapid strides have been taken both internally and in establishing links with the rest of the world. During the 1930s roads were built to connect Belize City with Corozal, Orange Walk, and Cayo (now San Ignacio). In the 1950s the Western Highway to Cayo was extended to Stann Creek, which has now also been linked with Punta Gorda. Road maintenance remains an expensive undertaking in a country with limited resources, much of its population dispersed in outlying districts, and a prolonged wet season. Nevertheless, considerable progress has already been made, and new roads are now being constructed or planned to enable the agricultural produce from the remoter villages to be brought to market. One example is the all-weather road designed to transport bananas from the plantations at Alabama to the jetty at Riversdale. This project is receiving assistance from the Canadian International Development Agency and should prove a real incentive to the banana producers.

Roads are not the only means of communication to have been developed in recent years. The international airport at Belize City has been expanded to accommodate jet aeroplanes, and small domestic planes use airstrips to provide a regular service throughout the country. Although Belize City has no deep water harbour, it remains the most important port and regular shipping routes are maintained with the United Kingdom, the United States and Jamaica. A feasibility study of deep water harbour facilities has recently been completed: this may become one of the most economically important developments in the future. The introduction of a telephone service and broadcasting by means of Radio Belize has also contributed to the development of communications between Belize City and the districts. In 1971 more ambitious plans for a national telecommunications system were announced and the Belize Telecommunications Authority set up. The new telephone system will cost over 5 million B.H. $ and will take three years to complete. It will provide a fully automatic dialling system for towns and a semi-automatic system for the rural areas. The whole scheme should be completed by 1976 and will be capable of expansion as the need arises.

Belmopan—the new capital city

Perhaps the most momentous decision ever made throughout the long history of Belize will prove to be that taken after the disastrous hurricane 'Hattie' in 1961. The destruction suffered by Belize City for the second time in thirty years persuaded the Government that the time had come to build a new capital. After detailed studies had been made a site was chosen in 1962 near the village of Roaring Creek, fifty miles inland from Belize City, at the junction of the Western Highway with the Hummingbird Highway to the south. After formal approval of this site had been given and the British Government had promised loans and grants amounting to over 16 million B.H. $, the initial surveys were made. The new capital is situated at a pleasant site near the Belize River valley and with views of the Mountain Pine Ridge foothills. The scheme was devised by a consortium of London consultants and is to be completed in several stages. It was envisaged that for the first few years the population would be about 5,000 but would eventually rise to 30,000. In 1965 Mr Anthony Greenwood, Secretary of State for the Colonies, unveiled a commemorative stela at the site; the following year the task of building the new capital was begun. The first stage of the project had to include all the essential services such as the water supply, generating plant and a telephone system. It also provided the first government buildings, homes for government officials, schools, a hospital and an ecumenical centre for the main religious organizations. Reinforced concrete has been used for all the buildings to enable them to withstand hurricane force winds. At the same time the architects have aimed at providing a pleasing appearance with the maximum use of natural ventilation. The government buildings have been designed with a Maya motif, which has been achieved by the use of plazas and pyramid type architecture. The name Belmopan given to the new capital also emphasizes the Maya theme since it is derived from the Mopan people who once inhabited the area.

In August 1970 Government Ministries and their Departments were transferred to Belmopan, and on 1 February 1971 the House of Representatives assembled for the first time in its new legislative chamber on Independence Hill, bringing Belmopan to life as the centre of government and the first modern capital city in Central America. By the time of her first birthday in August 1971, Belmopan's population was already 2,700 and work was almost ready to begin on the second stage. This was to provide recreational areas and some facilities for small light industries. Later plans include hotels, a library, museum and more schools. A site has even been earmarked for a possible university. Meanwhile the reconstruction of the Western Highway has been progressing steadily. By 1973 there will be a properly paved road from the new capital to Belize City and this should encourage the establishment of industries at Belmopan and the growth of agriculture in the area. It is unlikely that Belize City will lose its importance as the trading and mercantile centre of the country, but, after nearly three hundred years, it has ceased to be the administrative centre.

Public Finance

The construction of a new capital, the development of communications, the provision of public amenities and utilities such as water supplies and electricity, together with the provision of the social and welfare services expected in a modern community have all to be paid for from public finances. The management of the public money is one of the most important tasks of any government and is often entrusted, as in Belize, to the Prime Minister.

In its early days the economy of Belize was simple and static. The forest resources were exploited to the full and the settlers were able to obtain all their needs in exchange for the sale of forest products. The forest workers earned sufficient wages for their simple needs and often supplemented them with the produce of small gardens. The Maya Indians and the Carib communities based their way of life on subsistence farming or fishing. Public money was raised mainly by taxes on imports. There were occasional crises according to fluctuations in the sale of mahogany but, generally speaking, until the 1914–18 war the annual expenditure was usually balanced by the revenues at a level of around 500,000 dollars. The colonists were determined to keep the level of taxation low and they were able to maintain a balanced budget only by adhering to a static economy and by spending virtually nothing on the development of roads, ports and other essential modern facilities.

During the war the forest produce brought higher prices and for some years afterwards there was a greatly increased level of prosperity so that revenues rose to about one million dollars. Apart from the years of world depression and the devastation brought by the 1931 hurricane the revenues have risen fairly steadily. However, at the same time, there has been a corresponding increase in the costs of administering the government and the social services which, it is now acknowledged, are one of the responsibilities of modern government. As technical knowledge increases so does the desire for the latest improvements in living standards, medical services and above all educational opportunities. As a result the rate of expenditure has risen at a much faster rate than the yield from taxation can finance.

Aid from overseas

The answer to this problem of an unbalanced budget was found in the changing attitude of the Imperial Government to its responsibilities. Until the post-1918 period the colonies were expected to be entirely self-supporting financially. Gradually there emerged the recognition that assistance was needed to improve the social condition of the people in certain territories and an attempt was made to enlist the resources of science for this purpose. In 1929 the first small Colonial Development Fund was voted by Parliament, but its main aim was to relieve unemployment at home. The really significant step forward was taken in 1940 when a Colonial Development and Welfare Act was passed which allowed for the expenditure of five million pounds a year for ten years on development. The scope of the Act was later extended and for the first time the British Government was committed to a policy of promoting economic development and social welfare in her colonies.

Meanwhile, provision was made by means of grants-in-aid for colonies where the budget could not provide for the bare administrative necessities. After the 1931 hurricane Belize, already badly affected by the world depression, had no choice but to apply for a grant-in-aid in order to balance its local budget. Grants were not simply handed over to the colonial government: the necessary but hated condition of becoming a grant-aided territory was subjection to rigorous Treasury control. This entailed the submission of detailed estimates to the Treasury in London each year. The delays which accompanied this procedure often meant that constructional work was held over from one dry season to the next for lack of permission to proceed. Sir Alan Burns, Governor from 1934 to 1940, has written of the frustration of trying to revive the economy in these difficult conditions and has stressed the importance in such circumstances of the first small Development Fund. It was from this source that Sir Alan was able to obtain funds to assist the new sugar factory at Corozal in 1937. He also used it to start work on a number of important roads in spite of opposition to this expenditure from certain leading citizens. In his book *Colonial Civil Servant* Sir Alan refers to the opposition of the timber interests to the building of roads and the development of agriculture, on the grounds that this would put an end to the pool of casual labour from which the timber industry drew its workers. Whatever the truth of these charges it is certain that the measures taken made little real impact in the distressed circumstances of the late 1930s. Unemployment continued until the outbreak of the Second World War (1939-45) brought some improvement in the general economic position of the country. Yet, in spite of an increase in revenues during the war, the demands on the administration still exceeded the revenues.

Post-war conditions again aggravated the employment situation as they had done in 1918 and there was much hardship in Belize City in particular. Nevertheless in 1951 the budget was balanced for the first time for twenty years and for a short time Treasury control was relaxed. However in 1957 it became necessary to obtain a grant of over one million dollars in order to expand the administrative and social services. Ten years later Premier George Price was able to announce in his budget speech that the country was now freed from Treasury control, and the revenues could therefore be allocated as his Government decided. He took care to point out that the rising level of expenditure through the provision of better social services and schools placed a very heavy strain on the budget so that for some years to come the utmost caution would be necessary. The Premier was referring to the recurrent budget which is financed by locally raised revenues; the most important source of revenue came from customs and excise duties which produced more than 50% of the total. Income tax provided another 20-25% and the remainder was raised by a variety of other means such as licences, rents, land taxes and through the Post Office.

Specific projects, such as the recent reconstruction of the Belize International Airport, the improvements to the principal roads and the expensive construction of Belmopan, form part of a separate capital budget. A large proportion of the latter is earmarked for projects in the Development Plan. In 1967 capital expenditure of over seven million dollars was financed by five million dollars from Commonwealth Development Funds while the remainder was raised from local resources and loans.

The economic outlook

The most recent economic survey available, that for 1968, was optimistic about the continued growth in economic activity. It pointed to the notable advances made in agriculture, especially in rice production, and also to the construction and tourist industries. The development of hotels and beach facilities together with existing tourist amenities such as fishing and visits to the Mayan ruins should, in time, make the new nation of Belize an important tourist centre. But the most important step taken has undoubtedly been the decision to enter Carifta. The Caribbean Free Trade Association, or Carifta as it is generally known, was formed in 1968 with the aim of fulfilling the hopes of the people of the Caribbean territories 'for full employment and improved living standards'. The main intention is to widen the markets of the countries involved by removing barriers to trade. A great deal of preliminary work was done by Minister Hunter and Financial Secretary Rafael Fonseca in discussing the terms for Belize's entry to Carifta. It was only after prolonged discussion that the Cabinet decided to seek admission. On 1 May 1971 Belize became the twelfth member of Carifta and was given the status of a 'less developed' nation. This meant that a lengthy period would be allowed in which to phase out duties while certain industries would continue to receive protection

The decision to enter Carifta is regarded by farmers as a most exciting invitation to expand. Meanwhile the Government is doing much to encourage new enterprises by means of agricultural research and other measures designed to ensure the development of the land. It is hoped that the final achievement of independence will also bring increased investment from Canada and the United States, but, in the final analysis, only the people of Belize can generate the necessary energy to develop their own new nation.

15

The Road to Self-Government

The year 1871 marks a turning-point in the constitutional history of Belize. In that year the long-established representative system of government was abandoned and British Honduras, as it then was, became a Crown Colony. During the preceding half of the nineteenth century the simple methods of government evolved by the early settlers had gradually given way to a more sophisticated structure similar to that employed throughout the British Caribbean colonies. By 1861 the democratic Public Meeting, elected Magistrates and appointed Superintendent had developed into a Legislative Assembly, an Executive Council and Lieutenant-Governor. These more conventional institutions were in keeping with those usually established by the Colonial Office on behalf of the British Parliament.

Throughout the West Indies constitutional changes were taking place during the mid-nineteenth century. As the old social system in the sugar colonies broke down after emancipation in 1833 and the abolition of imperial protection in 1846, so each colony was gradually forced to abandon its representative institutions. In December 1870 the representative Legislative Assembly of British Honduras signed its own death warrant by abolishing the Assembly and replacing it by a Legislative Council. This action allowed the British Government to intervene and in April 1871 the first session of the Legislative Council under Crown Colony rule took place. Nevertheless one vestige of the past remained: since the legislature undertook its own reform, by virtue of its constituent powers, the Crown has never regained the power to legislate for the colony by Order-in-Council; this same privilege also applied to the Leeward Islands.

The loss of representative rights was soon bitterly regretted and the constitutional history of Belize since 1871 can best be interpreted as a prolonged struggle to win back some of those rights. Like other British colonies since the Second World War, it has attempted to free itself from imperial control in exchange for responsible self-government. At the same time an expanding population has led to an enormous growth in the complexity of local administration and government. A brief survey of these developments, affecting as they do every sector of the community, is important in itself as well as a prelude to an understanding of the work of the central government.

Local Government

It was not until the influx of refugees from Yucatán in the mid-nineteenth century that the need for some form of local government made itself felt. The problems which arose in Corozal and the neighbouring small villages caused the Northern District to be given its own paid Magistrate. This innovation was first suggested by the Superintendent in 1849 and the following year the necessary provision was made by the Public Meeting. The Magistrate was to receive £200 per annum and he was to be assisted by two police constables at £30 per annum. In addition there were to be two unpaid Magistrates, each with one constable. At the same Public Meeting it was also agreed to provide unpaid Magistrates for the Belize River and Sibún River areas and for the Southern District. At Stann Creek the constable was to have two paid assistants. In 1856 an Act sanctioned the payment of all District Magistrates out of the revenues which they were empowered to collect. Nine years later District Commissioners, as they became known, were appointed for Orange Walk and Stann Creek and, in 1882, for the Cayo and Toledo Districts.

Eventually the colony was divided, for administrative purposes, into six Districts, each with its full-time administrator. Among the duties of the District Commissioner were those of acting as Magistrate, Coroner and Postmaster in addition to supervising the work of the police and acting as Chairman of the Town Board where it existed. From time to time Orange Walk and Corozal have been united into one Northern District; the other administrative districts have always been Belize and Cayo, as well as Stann Creek and Toledo after the latter were separated from a single Southern District.

The problems posed by distance and poor communications during the period in which the local administrative system was gradually established ensured that the district capital became the most important centre of authority for villagers of the out-districts. There were few links between the villages and the central government in Belize City and gradually the District Commissioners were endowed with wider powers. Yet there was virtually no uniformity in the systems of rural local government. Wide variations in custom, language and pattern of settlement led to very diverse methods of village government, only now beginning to show a more uniform pattern. Until the recent introduction of statutory village councils the three most common forms of rural organization were the Alcalde system in the southern Maya and Carib villages, the looser 'Patron' or 'Mayor' system in the northern villages, and the completely informal Creole village organization.

Systems of village government

Of these the Alcalde system is perhaps the most interesting as it is the only non-Anglo-Saxon institution in the country. It was introduced by the Maya Indians who entered the country from Yucatán and Guatemala, but it has only been maintained in its full traditions in the southern and western parts of the country. The system was officially recognized in 1858 when a local Act was passed to give certain persons in the rural districts limited judicial powers; further authority was given to Alcaldes in 1884. The original system was, at least superficially, very democratic; annual elections were held in which the villagers elected the First Alcalde while the runner-up became Second Alcalde. A body of five men to form the Alcalde's Court were also elected. The work of this Court included the appointment of Officers of the Peace, the decision as to the amount of produce to be contributed towards village public works, the land to be cultivated and the date on which planting was to begin. A programme of communal labour or *fajina* for the cleaning of the village and other projects was also worked out. This programme was placed before the village for its approval and once this had been obtained any defaulters could be imprisoned.

It is obvious that under the original system the Alcaldes were men of considerable importance and, given the paternal family organization among the Maya, it was natural that the oldest and most respected citizens should be selected. The Alcalde's Court tried to ensure that minor village quarrels were settled without recourse to the District Commissioner except in cases of appeal or major crimes. However, when this system was regularized and delimited by the Government as late as 1952, it was almost inevitable that it should decline. The Inferior Court Ordinance of 1952 defined the duties of the Alcalde and laid down that the maximum fine to be imposed by this Court should be twenty-five dollars. Moreover the Alcalde's election was to be subject to the approval of the Governor in Council; both the Alcalde and his deputy were to be paid small stipends. Intervention by the central government has led to diminished confidence in the system; the Alcalde himself is regarded as an external official although his election is carried on in the traditional way. During the last fifteen years, as party politics have spread to the rural areas, the importance of the family and the respect for old age has so declined that a younger man without family support but with some government sponsorship can now become Alcalde. The obligation to cooperate in communal labour has weakened and, as a cash economy replaces subsistence farming, many people prefer to pay fines rather than contribute to the *fajina*. Nevertheless the Alcalde retains considerable prestige and there are still few appeals from his jurisdiction to a higher authority.

The Alcalde system was imposed on the Carib villages with less success, largely because of the more individual outlook of the Carib fisherman and farmer. Nevertheless in 1962 there were still three Alcaldes in the Stann Creek District as well as six in Cayo and eleven in Toledo. In the north and in certain villages in the west the much less formalized system of 'Patron' or 'Mayor' existed. These officials were also elected by the villagers but their main purpose was the protection of the community. As in the Alcalde system, the traditional 'Patron' or 'Mayor' belonged to the strongest families; his task was to settle disputes, to arrange the allocation of the *milpas* and to represent the village. But there were no communal taxes and the only common task was to keep the village clean. The administration of justice was much simpler as quarrels were normally settled within the family and only brought before the 'Patron' as a last resort. Since this type of village organization is less established than the Alcalde system it has been much easier for the government to introduce village councils and during the last few years the work of these councils has gradually ousted the 'Patron' from most villages in the north.

Local government in the Creole villages scarcely deserved that name. There was never any formal or permanent administrative machinery there. Small bodies of villagers formed committees to deal with the needs of the community as these arose. These casual arrangements were partly the result of the long absence of the men engaged in forestry work, which also had the effect of bringing Creole women into village affairs, unlike their Maya or Carib sisters. The rôle of the leader in the Creole villages was once the prerogative of the village teacher who often acted as lay preacher. He carried out certain functions for the central government too, since he represented such departments as the Post Office. But the expansion of staff in government departments has led to the withdrawal of these functions so that the local teacher is no longer necessarily the most important member of the village community.

The various village organizations fulfilled a definite rôle for many years, but they do not provide the basis for a system of local government to meet the needs of a modern society. This fact was recognized by the Commission of Enquiry on Constitutional Reform which published its report in 1951. The Commission pointed out the importance of an efficient system of local government and stated that: 'A sound and democratic system of local government is, in our opinion, the best foundation on which to build a solid democratic central structure'. The setting up of village councils was recommended for all villages with a population of more than 250. Such councils were already working successfully in Placentia, Seine Bight and other villages. It proposed that there should be at least five members on the council who should be elected annually with the power to levy certain local rates. Standard constitutions for the village councils were worked out by the Social Development Department and their main function now seems to be to act as self-help councils through which the government community development programme is carried out. Some training courses in leadership are organized by the same Department with the result that oratory sometimes tends to be regarded as the most important qualification for any potential leader. Another unfortunate result has been that where the village councils are supposed to function side by side with an existing institution such as the Alcalde's court, serious rivalry has developed. A further noticeable feature has been the tendency of the village councils to be influenced by national politics; some of them may become more concerned with impressing the central government than running the affairs of their own community. Inevitably in time the old institutions will cease to exist as the new councils receive statutory powers and continue to spread throughout the rural areas. Already by 1965 there were 86 village councils in operation, all linked with the Social Development Department.

Town and city government

Yet another important organ of local government are the Town Boards. As long ago as 1856 the Superintendent recommended that such a Board should be set up in Belize itself, but the suggestion was not carried out until 1865 when the Legislative Assembly passed a Bill to establish a Municipal Board. Until 1911 the Belize District Board was composed of nominated members and the Colonial Secretary acted as Chairman. This arrangement was superseded by the creation of the Belize Town Board in 1911 which was composed of eight elected and two nominated members. The Government Gazette for that year shows that voters had to be males over the age of twenty-one, who either owned property worth more than 60 dollars per annum, rented property to the value of 96 dollars, or had an annual salary of 300 dollars. The functions and powers of the Board have been changed from time to time, but its main responsibility has always been the running of the city. In its early days it seems to have been chiefly concerned with work pertaining to the appearance of the city such as laying out roads and draining lots. This was work of great importance and, in 1927, Governor Burdon not only congratulated the Town Board in his address to the Legislative Council but went on to announce that: 'The Government recognizes so fully the importance and value of this work that a grant-in-aid to the Town Board for its continuation is the only provision for works of progress contained in the Estimates for the coming year, all others being ruled out by want of money'. In particular he commended the Town Board for its work in transforming the Mesopotamia district from an area of swamp to one of decent housing. Today Belize City Council, as it is now known, has many functions relating to the care and cleanliness of the city; it has considerable powers in the collection of local rates and other revenue, and for some of its work extra money is granted from central government funds. There are nine elected members on the Council, all of whom receive a monthly salary.

The District Town Boards were established by the 1938 District Town Boards Ordinance and there are now Boards in seven towns: Corozal, Orange Walk, Punta Gorda, Monkey River, Stann Creek, San Ignacio and Benque Viejo. Originally the members of the District Town Boards were composed of five to seven nominated members, including the District Medical Officer, with the District Commissioner as Chairman. At Stann Creek in 1940 an elective element was added to the Town Board. The comparative prosperity of the Stann Creek District, due to its expanding citrus industry, had brought to the area a small middle class of business men and a few retired civil servants. Their experience and qualifications made an elected Town Board possible. Elsewhere the members of Town Boards tended to be landowners, chicle contractors or store owners—it was unusual for them to be professional men and more often than not they were Creoles even in the predominantly Mestizo towns of the north. Unlike the members of the Belize City Council those on the District Town Boards were unpaid and both their work and their budgets were strictly limited until 1952 when an annual grant was made available for sanitation purposes. Their main duties are the regulation of markets and the maintenance of local roads; both these functions are now statutory.

The Courtenay Constitutional Commission of 1951 recommended that the elective principle should be extended to all Town Boards. The continued presence of the local Medical Officer was no longer regarded as necessary, but it was agreed that the District Commissioner should continue to be an ex-officio member of the Board and that the Chairman should be elected by the members of the Board from among their number. Since these suggestions were adopted in 1955 there has been a rapid growth in party politics which now influences local government elections. In 1962 the Town Boards became directly responsible to the Ministry of Local Government and Social Development, thus freeing them from the control of the District Commissioner. Town Board elections are now carried out along party lines although their results do not always correspond with the national elections; the parties definitely compete for control of the Town Boards. Certain difficulties are therefore bound to arise when a party in opposition to the government gains control of a particular town. As the authority and status of the District Commissioner has declined, that of the local representative in the House of Representatives has increased, and certain matters which were formerly submitted to the District Officer now go from the elected member straight to the relevant Ministry or Department.

The main problem in the development of an efficient system of local government is one of size. Villages are so small and widely dispersed that it is not possible to weld them into larger administrative units, nor are they economically strong enough to have statutory powers as local authorities. The main function of the village councils must remain for the time being to act as community councils on a basis of self-help, with welfare projects administered through them by means of personnel working for the central government. The District Town Boards, on the other hand, already act as local authorities and are endowed with statutory powers, but their work is also limited in scale since the areas covered by their authority are so small. The result is that their financial capacity is restricted and it is difficult to attract the best officials. Until the size of the administrative units can be extended and the local budgets increased it is difficult for the central government to delegate further powers to local authorities. It is possible that the rôle of these authorities in the future may lie less in welfare projects than in the encouragement of specific economic projects which will enhance the prosperity and well-being of all the villagers.

Changes in the Constitution, 1862–1945

The constitutional changes made in British Honduras during the second half of the nineteenth century were not unique. The dependent territories of Great Britain were undergoing reform as the Colonial Office attempted to bring more systematic government to the expanding Empire. The colonies acquired during the Napoleonic wars were never granted representative forms of government but the term Crown Colony was not specifically applied to them until 1845. In fact this term described them perfectly. As the West Indian colonies gave up their representative institutions they too became Crown Colonies as did the tropical colonies where representative institutions were not practical. During this period the colonies in Australia and North America which had been settled by Europeans embarked on the constitutional steps towards responsible government. This dual systematization of the British Empire came about slowly as each colony had to be steered along its own individual path. When the West Indian colonies, apart from Bermuda, Barbados and the Bahamas, abandoned their traditional representative systems, they adopted instead mixed councils composed of official members holding their seats by virtue of their official posts, and unofficial members. In a few cases such as Dominica and Tobago attempts were made to have an elected majority on the council, but by 1898 every Legislative Council except the Jamaican was a fully nominated body.

In these circumstances it is perhaps not so surprising that the Legislative Assembly which opened with such high hopes in 1854 should have survived for only seventeen years. The granting of colonial status to British Honduras in 1862 seemed, at the time, a high point in her history. In retrospect the period between 1854 and 1871 was mainly one of unedifying squabbles within the Assembly which finally ended in deadlock. At first the Assembly functioned efficiently enough, but the constant threat of Indian invasions during the 1860s, and the audacious raids carried out by Marcos Canul, brought about an atmosphere of panic in the colony and dissension in the Assembly. The members of the Legislative Assembly resided in Belize, safe from the perils of life along the Rio Hondo or in Corozal. They were unwilling to provide extra taxes for the maintenance of a permanent frontier force, but the British Government insisted that the colony should shoulder its own responsibilities for defence. This particular issue came to the fore late in 1866 when the Assembly turned down the British offer of sharing the expense of an armed steamer to patrol the Hondo; the Government regarded the offer as sufficient protection and, as Lieutenant-Governor Austin pointed out in a speech conveying the Government's decision: 'The Colony must understand that it cannot be permitted to dictate to Her Majesty's Government the nature of the protection to be given by the Crown; if the Assembly sees fit to refuse cooperation with Her Majesty's Government they must prepare for that self-protection which is the correlative of such self-reliance'. Under the threat that the garrison would be withdrawn, the Bill to provide for the armed steamer was passed, but not without much ill-feeling.

By July of the following year Austin was writing to the Governor of Jamaica to say that proposals were being made which would reduce the elective element in the Assembly and that some men were even suggesting its complete abolition. He himself favoured strong government together with an increased population and new industry as a solution to the colony's problems. In his Blue Book for the year 1866 Austin expressed the opinion that the growth of agriculture and new towns required corresponding changes in the constitution especially since 'wealthy and intelligent electors have been to a great extent superseded by uneducated Petty Traders, Journeymen, and Labourers'. Seven members had deserted the Assembly entirely while several others rarely attended its meetings. In September he described the situation with even greater distaste, informing the Governor of Jamaica that: 'the present Legislative arrangements are almost a burlesque'. The arguments concerning the payment of troops continued and Lieutenant-General Longden, who took up his appointment in the autumn of 1867, was no better equipped to deal with the fractious Assembly. In July 1869 he reported that he had prorogued the Assembly after a session of five months during which frequent adjournments had to be made owing to the impossibility of obtaining a quorum of eleven members. Early in 1870 the suggestion was made that the Assembly was illegally constituted and so it was adjourned. The difficulties and delays in carrying out the necessary legislative business were finally brought to an end by the Act passed on 13 December 1870 by which the Legislative Assembly abolished itself.

The introduction of Crown Colony rule, 1871

The Assembly was replaced by a Legislative Council composed of five officials whose position automatically entitled them to a place on the Council. These were at first the Chief Justice, the Colonial Secretary, the Senior Officer commanding the troops, the Treasurer and the Attorney General. There were also to be four other members (known as the unofficial members) nominated by the Lieutenant-Governor who presided over the Council. In April 1871 the Queen's assent to the Act was published and an Executive Council was also created composed of virtually the same members. The first meeting of the Legislative Council took place on 13 April, thus bringing the long period of representative government to an end and, for the first time, imposing Crown Colony rule on British Honduras.

This constitutional change was by no means popular and it seems that, to some extent at least, it had come about as a result of the old rivalry between the landed and commercial classes. Since these two powerful groups in the community were by no means entirely self-exclusive this is not easy to substantiate. However it was certainly believed that the landowners favoured a stable economic policy directed by the Crown, while the merchants were more inclined towards an attitude of *laissez-faire*. Soon after the new system was introduced a drastic increase in import taxes from 4% to 10% indicated a definite victory for the landed section of the community. Moreover, three out of four unofficial members nominated by the Governor represented the landowning class, while only one represented commercial interests. During the next twenty years the value of representative government came to be more fully appreciated and the newspapers constantly lamented the days when elected members of the old Assembly controlled the revenues of the colony.

The promise that Crown Colony government would lead to firmer control and hence greater prosperity failed to materialize as did the prediction made by the American consular agent, Prindle, at the time of the transition that: 'British Honduras has seen its lowest ebb. The process of recuperation no doubt will be very slow, and the colony may never again see such palmy days as when in times of old the mahogany lords lived here and Belize was the entrepôt of this whole coast, . . . But I think there is a fair measure of prosperity in store'. In 1880 some of the inhabitants sent a memorial to the Secretary of State outlining their grievances and lamenting their error in surrendering their control of taxation; they stated that taxes had been greatly increased and far from any compensatory increase in economy and efficiency the reverse was the case. This memorial met with little sympathy in the Colonial Office, but one concerning the question of imperial troops in January 1887 did receive a more detailed reply.

The unofficial members of the Legislative Council had joined in a protest against the proposed withdrawal of the troops. The Secretary of State, Sir Henry Holland, expressed the hope that a treaty would be arranged with Mexico before the troops were finally withdrawn but he went on to examine the more serious issues involved: 'You will remind the Memorialists', he wrote, 'that the mother country cannot be held bound to incur the expense of protecting any and every Colony which has been established with a view to commercial advantage, in a position where it is liable to attacks from enemies for whose hostility this country is in no way responsible'. He then put an end to the allegation which had been circulating that the constitutional changes of 1870–1 had been made in exchange for a promise from Governor Cairns that permanent military posts would be maintained by imperial troops, and that was the reason the Legislative Assembly had agreed to resign its powers. Far from there being any truth in this suggestion Sir Henry Holland declared: 'The records of your office will show that there is no foundation for the statement that there was any such promise, and that the Legislative Assembly proposed its own dissolution without any suggestion from Sir W. Cairns'.

Now that the Imperial Government was in full control of the colony the need for supervision from Jamaica disappeared and in November 1884 the links between the two colonies were severed with the proclamation of Letters Patent which created the office of Governor and Commander-in-Chief of British Honduras. The one remaining link, which continued until 1911, was that appeals from the Supreme Court of British Honduras lay to the Supreme Court of Jamaica. This subordination to Jamaica had always been disliked by the people of the mainland colony and the change was welcomed. However resentment against the Crown Colony system of government continued and culminated in 1890 with a serious and lengthy crisis in the Legislative Council itself.

Dissatisfaction with the Legislative Council

Increasing dissatisfaction with Crown Colony rule, and in particular with the hated Governor Goldsworthy, was ventilated in the press during the late 1880s. The virtues of representative government were praised and the argument that further education was essential before it could operate was demolished in an editorial in the *Colonial Guardian* dated 30 November 1889. 'The people of British Honduras had already had a long training in the Representative system of Government when they were betrayed by their Representatives in 1870 and were handed over to the tender mercies of the autocratic system of Crown Government'. This theme of betrayal and the resultant iniquities from which the colonists were suffering ran through much of the public discussion at the time. Therefore the Hunter case, explosive as its implications were, presented itself as a suitable issue which could be exploited in the interests of the widespread desire for constitutional reform.

The problem came to a head with the legal proceedings which followed the seizure of C. T. Hunter's dredging equipment and the cancellation of one of his contracts during the absence on leave of Governor Goldsworthy in 1886.[1] The long drawn-out case took place in three stages. In the first Hunter was awarded damages of 20,000 dollars, the second was indecisive while the third stage, which took place in London, was the most controversial. The very act of removing the case to London on the grounds that no one in Belize could be trusted to act for Hunter was questionable, nor was there any good reason for the case to become a matter of equity rather than law. In the arbitration at London the person selected to represent the interests of the colony, Mr John Gentle, was a Belize resident but, since he held a mortgage on the property of Hunter's brother, he was by no means neutral in the case. The award of 30,000 dollars to Hunter by the London arbitrators was a serious blow to the taxpayers in the colony. Urged on by the *Colonial Guardian* which described the award as 'direct violation of the first principles of English law' the resistance to payment began. Since the necessary funds to pay the damages could only be raised through the Legislative Council, and the business men were firmly opposed both to the award and to any new tax designed to raise the money, complete deadlock was inevitable. The matter came before the

1.   See Chapter 14, pages 279–80

Legislative Council in April 1890 when the five unofficial members who were in a minority resigned. This unanimous action was strongly supported by the *Colonial Guardian* and it was soon realized that there would be no better opportunity for obtaining an unofficial majority on the Council.

At a public meeting held in June a committee was appointed to organize support. The evils of Crown government were attacked with renewed vigour and such a spirit of unity was engendered that the attempts of the government to bribe the unofficial members to return to their seats were treated with scorn. No one dared to accept one of the vacant seats and before long the situation had been brought to the attention of the British Parliament. The Colonial Secretary at the time was Lord Knutsford, formerly Henry Holland, who was already preoccupied with disgruntled colonists throughout the West Indies. Although Governor Goldsworthy left in the autumn of 1890 to take up an appointment in the Falkland Islands, the colonists' determination not to yield until they obtained an unofficial majority on the Legislative Council continued. Their resistance withstood considerable pressure from Lord Knutsford who refused to make any move on the desired railway project until the Legislative Council voted funds for a new survey. The whole affair was followed with considerable interest throughout the British West Indian colonies where demands for reform were mounting and opposition to Lord Knutsford was strong. But, though the difficulties of the colonists were similar, the constitution of British Honduras had evolved so differently that its people could insist on individual treatment. As the *Guardian* regularly pointed out, it was not the British Government that granted the colony representative government in the first place: only the treachery of their representatives in 1870 had yielded up this precious inheritance.

In July 1891 the Supreme Court ruled that the legislation which had been enacted by the boycotted council was illegal. This was hailed as a great victory, but nevertheless resistance continued until the following January when it was announced that there would in future be an unofficial majority on the Legislative Council. The new Council would be composed of three officials and at least five unofficials but the Governor would still preside and would continue to nominate the unofficial members. Thus the victory, although real, was only of minor importance and indeed was promptly criticized by the *Voice of St Lucia* which suggested that nothing less than the total removal of Crown Colony rule would be satisfactory. But the British Hondurans were contented with their achievement and for the next twenty years the composition of the Legislative Council remained unchanged.

The Legislature 1854–1954

Date	Legislative body	Elected	Nominated	Ex-Officio
1854–1870	Legislative Assembly	18	0	3
1871–1889	Legislative Council	0	4	5
1890–1891	Legislative Council	0	4	4
1892–1912	Legislative Council	0	5	3
1913–1935	Legislative Council	0	7	5
1936–1938	Legislative Council	5	2	5
1939–1945	Legislative Council	6	2	5
1945–1954	Legislative Council	6	4	3

From 1871 to 1954 the Lieut.-Governor or Governor acted as President and voted as an official. Except for the period 1871–1891 there was always a small unofficial majority on the Council.

The interest which had been aroused by the struggle between the unofficial members of the Legislative Council and the executive soon subsided and no changes of principle in the constitution were introduced until 1935. A few minor amendments were made but the attempt, during the 1920s, to obtain some fundamental alterations to the constitution came to nothing. In 1912 the Legislative Council was enlarged by the addition of two officials and two unofficials making twelve members in all. At the same time it became the practice for the unofficial members to resign their seats at the end of five years instead of holding them for life as previously. In fact this made little practical difference as they were eligible for re-appointment and the only result was that the unofficial members were less inclined to defy the Governor since their reappointment depended upon him.

Demands for reform

The aftermath of war had brought a gradual increase in the political consciousness of men throughout the colonial territories and in British Honduras the old demands for some element of elected representation were revived in 1921. At a meeting of the Legislative Council in November of that year the unofficial members unanimously voted for an amendment to the constitution which would provide for the elective principle to be restored to the Council. The Governor, in informing the Secretary of State of this vote, suggested that if all the unofficial members were to be elected then the officials should have a majority of at least one. He considered that the best solution might be to have four elected and three nominated unofficial members, leaving the same number of official members as before. When the Secretary of State replied to this despatch in January 1923 he suggested that a Franchise Commission should be appointed to consider the question. However he stated that where the elective principle was being introduced in the West Indies two requirements were made: the official majority must be retained and some members must be nominated. In the case of British Honduras, where there had long been an unofficial majority, he was willing to concede this point, but only provided that the Governor was endowed with certain reserve powers. This proved to be such a stumbling-block that no constitutional changes were made at all. Two Bills were drafted to alter the constitution but there was deep-rooted hostility to the concept of the Governor's reserve powers and the unofficial members prevented the Bill from proceeding.

Treasury control and restoration of the elective principle
The critical situation created by the 1931 hurricane was so great that there was little time for discussion of principles and the British Government seized the opportunity to impose Treasury control on the colony. The Ordinance of 1932 which put this unwelcome step into effect also gave the Governor reserve powers in matters affecting 'public order, public faith or other first essentials of good government'; thus financial pressure achieved what no amount of persuasion could achieve in 1924. Although the Council was obliged to yield in order to obtain the necessary financial assistance, the unofficial members promptly passed a resolution stating that they had agreed to the Ordinance only to secure the loan and that they realized the Bill was against the expressed wishes of the people. Moreover they made a request for the enactment of legislation on the lines of the 1924 proposals at the earliest possible date.

It was three years before the necessary legislation was passed. Referring to the proposed changes in his speech to the Legislative Council in April 1932 the Governor, Sir Harold Kittermaster, acknowledged the traditional independence of the people and said: 'I wish to take this opportunity of asking not only Honourable Members of this Council but also the people of this Colony as a whole to believe that no attack on their ancient liberties is contemplated or has been contemplated by the recent change in the Constitution. I recognize that the people of this Colony probably more than any unit in the Empire have won for themselves, by their history, a right to manage their own affairs'. Yet the rights actually granted by the Act passed on 11 April 1935 were very restricted. The membership of the new Council remained twelve with the Governor as President but now only two of the unofficial members were to be nominated and five were to be elected.

The qualifications for candidates and the franchise favoured the wealthier sections of the community to the exclusion of most of the population. Candidates had to be British subjects of three years' residence who possessed an income of 1,000 dollars a year, or 500 dollars in real property. The vote was restricted to British subjects with one year's residence and either an income of 300 dollars a year, the ownership of real property worth 500 dollars, or the payment of 96 dollars a year in rent for property. Since the 1931 hurricane and the world economic depression had caused so much poverty and hardship the qualifications imposed limited the electorate very seriously. In 1936 when the new arrangements came into force for the first time the number of voters was only 1,035, that is 1·8% of the population, although in the Belize District the proportion of voters rose to 3·99%. By 1948 the overall number of voters had risen to 2·8% of the population and in Belize District the figure reached 4·92%. But in the largely Indian-populated Toledo District the proportion of registered voters in 1948 was still as low as 1·42%. The 1936 Act divided the colony into four electoral divisions, but there was no attempt to make residence in a constituency a necessary qualification for election. The tendency therefore was for the wealthier and better educated Creoles of Belize City to dominate the outdistricts.

By the 1930s the real source of power in the colony lay in the hands of the Governor and the Executive Council. The long struggle between the Governor and the unofficial members of the Legislative

Council on questions of constitutional reform and financial control had made successive Governors wary of consulting the Council. The old-established families were nominated to seats on the Executive Council and they were also able to exert pressure through the Chamber of Commerce. The growing importance of local business men was scarcely reflected in the political scene until 1936; the Belize Town Board was the only institution which enabled the middle-class Creoles to make a contribution to government. The Governor preferred to nominate European-born clergy or lawyers to the Council than to make use of retired local civil servants. The first elections of 1936 showed a new trend when the manager of the Belize Estate Company was defeated by a local business man, Robert Turton. The manager had to be given one of the nominated seats on the council, but for Turton it was a great triumph as four years previously he had been refused a nominated seat.

The new constitution did nothing to alter the composition of the Legislative Council. Its members remained business men, although some of the elected members now belonged to the new, locally born middle classes rather than the wealthy old families. Even in 1959 the Constitutional Commissioner commented adversely on the membership of the Council, writing: 'I was astonished to find that there is among the unofficial members of the Legislative Assembly not a single lawyer, doctor, nor person with a university degree. This must be almost a unique condition of affairs'. It undoubtedly was unique in colonial legislatures, but it was also an accurate reflection of the domination of the political scene by the most powerful economic group in the colony—first the mahogany landowning interests and later the new business men and merchants.

The outbreak of the Second World War in 1939 brought all possibility of further constitutional development to an end for the duration of the war, but peace brought with it, as it had done in 1918, both economic depression and increased demands for political progress. The 1936 constitution had been altered only to increase the elected members on the Council. In 1938 the southern electoral division was divided into the more natural constituencies of Stann Creek and Toledo, thus increasing membership of the Council to fourteen. In 1945 the unofficial majority was further increased by the reduction of the officials from six to four, the two officials being replaced by two more nominated members. At the same time the qualifications for candidates were reduced to the same as those for voters.

Post–war Constitutional Developments, 1945–1970

After 1945 political agitation was in the air throughout the colonial territories. Universal suffrage and self-government became the battle cries of the colonies and the British Labour Government gradually began to abandon the burdens of an empire acquired over a period of two hundred years. India became self-governing in 1947, and from that time an attempt was made to prepare the smaller territories for some form of self-government either in a federation, as in the Rhodesias and the Caribbean, or as independent units. Once the principle of self-government had been recognized, political pressure was still required from the colonies to bring about the different stages towards their ultimate goal. The rate of progress varied according to how much agitation was aroused and the individual economic circumstances of each territory, since some evidence of economic viability was deemed an essential prerequisite for independence. Other considerations to be borne in mind by the British Government before it granted self-government included an adequately trained civil service and some assurance of protection for minority groups. But the general principle behind British colonial policy was stated by the Secretary of State, Mr Creech Jones, in 1948. He said: 'It is to guide the colonial territories to responsible self-government within the Commonwealth in conditions which ensure to the people concerned both a fair standard of living and freedom from oppression from any quarter'. This outline of the Labour government's policy was confirmed by the Conservatives when they returned to office in 1951.

It was clear that, against this background of political agitation and change, the concessions granted in the 1936 constitution would not satisfy the citizens of British Honduras for long. In the first place the demand for 'one man, one vote' was one of general appeal. The proportion of registered voters was still very low, despite the reduction of the age of women voters in 1945 from thirty to twenty-one, and the fall in the value of the dollar which reduced the property qualifications of voters. Secondly, there was a

L

general desire to introduce changes which would lead to a majority of elected members over the officials and nominated members in the Council.

The 1951 Report on Constitutional Reform

In 1947 certain proposals for constitutional reform were made by an elected member of the Legislative Council which were adopted as the basis for talks between a deputation of unofficial members and the Secretary of State which took place in July–August the same year. The same proposals were then placed before a five-man Commission of Enquiry appointed to submit recommendations for reform of the constitution to the Secretary of State and to consider changes in local government. When the first Chairman of the Commission, the Attorney General, resigned, W. H. Courtenay, a lawyer and unofficial member of the Executive and Legislative Councils, took his place. It was under Courtenay's chairmanship that the Report was finally presented in April 1951. It was approved by the Legislative Council a year later, but it was another two years before all the necessary procedures had been completed and the changes could be implemented.

This Report is of fundamental importance since it not only led to the establishment of a constitution which was a marked advance on the previous one, but because that constitution itself fell far short of self-government. The arguments put forward in the Report explain why. The Commission was composed of three unofficial members of the Legislative Council as well as the Government Surveyor and, at first, the Attorney-General. Their attitude was by no means revolutionary but one of acceptance and even deference towards British rule. This is made clear in the opening remarks of the Report where, speaking of British rule, it states: 'It has given to the Colony a stable government whose authority is unquestioned; it has maintained tranquillity in the Colony; it has established the rule of law and by the creation of a just administration and an upright judiciary, it has secured to every resident, whether a British subject or not, the right to go in peace about his daily work and to retain for his own use the fruit of his labours. Any advance in the political constitution of the Colony by the transfer of more power and greater responsibility to the people must be so designed as to preserve and maintain this record. We conceive it to be most desirable to avoid the errors made in other Colonies where the apparent premature extension of political responsibility has resulted in frequent political upheavals and given the impression to the outside world of instability in the Government'. The Report goes on to describe the social conditions of the colony, laying emphasis on the varying degrees of educational achievement among the different communities, and drawing attention to the interest and enthusiasm for reform shown in the city of Belize as compared with the rural districts. The conclusion is drawn that: 'It should be clear that the advance in general and political education has not been uniform among all the races which comprise the Colony's population, and that the lack of balance arising from the long lead which the largest group enjoys over the minorities calls for the establishment of a system which, while meeting the legitimate aspirations of the one does no violence to the interests of the other'. The recommendations made by the Report were all designed to ensure that these conditions were fulfilled.

The Legislature was not the only branch of government requiring reform, and the Report went on to consider in some detail the functions of the Executive Council. This Council had come into being through the exercise of the prerogative of the Crown rather than by an imperial or local Act. At the time of the enquiry it was composed of the Governor as President with three ex-officio members and four nominated ones. The ultimate responsibility for the administration of the colony lay with the Secretary of State who exercised his power through the Governor. The Executive Council merely acted in an advisory capacity to the Governor, who could disregard its advice since he, and not the Council, had to exercise responsibility. The Report argued that in a system where the Legislature was not fully responsible it could throw the administration into confusion by refusing to sanction expenditure or delaying business, but it did not have any responsibility in carrying policy into practice. 'The defects of the present system are obvious,' it declared. 'It is a political blind-alley and by its paternalism fails to engender a proper system of political responsibility by members of the Legislature'. It was for these reasons that the Commission went on to recommend the transfer of executive control in domestic matters from the Governor to the Executive Council, arguing that 'Unless however this change occurs, the hope of developing responsibility in the people and hastening the day when they will assume full conduct and control of their affairs will be deferred.

The sense of frustration likely to be engendered, at a time when other Colonies in the Caribbean and elsewhere are all on the forward march in political development, will be a bitter pill to swallow'.

The constitution which came into being as a result of this Report was largely based on its modest recommendations. In an effort to check the over-hasty development feared by the Commission members, they had suggested a system of electoral colleges in the districts whereby the district representatives would be elected by members of the Town Boards and village councils. This suggestion, alien to British democratic practices, was not adopted. The new constitution was created on the principle of universal suffrage for all literate British subjects over twenty-one. A Legislative Assembly replaced the Legislative Council just one hundred years after the first Legislative Assembly had been established. It was presided over by a Speaker nominated by the Governor and in addition there were fifteen members. Of these nine were to be elected, three for Belize City and six for the six districts. There were also to be three official members and three nominated ones. For the first time the elected members in the Assembly enjoyed a majority, of nine to six, over the combined official and nominated ones. At the same time the Executive Council was altered so that it became the chief instrument of policy. The Governor, who no longer sat in the Legislature, was to be Chairman but was required to consult the Council in the formulation of policy and to act according to its advice. The other members of the Council were to be drawn from the Legislative Assembly and were to include the three official members, two nominated and four elected; the last six were to be elected to the Executive Council by their colleagues in the Assembly.

Notwithstanding the definite improvements provided by these constitutional arrangements there was still some dissatisfaction with the lack of progress towards self-government; a more radical step in that direction was taken in January 1955 when a system of quasi-Ministerial government was introduced. Three of the elected members of the Executive Council were made responsible for the work of three Government departments: Natural Resources, Public Utilities and Social Services, the remaining three elected members acted as their assistants. Nevertheless the Governor retained his reserve powers and his control over the introduction of financial measures into the Legislature; in the Executive Council the nominated members still had a majority of one over the unofficial members.

Sir Hilary Blood's Report, 1959

The 1951 Commission recommended that after the new constitution had been in operation for five years it should be reviewed to see how desirable it was for further changes to be made. In 1959, therefore, exactly five years after the first elections under the new constitution, Sir Hilary Blood was appointed Constitutional Commissioner and charged with the task of enquiring into 'the working of the present constitution of British Honduras and to make recommendations for any changes which may be thought desirable'. The Commissioner found himself with the unenviable task of deciding whether or not British Honduras was ready to advance further towards self-government, and, if so, the rate at which the advance should be made. In the event he decided that the modest success of the quasi-Ministerial system justified further changes although he found definite indications against the granting of full internal self-government.

Sir Hilary's reasons for making only modest proposals were based on four arguments. In the first place he felt that since the colony was still grant-aided, control could not be delegated *in toto* to inexperienced politicians. Secondly, he regarded the shortage of an educated middle class from which to staff the government as a serious defect. His third cause of hesitation was the overwhelming success of one political party (PUP) in the two elections which had been held; he considered that there ought to be some evidence of the development of a democratic two-party system. Finally he thought that the threats from Guatemala could not be ignored. In concluding his Report Sir Hilary wrote: 'I am well aware that my proposals will not satisfy the political aspirations of the more advanced and vocal local reformers' and, indeed, they were some distance from the proposals made for full internal self-government by the political parties and were accordingly rejected.

Nevertheless the Constitutional Commissioner's Report formed the basis of discussion at the Constitutional Conference which was held in London in February 1960. At that conference the two main parties, PUP and NIP, formed a United Front in order to effect certain changes in the Commissioner's proposals which they regarded as: 'falling short of the aspirations of the people of British

Honduras'. However, the clash which was expected to occur between the different delegations from British Honduras failed to materialize and substantial agreement was reached on a constitution which, while not itself granting full internal self-government, paved the way for that step in a rather more advanced constitution than Sir Hilary Blood had envisaged. One notable event of the conference was the decision taken, at the request of all the unofficial members of the British Honduras delegation, to incorporate a declaration in the constitution affirming the desire of the people of British Honduras to remain within the Commonwealth.

The 1960 Constitution

The main features of the new constitution were based on the Blood Report. No changes were made to the existing franchise despite the fact that the Commissioner had recommended that provision should be made for postal and proxy voting: the conference agreed that this might lead to too many irregularities. The conference accepted the proposal for an increase in the elected members to the Legislative Assembly, in future to be eighteen from single member constituencies, as well as the reduction of ex-officio members to two. It was agreed that five members of the Assembly should be nominated and an elaborate procedure was adopted for their nomination. Two members were to be selected after consultation between the Governor and the First Minister and a third after consultation with the leader of the minority party. The other two nominated members were to be chosen after consultation with all the party leaders. This provision limited the discretion of the Governor to nominate at least three of the members himself, as had been suggested in the Report. It was further agreed that the Speaker should be elected by the Legislative Assembly, but the man selected was to be chosen from outside the Assembly. Finally it was decided that the Assembly should have a life of four years rather than the three years proposed in the Report or the five desired by the leading politicians.

The changes made in the Executive Council were designed to extend the system of Ministerial government already in operation. Only two members of the Executive Council were to be officials: the other six being unofficial members. One of these was to be a nominated member of the Legislative Assembly. There were to be five Ministerial posts with portfolios, including the Finance and First Ministers, and one post without portfolio. The Governor would appoint the leader of the party with the majority of seats as First Minister and the Legislative Assembly would elect the remaining five members to the Executive Council. The Governor would distribute portfolios in accordance with the advice of the First Minister.

Other measures included the change of title from Colonial Secretary to Chief Secretary, and steps were taken to ensure the continued independence of the judiciary. The conference made no proposals for the timing of further changes and the new constitution came into force after the general election of March 1961. At the time of this election the political parties declared their ultimate aim to be independence. Accordingly, in 1962, the British Government suggested that a further conference should be held the following year.

The 1964 Constitution

At the conference held in London in July 1963, the momentous decision was taken to hasten the stages of constitutional advancement and to bring into force a new constitution on 1 January 1964 which would grant full internal self-government to British Honduras.

In order to achieve this long-desired constitution several far-reaching changes had to be made, notably in connection with the powers of the Governor. These powers were now substantially reduced. The Governor continued to be appointed by the Crown, but the general power of disallowing acts of the Legislative Assembly disappeared except in cases where holders of government stock might be injured. In the executive sphere the Governor was now required to act with the advice of the Ministers except in certain special circumstances. In the legislative sphere his powers were restricted to measures concerning the same special responsibilities, but he could also reserve any bill for Her Majesty's pleasure which seemed inconsistent with British treaty obligations, was prejudicial to the Royal Prerogative, or was inconsistent with the British Honduras Constitution. The Governor's special responsibilities were stated to be 'defence, external affairs, internal security and the safeguarding of the terms of service of public officers. Further for so long as the Government of British Honduras continues to receive moneys from the United Kingdom Government in the form of grant-in-aid of the current revenues it will be necessary for the Governor to have a special responsibility for maintaining or securing the financial and economic stability of British Honduras or for ensuring that any condition attached to any financial grant or loan made by Her Majesty's Government is complied with'.

The Executive Council was replaced by a Cabinet headed by the Premier. The Ministers were to be appointed by the Governor on the advice of the Premier and there would be no official members. The Premier himself would also be appointed by the Governor and he would be the person with the support of the majority party in the new House of Representatives; he could be removed by the Governor if he failed to resign after a vote of no confidence. In order to assist the Governor with his special responsibilities certain committees were to be set up: one for internal security, an advisory one on the prerogative of mercy and another to keep the Minister informed on external affairs.

The new Legislature was to be a bicameral one known as the Assembly, comprising a Senate and House of Representatives. The eight Senators were to be appointed by the Governor in accordance with an elaborate formula of consultation. Five of them were to be selected on the advice of the Premier, two on the advice of the Leader of the Opposition and the last one after the Governor had consulted with other suitable persons. The Senate's powers included the initiation of legislation except in financial matters, and the power of delaying all but money bills for six months. Ministers could be selected from the Senate. The House of Representatives would comprise eighteen elected members and no official or nominated ones. The Speaker could be elected by the House from within or outside the House, but no Minister could become Speaker or Deputy Speaker. General elections were to be held at least every five years and the gap between sessions of the National Assembly should be no longer than six months. The constitution also incorporated certain safeguards with regard to the appointment and control of public officers. The Governor continued to be responsible, but in consultation with the Public Service Commission.

This constitution came into force at the beginning of 1964. It would now require few changes to make Belize entirely self-governing; certain powers and functions at present entrusted to the

Comparative Table of Post-War Constitutions

1954 Constitution

	Elected	Nominated	Ex-Officio
Legislative Assembly presided over by Speaker nominated by Governor	9	3	3
Executive Council chaired by Governor who votes	1 / 4	2	3

Special features
Membership system or quasi-Ministerial system introduced, but elected representatives do not have a majority on Executive Council.

1960 Constitution

	Elected	Nominated	Ex-Officio
Legislative Assembly	18	5	2
Executive Council chaired by non-voting Governor	5	1	2

Special features
Office of First Minister and full Ministerial system introduced. Elected members have majority on Executive Council.

1964 Constitution
National Assembly

	Elected	Appointed	Ex-Officio
House of Representatives presided over by Speaker elected by Members	18	0	0
Senate presided over by President elected by Members	0	8	0
The Cabinet chaired by Premier who is leader of majority party	All members are appointed and come from both Houses. No fixed number of Ministers.		

Special features
Full internal self-government. Governor has special responsibility for defence, foreign affairs and the civil service and internal security.

From *How we are Governed.*

Government Information Service, Belize City.

Governor would simply be transferred to members of the Cabinet. The final achievement of independence will take place at a time chosen by the Belize Government in full agreement with the British Government. When this happens the constitutional wheel will have turned full circle and the country which began its modern history as a small and isolated British settlement, independent of outside control, will once again be free to accomplish its own destiny. The constitutional history of the country is unique in a number of ways, and yet it conforms to a general pattern of British colonial constitutions in most respects and particularly in the developments which have taken place since 1945 on the long road towards self-government.

16

A Society in Transition

The strands from which history is made are always tangled; this is just as true of the history of Belize as of any other country. The central threads of constitutional, social and economic growth are of undoubted significance but there still remain the less tangible factors which play their part in the lives of the people and so in the history of a society. These factors include the religion practised by the people, the education provided for them and their cultural and leisure activities. These themes in the history of Belize must therefore be considered, however briefly. The more novel contribution made during the last twenty years by the growth of the trade union movement and political parties must also be emphasized even if these developments are too recent for accurate historical assessment to be possible.

Religion and Education

Until the middle of the nineteenth century the Anglican Church was not only the established Church of British Honduras, and therefore supported by public funds, but was without doubt the most influential of the different religious bodies in the country. The first Anglican chaplain had been appointed as early as 1776 and, after the erection of St John's Church and its consecration in 1826, the Anglican clergy played an important rôle in the hierarchical colonial society. Few of these clergy were concerned with missionary work; they seem to have considered it their primary duty to minister to the more prosperous sections of the community in the town of Belize itself. Occasionally one of the clergy took some interest in the welfare of the slaves, but this usually led to criticism from the mahogany cutters who owned them. The more active missionary work of the Nonconformists, particularly among the slaves and Caribs, naturally led to a decline in the influence of the Anglican Church in the mid-nineteenth century. Nevertheless, in 1845, a second Anglican Church, St Mary's, was planned and subscriptions were raised. The protests from the Presbyterians were so great that public funds were also allotted for the building of a Presbyterian Church.

However, during the next twenty years, there were new forces at work in the religious life of the colony which were to lead to far-reaching changes. Firstly, the Anglican Church was itself torn by internal differences. A struggle over forms of worship, expressed in the controversy between High and Low Church, took place wherever there were Anglican dioceses. In British Honduras there was a tendency for the Superintendents to regard themselves as the Supreme Heads of the Church and to make pronouncements on various aspects of Church government. In 1855, for instance, Superintendent Stevenson wrote to the Governor of Jamaica recommending that only a liberal-minded clergyman should be appointed to British Honduras as the people had definite evangelical leanings. The Superintendent's insistence on a degree of control over such matters as clerical appointments and salaries did nothing to help the harmony of the Church. Moreover the growing strength of the Nonconformists made itself felt over the question of Dissenters' marriages and burials; Dissenters who refused to take oaths in the law courts caused other difficulties.

The last and most important of the new religious pressures was caused by the influx of the Yucatecan refugees and the subsequent growth of the Roman Catholic Church. The majority of the new arrivals in the northern parts of the colony were already members of that Church. Even those Indians who did not belong to the Catholic faith were predisposed in its favour; its elaborate ceremonies and rituals were calculated to appeal to the Indian far more than the formal austerity practised by the members of the Anglican Church. In 1851 the first two Jesuit priests were sent by the Vicar Apostolic of Jamaica to preach the faith and to convert the heathen.

From these humble beginnings the Roman Catholic Church soon established a strong position so that in 1856 it was already second in importance to the Anglican Church in the capital. It was the missionary zeal of the Jesuits and the readiness of the priests to leave the city for the remote and backward villages which was responsible for the increasing strength of the Catholic Church and which has since brought it to its present predominant position in the country.

All these factors—internal dissension among the Anglicans, the Nonconformist strength and the arrival of the Roman Catholic Church—played their part in the events leading to the disestablishment of the Anglican Church in British Honduras. A committee set up to enquire into public expenditure reported in 1866 that, since the Church of England and the Presbyterian Church were supported by only a fraction of the community, there seemed no reason for the poorer Catholic, Methodist and Baptist Churches to support the two wealthier ones. Accordingly the Anglican and Presbyterian Churches were disendowed, so saving the local Treasury the sum of 8,600 dollars a year. Five years later both Churches were completely disestablished by ordinance. This seems to have had a more beneficial effect on the Anglican Church than might have been anticipated, for the colony was now regarded as a suitable field for missionary work and was henceforward served by the various English missionary societies. In 1880 the British Honduras diocese was separated from Jamaica and Bishop Tozer of Zanzibar became the first Bishop of the new diocese.

Meanwhile the Catholic Church was also increasing its congregation and in 1893 Pope Leo XIII created the Vicariate of Belize. Unfortunately the English Jesuits who had accomplished so much for the faith were too few in number to carry on their work, so in the same year that Belize became a Vicariate, the American Society of Jesus from Missouri Province took over responsibility for its administration, and has continued its work to the present day. Even though a Bishopric was created in 1956 it is still the Missouri Jesuits who control the Catholic Church in Belize. They have been greatly helped in their task of creating an efficient, solidly based diocese by the devoted work of several Orders of Nuns, notably the Pallotine Sisters, the Holy Family and the Sisters of Mercy. The priests and nuns have carried their faith into the most inaccessible parts of the country and to members of every ethnic community. By setting up village schools wherever they preached the Roman Catholic faith, they have created a lasting bastion of their religion which has enabled it to grow to its present position of dominance. According to the 1960 census the Catholic Church included 60% of the total population among its members. In every district except Belize the Catholics were in the majority. The Anglican Church had lost ground not only to the Wesleyans, who formed 11·6% of the Christian population, but also to the new evangelical churches. This decline has been particularly evident since 1946, for until that year the Anglican Church still numbered 21% of the population among its congregation.

Church and Government in education

Very few of those who correctly filled in their census returns in 1960 stated that they belonged to no religious organization. In view of the part played by the various denominations in the educational system of Belize this is hardly surprising. The Jesuits regard education as the basic tool by which they extend their faith and it therefore follows that every good Catholic must send his children to a Catholic school. It is for this reason that the missionaries established so thorough a network of schools throughout Belize. Given this fervent belief in the value of education and the importance of the Church's rôle in society, it follows that the Catholic Church regards the possibility of any government interference in the realms of education with misgiving.

As the Protestant Churches were the first in the field of education, establishing several schools early in the nineteenth century, they too have continued to maintain their own schools. The shortage of public money available for education has allowed the denominations to retain their control over the system. Equally important in very recent years has been the attitude of the present Government which has consistently affirmed the responsibility of the Churches for education and insisted that government control is against its principles. The PUP Government has described itself as a Christian Democrat Government and has declared that 'it will sustain the Church State School system'; the same attitude to education is held by the main opposition party.

The denominational nature of the educational system, although it has led to some fragmentation of vital resources and effort, is deep-rooted in the history of Belize. The wealthier merchants and mahogany cutters of the nineteenth century sent their children to Britain or to Jamaica for their education: apart from providing the free schools they left all education in the hands of the churches. In 1868 the original free schools were abolished and an attempt was made to provide for education throughout the colony and not just in the town of Belize. Although the powers hitherto vested in the Board of Education were then transferred to the Executive Council, the Government played little part in education. Its rôle was limited to giving grants to the elementary schools on the basis that such sums should be matched by a similar amount from the church concerned. Secondary education, limited as it was, was entirely in the hands of the churches. The annual expenditure on education in the period when the revenue was locally controlled, never exceeded 3·3% of the budget. Yet when the Imperial Treasury obtained control in 1932, in a period of extreme financial difficulty, the expenditure on education was immediately raised to 9% of the budget.

The Easter Report, 1934

The churches were by no means reluctant to assume the greater part of the responsibility for education since they regarded it as an essential part of their religious activities. It was for this reason that there was so much duplication of effort, particularly in the rural areas. In small villages, Catholic and Protestant schools were often established side by side in places where the number of children and the resources available could barely support one school. In 1934 a thorough investigation of the educational system of British Honduras was made by B. H. Easter, Director of Education in Jamaica, at the request of the colonial government. Easter was shocked at the low proportion of the country's resources which had been spent on education. As a result of Easter's enquiry, the Supervisor of negro education in Georgia, J. C. Dixon, was appointed as an adviser to see how Easter's proposals for the use of 'Jeanes' agent-teachers could best be implemented.[1] Dixon condemned the widespread opposition to using local people as teachers. Reluctantly asking 'whether education of the children or promotion of church interest . . . are the objectives of the church', he was forced to conclude that 'education is an appendage to the church'.

1. This system was used in the southern states of the U.S.A. In British Honduras Jeanes teachers acted mainly as supervisors to teachers in the rural areas.

The initiative shown by the administration in the appointment of both Easter and Dixon was followed up in several ways during the 1930s. Amongst other reforms, a Superintendent of Education was appointed and the Inspector of Schools was required to hold professional qualifications for the first time. Some government scholarships from primary to secondary schools and from there to university were instituted, and provision was made for primary school teachers to receive training in Jamaica. During the last ten years or so, great efforts have been made to improve the standards of education. The present Government has pledged itself to carry out three main objectives: 'to improve the quality of education at all levels; to orient the system of education to meet the needs of the country's development; to improve and expand training at the university and professional levels'. These are laudable aims which present the Government with many problems in the organization of the educational system before they can be fully implemented.

Recent developments in education

An ordinance of 1962 gave the Government general control over education, but with more specific powers at the primary level. Nevertheless management of these schools remains in the hands of the local ministers of religion and each denomination has its own general manager of schools. Governmental responsibility now resides in the Minister of Education and Housing, who is assisted in professional matters by the Chief Education Officer. The latter is head of the Department of Education which has a separate staff from that of the Ministry. The Department works with the denominational authorities but its legal powers in secondary education are extremely limited.

Both the UNESCO mission and the Tripartite Mission of 1966 criticized the education available in Belize as too literary in content and recommended greater emphasis on the more practical, vocational aspects of education. The present Government is taking steps to remedy this and many important educational projects have been initiated in the last few years. In 1965 one teachers' training college was formed by a merger between the government college and a Catholic one. Belize Technical College, the only government-controlled secondary school, is being reorganized; a new system of junior secondary schools has been begun; vocational training is being expanded and the old Board of

Education has been replaced by a National Council for Education. Considerable contributions have been made from government funds to science laboratories for certain secondary schools which, it is hoped, will be used by pupils from different schools. More scholarships are being granted to secondary school pupils but still only a small percentage of the age group transfer from primary to secondary schools.

Denominational control of the schools has led to a more serious problem. Traditionally the secondary schools have been and continue to be staffed largely by aliens. The Catholic schools have been mainly staffed by American Jesuits, while the Protestant schools have been staffed by clergy from Britain or the West Indies. Naturally as the number of local graduates enter the teaching profession this position will change. In the Jesuit schools American textbooks and teaching methods have been used even if the pupils have also been taught for the standard English examinations. The Protestant schools, on the other hand, have had a bias towards the British system of education. They have followed the example set by the Protestant Churches in establishing certain British standards based on middle-class values and attitudes to society. The Catholic schools have been more ready to embrace Latin American attitudes and to welcome the Spanish-speaking Indians into their midst. The result has been that the educational system, which ought to be a force for unity in society, has actually accentuated the social and cultural differences between the different communities. One more hopeful sign for the future is the recent decision of the different denominations to plan an ecumenical centre and secondary school for the new capital. The experiment at Belmopan may therefore encourage a more unified approach to the problems of education in the future.

Culture and Leisure

The divisive nature of the educational system is all the more remarkable in view of the strenuous efforts made during the last few years to imbue the different communities with a sense of their common identity as Belizeans. It was with this aim that the PUP Government so speedily introduced the emblems of nationality: a flag, an anthem and a name for the country. For the same reason there has been considerable emphasis on cultural activities: arts festivals have been organized and local artists encouraged to write poetry and plays or to exhibit their works of art. Radio Belize is also playing an important part in creating a feeling of national unity and has an extremely valuable function in bringing national news to the small, remote villages in the interior. It is owned by the Government and forms part of the Ministry of Information and Broadcasting. Since the introduction of commercial broadcasting in 1964 it has been able to operate for much longer hours and is now on the air throughout the day using both English and Spanish.

The Ministry of Information also carries out useful work apart from its main task of making government information available. Its mobile film unit is used throughout the country to take educational films to the villages. Two of the most important institutions for furthering cultural activities and educational interest throughout the country are the British Council and the Extra-Mural Department of the University of the West Indies. The British Council maintains its own library and reading room in Belize City where the latest newspapers and periodicals from Great Britain can be read. It also runs its own film unit and takes films to the schools. In addition to offering various scholarships the British Council organizes visits to the country by important British lecturers and artists.

The University of the West Indies has a permanent extra-mural tutor in Belize and he is much concerned with adult education work. At present only a small proportion of secondary school leavers proceed to a university or to further education, but those who obtain scholarships to study abroad usually go to the University of the West Indies or to American or British universities. Optimism in the future potential of Belizean youth has been shown by setting aside an area at Belmopan for the construction of a university at some unspecified date.

There has been an excellent library in Belize since 1935 when the Carnegie Foundation helped to equip a modern building. Today the central library, together with the national collection of archives, is housed in the Bliss Institute in Belize City and there is a separate reference library in another building. The library service is entirely free, being subsidized by the government. It aims to operate a service throughout the country and in 1965 there were no fewer than 66 centres of operation; there were also more than 18,000 library members. In that same year the Chief Librarian was also appointed Archivist, and a definite policy was adopted of caring for the nation's archives and making them available to scholars.

The Bliss Institute not only contains the main library and archives, but is also used as a museum for Maya artefacts. It is the centre of much extra-mural activity as it has lecture rooms and a theatre which is used for plays and concerts. The institute is named after the country's most bizarre benefactor, Baron Bliss. A wealthy Englishman whose title was an ancestral Portuguese one, Baron Bliss was a keen fisherman attracted by the tales of the huge fish along the Belizean coastline. Unfortunately the Baron was taken ill and died in 1926 without ever setting foot in the country, but before dying he drew up a will in which he left all his money to the colony apart from a few annuities. A trust was appointed to administer the will, and hopes were expressed that the Baron's generosity would alter the entire course of history. Governor Burdon told the Legislative Council that the future prosperity of the country was assured by the Baron's munificence. Unfortunately the Governor did not appreciate that the British Government would be able to claim a substantial sum in estate duties. The will was somewhat unusual for, after providing for a permanent memorial for himself and for an annual regatta, the Baron laid down that the residue must be spent on capital projects and not be used for current expenditure. As a result there is no provision for the maintenance of buildings set up by the Bliss Trust, nor can any money be spent on building schools. Despite these restrictions many worthwhile projects have been assisted or entirely carried out with funds from the Trust. Among these have been the construction of a promenade on the foreshore, improvements to roads and to water-supplies, the recently built markets at Corozal and Stann Creek towns and the Bliss Institute itself.

Recreational facilities

Facilities for recreation have never been abundant and are mainly limited to pastimes associated with the sea: swimming, fishing and yachting. The natural reef provided by the Cays has made the coastal waters a paradise for fishermen, and there is also plenty of sport to be found in the rivers. Bathing facilities in Belize City itself have, until recently, been very limited, but new bathing beaches are now being prepared. Boating of all kinds has always been extremely popular and the skill with which the smallest boats are manœuvred testifies to long experience in their handling. Horse racing is also a popular pastime and the construction of a track and stadium in Belize City has recently been completed.

Indoor amusements are less well provided for. There is no permanent theatre company or symphony orchestra in the country, but occasional visits are paid by touring companies. Cinemas provide the most popular entertainment, and in the absence of television the two cinemas in Belize City and the smaller ones in the other towns can count on regularly full houses. Films from the United States provide the bulk of the film repertoire.

Newspapers

Unfortunately from the historian's point of view newspapers in British Honduras have always had a rather chequered existence, many newspapers surviving for only a year or so. The first newspaper of which copies still remain, *The Honduras Gazette and Commercial Advertiser*, was published between July 1826 and June 1827. Equally short-lived were *The New Era and British Honduras Chronicle*, February 1871–May 1872, and *The Observer*, February 1885–1886. One of the better newspapers was *The Colonial Guardian* which was published 1882 to 1913 under one editor, Dr Frederick Gahné. *The Guardian* expressed definite political views in its weekly editorials, but most other newspapers limited themselves to advertisements and descriptions of social events among the colonial society. As more attention was paid to news of European happenings than to matters of local interest it is perhaps not surprising that few newspapers lasted more than a year or so. One other exception was *The Clarion* which circulated as a weekly paper from 1897 until 1935, and thereafter as a daily until 1961. In 1970 there are two leading newspapers, both organs of their respective political parties. *The Belize Billboard* was first published in 1946 and proved an indisputable asset to the emerging labour movement; the leader of the present opposition party, Philip Goldson, has always been associated with the paper, which is now the mouthpiece of the National Independence Party. *The Belize Times*, which has only been functioning since 1959, is the People's United Party answer to *The Billboard*. At times both papers have been sufficiently tendentious to be warned by the Speaker of the House of Representatives that the reporting of the proceedings of that House must be regarded as a privilege not to be treated lightly. The only paper currently in circulation which is not an organ of a political party is that sponsored by the local Chamber of Commerce, *The Reporter*. None of these papers attempts to print much world news. For major events outside the country, Belizeans tend to rely on Radio Belize and papers imported from Britain and the United States.

The Development of Trade Unions and Political Parties

The appearance of trade unions and political parties during the last twenty years are outward signs that both the labour movement and politics are following the usual line of development in all modern societies. Their emergence, although of profound significance for the future, is so recent and involves so many individuals still active in public life, that it is impractical here to do more than outline the salient facts of their growth.

The first trade union of any real importance in the country was the General Workers Union which was founded in 1939. Membership rose slowly from only 2,000 in the period between 1947 and 1950 to 12,000 in 1955, the year of peak membership for all the trade unions. The rapid rise in membership in the early 1950s can be attributed to the political awakening of the people and the rôle played by the General Workers Union in the formation of the People's United Party. Another general union was formed in Stann Creek in 1950 by a breakaway movement but its membership was only numbered in hundreds. Other small and specialized unions were formed at that period, but the tendency of the unions to engage in political rather than industrial pressure has led to some confusion of purpose. The extremely close relations between the early unions and the PUP did little to win the unions recognition from the employers. Moreover the complete split which occurred in the PUP in 1956 demoralized union support. It led to the formation of a new union, the Christian Democratic Union, which claimed to have about 1,600 members between 1956 and 1957. No fewer than nine unions were formed in the years between 1946 and 1960: of these only four unions survived into the 1960s, comprising a total membership of 2,200 out of a wage-earning population of 21,000.

From 1961 the PUP has sought to encourage the development of regional unions under the general supervision of the elected representatives in the Districts. One example of this trend was the formation of the Northern Cane Workers Union sponsored by Senator Ken, but it has not been widely successful and the early ties between the unions and parties have now been relinquished with a beneficial effect on industrial relations. Few of the unions' supporters are actually paid-up due-paying members because of widespread unemployment and the seasonal nature of much work. As a direct consequence of the poverty of the unions, conciliation rather than litigation between the unions and the employers is the general rule. The bargaining that takes place is conducted on an independent basis and the use of government machinery to fix wage levels seems to be limited to the citrus and timber industries. Lack of union funds also has the effect of drawing the somewhat fragmented unions into larger organizations with international affiliations. As the wage-earning population increases and the advantages of union membership come to be more fully appreciated the unions will increase in strength.

The emergence of the General Workers Union as a force representing the masses in the post-war years was of great importance since the labour movement became closely linked with the first political party. The post-war feelings of restlessness and frustration which were as common in Belize as in other parts of the dependent territories, were conducive to a widening in the political horizons. At the end of the war the colony's government was still controlled by a few men and the proportion of registered voters to the population was only 1·3%. The constitutional changes of 1945 did bring about some small improvements but the demand for universal suffrage was becoming more insistent. The unofficial members on the Legislative Council were beginning to challenge the Executive on every possible occasion. Thus in 1946 the Governor was forced to use his reserve powers in a crisis over an Income Tax Bill, with the result that the unofficial members walked out of the Council. After this incident some attempt was made by the Governor and Executive Council to improve relations with the members of the Legislative Council and a standing Finance Committee was appointed. Moreover two of the unofficial members, W. H. Courtenay and J. Espat, were appointed to the Executive. In the following year, 1947, a delegation of unofficial members including Courtenay, visited London to discuss the future of the colony at the Colonial Office. Their visit was extremely successful for it led to the setting up of the Constitutional Commission to consider reforms, and also won the remission of the outstanding part of the Hurricane Reconstruction Loan which had been recommended by the Moyne Commission as long before as 1938. The unofficial members were by no means radicals, but rather conservatives trying to obtain a larger share in the government of the country. They valued the British colonial connection and during the 1950s were to become apologists for it; but they played their part in directing attention to the defects of the colonial government as it stood at that time.

The West Indian Federation

There were other influences at work which stimulated an interest in politics. For the first time there was a newspaper, *The Belize Billboard*, to encourage the labour movement and to formulate the opinions of the masses, although it lacked a definite political ideology. There were also several important issues before the public which were controversial enough to create an interest in the political processes. The first of these was the question of a West Indian Federation which was thoroughly discussed at the Montego Bay conference in 1947. The British Honduran delegates to the conference expressed little enthusiasm for the idea of a federation and though they participated in later conferences, when the short-lived West Indian Federation came into being eleven years later British Honduras was not associated with it. Closely linked with the question of federation was that of immigration. One of the main objections to the idea of federating with the West Indian islands was the possibility that British Honduras would be flooded by immigrants without the necessary employment or social provisions being found for them. Immigration was the subject of the Settlement Commission's Report which was published in 1948. The Commission, under the chairmanship of Sir Geoffrey Evans, was set up to examine how far it would be possible for British Guiana and British Honduras to absorb some of the surplus population from the West Indian islands and from Europe. The Commission carried out an extremely detailed study of the development measures which would have to be taken if a carefully phased immigration scheme were carried out. C. W. Greenidge, a former Chief Justice of British Honduras, was a member of the Commission who continued to take an interest in the colony and its problems after the presentation of the Report. Greenidge became convinced that unless pressure was brought to bear at the Colonial Office the Report would remain a dead letter, like so many earlier development schemes. In private letters to Grantley Adams, Prime Minister of Barbados, he tried to enlist support for the scheme and mentioned that over 50,000 immigrants could be catered for in British Honduras. While proponents of the scheme sought to exert pressure on Colonial Secretary Creech Jones, opposition to large-scale immigration and to federation was mounting in British Honduras itself.

These issues were presented to the people and public opinion was mobilized in a variety of ways. Mass meetings were held in a so-called Open Forum on the 'Battlefield' not dissimilar to the meetings held by Eric Williams of Trinidad in his famous University of Woodford Square. Jesuits from St John's College formed a Christian Social Action Group and even the College's Alumni Association became a centre for political interest. One of its most enthusiastic supporters was George Price who was elected to the Belize City Council in 1947. The following year two other aspiring politicians, Leigh Richardson and Philip Goldson, gave up their jobs to devote themselves to running *The Belize Billboard*. In 1948, when Guatemala renewed her threats towards the country and refused to accept the British suggestion of arbitration before the new International Court, her propaganda became so provocative that the British Government was obliged to send a warship to Belize, thus bringing the problem to the attention of the world press. As a result a resolution expressing loyalty to the British Crown was unanimously passed in the Legislative Council and confirmed by popular acclaim in meetings held throughout the colony. In spite of these expressions of loyalty the general trend of the period was anti-colonial in flavour. It found articulate expression in the speeches of the young and emerging political leaders rather than among the masses whose discontent the activists sought to mobilize.

Devaluation and the anti-colonial movement
The opportunity came in December 1949 with the devaluation of the B.H. dollar. But devaluation was only the catalyst in an already potentially explosive situation. It is an exaggeration to say that modern politics in Belize can be specifically dated to 31 Decem-

ber 1949, but devaluation was certainly an issue which seemed tailor-made to exploit the current interest in political matters. In whatever light devaluation was examined both the constitutional and the economic issues arising from it could be presented in such a way as to appeal to a new, nationalist and anti-colonial movement.

The devaluation of the pound sterling in relation to the U.S. dollar in September 1949 left British Honduras in a disadvantageous trading position in the sterling area. As a result the already serious economic situation of the colony worsened and unemployment increased. The initial exemption of the B.H. dollar from devaluation was not thought likely to be continued and a period of uncertainty ensued. The traditional trade with the United States was threatened by the possible devaluation which would lead to a rise in the cost of all imports from America. As the colony still depended largely on American foodstuffs the cost of living would rise at a time of unemployment. Official attempts to allay fears of a possible devaluation were not very successful, and the financial activities of the business community, among whom were several members of the Legislative Council, did nothing to help. Funds were transferred to Britain and many merchants took advantage of the existing exchange rates by purchasing goods ahead of requirements. However the visit by Lord Listowell, Minister of State for the Colonies, in October did much to restore confidence to the B.H. dollar. In public meetings and in the Legislative Council he assured his audiences that the British Government had decided not to devalue the dollar. Further assurances were made in Parliament in November, yet only a few weeks later Governor Garvey had to inform the Legislative Council that the dollar was indeed to be devalued. In an attempt to reduce the serious effects of this decision the Government had decided to introduce subsidies and price controls. No measures for economic development were announced although it was argued that devaluation was an essential precursor of any such development.

The unofficial members were perhaps not altogether opposed to devaluation, but they were certainly indignant that they had not been treated with more confidence by the Government, and that no funds were being made available to provide employment. They therefore refused to play any part in the decision and opposed the necessary Bill so that the Governor had once again to use his reserve powers to pass it. Their genuine concern at the situation was expressed in a cable to C. W. Greenidge requesting his assistance in obtaining development funds. The cable was dated 13 January 1950 and said: 'Grave situation exists B.H. following devaluation of local dollar which will worsen if immediate steps not taken provide work for large number unemployed stop. Government efforts to limit inevitable rise in living costs by controls and subsidies ineffectual because of lack of purchasing power of majority of people stop. Control of help only if employment of labour at living wage provided stop.' Having urged the immediate expenditure of £100,000 on building a road, the cable concluded 'conditions of unrest fruitful ripe for communist and other subversive influence stop. Fear serious disorder as result widespread suffering and hardship if immediate help not forthcoming'.

Yet, in spite of their expressed opposition to devaluation, the unofficial members of the Legislative Council were regarded by the masses as party to it and their protestations disregarded. As their cable shows they were clearly aware of the possibility of serious trouble, and self-interest undoubtedly played a part in making their gestures of protest. On the night of devaluation it was the young and rising politicians who seized their opportunity and formed the People's Committee with the intention of exploiting the situation and forcing an end to colonial rule. The situation provided the Committee with immediate urban support and it soon won over the General Workers Union to its cause—a useful acquisition to any party in view of the strength of the union's district branches.

From the beginning the leaders of the new movement showed their anti-colonial feelings and their opposition to joining a West Indian Federation. But the movement was not based on a specific ideology: although it sought support from the workers it never embraced socialist principles. In fact, there was considerable support for secession from Britain in favour of some sort of alliance with the United States. The American Consul in Belize was very popular and 'God Bless America' was frequently sung at party rallies. George Price's personal feelings toward Central America at that time were expressed in February 1950 in *The Billboard* where he declared, 'People do not consider themselves part and parcel of the British West Indies, but rather a part and parcel of Central America on the mainland, with whom we have long had existing economic and commercial ties.'

The formation of political parties

A definite threat of disturbance was in the air. The public meetings at the 'Battlefield' had to be curtailed although the Governor's fears of anarchy or communist infiltration were ill-founded. Nevertheless it was decided to call off a proposed visit by Princess Alice, a member of the British royal family. The loyal members of the Legislative Council were disappointed at the decision and they were denounced by the People's Committee as 'colonialist devaluationists'. The Committee organized its own celebrations on the anniversary of the battle of St George's Cay in 1950. By introducing the symbols of a flag and an anthem they converted the day into a National Day. Shortly after this on 29 September the People's Committee dissolved itself and the People's United Party was born. The first leaders of the PUP, as it soon became known, were John Smith, Leigh Richardson as Chairman, George Price as Secretary and Philip Goldson. The new party's first success came in winning a majority position on the Belize City Council. At first there was no real opposition to the PUP but this emerged in August 1951 after its members on the Council refused to allow a portrait of the King to be hung in the City Hall. The incident seemed small enough in itself, but it infuriated the loyalist members of the Legislative Council who advised the Governor to dissolve the City Council and nominate one in its stead. This action, combined with the imprisonment of Richardson and Goldson for seditious writing in *The Billboard*, only served to increase support for the PUP. Opposition was ineffectual. Most of the unofficial members of the Council joined the National Party under Herbert Fuller but, in comparison with the PUP, this new party was not well organized even in Belize City itself. Its weakness was so marked that the colonial administration felt itself called upon to try to reduce the PUP's influence by appointing a public relations officer and establishing an official paper, *The British Honduran*.

The National Party and the administration were accused of delaying the introduction of constitutional reforms and, once the 1951 proposals had been accepted, of putting them into force. The first elections under the new constitution were held on 28 April 1954 and were the first real test of the party organizations. The introduction of universal suffrage increased the number of registered voters from 1,772 in 1948 to almost 21,000. It also had the effect of greatly increasing the percentage of rural voters: the PUP, which commanded the support of the General Workers Union, clearly had an advantage in getting the rural voters to the polls and teaching the illiterate to sign their names in order to comply with the regulations. The PUP contested all nine constituencies but the National Party only contested six. Of the National Party candidates only one was a mestizo by birth, the others were either Creoles or of West Indian origin—a fact which did not help their cause. In the event the PUP won an overwhelming victory, gaining eight out of nine seats in the new Assembly and obtaining 65% of the total vote.

The defeat of the National Party in the 1954 elections led to its virtual withdrawal from politics for the next three years. The vacuum was filled to some extent by the growing factionalism within the PUP. As early as 1951 John Smith had resigned from the party because of his objections to Price's pro-Central American policy. Moreover now the PUP had access to the processes of government, certain of its attitudes had to be clarified. The introduction of the quasi-ministerial system in January 1955 assisted this change. George Price showed his unwillingness to participate in a colonial government by speaking as little as possible in the Legislative Council, by refusing to join an Executive Council delegation to London and by taking only a minor post. Richardson and Goldson, on the other hand, in their semi-ministerial posts cooperated in working the new constitution and gradually came to appreciate that it was desirable for the country to maintain and even increase her economic links with Britain and the West Indies. A split in the party became inevitable and it took place in the summer of 1956. The immediate cause of the break was the allegation of misuse of funds made against Nicholas Pollard, Secretary of the General Workers Union. Pollard was supported by Price and at the party conference which took place in September 1956 Richardson and Goldson realized, too late, the need for mass support from the rank and file of the party. Price and Pollard together retained control of the PUP and formed a new union (Christian Democratic Union) while the dissidents created the Honduras Independent Party and retained control of the General Workers Union. But time was short before the elections of March 1957 and the PUP retained its superior party organization. Moreover, neither the new party nor the National Party could oppose Price's anti-Federation policy with any chance of success, and despite the lack of General Workers Union support in the rural constituencies the PUP won all nine seats. The electorate showed its apathy by abstaining from voting and the total poll was only 53% as against 70% in 1954.

The road to self-government

After the elections in 1957 Price took over the leadership in the Legislative Assembly and succeeded Richardson in the Executive Council as Member for Natural Resources. By the end of the year his interest in the Organization of Central American States (ODECA) had caused some suspicion. In November he led a delegation to London to request more financial assistance and further constitutional progress, but the discovery that he was engaged in talks with the Guatemalan Minister in London at the same time led to the breakdown of talks. On his return to Belize Price received a hero's welcome and in spite of his dismissal from the Executive Council he retained his hold over the majority of the party. Two of the PUP members of the Legislative Assembly, De Paz and Jeffrey, defected, leaving Price as leader of a minority group. In July 1958 the two opposition parties merged to form the National Independence Party (NIP) under the leadership of Fuller. Meanwhile Leigh Richardson had left the country and Philip Goldson was so busy editing *The Billboard* that he abandoned his political rôle for a time, only resuming it late in 1961 when he took over NIP's leadership from the invalid, Fuller.

The opportunity for a more constructive phase in political development presented itself in 1960 when a temporary United Front was formed by all parties to press for the implementation of greater constitutional reforms than those proposed by Sir Hilary Blood. This step was initiated by W. Courtenay and was welcomed by the NIP leaders who wanted to show that they had a responsible part to play in the development of the country, and by Price who needed to win some official support. The formation of the United Front was of considerable importance in convincing the British Government that the party leaders could conduct themselves responsibly in the interest of their country, and a more advanced constitution was the reward, to be followed in 1964 by the granting of full internal self-government.

Since then the PUP has maintained its dominant position in politics and in 1964 George Price became Premier of the first PUP

Government. One of his main aims as Premier has been to create an atmosphere of national unity as a necessary condition for complete independence. It is known that independence will be granted by the British Government as soon as the Belize Government considers that the appropriate time has arrived. But in rejecting the Webster proposals in 1968, the Prime Minister made it clear that independence requires certain safeguards. Speaking to the nation on 12 May 1968 he said: 'We must be mindful also that sovereign independence without adequate guarantees of our defence and external affairs and without assistance for our economic growth is an independence that would rest on a weak, shifting foundation'. Once the guarantees are ensured and independence achieved, the new sovereign nation of Belize may well fulfil its prospective rôle as a bridge between the Commonwealth Caribbean territories and the Central American countries, a rôle of undoubted importance in the modern world. The future of an independent Belize is likely to be even more exciting than her past.

Appendix I

Administrators in British Honduras, 1786–1972

Superintendents, 1786–1862

1786–1790	Colonel Marcus Despard.
1790–1791	Colonel Peter Hunter.
1791–1796	Government by the Magistrates.
1796–1800	Major Thomas Barrow.
1800–1801	Brigadier General Sir Richard Bassett.
1802	Captain B. H. Luson (Acting).
1802	Captain C. McDonell (Acting).
1803–1805	Colonel Thomas Barrow.
1805–1806	Lieutenant-Colonel Gabriel Gordon.
1806–1809	Lieutenant-Colonel Alexander Hamilton.
1809–1814	Lieutenant-Colonel John Smyth.
1814–1822	Major George Arthur (appointed Lieutenant-Colonel 1816).
1822	Major General Pye (Acting).
1823–1829	Major General Edward Codd.
1829	Lieutenant-Colonel Alexander McDonald (Acting).
1830–1836	Lieutenant-Colonel Francis Cockburn.
1836	Major John Anderson (Acting).
1837–1843	Colonel Alexander McDonald.
1843–1851	Colonel Charles St John Fancourt.
1851–1853	Philip Wodehouse.
1853–1854	George Berkeley (Colonel Secretary, Acting).
1854–1857	William Stevenson.
1857–1862	Frederick Seymour.

Lieutenant-Governors, 1862–1884

1862–1863	Frederick Seymour.
1863–1864	George Berkeley (Colonial Secretary, Administering).
1864–1867	John G. Austin.
1867–1870	James R. Longden.
1870–1874	William Wellington Cairns.
1874–1876	Major Robert Mundy.
1876–1877	Captain Charles Mitchell (Administering).
1877–1882	Sir Frederick P. Barlee.
1882–1883	Colonel Robert Harley (Administering, appointed Lieut-Gov. May 1883).
1883	Major General Robert Turton (Administering).
1883–1884	Henry Fowler (Colonial Secretary, Administering).

Governors, 1884–1972

1884–1891	Sir Roger Goldsworthy (promoted from Lieut-Gov. 31 Oct. 1884).
1891–1897	Sir Alfred Moloney.
1897–1904	Colonel Sir David Wilson.
1904–1906	Sir Bickham Sweet-Escott.
1906–1913	Colonel Sir Eric Swayne.
1913–1918	Sir Wilfred Collett.
1918	W. Hart Bennett.
1919–1925	Sir Eyre Hutson.
1925–1931	Sir John Burdon.
1932–1934	Sir Harold Kittermaster.
1934–1939	Sir Alan Burns.
1940–1946	Sir John Adams Hunter.
1947–1948	Sir E. G. Hawkesworth.
1949–1952	Sir Ronald Garvey.
1952–1955	Sir Patrick Renison.
1955–1961	Sir Colin Thornley.
1961–1966	Sir Peter Stallard.
1966–1971	Sir John Paul.
1972	R. N. Posnett.

Appendix II

Population figures

These figures are far from reliable since they were often mere estimates.
The census of 1861 was the first attempt to obtain an accurate result.

Date	Whites	Free coloureds & free blacks	Slaves	Total	Source
1742	400	..	? mentioned but no number given	400?	A.B.H. vol. 1 p. 70
1745	50	..	120	170	A.B.H. vol. 1 p. 73
1754	..	..	..	500 escaped to Mosquito Shore	A.B.H. vol. 1 p. 80
1765	..	..	..	1,500	A.B.H. vol. 1 p. 93
1779	101	40	250	391 on St George's Key (i.e. excludes those up-river in mahogany camps)	A.B.H. vol. 1 p. 129
1790	260	377	2,024	2,661	C.O. 123–9 Return of Inhabitants
1806	222	877	2,527	3,626	C.O. 123–17 —do—
1823	217	1,422	2,468	4,107	C.O. 123–35 Census
1829	250	2,266	2,127	4,643	C.O. 128–10 Census
1831	265	1,591 (excludes free coloured)	2,027	3,883 (excludes free coloured)	C.O. 128–12 Census
1841	235	8,000 (includes former slaves)	..	8,235	P.P. 1844 XLVI (591)
1845	..	..	..	10,809	Blue Book for 1845
1861	..	..	..	25,635	A.B.H. vol. 3 p. 238
1881	..	..	..	˙27,542	„ „ p. 348
1901	..	..	..	37,479	Report of B.G.&B.H. Settlement Commission Cmd. 7433
1911	..	..	..	40,458	„
1921	..	..	..	45,317	„
1931	..	..	..	˙51,347	„
1946	..	..	..	59,220	„
1960	..	..	..	90,343	1960 Census
1970	..	..	..	119,645	1970 Census— provisional figures

Appendix III

Select Bibliography

Manuscripts

The single most important source for this history is the Original Correspondence from Belize to the Secretary of State to be found among the Colonial Office records in the Public Record Office. C.O. 123 volumes 1–112 cover the period from 1744 to 1862 while volumes 113–388 continue the series to 1946. In addition to the official despatches, these records contain many enclosures from Belize, draft despatches from the Secretary of State and memoranda drawn up by Colonial Office officials. Other important records listed under British Honduras include C.O. 124, Entry Books of Correspondence; C.O. 125, Acts; C.O. 126, Sessional Papers; C.O. 128, Blue Books. C.O. 137 contains the Original Correspondence from Jamaica and is especially helpful for the period 1841–84 when despatches from Belize were forwarded via Jamaica with the Governor's comments. Board of Trade material in B.T. 5 and 6 is useful and the Admiralty and Treasury records contain some relevant material. The Foreign Office records were used to supplement the C.O. despatches where necessary, the most important series being F.O. 15, Central America and Guatemala; F.O. 50, Mexico; F.O. 72, Spain; F.O. 96 and 97, Central America misc.; F.O. 391, Hammond Papers.

The Arthur papers in the possession of the Royal Commonwealth Society include the private letters of Sir George Arthur written during his Superintendency at Belize and are undoubtedly the most valuable collection of relevant private papers. The records of the Baptist and Methodist Missionary Societies throw some light on the early work of the missionaries in the settlement. The papers of Lord Clarendon and Henry Taylor in the Bodleian Library, Oxford, provide a useful supplement to the official records, as do the more recent Greenidge papers in Rhodes House Library. The Archives in Belize are a more valuable collection than might be supposed considering the ravages caused by termites and hurricanes. They include an incomplete series of despatches both inwards and outwards from 1821 onwards; but as these are duplicated in London and often in Jamaica they are of less value than the miscellaneous volumes bound according to subject matter. The latter include local correspondence from some of the Districts, military correspondence, material relating to the Indian raids on the colony and Minutes of both the Council and Legislative Assembly. Earlier records are housed in the Registry and include some eighteenth-century records of Magistrates' meetings, Magistrates' Letter Books and private records dealing with wills, contracts and manumissions. There are also Court records dating back to 1790 which contain valuable information on the punishments awarded. Extracts from many of these records were made by a team of amateurs who helped to compile the *Archives of British Honduras*; edited by Sir John Burdon. Unfortunately the importance of dating documents and of careful quotation was not always appreciated with the result that these printed *Archives* must be used with caution.

Despatches from the United States Consul in Belize to Washington from 1847 to 1906 were studied on microfilm T334 obtained from the U.S. National Archives and give a useful picture of Belize from an American viewpoint. Few newspapers in Belize have had long runs, but of those extant in the British Museum Newspaper Library at Colindale the most important are the *Colonial Guardian* 1882–1913, the *Clarion* 1897–1935 and, more recently, the *Belize Billboard* from 1957 and the *Belize Times* from 1959.

Printed Sources

The most useful source material for the early history of the settlement is contained in the *Calendar of State Papers Colonial; American and West Indies from 1574–1737* (43 vols.) The *Acts of the Privy Council, Colonial Series*, 1613–1783 (5 vols.) and the *Journal of the Commissioners for Trade and Plantations 1704–83* (14 vols.) are also useful. For the nineteenth century the Parliamentary Papers and Debates are essential, details of the most relevant ones being found in the references below. The Government Gazettes for the late nineteenth and early twentieth centuries were printed in Belize and are a useful source of information, as are the Minutes of the Proceedings of the Legislative Council.

Secondary Works

The most important books, articles and theses are cited in the list of references (Appendix IV), but the following select list should also be noted. A detailed bibliography for the history of Belize would include many works of more general application to Caribbean and Central American history.

Bianchi, W. J. *Belize: The Controversy between Guatemala and Great Britain over the Territory of British Honduras in Central America*, New York 1959.

Bloomfield, Louis. *The British Honduras-Guatemala Dispute*, Toronto 1953.

Chamberlain, R. S. *The Conquest and Colonization of Honduras 1502–1550*, Carnegie Institute of Washington 1953.

Clegern, W. New Light on the Belize Dispute, *American Journal of International Law*, vol. 52 no. 2, 1958.

Clegern, W. British Honduras and the Pacification of Yucatan, *The Americas*, vol. 18 no. 3, 1962.

Crowe, Frederick. *The Gospel in Central America*, 1850.

Defence of the Settlers of Honduras against the Unjust and Unfounded Representations of Colonel George Arthur. Jamaica 1824.

Fowler, Henry. *A Narrative of a Journey across the Unexplored Portion of British Honduras*, Belize 1879.

Furley, P. A. ed. *Report on Edinburgh University Expedition to British Honduras and Yucatan 1966.* Edinburgh 1968.

Griffith, William J. *Empires in the Wilderness*, University of North Carolina 1965.

Hodgson, Colonel R. *Some Account of the Mosquito Territory*, 2nd. ed. 1822.

Honduras Almanacks. Vols. for 1826 and 1830 in Rhodes House Library, for 1828, 1829 and 1830 in Royal Commonwealth Society.

Humphreys, R. A. Anglo-American Rivalries in Central America, *Transactions Royal Historical Society*, 5th series vol. 18 1968.

Jones, N. S. Carey, *The Pattern of a Dependent Economy: the National Income of British Honduras*, Cambridge 1953.

Manning W. R. *Diplomatic Correspondence of the United States. Inter-American Affairs 1831–60 (12 vols)*, Washington 1932–9.

Means, P. A. *History of the Spanish Conquest of Yucatan and of the Itzas*, Cambridge, Mass. 1917.

Oman, Sir Charles, *Colonel Despard and Other Studies*, London 1922.

Reed, Nelson. *The Caste War of Yucatan*, Stanford 1964.

Taylor, D. M. *The Black Carib of British Honduras*, New York 1951.

Thompson, J. Eric S. *The Maya of Belize: Historical Chapters since Columbus*, Belize 1972.

Uring, Capt. Nathaniel. *A History of his Voyages and Travels*, London 1726.

Waddell, D. A. G. *British Honduras: a Historical and Contemporary Survey*, O.U.P. 1961.

Williams, Mary W. *Anglo-American Isthmian Diplomacy 1815–1915*, Washington 1916.

Young, T. *Narrative of a Residence on the Mosquito Shore 1839–41*, London 1842.

There are also many official reports and publications which are essential to an understanding of recent history, but lists of these are readily available from H.M.S.O. or the Government Information Service Belize, and also in *A Bibliography of British Honduras 1900–70* compiled by Clarence Minkel and Ralph Alderman, Research Report no. 7, Latin American Studies Center, Michigan State University.

Appendix IV

List of References

Each entry in the following list of references is preceded by a set of numbers. Those printed in bold type relate to the page number; the other numerals provide a key to the appropriate line(s) of text on that page, exclusive of any headings.

There follows a key to the abbreviations used in this list.

A.B.H.	Archives of British Honduras 3 vols. ed. Sir John Burdon, 1931–5
Adm.	Admiralty Records (Public Record Office—P.R.O.).
A.P.	Arthur Papers, the papers of Sir George Arthur in the Royal Commonwealth Society Library.
A.P.L.B.	Arthur Papers Letter Books.
B.H.	Series of papers bound according to subject in the Belize Archives.
B.M. Add. MSS.	Additional manuscripts in the British Museum
B.T.	Board of Trade Records (P.R.O.).
C.O.	Colonial Office Records (P.R.O.).
C.S.P.Col.	Calendar of State Papers Colonial, America and West Indies, 1574–1737.
F.O.	Foreign Office Records (P.R.O.).
G.I.S.	Government Information Service, Belize.
Leg. Co.	Legislative Council.
Mags.	Magistrates.
M.M.	Records of Magistrates Meetings, 1793–1837, in the Registry, Belize City.

MSS. Br. Emp.   Papers relating to the British Empire in Rhodes House Library, Oxford.

MSS. Clar.   The papers of Lord Clarendon in the Bodleian Library, Oxford.

P.D.   Parliamentary Debates.

P.M.   Public Meeting.

P.P.   Parliamentary Papers.

P.R.O.   Public Record Office.

Chapter 1

3–5: incl.   This geographical introduction is based largely on information from D. H. Romney ed., *Land in British Honduras*, Colonial Research Publication no. 24 H.M.S.O. (1959).

8: 23–5   K. Duncan, *Some Aspects of the Economic Geography of the Forests of British Honduras*, M.A. thesis (Edinburgh 1966).

8: 30–2   For description of early forest exploitation see Captain Henderson, *An Account of the British Settlement of Honduras* (London 1809), Ch. 3.

Chapter 2

12: 5–10   R. MacNeish, 'The Origins of New World Civilization', *Scientific American*, vol. 211, no. 5 (1964).

13: 6–9   J. Eric S. Thompson, *The Rise and Fall of Maya Civilization* (London 1956), pp. 36–8.

14: 26–35   Michael D. Coe, *The Maya* (London 1966), p. 26.

18: 28–31   ibid. p. 115

19: 1–4   Norman Hammond, *The Times*, 17 September 1968.

23: 28–31   Coe, op. cit., pp. 91–2.

31: 10–11   ibid. p. 170.

33: 22–5   ibid. pp. 144–7.

34: 24   J. Eric S. Thompson, *Maya Archaeologist* (London 1963).

36: 20–2   ibid. p. 182.

37: 7–11   N. Hammond, 'Excavations at Lubaantun 1970', *Antiquity* XLV (1970), pp. 216–23, and by the same author, 'The Planning of a Maya Ceremonial Center', *Scientific American*, vol. 226, no. 5 (1972).

38: 4–10   Thompson, *Maya Archaeologist*, p. 182.

38: 14–15   Adrian Digby, *Maya Jades* (British Museum 1964), p. 19.

38: 16–17   See p. 18 above.

38: 22–6   David Pendergast, 'The ROM British Honduras Expedition', *Journal of the Royal Ontario Museum* vol. 1, no. 9 (1967) and *Altun Ha, A Guidebook to the Ancient Maya Ruins* (B.H. 1969).

Chapter 3

42: 25–9   Bernal Diaz, *True History of the Conquest of New Spain*, vol. 2, Hakluyt Series II MDCCCCVIII vol. XXIII, p. 15.

44: 3–5   ibid. pp. 44–55.

44: 23–6   Robert S. Chamberlain, *The Conquest and Colonization of Yucatan 1517–50* (1966), p. 20.

45: 1–3   S. G. Morley, *The Inscriptions of Peten* (Washington 1938), vol. 1, p. 18.

46: 32–4   ibid. vol. 1, pp. 28 & 36.

46: 36 to
47: 3   Doris Z. Stone, *Some Spanish Entradas 1524–1695* (Middle American Research Series no. 4, 1932).

47: 28–30   *Hakluyt's Principal Navigations* vol. X, MDCCCCIV, A Voyage of Master William Parker, pp. 279–80.

48: 26–7   E. O. Winzerling, *The Beginning of British Honduras, 1506–1765* (New York 1946), ch. 3.

48: 37 to
49: 1   For detailed survey of Providence Island colony see A. P. Newton, *The Colonizing Activities of the English Puritans* (Yale 1914).

49: 38–40   Winzerling, op. cit., p. 39.

50: 15–17   C. S. P. Col. 1574–1660, 23 June 1636.

50: 18–20   Winzerling, op. cit., p. 45.

51: 10–13   P. F. de Charlevoix, *Histoire de l'isle Espagnole ou de St Domingue* (1730), p. 10.

51: 27–30   G. Bridges, *The Annals of Jamaica* (London 1828), vol. 2, p. 134.

51: 31–5   H. H. Bancroft, *History of Central America* (San Francisco 1883), vol. 2, p. 624.

51: 36–8   F. Asturias, *Belice* (Sociedad de Geographia y Historia de Guatemala 1925).

51: 40 to
52: 1   J. A. Calderón Quijano, *Belice 1663–1821* (Seville 1944), pp. 33–5.

Chapter 4

53: 6–21   For account of logwood trade see A. M. Wilson, *The Logwood Trade in the 17th and 18th centuries* in *Essays in the History of Modern Europe*, ed. D. C. McKay (New York 1936).

54: 7–11   C. H. Haring, *The Buccaneers in the West Indies in the 17th century* (London 1910) and J. Esquemeling, *The Buccaneers of America* (London 1893), for description of buccaneering activities.

54: 31–6   *Dampier's Voyages*, vol. 2, *Two Voyages to Campeachy*, ed. J. Masefield (1906), pp. 149–50.

55: 3 to
57: 6   ibid. pp. 178–9.

57: 36 to
58: 6   C.S.P.Col. 1669–74, no. 310, Gov. Modyford to Sec. Arlington, 31 Oct. 1670.

58: 15–17   ibid. no. 580, Gov. Lynch to Sec. Arlington, 2 July 1671.

58: 17–19   ibid. no. 954, Lynch to Sec. of Council, 5 Nov. 1672.

58: 32–4	ibid. no. 954, Depositions enclosed in Lynch's letter.
59: 18–21	C.S.P.Col. 1681–5 no. 668, Lynch to Lords of Trade, 29 Aug. 1682.
59: 29–30	ibid. no. 769, Lynch to Sec. of Council, 6 Nov. 1682.
59: 27–9	A.B.H. vol. 1, p. 60.
59: 35–7	C.S.P.Col. 1696–7 no. 163, Gov. Beeston to Duke of Shrewsbury, 24 Aug. 1696.
60: 36 to **61:** 2	C.S.P.Col. 1685–8 no. 1,066, Gov. Molesworth to William Blathwayt, 17 Dec. 1686.
61: 12–13	C.S.P.Col. 1699 no. 791, Council of Trade to Lords Justices, 15 Sept. 1699.
61: 34 to **62:** 3	C.S.P.Col. 1717–18 no. 104, Council of Trade to Sec. Addison, 25 Sept. 1717.

Chapter 5

67: 9–19	John Atkins, *A Voyage to Guinea, Brazil and the West Indies* (London 1735), pp. 227–8.
67: 20–6	L. Galvez to A. Valdes, 8 Oct. 1789, quoted by Calderón Quijano op. cit., p. 360.
67: 29–30	R. Llobet, Diary, quoted Quijano, p. 366.
68: 1–5	Plan of south point of Belize River, 13 July 1787, A.B.H. vol. 1, facing p. 163.
68: 22–4	For population estimates see Appendix II.
69: 22–6	A.B.H. vol. 1, p. 13.
69: 31	Calderón Quijano, op. cit., p. 111.
69: 40 to **70:** 1	A.B.H. vol. 1, pp. 14–16, for British version of Spanish attacks.
70: 32–6	B.M. Add. MSS. 32, 849 ff 441–54, B. Keene to Sir T. Robinson, 31 July 1754.
71: 14–16	B.M. Add. MSS. 36, 807 Sir James Gray to Earl of Egremont, 29 Dec. 1761.
71: 33–9	These incidents are detailed in A.B.H. vol. 1, pp. 88–99.
73: 2–9	C.O. 123 vols. 1–3 passim.
74: 35 to **75:** 2	Hunter to Sec. Grenville, 18 May 1790, C.O. 123/9.
75: 31–2	For this meeting and events leading up to Battle of St George's Cay see A.B.H. vol. 1, pp. 230–52.
77: 25–9	Barrow to Earl of Balcarres, 23 Sept. 1798, C.O. 137/10 and Capt. Moss to Admiral Hyde Parker, 27 Sept. 1798, Adm. 1/248.
78: 36–7	J. McLeish, *British Activities in Yucatan and on the Mosquito Shore in the 18th century* (Unpublished London M.A. thesis 1926), p. 266 and A. R. Gibbs, *British Honduras* (London 1883), pp. 53–4

Chapter 6

79: 3–5	57 Geo. III C 53.
80: 26–32	Proclamation, 1 Feb. 1809, C.O. 123/18.

80: 35–7	Smyth to Liverpool, 31 Aug. 1810, C.O. 123/19.
81: 6–10	Dyer to Jenkinson, 18 Apr. 1810, C.O. 123/19.
81: 23–8	Stephen, Minute on Law Officers' opinions on certain Acts passed in Honduras, 31 July 1846, C.O. 323/61.
82: 35–7	Memorial of H.M.'s Subjects, 29 Sept. 1783, C.O. 123/3.
86: 23–4	P. Hunter, Memo., 2 Aug. 1791, C.O. 123/13.
87: 23–5	Order-in-Council to Trelawney, 14 June 1744, C.O. 137/48.
88: 6–11	Burnaby's Laws, 9 Apr. 1765, A.B.H. vol. 1, pp. 100–6.
89: 17–24	ibid. 15 May 1766, p. 112.
89: 28–33	Parry to Sec. Stephens, 12 Dec. 1768, Adm. 1/238.
91: 29–34	Draft to Hunter, 16 Oct. 1789, C.O. 123/8.

Chapter 7

96: 11–16	Stephen to Glenelg, 4 Oct. 1838, C.O. 123/54.
97: 1–3	H. L. Osgood, *The American Colonies in the 18th century* (New York 1924), vol. 1, p. 34.
97: 22–7	Papers relating to the appointment of Major Arthur as Commandant at Honduras 1814, P.P. 1826–7 (37) XV 489.
97: 30–7	Liverpool to Smyth, 15 June 1810, C.O. 124/3.
98: 23–8	Hamilton to Coote, 26 Nov. 1807, C.O. 123/17.
99: 33–6	Hyde to Arthur, 15 Nov. 1819, A.P. Box 10 f.7.
100: 1–3	Codd to Murray, 1 Jan. 1829, A.B.H. vol. 2, p. 304.
100: 25–9	Arthur to Bathurst, 31 July 1819, C.O. 123/28.
101: 17–20	Law Officers to Bathurst, 24 Aug. 1822, C.O. 123/32.
102: 10–12	Magistrates to Sec. Luson, 4 Sept. 1801, C.O. 123/15.
103: 1–5	Murray to Cockburn, 28 Oct. 1829, C.O. 124/3.
104: 29 to 105: 4	Taylor to Spedding, 13 Sept. 1836, Bodley MSS. Eng. Letters d8 f254.
106: 32–6	P.M., 28 Feb. 1809, A.B.H. vol. 2, p. 127.
107: 3–5	Arthur to Gascoyne, 12 Nov. 1819, A.P.L.B. 7.
108: 7–14	Goderich to Cockburn, 18 Oct. 1832, C.O. 123/43.
109: 10–14	Bathurst to Arthur, 30 Nov. 1819, C.O. 124/3.
109: 33–40	Goderich to Cockburn, 21 March 1833, C.O. 124/3.
110: 18–22	Macdonald to Normanby, 24 Sept. 1839, C.O. 123/55.
111: 15–29	Fancourt to Elgin, 16 Jan. 1844, C.O. 123/67.
112: 3–9	ibid. 20 March 1846, C.O. 123/71.
112: 32 to 113: 4	P.M. 29 Oct. 1808, A.B.H. vol. 2, p. 123.
113: 11–14	Arthur to Bathurst, 2 Dec. 1814, C.O. 123/23.
113: 33 to 114: 1	P.M., 24 July 1820, A.B.H. vol. 2, p.232.
114: 8–14	Goderich to Cockburn, 18 Oct. 1832, C.O. 123/43.
114: 18–21	Taylor to Hope, 15 Oct. 1841, C.O. 123/59.
115: 25–30	Arthur to Hyde, 22 Oct. 1819, A.P.L.B. 12.

117: 31–7   Fancourt to Stanley, 15 Apr. 1844, C.O. 123/68.

118: 8–26   Fancourt to Grey, 10 Aug. 1848, C.O. 123/74.

119: 7–10   Taylor, Minute, 8 Dec. 1851, C.O. 123/83.

119: 39 to   Stevenson to Berkeley, 17 Feb. 1855, C.O. 123/90.
120: 1

120: 5–12   Grey to Wodehouse, 4 Jan. 1853, C.O. 123/87.

120: 22–8   Law Officers to Liverpool, Feb. 1812, C.O. 123/21.

122: 1–3   Bathurst to Arthur, 11 Jan. 1817, C.O. 124/3.

123: 13–32   Third Report of Commission of Enquiry into the Administration of Criminal and Civil Justice in the West Indies. (Honduras and Bahamas) 1829 (334) XXIV 187.

Chapter 8

128: 8–12   Cockburn to Stanley, 29 Oct. 1833, C.O. 123/44.

130: 9–11   Arthur to Bathurst, 2 April 1818; B.T. to Goulburn. 7 July 1818, C.O. 123/27.

130: 16–17   Petition of Committee to P.M. 15 Nov. 1833, C.O. 123/44.

130: 18–19   Lefevre to Ewing, 25 July 1834, C.O. 124/4.

130: 20-6   B.T. Minutes, 20 Aug. 1817, B.T. 5/20 1817–18; Bathurst to Arthur, 6 Sept. 1817, C.O. 124/3.

130: 26–30   Arthur to Gascoyne, 17 July and 31 Oct. 1818, A.P.L.B. 7.

130: 37 to   Arthur to Gascoyne, Jan. 1821, A.P.L.B. 7.
131: 2

131: 33–4   Arthur to Gascoyne, 31 Oct. 1818, A.P.L.B. 7.

132: 3–5   Committee of Trade, 18 April 1820, B.T. 5/28.

133: 3–4   Proclamations, 8 and 9 Nov. 1832, encl. Cockburn to Goderich, 24 Nov. 1832, C.O. 123/43.

133: 19–22   P.M. Petition, 2 March 1841, C.O. 123/59.

133: 30–3   Edward Chaloner, *The Mahogany Tree in the West Indies and Central America* (Liverpool 1850), ch. 1.

133: 37 to   Memorial Hyde and Company to Earl Grey, 15 Nov.
134: 3   1847, C.O. 123/73.

134: 6–10   Earl Grey to Hyde, 13 June 1848, C.O. 123/73.

135: 29–30   R. A. Humphreys, introd. to *British Consular Reports on Latin America* (1940), p. xi.

136: 14-24   Guatemalan Consular Reports 1826 B.T. 6/47.

137: 15–17   For full discussion of Chatfield's rôle in Central American affairs see Mario Rodriguez, *A Palmerstonian Diplomat in Central America, Frederick Chatfield Esq.* (Univ. of Arizona 1964).

139: 26-31   C. Dashwood to J. Backhouse, 28 Jan. 1830, F.O. 15/10.

139: 38 to   For survey of trade between B.H. and Central America
140: 3   see R. A. Naylor, *British Commercial Relations with Central America* 1821–51 (Tulane Ph.D. 1958).

141: 14–17   James Stephen to Vernon Smith memo. on reverse of Macdonald's despatch no. 19, 17 Dec. 1839, C.O. 123/55.

141: 21–5   Meeting, 10 April 1765, A.B.H. vol. 1, p. 107.

141: 27–31	ibid. 15 May 1766, p. 112.
142: 10–12	Proclamation, 28 Oct. 1817, C.O. 123/28.
142: 17–21	Arthur to Bathurst, 14 June 1819, C.O. 123/28; ibid. 13 Sept. 1820, C.O. 123/29.
143: 5–26	For full account of dispute see present author's unpublished thesis, *Social and Administrative Developments in British Honduras 1798–1843*, N. D. Leon (Oxford B.Litt. 1958), pp. 320–3.
144: 4–8	Normanby to Macdonald, 29 June 1839, C.O. 123/55.
144: 13–14	Stanley to Elgin, 11 May 1843, C.O. 123/65.

Chapter 9

147: 23–5	See H. H. Bancroft, op. cit., vol. 2, p. 626.
148: 2–20	John Armstrong, *A Candid Examination of the Defence of the Settlers of Honduras* (London 1824).
149: 15–19	Arthur to Bathurst, 7 Nov. 1816, C.O. 123/25.
151: 2–4	Henderson, op. cit., pp. 56–8.
151: 15–19	Armstrong, op. cit., pp. 61–3.
151: 25–38	A.B.H. vol. 1, pp. 121–4.
152: 6–8	Summary Court, 16 Feb. 1795, MMA 1 1793–6.
152: 17–23	Arthur to Bathurst, 16 May 1820, C.O. 123/29.
152: 32–3	ibid. 7 Oct. 1820, C.O. 123/29.
153: 6–9	ibid. 7 Nov. 1816, C.O. 123/25.
153: 9–18	ibid. 7 Oct. 1820, C.O. 123/29.
153: 23–7	Summary Court Records 1817–21 f43, 7 Aug. 1817.
155: 5–16	*Honduras Gazette*, 19 May 1827.
155: 35 to **156**: 4	Manumission Returns 1826–30, C.O. 123/42.
156: 34–40	P.P. 1829 (334) XXIV 187 Appendix to Report.
157: 20–3	Arthur to Magistrates, 28 Sept. 1821, A.P.L.B. 12.
157: 33 to **158**: 38	For full account see Report of Commissioners of Legal Enquiry on the case of the Indians at Honduras, P.P. 1828 (522) XXVI 1 and Papers relating to the Honduras Indians, P.P. 1830 (583) XXI 393.
159: 22–5	Newport to Horton, 12 Jan. 1825, C.O. 123/36.
160: 4–5	Returns of Baptism and Marriage, C.O. 123/34.
161: 26–9	Cockburn to Goderich, 10 Jan. 1833, C.O. 123/44.
161: 31–5	Draft to Cockburn, 20 March 1833, C.O. 123/44.
162: 17–23	Grey to Fancourt, 30 Oct. 1847, C.O. 123/74.
162: 38 to **163**: 2	Cockburn to Goderich, 10 Jan. 1833, C.O. 123/44.
163: 15–17	Instructions to Inspectors of Schools in West Indies receiving grants for Negro Education, P.P. 1837 (393) XLIII 311.
163: 17–20	Macdonald to Elgin, 15 May 1843, C.O. 123/65.
164: 20-4	Macdonald to Glenelg, 18 March 1839, C.O. 123/55.

Chapter 10

165: 14–18	See Appendix II.
166: 10–13	See W. L. Mathieson, *British Slavery and its Abolition* (1926), p. 39 & pp. 188–90.
166: 27–30	Arthur to Bathurst, 16 Feb. 1815, C.O. 123/24.
167: 14–17	ibid. 5 March 1822, C.O. 123/31.
167: 23–31	Hyde to Bathurst, 3 Feb. 1827, C.O. 123/38.
167: 35–6	P.D. New Series, vol. XVII, 12 June 1827, cols. 1242–1256.
168: 1–3	Lushington to Stephen, 28 Oct. 1827, C.O. 123/38.
168: 25–9	P.M. 3 March 1828, A.B.H. vol. 2, p. 298.
168: 33–4	P.M. 6 July 1829, C.O. 123/40.
168: 37–9	P.M. 4 July 1831, C.O. 123/42.
171: 22–5	Cockburn to Spring Rice, 11 Aug. 1834, C.O. 123/45.
171: 35 to **172:** 1	Aberdeen to Cockburn, 29 Dec. 1834, printed in P.P. 1835 (278 II) L 393.
172: 6–12	MSS. Br. Emp. S22 G39, Analysis of West Indian laws re Apprenticeship—Honduras.
172: 25–30	Cockburn to Lefevre, 24 July 1834, C.O. 123/45.
173: 34–6	Aberdeen to Cockburn, 10 Apr. 1835, C.O. 124/5.
174: 5–8	Quoted by W. L. Burn, *Emancipation and Apprenticeship in the British West Indies* (1937), p. 172. See also for detailed account of apprenticeship system.
174: 9–12	Maskall's report encl. Cockburn to Aberdeen, 1 July 1835, C.O. 123/46.
175: 1–4	Account of averages of sales in colonies affected by abolition of slavery. P.P. 1837–8 (64) XLVIII 329.
176: 12–16	Walker to Macdonald, 12 Feb. 1838, C.O. 123/52.
178: 17–21	John L. Stephens, *Incidents of Travel in Central America Chiapas and Yucatan* (New York 1867), p. 12.

Chapter 11

184: 12–17	Arthur to Angas, 2 Oct. 1822, A.P.L.B. 7.
185: 4–6	Codd to Goderich, 24 Nov. 1827, C.O. 123/38.
185: 10–11	Villiers to Palmerston, 27 Feb. 1836, F.O. 72/457.
187: 16–20	Wright to Codd, 14 Oct. 1823, C.O. 123/34.
188: 6–8	Cooke to Huskisson, 1 Feb. 1828, C.O. 123/39.
188: 12–17	*Honduras Gazette*, 24 Nov. 1827.
188: 19–31	Taylor Memo., 29 Aug. 1829, C.O. 123/40.
189: 9–12	Cockburn to Goderich, 26 Jan. 1833, F.O. 15/13.
190: 35 to **191:** 2	Cockburn to Aberdeen, 17 Apr. 1835, C.O. 123/46.
191: 9–13	Taylor Memo., 20 Jan. 1835, C.O. 320/10.
191: 22–5	Miller Memo., Feb. 1835, C.O. 123/47.
191: 29 to **192:** 4	Note: Villiers to Martinez de la Rosa, 5 Apr. 1835, F.O. 72/441.

192: 22–3	Chatfield to Palmerston, 10 Jan. 1835, F.O. 15/16.
193: 8–11	ibid., 10 Aug. 1839, F.O. 15/22.
193: 37 to **194**: 4	ibid., 20 July 1847, F.O. 15/46.
194: 8–10	ibid., 24 Feb. 1849, F.O. 15/57.
196: 1–3	Stephen Minute attached Taylor's Memo. on Mosquito Shore, 28 Apr. 1840, C.O. 123/57.
198: 38 to **199**: 5	Palmerston draft to Bulwer, 14 March 1850, F.O. 5/509.
199: 35 to **200**: 3	Clarendon to Crampton, 6 Jan. 1854, MSS. Clarendon dep. c 127.
200: 20–2	Palmerston to Clarendon, 22 Apr. 1854, MSS. Clarendon dep. c 15.
200: 24–6	Aberdeen to Clarendon, 17 Apr. 1854, MSS. Clarendon dep. c 14.
200: 36–9	Crampton to Clarendon, 6 March 1854, encl. in Hammond to Merivale, 26 Apr. 1854, C.O. 123/89.
201: 16–20	Clarendon to Crampton, 25 Jan. & 8 Feb. 1856, MSS. Clarendon dep. c 135.
204: 19–24	Draft Instructions to Wyke, 16 Feb. 1859, F.O. 15/114.
205: 25–37	Wyke to Malmesbury, 30 Apr. 1859, F.O. 15/114.
205: 39 to **206**: 9	Taylor Memo., 19 June 1859, C.O. 123/98.
206: 24–37	Aycinena to House of Representatives, 4 Jan. 1860, printed by W. Clegern, *Hispanic American Historica Review* vol. XL, Nov. 1960, pp. 570–81.
207: 11–15	Wyke to Russell, 7 Feb. 1860, F.O. 15/114.
207: 21–7	Russell to Hall, 15 Dec. 1859, F.O. 15/114.
207: 31–6	Wyke to Russell, 7 Feb. 1860, F.O. 15/114.
208: 3–8	Russell to Hall, 7 Apr. 1860, F.O. 15/114.
208: 15–20	Wray to Russell, 7 Jan. 1861, F.O. 15/115.
208: 36–40	Gladstone Minute, 3 Apr. 1861, F.O. 15/115.
209: 5–8	Russell to Gladstone, private, 24 Oct. 1861, B.M. Add MSS. 44, 292 f 40.
209: 19–22	Hammond to Mathew, private, 16 June 1862, F.O. 15/143.
209: 32–9	Aycinena to Mathew, 10 Feb. 1863, F.O. 15/144 A.
210: 22–5	Martín to Russell, 25 Apr. 1864, Russell to Martín 3 May 1864, F.O. 15/144 A.
10: 36 to **211**: 3	Stanley to Martín, 30 July 1866, F.O. 15/145.
211: 13–18	ibid., 3 Jan. 1867, F.O. 15/146.
212: 17–28	Earl Grey Minute, 13 Dec. 1848 on despatch from Charles Grey, 6 Nov. 1848, C.O. 123/74, and Taylor Minute, 28 Dec. 1848 ibid.
212: 32–6	Taylor Minute, 26 July 1850, C.O. 123/80.
213: 10–12	Pakington to Charles Grey, 16 Nov. 1852, C.O. 123/85.

Chapter 12

219: 21–3	Scarlett to Russell, 9 March 1865, F.O. 15/144 A.
219: 31–7	Russell to Scarlett, 1 July 1865, F.O. 15/144 B.
220: 12–16	Scarlett to Castillo, 6 March 1866, F.O. 15/145.
220: 33–5	Hodge to Austin, 2 May 1866, B.H. vol. 93 Indian Raids 1866–8.
221: 11–14	Ohlafen to Austin, 1 July 1866, ibid.
221: 22–6	Carnarvon to Grant, 13 Oct. 1866, F.O. 15/145.
222: 4–13	McKay to Austin, 24 Dec. 1866, A.B.H. vol. 3, p. 275.
222: 17–23	Court of Enquiry, 25 June 1867, A.B.H. vol. 3, p. 290.
223: 23–6	Miller Report, 16 March 1887, printed in Correspondence re Boundaries of B.H., Guatemala and Mexico 1872–87, Cmd. 5622.
223: 30–6	Carmichael to Longden, 15 Nov. 1867, B.H. vol. 93 op. cit.
224: 25–32	Johnston to Cairns, 11 Sept. 1872, A.B.H. vol. 3, pp. 327–8.
225: 2–6	See W. Clegern, *British Honduras. Colonial Dead End 1859–1900* (Baton Rouge 1967), p. 142.
225: 22–5	*Government Gazette*, 9 June 1882.
225: 27–31	*Colonial Guardian*, 16 June 1883.
226: 4–22	See Clegern, op. cit., pp. 143–7.
226: 31 to **227**: 4	For this section see Cmd. 5622 op. cit.
229: 22–8	Medina to Granville, July 1880, F.O. 15/207.
230: 8–10	For this section and events to 1900 see R. A. Humphreys *The Diplomatic History of British Honduras* (O.U.P. 1961), pp. 154–65.
232: 29–32	Treasury to F.O., 1 July 1887, Cmd. 5622 op. cit.
232: 34–5	Clegern, op. cit., pp. 125–9.
234: 32–5	P.P. Treaty Series, no. 9 (1932), Cmd. 4050.
235: 23–7	C.O.I. pamphlet, *British Honduras: the Guatemalan claim* (June 1960).
238: 26–9	Leg. Co. Proceedings and Minutes for 1948, no. 1, 16 March 1948.
239: 7–11	*The Times* 28 & 29 Nov. 1957.
239: 32–6	Report of B. H. Conference, 1960. Cmd. 984.
240: 4–24	Price to Belize Men's Meeting, 5 Aug. 1962, *The Premier Speaks* (G.I.S. Belize).
240: 27–33	C.O.I., *British Honduras*, Aug. 1964 & *The Times*, 16 Apr. 1962.
240: 29–31	*The Times*, 20 March 1963.
241: 13–16	Draft Treaty between U.K. and Guatemala relating to resolution of the dispute over British Honduras (Belize), Apr. 1968.
241: 31–4	*Belize Times*, 12 May 1968.

Chapter 13

244: 6–7	B.H. Report 1964-1965 (Belize City 1967).
245: 20–2	*Colonial Guardian*, 7 Jan. & 5 Aug. 1882.
246: 5–9	Leas to Seward, 13 Jan. 1863, U.S. Consular Reports from Belize (microfilm from U.S. National Archives), T 334/1.
247: 3–5	*The Colonist*, 5 Aug. 1865.
247: 15–19	Prindle to Seward, 1 Oct. & 6 Nov. 1867, T 334/3.
247: 29–35	ibid., 10 Jan., 8 Feb., & 6 March 1868, T 334/3.
245: 9–10	ibid., 6 June 1869, T 334/4.
249: 17–20	For full account of Toledo settlement see D. Holdridge, Toledo: Tropical Refugee Settlement in B.H., *Geographical Review*, vol. 30 no. 3, July 1940, & D. Rosenberger, *An Examination of the perpetuation of Southern U.S. institutions in B.H. by a Colony of Ex-Confederates* (Unpublished Ph.D. New York State Univ.).
249: 32–3	P.M. 16 July 1850, A.B.H. vol. 3, p. 137.
249: 35–7	Super. to Gov. Jamaica, 16 Nov. 1857, A.B.H. vol. 2, p. 198 & Super's speech, 21 Jan. 1858, ibid. p. 200.
253: 6–19	For full story see Porter to Col. Sec., 6 April 1889, F.O. 15/256 f 287-90.

Chapter 14

260: 28–36	Harley, Leg. Co. 16 Jan. 1872, *Government Gazette* 1871.
261: 21 to **262**: 7	For full account of changes in forestry see K. Duncan op. cit.
263: 20–2	*The Clarion*, 26 Nov. 1931.
263: 23–4	Brown to Col. Sec., 16 Nov. 1931, Leg. Co. Minutes 1928-35.
263: 29–33	Message no. 3, 30 March 1932, ibid.
267: 2–3	Blue Book 1867, A.B.H. vol. 3, pp. 305-6.
267: 28–34	For Barlee's measures see Clegern, op. cit., pp. 60-3.
268: 2–4	D. Morris, *The Colony of British Honduras* (London 1883).
268: 26–9	*Land in B.H.*, op. cit., pp. 118-19.
269: 4–5	13 Dec. 1879, A.B.H. vol. 3, p. 343.
271: 16–22	Burdon, Leg. Co., 28 Feb. 1928, Leg. Co. Minutes 1928-35.
272: 14–15	Cairns, Leg. Co., 21 Nov. 1872, Supplement to *Government Gazette* 1871.
273: 6–9	*Land in B.H.*, op. cit., p. 57.
273: 24–31	Hunter to House of Representatives, 7 Jan. 1966 (printed G.I.S. Belize City).
274: 22–4	Gordon, *Economic Development Programme of B.H.* (International Bank 1954), p. 15.
274: 28–33	Report of the British Guiana and B.H. Settlement Commission (Cmd. 7533 1948), p. 237.
275: 12–19	ibid. p. 237.

276: 2–5   15 May 1766, A.B.H. vol. 1, p. 113.

276: 7–9   12 June 1784, ibid., p. 115.

276: 14–16   18 May 1825, ibid., vol. 2, p. 285.

276: 24–7   15 March 1855, ibid., vol. 3, p. 182.

276: 32 to   5 June 1860, ibid., p. 226.
277: 9

277: 24–7   Report of Settlement Commission, op. cit., p. 270, and *Colonial Guardian* 21 May 1892.

279: 11–17   Barlee, Leg. Co., 29 July 1880, *Government Gazette* 1880 & 10 June 1881, Supplement to *Gazette* 1881.

280: 9–11   For full account of Hunter case see Clegern, op. cit., pp. 76–83.

280: 38 to   *Colonial Guardian* 21 June 1884.
281: 2

281: 21–39   W. Clegern, ed., *Maudslay's Central America* (New Orleans 1962), p. 90.

282: 20–6   A. Moloney, Minute on railway, cable and boundary questions of B.H., Jan. 1896, printed West Indies no. 75.

286: 35–9   A. Burns, *Colonial Civil Servant* (Allen & Unwin 1949), p. 130.

Chapter 15

289: 28 to   Martin Wight, *The Development of the Legislative Council*
290: 3   (1946), p. 60.

290: 20–3   P.M. 16–25 July 1850, A.B.H. vol. 3, p. 137.

290: 28–30   Super. to Gov. Jamaica, 17 March 1856, ibid., p. 188.

291: 17–22   For full account of alcalde system see C. Grant, 'Rural Local Government in Guyana & B.H.', *Social and Economic Studies*, vol. 16 no. 1 March 1967.

294: 22–3   26 Jan. 1865, A.B.H. vol. 3, p. 259.

294: 37 to   Burdon, Leg. Co., 28 Feb. 1927, *Government Gazette* 1927.
295: 5

298: 5–11   Austin to Leg. Assembly, 19 Nov. 1866, A.B.H. vol. 3, p. 273.

298: 26–8   Austin to Gov. Jamaica, 4 Sept. 1867, ibid., p. 295.

298: 35–7   25 March 1870, ibid., p. 319.

298: 39–40   13 Dec. 1870, ibid., p. 323.

299: 10–13   See T. D. Vickers, *The Legislature of British Honduras* (B.H. 1955).

299: 34–9   Prindle to Davis, 19 Apr. 1871, T 334/4.

300: 1–5   Memorial to Sec. of State, Sept. 1880, A.B.H. vol. 3, p. 345.

300: 10–27   Holland to Goldsworthy, 13 Apr. 1887, *Government Gazette* 1887.

300: 30–2   1 Nov. 1884, *Government Gazette* 1884.

301: 32–4   *Colonial Guardian*, 1 March 1890.

302: 1–5   ibid., 10 & 17 May 1890.

302: 35-9	Moloney, Leg. Co., 25 March 1892, *Government Gazette* 1892.
303: 19-32	For changes in the constitution see Vickers, op. cit., and Report of Commission of Enquiry on Constitutional Reform 1951, W. H. Courtenay, Chairman.
305: 33-7	For detailed account of political background see C. Grant, *Political changes in B.H.* (Unpublished Ph.D. Edinburgh 1969).
306: 21-5	Sir Hilary Blood, Report of Constitutional Commissioner 1959.
312: 4-10	Report of B.H. Constitutional Conference, Feb. 1960, Cmd. 984.
313: 16-20	Report of B.H. Constitutional Conference, July 1963, Cmd. 2124.

Chapter 16

318: 21-5	Stevenson to Gov. Jamaica, 13 July 1855, A.B.H. vol. 3, p. 183.
319: 19-20	10 June 1871, ibid., p. 325.
320: 32-4	PUP Manifesto 1964.
321: 24-7	B. H. Easter, Report of an Enquiry into the Educational System of B.H., 1933-4 (Belize City 1935).
321: 32-6	Quoted by Ashcroft & Grant 'The Development and Organization of Education in B.H.' *Comparative Education Review*, vol. XII, no. 2, June 1968.
322: 10-14	1964-70 Development Plan (Belize City), p. 93.
325: 16-17	Message no. 12 1926, Leg. Co. Proceedings 1924-7.
330: 5-8	Greenidge to Adams, July-Aug. 1948, MSS. Br. Emp. s 285, Box 21, ff. 1, 16 & 18.
332: 1-13	Cable to Greenidge, ibid. Box 20, file 2, ff 3-9.
332: 35-40	*The Belize Billboard*, 5 Feb. 1950.
333: 8-13	For full account of these events see Grant, *Political Changes*, op. cit.

Index

Abbs, Lieutenant, 223, 227
Aberdeen, Earl, 171, 190, 196, 200
Abolition Act (1833), 146–7, 169–71
Adams, Grantley, 330
Agent, 81, 84, 91, 107
Agriculture, 5, 8–9, 248, 259–60;
    development 266–72, 286–8
Aid, overseas, 286–7
Altun Ha, 26, 38–40
Anglican Church, 159–61, 317–19, *see
    also* Religion
Anti-Slavery Society, 148, 172
Armstrong, Rev. John, 147–8, 151, 159
Arthur, Colonel George (Super-
    intendent): appointment, 97, 99; use
    of proclamations, 101, 146–7;'
    Career, 103–4; attitude to Magis-
    trates, 106–9; to Public Meeting 102,
    113–15; to Courts, 121–2, 124; to
    economy, 130–2, 142; to slavery,
    146–7, 149, 152–3, 156–9, 162; to
    coloured people, 167; to boundary
    question, 184
Asiento, 61, 64–5
Atkins, John, 67–8
Austin, John (Lieutenant Governor),
    219, 221–2, 247, 298
Aviation: airport facilities, 9, 283, 287
Aycinena, Pedro de, 204–10

Balcarres, Earl (Governor, Jamaica),
    75–6, 92, 96
Banana Cultivation, 8, 267–8, 283
Banks, 263, 274, 276–8
Baptists, 160–2, 318–20, *see also*
    Religion
Barbados, 48, 57, 149, 155, 166, 175,
    245, 297, 330
Barker, Capt. Andrew, 47
Barlee, Frederick (Lieutenant
    Governor) 225, 245, 259, 267, 272,
    279–80
Barrios, President, 232
Barrow, Lieut. Col. Thomas (Super-
    intendent), 75–6, 92, 96, 154

Basset, Richard (Superintendent), 102,
    106
Bathurst, Earl (Secretary State
    Colonies), 100, 108–9, 113, 121–2,
    124, 142, 167
Bay Islands, 87, 137, 192, 194–5, 197–
    201, *see also* Bonacca, Ruatan
Belize Estate and Produce Company,
    262–4, 275, 306
Bell, Philip, 49–50
Belmopan: new capital city, 283–4
Bennett, Marshall, 107, 130, 137, 155,
    190
Bermuda, 171, 175, 297
Birthrate, 244
Black River, 70, 72, 85
Bliss, Baron, 324–5
Blood, Sir Hilary, 311–12, 335
Bonacca, 42, *see also* Bay Islands
Boundaries, 74, 86, 181–6, 219–20, 223,
    234–5, *see also* Guatemala, Mexico
Bowen, Manfield, 157
British Council, 324
British Guiana, 171, 175, 177, 250, 329
Buccaneers, 53–7
Buchanan, James (U.S. Secretary of
    State), 199–201
Bulwer, Sir Henry, 198–9
Burdon, Sir John (Governor), 294
Burnaby, Admiral, 71–2, 87–9
Burnaby's Code, 87–9, 106, 112, 114,
    120, 141
Burns, Sir Alan (Governor), 286

Cairns, W. W. (Lieutenant Governor),
    300
Camock, Capt. Sussex, 49–50
Campeche, Bay of: 42, 47; Spanish
    logwood cutting, 53; British
    settlements, 54–8, 87; Spanish attacks
    on, 59–64, 67, 69
Canals, 279–80
Canning, George (Foreign Secretary),
    135–6, 183, 187
Canul, Marcos, 219–24, 297